Enterprise Application Development with C# 10 and .NET 6

Second Edition

Become a professional .NET developer by learning expert techniques for building scalable applications

Ravindra Akella

Arun Kumar Tamirisa

Suneel Kumar Kunani

Bhupesh Guptha Muthiyalu

BIRMINGHAM—MUMBAI

Enterprise Application Development with C# 10 and .NET 6

Second Edition

Group Product Manager: Richa Tripathi
Publishing Product Manager: Kunal Sawant
Senior Editor: Ruvika Rao
Technical Editor: Pradeep Sahu
Copy Editor: Safis Editing
Project Coordinator: Deeksha Thakkar
Proofreader: Safis Editing
Indexer: Manju Arasan
Production Designer: Sinhayna Bais
Marketing Coordinator: Sonakshi Bubbar
Business Development Executive: Kriti Sharma

First published: March 2021
Second edition: June 2022

Production reference: 1310522

Published by Packt Publishing Ltd.
Livery Place
35 Livery Street
Birmingham
B3 2PB, UK.

ISBN 978-1-80323-297-3

www.packt.com

To my wife, Srividya, and my son, Vaarush, for their love and support.

– Ravindra Akella

To my family for their love and support.

– Arun Kumar Tamirisa

To my parents, Rajaiah and Mahalakshmi, for their love, endless support, and encouragement.

– Suneel Kumar Kunani

To my parents, Mrs. Geetha Rani and Mr. Muthiyalu, for inspiration. To my wife, Aparna, and my children, Tarak and Yashvak, for their continued support and love. To my sister, Janani, for encouragement throughout the long process of writing this book.

– Bhupesh Guptha Muthiyalu

Contributors

About the authors

Ravindra Akella works as a senior software engineer at Microsoft and has more than 15 years of software development experience, specializing in .NET and web-related technologies. He has led software architecture, design, development, and delivery of large complex solutions using the Azure cloud and related technologies. He is a tech-savvy developer who is passionate about embracing new technologies.

I want to thank the people who have been close to me and supported me, especially my wife, Srividya, and my parents. Also, thanks to the editors and the team at Packt for their help and support throughout the process.

Arun Kumar Tamirisa is a senior consultant currently working at Microsoft with over 16 years' experience in IT, designing and developing highly scalable and reliable, large, and complex applications using the Microsoft .NET and Azure technology stack. He has extensive experience working with both client-side and server-side technologies and is passionate about learning and solving complex problems.

I want to express my gratitude to my family members for their unconditional love and support. My sincere thanks to the Packt team for their continuous support throughout the journey of writing this book.

Suneel Kumar Kunani is a passionate developer who strives to learn something new every day. With over 16 years of experience in .NET and Microsoft technologies, he works on architecting and building mission-critical, highly scalable, and secure solutions at Microsoft. He loves to teach and evangelize about the best practices in building distributed cloud solutions.

I would like to first and foremost thank my family for their support, patience, and encouragement throughout the long process of writing this book. I would like to extend my thanks to the Packt team, the co-authors, and the technical reviewers who made the journey of writing this book so pleasant. I am thankful to my managers and colleagues who supported and encouraged me in writing this book.

Bhupesh Guptha Muthiyalu is a Microsoft Certified Professional and works at the company as a software engineering manager. He has over 17 years of software development experience on the .NET technology stack. His current role involves designing systems that are resilient to the iterations and changes required by businesses, validating architectural innovations, delivering solutions with high quality, managing the end-to-end ownership of products, and building diverse teams with the capabilities to fulfill customer objectives. He is passionate about creating reusable components and identifying opportunities to make a product better.

I would like to first and foremost thank my family for their support, patience, and encouragement throughout the long process of writing this book. I would like to extend my thanks to the Packt team, the co-authors, and the technical reviewers for the great partnership and collaboration. I am thankful to my managers and peers who supported and inspired me to write this book.

About the reviewer

Vibhu Banga is currently a portfolio architect for a healthcare company in Hyderabad, India. His previous job for more than 10 years was as a developer/architect for Microsoft where he had delivered projects for customers on the Microsoft tech stack. He has been an active member in the open source dotnet community. He is a Microsoft Certified Azure Architect and DevOps Expert. Vibhu has contributed to open source projects related to building ERP solutions for retailers, brands, and the automobile industry under the free Apache license, all of which were developed in .NET 6.0.

> *I am deeply indebted to my friend, Ravindra, who was confident that I could take on this heavy job of being a technical reviewer, as this is my first book. I am also thankful to my parents and my loving wife for providing me all the support I need and tolerating my busy schedule and still standing by my side. I had no time to take my wife out for vacations or celebrations, but she still supported me and has always been the strongest pillar for me.*

Table of Contents

3

Introducing C# 10

Part 2: Cross-Cutting Concerns

4

Threading and Asynchronous Operations

5

Dependency Injection in .NET 6

6

Configuration in .NET 6

7

Logging in .NET 6

8

All You Need to Know about Caching

Part 3: Developing Enterprise Applications

9

Working with Data in .NET 6

10

Creating an ASP.NET Core 6 Web API

11

Creating an ASP.NET Core 6 Web Application

Part 4: Security

12

Understanding Authentication

13

Implementing Authorization in .NET 6

Part 5: Health Checks, Unit Testing, Deployment, and Diagnostics

14
Health and Diagnostics

15
Testing

16

Deploying the Application in Azure

Index

Other Books You May Enjoy

Preface

.NET 6 is an open source, free, and full stack framework to write applications targeting any platform. The framework offers you the opportunity to write applications with ease, including for the cloud. As software developers, we are entrusted with the responsibility of building complex enterprise applications. In this book, we will learn about various advanced architectures and concepts for building enterprise applications using C# 10 and .NET 6.

This book can be used as a reference while building an enterprise application using .NET 6. Complete with step-by-step explanations of essential concepts, practical examples, and self-assessment questions, you will get in-depth coverage of and exposure to every important component of .NET 6 required to build a professional enterprise application.

Who this book is for

This book is for intermediate to expert-level developers who are already familiar with .NET classic or .NET Core and C#.

What this book covers

Chapter 1, Designing and Architecting the Enterprise Application, first discusses commonly-used enterprise architectures and design patterns, and then covers designing and architecting an enterprise application into a three-tier application consisting of a UI layer, service layer, and database.

Chapter 2, Introducing .NET 6 Core and Standard, talks about the new features in C# 10, which was released with .NET 6.

Chapter 3, Introducing C# 10, starts from our awareness that runtime is where your code runs. In this chapter, you will learn about the core and advanced concepts of .NET 6 runtime components.

Chapter 4, Threading and Asynchronous Operations, helps you learn about threads, thread pools, tasks, and async/await in detail and how .NET allows you to build asynchronous applications.

Chapter 5, Dependency Injection in .NET 6, helps us to understand what dependency injection is and why every developer is flocking toward it. We will learn how dependency injection works in .NET 6 and list the other options that are available.

Chapter 6, Configuration in .NET 6, teaches you how to configure .NET 6 and use the configuration and settings in your applications. You will also learn about extending the .NET 6 configuration to define your own sections, handlers, providers, and so on.

Chapter 7, Logging in .NET 6, discusses the events and logging APIs in .NET 6. We will also take a deep dive into logging using Azure and Azure components and learn how to do structured logging.

Chapter 8, All You Need to Know about Caching, discusses the caching components available in .NET 6 and the best industry patterns and practices.

Chapter 9, Working with Data in .NET 6, discusses two possible data providers: SQL and databases such as RDBMS. We will also discuss at a high level how NoSQL databases can be used for storage and data handling using .NET 6. This chapter will discuss .NET Core's interface with files, folders, drives, databases, and memory.

Chapter 10, Creating an ASP.NET Core 6 Web API, develops the service layer of our enterprise application by using an ASP.NET 6 Web API template.

Chapter 11, Creating an ASP.NET Core 6 Web Application, develops the web layer of our enterprise application by using an ASP.NET 6 MVC web application template and Blazor.

Chapter 12, Understanding Authentication, discusses the most common authentication patterns in the industry and how you could implement them using .NET 6. We will also cover implementing custom authentication.

Chapter 13, ImplementingAuthorization in .NET 6, discusses the different methods of authorization and how ASP.NET 6 lets you handle it.

Chapter 14, Health and Diagnostics, discusses the importance of monitoring the health of an application, building a `HealthCheck` API for .NET apps, and Azure applications for capturing the telemetry and diagnosing the problem.

Chapter 15, Testing, discusses the importance of testing. Testing is an essential part of development, and no application can be shipped without proper testing, so we will also discuss how we can unit test our code. We will also learn how to measure the performance of an application.

Chapter 16, Deploying the Application in Azure, discusses the deployment of applications in Azure. We will check-in our code to the source control of our choice, and then the CI/CD pipeline will kick in and deploy the application in Azure.

To get the most out of this book

You need to have the .NET 6 SDK installed on your system; all the code samples have been tested using Visual Studio 2022/Visual Studio Code on the Windows OS. It is recommended to have an active Azure subscription to further deploy the enterprise application. A free account can be created at `https://azure.microsoft.com/en-in/free/`.

Software/hardware covered in the book	Operating system requirements
.NET 6	Windows, macOS, or Linux
Visual Studio 2022	
Visual Studio Code	
An Azure subscription	

If you are using the digital version of this book, we advise you to type the code yourself or access the code from the book's GitHub repository (a link is available in the next section). Doing so will help you avoid any potential errors related to the copying and pasting of code.

Download the example code files

You can download the example code files for this book from GitHub at `https://github.com/PacktPublishing/Enterprise-Application-Development-with-C-10-and-.NET-6-Second-Edition`. If there's an update to the code, it will be updated in the GitHub repository.

We also have other code bundles from our rich catalog of books and videos available at `https://github.com/PacktPublishing/`. Check them out!

Download the color images

We also provide a PDF file that has color images of the screenshots and diagrams used in this book. You can download it here: `https://static.packt-cdn.com/downloads/9781803232973_ColorImages.pdf`.

Conventions used

There are a number of text conventions used throughout this book.

`Code in text`: Indicates code words in text, database table names, folder names, filenames, file extensions, pathnames, dummy URLs, user input, and Twitter handles. Here is an example: "`WriteMinimalPlainText` will just emit the overall status of the health check services."

A block of code is set as follows:

```
app.UseEndpoints(endpoints =>
{
    endpoints.MapControllerRoute(
        name: "default",
        pattern: "{controller=Products}/{action=Index}/{id?}");
```

When we wish to draw your attention to a particular part of a code block, the relevant lines or items are set in bold:

```
app.UseEndpoints(endpoints =>
{
        "{controller=Products}/{action=Index}/{id?}");
    endpoints.MapHealthChecks("/health");
});
```

Any command-line input or output is written as follows:

```
dotnet new classlib -o MyLibrary
```

Bold: Indicates a new term, an important word, or words that you see onscreen. For instance, words in menus or dialog boxes appear in **bold**. Here is an example: "Let's add a custom event tracking when the user clicks on the **Add to Cart** button on the **Product Details** page."

Tips or Important Notes
Appear like this.

Get in touch

Feedback from our readers is always welcome.

General feedback: If you have questions about any aspect of this book, email us at customercare@packtpub.com and mention the book title in the subject of your message.

Errata: Although we have taken every care to ensure the accuracy of our content, mistakes do happen. If you have found a mistake in this book, we would be grateful if you would report this to us. Please visit www.packtpub.com/support/errata and fill in the form.

Piracy: If you come across any illegal copies of our works in any form on the internet, we would be grateful if you would provide us with the location address or website name. Please contact us at copyright@packt.com with a link to the material.

If you are interested in becoming an author: If there is a topic that you have expertise in and you are interested in either writing or contributing to a book, please visit authors.packtpub.com.

Share Your Thoughts

Once you've read *Enterprise Application Development with C# 10 and .NET 6*, we'd love to hear your thoughts! Scan the QR code below to go straight to the Amazon review page for this book and share your feedback.

https://packt.link/r/1-803-23297-8

Your review is important to us and the tech community and will help us make sure we're delivering excellent quality content.

Part 1: Fundamentals

In this part, we will learn about the advanced concepts of C# 10 and .NET 6's fundamental components.

This part comprises the following chapters:

- *Chapter 1, Designing and Architecting the Enterprise Application*
- *Chapter 2, Introducing .NET 6 Core and Standard*
- *Chapter 3, Introducing C# 10*

1

Designing and Architecting the Enterprise Application

Enterprise applications are software solutions designed to solve large and complex problems for enterprise organizations. They enable *Order-to-Fulfillment* capabilities for enterprise customers in the IT, government, education, and public sectors. They empower them to digitally transform their businesses with capabilities such as product purchasing, payment processing, automated billing, and customer management. When it comes to enterprise applications, the number of integrations is quite high, and the volume of users is also very high as, typically, applications are targeted at a global audience.

To ensure that enterprise systems remain highly reliable, highly available, and highly performant, getting the design and architecture right is very important. Design and architecture form the foundation of any good software. They form the basis of the rest of the software development life cycle; therefore, it is very important to, first, get the right design to avoid any rework later, which could prove very expensive, depending on the changes required. So, you need a flexible, scalable, extensible, and maintainable design and architecture.

In this chapter, we will cover the following topics:

- A primer on common design principles and patterns
- Understanding common enterprise architectures
- Identifying enterprise application requirements (business and technical)
- Architecting an enterprise application
- Solution structuring for an enterprise application

By the end of this chapter, you will be able to start designing and architecting enterprise applications.

A primer on common design principles and patterns

Every piece of software in the world solves at least one real-world problem. As time goes by, things change, including what we expect from any specific software. To manage this change and deal with various aspects of software, engineers have developed several programming paradigms, frameworks, tools, techniques, processes, and principles. These principles and patterns, proven over time, have become guiding stars for engineers to build quality software.

Principles are high-level abstract guidelines to be followed while designing. They are applicable regardless of the programming language being used. They do not provide implementation guidelines.

Patterns are low-level specific implementation guidelines that are proven, reusable solutions for recurring problems. First, let's start with design principles.

Design principles

Techniques become principles if they are widely accepted, practiced, and proven to be useful in any industry. Those principles become solutions to make software designs more understandable, flexible, and maintainable. In this section, we will cover the SOLID, KISS, and DRY design principles.

SOLID

The SOLID principles are a subset of the many principles promoted by an American software engineer and instructor, Robert C. Martin. These principles have become the de facto standard principles in the OOP world and have become part of the core philosophy for other methodologies and paradigms.

SOLID is an acronym for the following five principles:

1. **Single-responsibility principle (SRP)**: An entity or software module should only have a single responsibility. You should avoid granting multiple responsibilities to one entity.

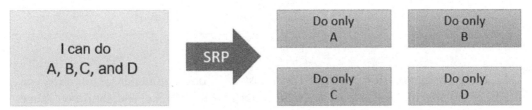

Figure 1.1 – SRP

2. **Open-closed principle (OCP)**: Entities should be designed in such a way that they are open for extension but closed for modification. This means the regression testing of existing behaviors can be avoided; only extensions need to be tested.

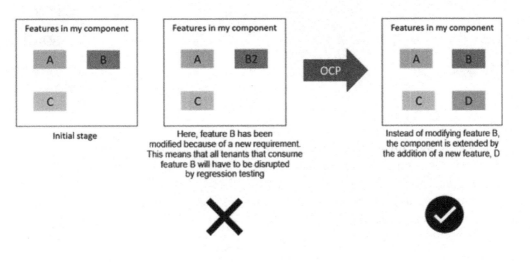

Figure 1.2 – OCP

3. **Liskov substitution principle (LSP)**: Parent or base class instances should be replaceable with instances of their derived classes or subtypes without altering the sanity of the program.

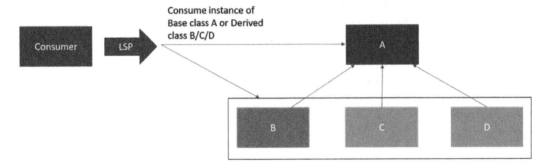

Figure 1.3 – LSP

4. **Interface segregation principle (ISP)**: Instead of one common large interface, you should plan multiple, scenario-specific interfaces for better decoupling and change management:

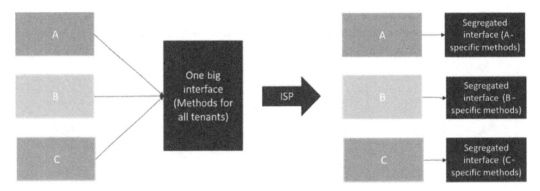

Figure 1.4 – ISP

5. **Dependency inversion principle (DIP)**: You should avoid having any direct dependency on concrete implementations. High-level modules and low-level modules should not depend on each other directly. Instead, both should depend on abstractions as much as possible. Abstractions should not depend on details, and details should depend on abstractions.

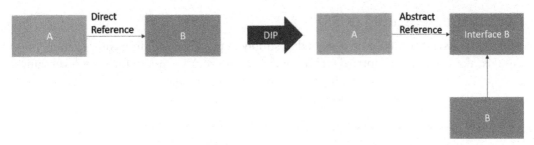

Figure 1.5 – DIP

Don't Repeat Yourself (DRY)

With DRY, a system should be designed in such a way that the implementation of a feature or a pattern should not be repeated in multiple places. This would result in maintenance overhead, as a change in requirements would result in modifications being needed at multiple places. If you fail to make a necessary update in one place by mistake, the behavior of the system will become inconsistent. Rather, the feature should be wrapped into a package and should be reused in all places. In the case of a database, you should look at using data normalization to reduce redundancy.

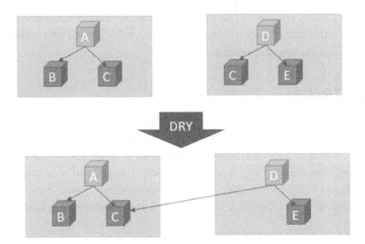

Figure 1.6 – DRY

This strategy helps in reducing redundancy and promoting reuse. This principle helps an organization's culture too, encouraging more collaboration.

Keep it simple, stupid (KISS)

With KISS, a system should be designed as simply as possible, avoiding complicated designs, algorithms, new untried technologies, and more. You should focus on leveraging the right OOP concepts and reusing proven patterns and principles. Include new or non-simple things only if it is necessary and adds value to the implementation.

When you keep it simple, you will be able to do the following better:

- Avoid mistakes while designing/developing.

- Keep the train running (there is always a team whose job is to maintain the system, even though they are not the team that developed the system in the first place).

- Read and understand your system code (your system code needs to be understandable to people who are new to it or for people who will use it in the future).

- Do better and less error-prone change management.

With this, we are done with our primer on common design principles; we have learned about SOLID, DRY, and KISS. In the next section, we'll look at some common design patterns in the context of real-world examples to help you understand the difference between principles and patterns and when to leverage which pattern—a skill that's essential for good design and architecture.

Design patterns

While following design principles in the OOP paradigm, you might see the same structures and patterns repeating over and again. These repeating structures and techniques are proven solutions to common problems and are known as **design patterns**. Proven design patterns are easy to reuse, implement, change, and test. The well-known book, *Design Patterns: Elements of Reusable Object-Oriented Software*, comprising what is known as the **Gang of Four** (**GOF**) design patterns, is considered the bible of patterns.

We can categorize the GOF patterns as follows:

- **Creative**: Helpful in creating objects
- **Structural**: Helpful in dealing with the composition of objects
- **Behavioral**: Helpful in defining the interactions between objects and distributing responsibility

Let's look at these patterns with some real-life examples.

Creational design patterns

Let's take a look at some creational design patterns, along with relevant examples, in the following table:

Pattern	Example
Abstract Factory: This pattern is used to create objects without specifying concrete types. Use this pattern when a family of related products is involved.	The `DbProviderFactory` class is an abstract factory/class. `System.Data.SqlClient.SqlClientFactory`, `System.Data.EntityClient.EntityProviderFactory`, and others are concrete factories implementing operations declared in the abstract factory/class and are responsible for creating concrete objects.
Builder: This pattern is used to create complex objects through a step-by-step process. Use this pattern to build a product of the same type as another but with different data.	`SqlConnectionStringBuilder` helps in building a connection string step by step by specifying `DataSource` (SQL Server), `InitialCatalog` (a database), and so on.
Factory Method: This pattern is used to construct classes with a component of a type that has not been predetermined. For instance, it is used to define an interface for creating an object. Instantiation is deferred to subclasses.	The `System.Convert` class provides multiple overloaded methods, and depending on the one you choose, the subclass will decide which class to instantiate to convert from one type to another.
Prototype: This pattern is used to create concrete types of objects using its prototype (existing objects). The class creates a clone of itself or an existing object and returns it as a prototype. The caller can enhance and operate on the new returned object.	`DataTable.Clone()` clones the structure of `DataTable` (an existing object), including all `DataTable` schemas and constraints, to make a new object.
Singleton: This pattern is used for scenarios where only one instance of a class is allowed. It is generally used to protect multiple instances of expensive resources. There should be no public constructor and the implementation should be thread-safe to ensure that only one thread will create an instance.	You create only one instance of `Logger` or a database connection and use it across your application with global access.

Table 1.1 – Creational design patterns

Structural design patterns

The following table includes some examples of structural design patterns:

Pattern	Example
Adapter: This pattern is used so that two incompatible interfaces can work together. It increases reusability by converting one interface into another interface that is expected by the client.	Runtime callable wrappers help .NET clients consume COM objects by acting as adapters between two incompatible interfaces.
Bridge: This pattern is used when you want to separate an abstraction from its implementation so that they can be extended independently of each other. This pattern is used for the new version (the client already has the old version and can move to the new version without breaking); the adapter pattern is used with existing systems.	This example involves List and LinkedList classes implementing ICollection. Assume that a client has been using List via ICollection and now wants to move to LinkedList. The client sends a LinkedList instance to the abstraction instead of the List instance. Abstractions run the method on the LinkedList instance and return the results to the client. The client then just works on the results that are returned.
Composite: This pattern is used to compose objects into a tree structure and, at the same time, see them as individual objects. Generally, this can be very well implemented by using a "has-a" relationship between objects. Composite will have methods to add to, remove from, and get from the tree, as well as to iterate through leaves.	In a filesystem, the directory is a composite object and the files inside the directory are leaves. You can add files, remove files, get files from directories, and iterate through files in directories.
Decorator: This pattern is used to extend the functionality of a certain entity. Following the SRP, a new decorator class wraps the original class. Use this pattern to add responsibility at runtime to an interface by wrapping the original code.	In .NET, the Stream class is an abstract class, and BufferedStream, CryptoStream, and GZipStream are decorators that wrap the original Stream class and extend the functionality to buffer or GZip.
Facade: This pattern is used to define a higher-level interface and hide internal complexity behind a single clean interface. This makes it easier for modules to interact and enables parallel development as well.	The foreach loop is a higher-level interface. It hides the internal complexity of iterating through items and executing a block of statements for each item.
Flyweight: This pattern is used to share common data among objects. It helps in avoiding object explosions at runtime and reduces the memory footprint.	Take the example of a Word document and characters in the document. Instead of creating an object for each character, you would use 26 classes, with one object for each character/class. If the word **Book** is to be displayed, instead of creating one object for each character, you would reuse the character object for the letter "o" to avoid object explosions.
Proxy: This pattern is used for controlled access to a functionality. The proxy class and the class being hidden share the same interface. This allows you to perform operations before or after a request is processed by the original object.	A Proxy class in Windows Communication Foundation enables client applications to communicate with a service by sending and receiving messages.

Table 1.2 – Structural design patterns

Behavioral design patterns

The following table includes some examples of behavioral design patterns:

Pattern	Example
Chain of Responsibility: This pattern is used to decouple senders and receivers. Once a request is received, each handler will decide whether to process it or send it to the next receiver in the chain. Requests can go unhandled sometimes.	Take the example of an ASP.NET Core middleware sequence, such as AUTH | Controller | Serializer (each request goes through this chain/pipeline, where each handler does some processing before deciding to pass on to the next handler).
Command: This pattern is used to encapsulate the operations of a request into a command object and execute it as a transaction.	ADO.NET commands, such as ExecuteNonQuery and ExecuteReader, encapsulate the operation of a request and execute it as a transaction.
Interpreter: This pattern is used to evaluate/interpret instructions.	An example of where this is used would be the .NET compiler interpreting code.
Iterator: This pattern is used to traverse and access items in a collection or container. This helps in decoupling common behavior from the nature of the container.	Take the example of collections or lists. You can traverse the items in a collection such as a list sequentially without knowing the underlying representation.
Mediator: This pattern is used for interaction between multiple entities. It promotes loose coupling as none of the involved entities have to know about each other; they interact via a mediator.	Take the examples of email or chat apps. In both these examples, users interact with each other only via an intermediate mediator such as mail servers and chat rooms.
Memento: This pattern is used for scenarios where state restoration must be managed.	Examples include undo and redo in Word and SQL transactions.
Observer: This pattern is used for scenarios where an object maintains a list of its dependents, called observers, with a one-to-many relationship. In the case of a change event, all the dependents are notified of the change.	Take the example of ASP.NET MVC: when the state of the model changes, the corresponding view gets updated; the view is the observer.
State: This pattern is used for changes of behavior at runtime, due to a change in the state of an object.	A SQL connection changes behavior at runtime when it transitions to different states such as open, connecting, and closed.
Strategy: This pattern is used for scenarios where the internal steps/algorithms can be selected at runtime.	An example would be an order shipping calculator, where the calculator must determine the shipping cost at runtime.
Template Method: This pattern is used for scenarios where a superclass/abstraction defines the skeleton of an operation in terms of its high-level steps. The general workflow of the operation is implemented once in the template class. Subclasses can implement any variations.	Take the example of interviews and hiring events. The high-level design template is like the basic first round of a hiring process. Any subsequent stages in the hiring process become more detailed and advanced; so it is with the Template Method pattern.
Visitor: This pattern is used for scenarios where there is a need to separate an algorithm from the object structure on which it depends. You can add a new operation without changing the existing structure.	C# extension methods allow you to add new methods to an existing class without the need for the modification of the existing class.

Table 1.3 – Behavioral design patterns

Sometimes, you can become overwhelmed by all these patterns being inside the table. But really, any design is a good design until it violates the basic principles. One rule of thumb that we can use is to *go back to the basics*, and in design, principles are the basics.

Figure 1.7 – Patterns versus principles

With this, we are done with our primer on common design principles and patterns. By now, you should have a good understanding of the different principles and patterns, where to use them, and what it takes to build a great solution. Now, let's spend some time looking at common enterprise architectures.

Understanding common enterprise architectures

There are a few principles and architectures that are commonly practiced when designing enterprise applications. First and foremost, the goal of any architecture is to support business needs at the lowest cost possible (costs being time and resources). A business wants software to enable it rather than act as a bottleneck. In today's world, availability, reliability, and performance are the three KPIs of any system.

In this section, first, we will look at the issues with monolithic architectures, and then we will see how to avoid them by using widely adopted and proven architectures for developing enterprise applications.

Consider a classical monolithic e-commerce website application, such as the one shown in the following diagram, with all the business providers and functionality in a single app and data being stored in a classical SQL database:

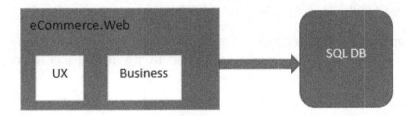

Figure 1.8 – A monolithic app

The monolithic architecture was widely adopted 15–20 years ago, but plenty of problems arose for software engineering teams when systems grew and business needs expanded over time. Let's look at some of the common issues with this approach.

Common issues with monolithic apps

Let's take a look at the scaling issues:

- In a monolithic app, the only way to horizontally scale is by adding more compute to the system. This leads to higher operational costs and unoptimized resource utilization. Sometimes, scaling becomes impossible due to conflicting needs in terms of resources.

- As all the features mostly use single storage, there is the possibility of locks leading to high latency, and there will also be physical limits as to how far a single storage instance can scale.

Here is a list of issues associated with availability, reliability, and performance:

- Any changes in the system will require the redeployment of all components, leading to downtime and low availability.

- Any non-persistent state, such as sessions stored in a web app, will be lost after every deployment. This will lead to the abandonment of all workflows that were triggered by users.

- Any bugs in a module, such as memory leaks or security bugs, make all the modules vulnerable and have the potential to impact the whole system.

- Due to the highly coupled nature and sharing of resources within modules, there will always be unoptimized use of resources, leading to high latency in the system.

Lastly, let's see what the impact on the business and engineering teams is:

- The impact of a change is difficult to quantify and requires extensive testing. Hence, it slows down the rate of delivery to production. Even a small change will require the entire system to be deployed again.

- In a single highly coupled system, there will always be physical limits on collaborations across teams to deliver any features.

- New scenarios such as mobile apps, chatbots, and analysis engines will take more effort as there are no independent reusable components or services.

- Continuous deployment is almost impossible.

Let's try to solve these common problems by adopting some proven principles/ architectures.

Separation of concerns/single-responsibility architecture

Software should be divided into components or modules based on the kind of work it performs where every module or component owns a single responsibility from the entire software's responsibility. Interaction between components happens via interfaces or messaging systems. Let's look at the n-tier and microservices architecture and how the separation of concerns is taken care of.

N-tier architecture

N-tier architecture divides the application of a system into three (or n) tiers:

- **Presentation** (known as the UX layer, the UI layer, or the work surface)

- **Business** (known as the business rules layer or the services layer)

- **Data** (known as the data storage and access layer)

Figure 1.9 – N-tier architecture

These tiers can be owned/managed/deployed separately. For example, multiple presentation layers, such as the web, mobile, and bot layers, can leverage the same business and data tier.

Microservices architecture

Microservices architecture consists of small, loosely coupled, independent, and autonomous services. Let's see their benefits:

- Services can be deployed and scaled independently. An issue in one service will have a local impact and can be fixed by just deploying the impacted service. There is no compulsion to share technology or frameworks.

- Services communicate with each other via well-defined APIs or messaging systems such as the Azure service bus.

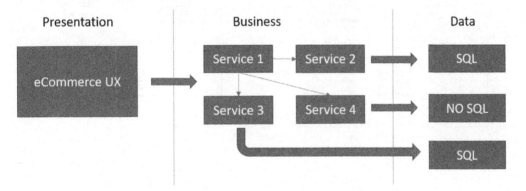

Figure 1.10 – Microservices architecture

As you can see in the preceding diagram, a service can be owned by independent teams and have its own cycle. Services are responsible for managing their own data stores. Scenarios demanding lower latency can be optimized by bringing in a cache or high-performance NoSQL stores.

Stateless services architecture

Services should not have any state. State and data should be managed independently from services, that is, externally through a data store such as a distributed cache or a database. By delegating the state externally, services will have the resources to serve more requests with high reliability. The following diagram shows an example of stateful services on the left-hand side. Here, state is maintained in each service through an in-memory cache or session provider, whereas a stateless service, as shown on the right-hand side, manages state and data externally.

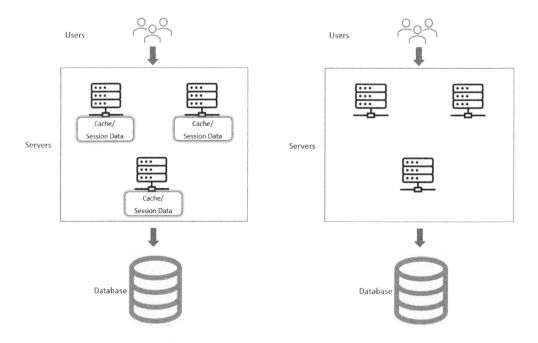

Figure 1.11 – Stateful (left) versus stateless (right)

Session affinity should not be enabled as it leads to sticky session issues and will stop you from getting the benefits of load balancing, scalability, and the distribution of traffic.

Event-driven architecture

The main features of event-driven architectures are listed as follows:

- In an event-driven architecture, communication, which is generally known as **publisher-subscriber communication**, between modules, is primarily asynchronous and achieved via events. Producers and consumers are totally decoupled from each other. The structure of the event is the only contract that is exchanged between them.

- There can be multiple consumers of the same event taking care of their specific operations; ideally, they won't even be aware of each other. Producers can continuously push events without worrying about the availability of consumers.

- Publishers publish events via a messaging infrastructure such as queues or a service bus. Once an event has been published, the messaging infrastructure is responsible for sending the event to eligible subscribers.

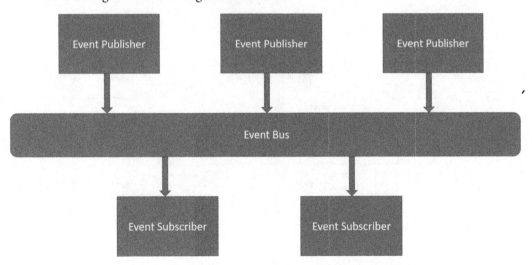

Figure 1.12 – Event-driven architecture

This architecture is best suited for scenarios that are asynchronous in nature. For example, long-running operations can be queued for processing. A client might poll for status or even act as a subscriber for an event.

Resiliency architecture

As the communication between components increases, so does the possibility of failures. A system should be designed to recover from any kind of failure. We will cover a few strategies for building a fault-tolerant system that can heal itself in the case of failures.

If you are familiar with Azure, you'll know that applications, services, and data should be replicated globally in at least two Azure regions for planned downtime and unplanned transient or permanent failures, as shown in the following screenshot. In these scenarios, choosing Azure App Service to host web applications, using REST APIs, and choosing a globally distributed database service, such as Azure Cosmos DB, is wise. Choosing Azure paired regions will help in **business continuity and disaster recovery (BCDR)**, as at least one region in each pair will be prioritized for recovery if an outage affects multiple regions.

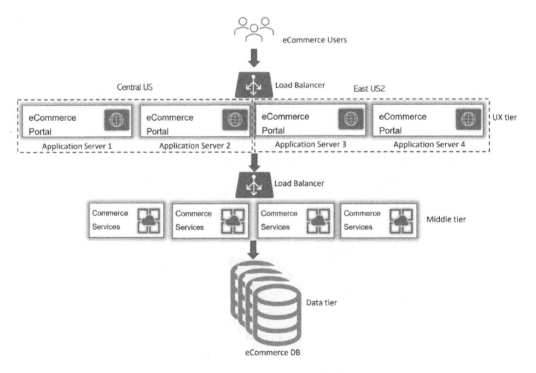

Figure 1.13 – Resiliency architecture

Now, let's see how to tackle different types of faults.

Transient faults can occur in any type of communication or service. You need to have a strategy to recover from transient faults, such as the following:

- Identify the operation and type of transient fault. Then, determine the appropriate retry count and interval.
- Avoid anti-patterns such as endless retry mechanisms with a finite number of retries or circuit breakers.

If a failure is not transient, you should respond to the failure gracefully by choosing some of the following options:

- Failing over
- Compensating for any failed operations
- Throttling/blocking the bad client/actor
- Using a leader election to select a leader in the case of a failure

Here, telemetry plays a big role; you should have custom metrics to keep a tab on the health of any component. Alerts can be raised when a custom event occurs or a specific metric reaches a certain threshold.

With this, we are done with our coverage of common enterprise architectures. Next, we will look at the requirements of enterprise applications and their different architectures through the lens of the design principles and common architectures that we learned about earlier.

Identifying enterprise application requirements (business and technical)

In the next few chapters, we will build a working e-commerce application. It will be a three-tier application consisting of a UI layer, a service layer, and a database. Let's look at the requirements for this e-commerce application.

The solution requirements are the capabilities to be implemented and made available in the product to solve a problem or achieve an objective.

The business requirements are simply the end customer's needs. In the IT world, *business, generally, refers to customers*. These requirements are collected from various stakeholders and documented as a single source of truth for everyone's preference. Eventually, this becomes the backlog and scope of work to be completed.

The technical requirements are the technology-related aspects that a system should implement, such as reliability, availability, performance, and BCDR. These are also known as **quality-of-service** (**QoS**) requirements.

Let's break the typical business requirements for an e-commerce application site down into the following categories: **Epic**, **Feature**, and **User Story**.

The application's business requirements

The following screenshot, from Azure DevOps, shows a summary of the backlog of our business requirements. You can see the different features that are expected in our application along with the user stories.

Epic	⌄ 🏰 eCommerce web site for customers to purchase products
Feature	⌄ 🏆 eCommerce application should have feature for users to register
User Story	🃏 As a customer, I want to sign up with email id/password or phone number/OTP, so that I can get access to the eCommerce application
Feature	⌄ 🏆 eCommerce application should have feature to authenticate and authorize the user
User Story	🃏 As a customer, I want to log in using email id/password or phone number/OTP, so that I can start purchasing
User Story	🃏 As an administrator, I want to log in using email id/password or phone number/OTP, so that I can add or delete products to/from the catalog
Feature	⌄ 🏆 eCommerce application should have feature to search and sort products
User Story	🃏 As a customer, I want to search products across all categories or selected categories, so that I can select the products easily for purchase
User Story	🃏 As a customer, I want to sort products in search results by price/customer-reviews/newest-arrivals, so that I can select the products easily for purchase
Feature	⌄ 🏆 eCommerce application should have feature to add products to cart or buy directly
User Story	🃏 As a customer, I want to add products to cart and stay in same page, so that I can continue shopping
User Story	🃏 As a customer, I want to buy product directly, so that I can complete my purchase quickly if I am buying only one product
Feature	⌄ 🏆 eCommerce application should have feature to review and submit the order
User Story	🃏 As a customer, I want to review the cart and edit the product and its quantity, so that I can submit the final order
Feature	⌄ 🏆 eCommerce application should have feature to send notifications
User Story	🃏 As a customer, I want to receive email notifications with summary of products, so that I can have it as confirmation
Feature	⌄ 🏆 eCommerce application should have feature to search orders
User Story	🃏 As a customer, I want to search Orders placed in the last 30/60/90/All days, so that I can refer to them any time to create a copy or check what products I purchased
User Story	🃏 As a regular customer, I want to search and resubmit past orders, so that I save time purchasing products I buy often
Feature	⌄ 🏆 eCommerce application should have feature to generate and download invoice
User Story	🃏 As a customer, I want to see and download my invoice, so that I have the proof of bill paid for that shipment
Feature	⌄ 🏆 eCommerce application should have feature to Support customers when they need
User Story	🃏 As a customer, I want to see detailed warning message and error messages in case of unexpected issue with application, so that I know why it failed
User Story	🃏 As a customer, I want to get support via chat, so that I can resolve my issues faster

Figure 1.14 – Requirement backlog from Azure DevOps

The application's technical requirements

Having seen the business requirements, let's now go through the technical requirements:

- The e-commerce application should be **highly available**, that is, available for 99.99% of the time during any 24-hour period.

- The e-commerce application should be **highly reliable**, that is, reliable for 99.99% of the time during any 24-hour period.

- The e-commerce application should be **highly performant**, that is, 95% of operations should take less than or be equal to 3 seconds during any 24-hour period.

- The e-commerce application should be **highly scalable**: It should automatically scale up/down based on the varying load.

- The e-commerce application should have **monitoring and alerts**: An alert should be sent to a support engineer in the case of any system failures.

Here are the **technical aspects** and requirements that have been identified for the e-commerce application:

The frontend

- A web application (e-commerce) using ASP.Net 6.0

The core components

- Logging/caching/configuration in C# 10.0 and .Net 6.0

The middle tier

- An Azure API gateway to implement authentication

- A user management service through an ASP.NET 6.0 web API to add/remove users

- Product and pricing services through an ASP.NET 6.0 web API to get products from the data store

- A domain data service through an ASP.NET 6.0 web API to get the domain data, such as country data

- A payment service through an ASP.NET 6.0 web API to complete payments

- An order processing service through an ASP.NET 6.0 web API to submit and search orders

- An invoice processing service through an ASP.NET 6.0 web API to generate invoices

- A notification service through an ASP.NET 6.0 web API to send notifications such as emails

The data tier

- A data access service through an ASP.NET 6.0 web API to talk to Azure Cosmos DB to read/write data

- Entity Framework Core to access data

Azure Stack

- Azure Cosmos DB as a backend data store

- Azure Service Bus for asynchronous message processing

- Azure App Service to host the web application and web APIs

- Azure Traffic Manager for high availability and responsiveness

- Azure Application Insights for diagnostics and telemetry

- Azure paired regions for better resiliency

- Azure resource groups to create **Azure Resource Manager** (**ARM**) templates and deploy them to the Azure subscription

- Azure Pipelines for **continuous integration and continuous deployment (CI/CD)**

We are now done with the requirements of the enterprise application. Next, we will look at how to architect an enterprise application.

Architecting an enterprise application

The following architectural diagram depicts what we are building. We need to bear in mind all of the design principles, patterns, and requirements that we have seen in this chapter when we are architecting and developing the application. The following diagram shows the proposed architecture for our e-commerce enterprise application:

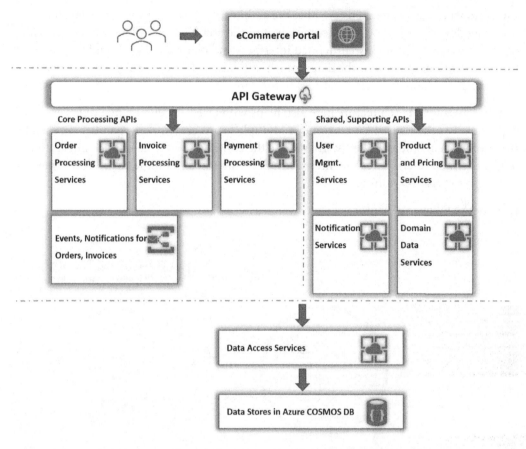

Figure 1.15 – The e-commerce application's three-tier architecture

Separation of concerns/SRP has been taken care of at each tier. The presentation tier, containing the UI, is separated from the services tier containing the business logic. This is again separated from the data access tier containing the data store.

The high-level components are unaware of the low-level components consuming them. The data access tier is unaware of the services consuming it, and the services are unaware of the UX tier consuming them.

Each service is separated based on the business logic and functionality it is supposed to perform.

Encapsulation has been taken care of at the architecture level and should be taken care of during development, too. Each component in the architecture will be interacting with other components through well-defined interfaces and contracts. We should be able to replace any component in the diagram without having to worry about its internal implementation and whether it adheres to the contracts.

The loosely coupled architecture here also helps with faster development and faster deployment to the market for customers. Multiple teams can work, in parallel, on each of their components independently. They share the contracts and timelines for integration testing at the start, and once the internal implementation and unit tests are done, they can start with integration testing.

Refer to the following diagram:

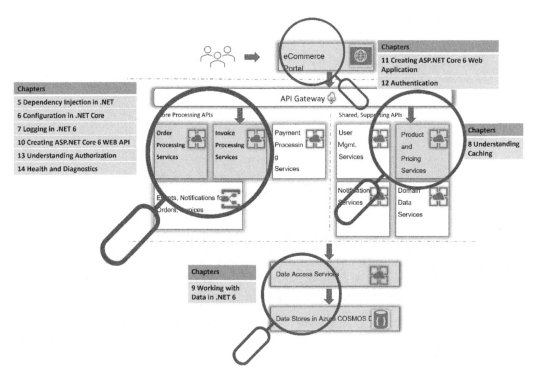

Figure 1.16 – The eCommerce application's three-tier architecture with highlighted chapters

From the preceding diagram, we can identify the chapters in which different parts of the e-commerce application that we will build will be covered. They can be explained as follows:

- Creating an ASP.NET web application (our e-commerce portal) will be covered in *Chapter 11, Creating an ASP.NET Core 6 Web Application.*

- Authentication will be covered in *Chapter 12, Understanding Authentication.*

- The order processing service and the invoice processing service are the two core services for generating orders and invoicing. They will be the heart of the e-commerce application as they are the ones that are responsible for the revenue. Creating an ASP.NET Core web API will be covered in *Chapter 10, Creating an ASP.NET Core 6 Web API,* and cross-cutting concerns will be covered in *Chapter 5, Dependency Injection in .NET 6, Chapter 6, Configuration in .NET 6,* and *Chapter 7, Logging in .NET 6,* respectively. The DRY principle will be taken care of by reusing core components and cross-cutting concerns instead of repeating implementations.

- Caching will be covered as part of the product pricing service in *Chapter 8, All You Need to Know about Caching.* Caching will help us to improve the performance and scalability of our system, with temporary copies of frequently accessed data being available in memory.

- Data storage, access, and the number of providers will be covered as part of the data access layer in *Chapter 9, Working with Data in .NET 6.* The kind of architecture that we have adopted, where data and access to it are separate from the rest of the application, gives us better maintenance. Azure Cosmos DB is our choice to scale throughput and storage elastically and independently across any number of Azure regions worldwide. Additionally, it is secure by default and enterprise-ready.

This concludes our discussion on architecting our enterprise application. Next, we will look at the solution structure for our enterprise application.

Solution structuring of the application

To keep things simple, we will go with a single solution for all our projects, as shown in the following screenshot. The other approach of having separate solutions for the UI, shared components, and web APIs can also be considered when the number of projects in the solution explodes and causes maintenance issues. The following screenshot shows our application's solution structure:

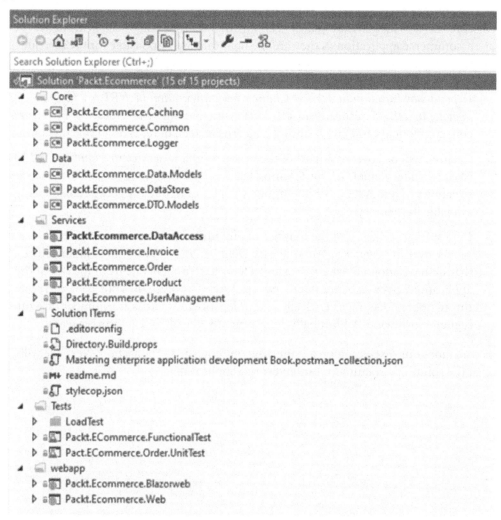

Figure 1.17 – The solution structure of the e-commerce application

Here, we have adopted separation of concerns by having separate folder structures and projects for UX, Service, Data, Core, and Testing.

Summary

In this chapter, we learned about common design principles such as SOLID, DRY, and KISS. Also, we looked at various design patterns with real-world examples. Then, we looked at different enterprise architectures, identified the requirements for the e-commerce application that we are going to build, and applied what we learned to architect our e-commerce application. You can now apply what you have learned here when you design any application.

In the next chapter, we will learn about .NET 6 Core and Standard.

Questions

1. What is the LSP?

    a. Base class instances should be replaceable with instances of their derived type.

    b. Derived class instances should be replaceable with instances of their base type.

    c. Designing for generics that can work with any data type.

    Answer: a

2. What is SRP?

    a. Instead of one common large interface, plan for multiple scenario-specific interfaces for better decoupling and change management.

    b. You should avoid taking a direct dependency approach on concrete implementation. Instead, you should depend on abstractions as much as possible.

    c. An entity should only have a single responsibility. You should avoid empowering one entity with multiple responsibilities.

    d. Entities should be designed in such a way that they should be open for extension but closed for modification.

    Answer: c

3. What is OCP?

    a. Entities should be open to modification but closed for extension.

    b. Entities should be open to extension but closed for modification.

    c. Entities should be open to composition but closed for extension.

    d. Entities should be open to abstraction but closed for inheritance.

    Answer: b

4. Which pattern is used to make two incompatible interfaces work together?

    a. Proxy

    b. Bridge

    c. Iterator

    d. Adapter

    Answer: d

5. Which principle ensures that services can be deployed and scaled independently and that an issue in one service will have a local impact, which can be fixed by just redeploying the impacted service?

    a. The domain-driven design principle

    b. The single-responsibility principle

    c. The stateless service principle

    d. The resiliency principle

    Answer: b

2

Introducing .NET 6 Core and Standard

.NET is a developer platform that offers libraries and tools for building many different types of applications, such as web, desktop, mobile, games, **Internet of Things (IoT)**, and cloud applications. Using .NET, we can develop applications targeting many operating systems, including Windows, macOS, Linux, Android, iOS, and so on, and it supports processor architectures such as x86, x64, ARM32, and ARM64.

.NET also supports application development using multiple programming languages, such as C#, Visual Basic, and F#, using popular **integrated development environments (IDEs)** such as Visual Studio, Visual Studio Code, and Visual Studio for Mac.

After .NET 5, .NET 6 is now a major release that includes C# 10 and F# 6, adds many language features, and includes many performance improvements.

The following topics are covered in this chapter:

- Introducing .NET 6
- Understanding the core components of .NET 6
- Setting up the development environment
- Understanding the CLI
- What is .NET Standard?
- Understanding .NET 6 cross-platform and cloud application support

This chapter will help us understand a few core components, libraries, and tools that are included in .NET for developing the applications.

Technical requirements

A Windows, Linux, or Mac machine is required and install the respective SDK from https://dotnet.microsoft.com/download/dotnet/6.0.

Introducing .NET 6

In 2002, Microsoft released the first version of .NET Framework, a development platform to develop web and desktop applications. .NET Framework offers many services, including managed code execution, a vast set of APIs via a base class library, memory management, a common type system, language interoperability, and development frameworks such as ADO.NET, ASP.NET, WCF, WinForms, and **Windows Presentation Framework** (**WPF**). Initially, it was released as a separate installer, but it was later integrated and shipped with the Windows operating system. .NET Framework 4.8 is the latest version of .NET Framework.

In 2014, Microsoft announced an open source, cross-platform implementation of .NET called **.NET Core**. .NET Core was built from scratch to make it cross-platform and it is currently available on Linux, macOS, and Windows. .NET Core is fast and modular and offers support side by side so that we can run different versions of .NET Core on the same machine without affecting other applications.

.NET 6 is an open source, cross-platform implementation of .NET with which you can build applications that can run on Windows, macOS, and Linux operating systems. With .NET 6, Microsoft's unified platform to develop browser, cloud, desktop, IoT, and mobile applications in order to use the same .NET libraries and share code easily.

To learn more about new features in .NET 6, you can visit https://docs.microsoft.com/en-us/dotnet/core/whats-new/dotnet-6.

> **Note**
> .NET 6 is a **long-term support** (**LTS**) release; it is supported for 3 years from the generally available date. It is recommended to migrate, particularly .NET 5 apps to .NET 6. For more details, you can visit https://dotnet.microsoft.com/en-us/platform/support/policy/dotnet-core.

Next, let's understand the core features of .NET.

Understanding the core features

The following are a couple of the core features of .NET that we will understand more in depth:

- **Open source**: .NET is a free (with no licensing costs, including for commercial use) and open source developer platform that offers many development tools for Linux, macOS, and Windows. Its source code is maintained by Microsoft and the .NET community on GitHub. You can access the .NET repositories at `https://github.com/dotnet/core/blob/master/Documentation/core-repos.md`.

- **Cross-platform**: .NET applications run on many operating systems, including Linux, macOS, Android, iOS, tvOS, watchOS, and Windows. They also run consistently across processor architectures, such as x86, x64, ARM32, and ARM64.

With .NET, we can build the following types of applications:

Application Types	Description
Web	Web applications, Blazor-based SPA applications, REST-based API and gRPC service applications
Microservices	Independently deployable, highly scalable microservices that run on Docker containers
Cloud	Serverless functions and cloud-native applications
Mobile	Native mobile applications for iOS, Android, and Windows
Desktop	WinForms and WPF for Windows
Internet of Things (IoT)	IoT applications that can run on Raspberry Pi and Hummingboard
Games	2D and 3D games for Windows, Android, and iOS
Machine Learning	Build custom machine learning models and easily integrate with .NET applications

Table 2.1 – Application types

- **Programming languages**: .NET supports multiple programming languages. Code written in one language is accessible in other languages. The following table shows the supported languages:

Supported Languages	Description
C#	Simple, modern, object-oriented, and type-safe programming language
F#	Functional, object-oriented programming language for .NET
Visual Basic	Simple, type-safe, object-oriented programming language

Table 2.2 – Supported Languages

- **IDEs**: .NET supports multiple IDEs. Let's understand each one:

  a. **Visual Studio** is a feature-rich IDE available on the Windows platform to build, debug, and publish .NET applications. It is available in three editions: Community, Professional, and Enterprise. Visual Studio 2022 Community Edition is free for students, individual developers, and organizations contributing to open source projects.

  b. **Visual Studio for Mac** is free and available for macOS. It can be used to develop cross-platform applications and games for iOS, Android, and the web using .NET.

  c. **Visual Studio Code** is a free, open source, lightweight yet powerful code editor available on Windows, macOS, and Linux. It has built-in support for JavaScript, TypeScript, and Node.js and, with extensions, you can add support for many popular programming languages.

  d. **Codespaces** is a cloud development environment powered by Visual Studio Code and hosted by GitHub to develop .NET applications.

- **Deployment models**: .NET supports two modes of deployment:

  a. **Self-contained**: When a .NET application is published in self-contained mode, the published artifact contains the .NET runtime, libraries, and the application and its dependencies. Self-contained applications are platform-specific, and the target machine need not have the .NET runtime installed. The machine uses the .NET runtime shipped along with the application to run the application.

  b. **Framework-dependent**: When a .NET application is published in framework-dependent mode, the published artifact contains only the application and its dependencies. The .NET runtime must be installed on the target machine to run the application.

Next, let's understand the application frameworks offered by .NET.

Understanding application frameworks

.NET simplifies application development by offering many application frameworks. Each application framework contains a set of libraries to develop targeted applications. Let's understand each in detail:

- **ASP.NET Core**: This is an open source and cross-platform application development framework that lets you build modern, cloud-based, internet-connected applications, such as web, IoT, and API applications. ASP.NET Core is built on top of .NET Core, hence you can build and run across platforms, such as Linux, macOS, and Windows.

- **Blazor**: This is an application framework to build interactive client-side web UI using C# instead of JavaScript. Blazor applications can re-use code and libraries from the server side and run in the browser using WebAssembly or handle Client UI events on the server using SignalR.

- **WPF**: This is a UI framework that lets you create desktop applications for Windows. WPF uses **Extensible Application Markup Language (XAML)**, a declarative model for application development.

- **Entity Framework (EF)** Core: This is an open source, cross-platform, lightweight, **object-relational mapping (ORM)** framework to work with databases using .NET objects. It supports LINQ queries, changes tracking, and schema migrations. It works with popular databases, such as SQL Server, SQL Azure, SQLite, Azure Cosmos DB, MySQL, and many more.

- **Language-Integrated Query (LINQ)**: This adds query capabilities to .NET programming languages. LINQ allows you to query data from a database, XML, in-memory arrays, and collections with the same API.

- **.NET MAUI**: The .NET Multi-platform App UI is a cross-platform framework to create native mobile and desktop applications using C# and XAML. Using .NET MAUI, you can develop applications targeting Android, iOS, macOS, and Windows using the same code base.

> **Note**
> .NET MAUI is currently in preview, and is not recommended for production use. For more information, you can refer to `https://docs.microsoft.com/en-us/dotnet/maui/what-is-maui`.

In the next section, let's understand the core components of .NET.

Understanding the core components of .NET

.NET has two major components: a runtime and base class libraries. The runtime includes a **garbage collector** (**GC**) and the **just-in-time** (**JIT**) compiler, which manages the execution of .NET applications and **base class libraries** (**BCLs**), also known as **runtime libraries** or **framework libraries**, which contain the fundamental building blocks for .NET applications.

The .NET SDK is available for download at `https://dotnet.microsoft.com/download/dotnet/6.0`. It contains a set of libraries and tools to develop and run .NET applications. You can choose to install either the SDK or the .NET runtime. To develop .NET applications, you should install the SDK on the development machine and the .NET runtime to run .NET applications. The .NET runtime is included in the .NET SDK, hence you don't have to install the .NET runtime separately if you have already installed the .NET SDK.

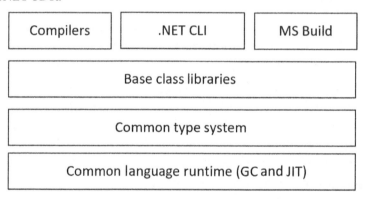

Figure 2.1 – Visualization of the .NET SDK

The .NET SDK contains the following components:

- **Common Language Runtime** (**CLR**): CLR executes the code and manages memory allocation. .NET applications, when compiled, produce an **intermediate language** (**IL**). CLR uses a JIT compiler to convert compiled code to machine code. It is a cross-platform runtime that is available for Windows, Linux, and macOS.

- **Memory management**: The GC manages the allocation and release of memory for .NET applications. For every new object created, memory is allocated in the managed heap and when there is not enough free space available, GC checks for objects in the managed heap and removes them if they are no longer used in the application. For more information, you can refer to `https://docs.microsoft.com/en-us/dotnet/standard/garbage-collection`.

- **JIT**: When .NET code is compiled, it is converted to IL. IL is platform- and language-independent, so when the runtime runs the application, JIT converts IL into machine code that the processor understands.

- **Common type system**: This defines how types are defined, used, and managed in CLR. It enables cross-language integrations and ensures type safety.

- **Base class library**: This contains implementations for primitive types such as `System.String` and `System.Boolean`, collections such as `List<T>` and `Dictionary<Tkey, Tvalue>`, and utility functions to perform I/O operations, HTTP, serialization, and many more. It simplifies .NET application development.

- **Roslyn compilers**: Roslyn is an open source C# and Visual Basic compiler with rich code analysis APIs. It enables building code analysis tools with the same API used by Visual Studio.

- **MSBuild**: This is a tool to build .NET applications. Visual Studio uses MSBuild to build .NET applications.

- **NuGet**: This is an open source package manager tool with which you can create, publish, and reuse code. A NuGet package contains compiled code, its dependent files, and a manifest that includes package version number information.

In the next section, let's understand how to set up the development environment to create and run .NET applications.

Setting up the development environment

Setting up a development environment is very easy. You will need the .NET SDK to build and run .NET applications. Optionally, you can choose to install IDEs that support .NET application development. You need to perform the following steps to set up the .NET SDK on your machine:

> **Note**
>
> .NET 6 is supported by Visual Studio 2022 and Visual Studio 2022 for Mac. It is not supported on earlier versions of Visual Studio. Visual Studio Community Edition is free for individual developers, classroom learning, and for unlimited users in organizations contributing to research or open source projects. It offers the same features as Professional Edition, but for advanced features such as advanced debugging and diagnostics tools, testing tools, and more, you need to have Enterprise Edition. To compare features, you can visit `https://visualstudio.microsoft.com/vs/compare`.

1. On a Windows machine, download and install Visual Studio 17.0 or later from `https://visualstudio.microsoft.com`.

2. In the installation options, from **Workloads**, you can select ASP.NET and web for web/API applications, Azure development, Mobile development with .NET for iOS, Android, windows, and .NET desktop development for windows applications, as shown in the following screenshot:

Figure 2.2 – Visual Studio installation, workload selection

3. Confirm the selection and proceed to complete the installation. This will install Visual Studio and the .NET 6 SDK on your machine.

> **Note**
> Azure development workload includes SDKs and tools to develop and support applications targeting Azure Services. It includes tools for Container development, Azure resource manager, Azure Cloud Services, Service Fabric, Azure Data Lake and Stream Analytics, Snapshot Debugger, and many more.

Alternatively, you can also perform the following steps to set it up:

1. Download and install the .NET 6 SDK for Windows, macOS, and Linux from `https://dotnet.microsoft.com/download/dotnet/6.0`. .NET Core supports side-by-side execution, and hence we can install multiple versions of .NET Core SDKs on a development machine.

2. From Command Prompt, run the `dotnet --version` command to verify the installed version, as shown in the following screenshot:

```
C:\>dotnet --version
6.0.101

C:\>dotnet

Usage: dotnet [options]
Usage: dotnet [path-to-application]

Options:
  -h|--help            Display help.
  --info               Display .NET information.
  --list-sdks          Display the installed SDKs.
  --list-runtimes      Display the installed runtimes.

path-to-application:
  The path to an application .dll file to execute.
```

Figure 2.3 – Command-line output of the dotnet command

3. Optionally, you can download and install Visual Studio Code from `https://code.visualstudio.com` to use it to develop the .NET application.

Now that we understand how to set up a development environment for .NET, in the next section, let's understand what the .NET CLI is and how it helps to create, build, and run .NET applications from the command line.

To set up an e-commerce application, you can refer to `https://github.com/PacktPublishing/Enterprise-Application-Development-with-C-10-and-.NET-6-Second-Edition/blob/main/README.md`.

Understanding the CLI

The .NET CLI is a cross-platform, command-line interface tool available to develop, build, run, and publish .NET applications. It is included in the .NET SDK.

The CLI command structure contains `command driver` (dotnet), `command`, `command-arguments`, and `options`, and this is a common pattern for most CLI operations. Refer to the following command pattern:

```
driver command <command-arguments> <options>
```

For instance, the following command creates a new console application. `dotnet` is the driver, `new` is the command, and `console` is a template name as an argument:

```
dotnet new console
```

The following table illustrates a few commands and a short description of the commands that are supported by the CLI:

Command	Description
new	Creates a new .NET project or file
build	Builds a .NET project
publish	Publishes the application and its dependencies to a folder for deployment
run	Builds and runs a .NET application
test	Runs unit tests using a specified test runner in the project
restore	Restores dependencies specified in a .NET project
clean	Cleans build outputs of a .NET project
pack	Creates a new NuGet package
help	Shows command-line help
add package	Adds a package reference to a project file
add reference	Adds a project to the project references
remove package	Removes a package reference from a project file
remove reference	Removes a project from the project references
list reference	Lists a project in the project references

Table 2.3 – CLI commands

Let's create a simple console application and run it using the .NET CLI:

> **Note**
>
> To perform the following steps, as a prerequisite, you should have the .NET SDK installed on your machine. You can download and install it from https://dotnet.microsoft.com/download/dotnet/6.0.

1. In Command Prompt, run the following command to create a console application with a project named HelloWorld:

```
dotnet new console --name HelloWorld
```

2. This command will create a new project called HelloWorld based on the console application template. Refer to the following screenshot:

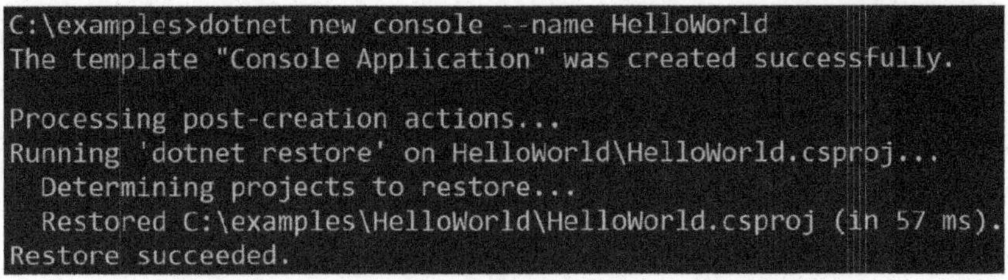

```
C:\examples>dotnet new console --name HelloWorld
The template "Console Application" was created successfully.

Processing post-creation actions...
Running 'dotnet restore' on HelloWorld\HelloWorld.csproj...
  Determining projects to restore...
  Restored C:\examples\HelloWorld\HelloWorld.csproj (in 57 ms).
Restore succeeded.
```

Figure 2.4 – Command-line output of the new console application

3. Run the following command to build and run the application:

```
dotnet run --project ./HelloWorld/HelloWorld.csproj
```

4. The preceding command will build and run the application and print the output onto the command window, as follows:

```
C:\examples>dotnet run --project ./HelloWorld/HelloWorld.csproj
Hello World!
```

Figure 2.5 – Command-line output of the console application when run

In the preceding steps, we created a new console application and ran it using the .NET CLI.

Overview of global.json

On the developer machine, if multiple .NET SDKs are installed in the global.json file, you can define the .NET SDK version to be used to run the .NET CLI commands. In general, the latest version of the SDK is used when no global.json file is defined, but you can override this behavior by defining global.json.

Running the following command will create a global.json file in the current directory. Depending on your requirements, you can choose a version for which you want to configure:

```
dotnet new globaljson --sdk-version 2.1.811
```

The following is an example global.json file that is created by running the preceding command:

```
{
  "sdk": {
    "version": "2.1.811"
  }
}
```

Here, `global.json` is configured to use the .NET SDK version 2.1.8.11. The .NET CLI uses this SDK version to build and run applications.

For more information on the .NET CLI, you can refer to `https://docs.microsoft.com/en-us/dotnet/core/tools`.

In the next section, let's understand what .NET Standard is.

What is .NET Standard?

.NET Standard is a set of API specifications that are available for multiple .NET implementations. New APIs are added with each new version of .NET Standard. Each .NET implementation targets a specific version of .NET Standard and has access to all the APIs supported by that .NET Standard version.

Libraries that are built targeting .NET Standard can be used in applications that are built using .NET implementations, which support those versions of .NET Standard. So, when building libraries, targeting higher versions of .NET Standard allows more APIs to be used, but can be used only in applications built using the versions of .NET implementations that support it.

The following screenshot lists the various versions of .NET implementations that support .NET Standard 2.0:

Version: .NET Standard 2.0	Available APIs: 32,638 of 37,118

.NET Implementation	Version Support
.NET and .NET Core	× 1.0 × 1.1 ✓ 2.0 ✓ 2.1 ✓ 2.2 ✓ 3.0 ✓ 3.1 ✓ 5.0 ✓ 6.0
.NET Framework	× 4.5 × 4.5.1 × 4.5.2 × 4.6 ✓ 4.6.1 ✓ 4.6.2 ✓ 4.7 ✓ 4.7.1 ✓ 4.7.2 ✓ 4.8
Mono	× 4.6 ✓ 5.4 ✓ 6.4
Xamarin.iOS	× 10.0 ✓ 10.14 ✓ 12.16
Xamarin.Android	× 7.0 ✓ 8.0 ✓ 10.0
Universal Windows Platform	× 8.0 × 8.1 × 10.0 ✓ 10.0.16299 ✓ TBD
Unity	✓ 2018.1

Figure 2.6 – .NET Standard 2.0-supported .NET implementations

For example, if you develop a library targeting .NET Standard 2.0, it has access to over 32,000 APIs, but it is supported by fewer versions of .NET implementations. If you want your library to be accessible by the maximum number of .NET implementations, then choose the lowest possible .NET Standard version, but then you'd need to compromise on the APIs available.

Let's understand when to use .NET 6 and .NET Standard.

Understanding the use of .NET 6 and .NET Standard

.NET Standard makes it easy to share code between different .NET implementations, but .NET 6 offers a better way to share code and run on multiple platforms. .NET 6 unifies the API to support desktop, web, cloud, mobile, and cross-platform console applications.

.NET 6 implements .NET Standard 2.1, so your existing code that targets .NET Standard works with .NET 6; you need not change the **target framework moniker** (**TFM**) unless you want to access new runtime features, language features, or APIs. You can multitarget to .NET Standard and .NET 6 so that you can access new features and make your code available to other .NET implementations.

If you are building new reusable libraries that need to work with .NET Framework as well, then target them to .NET Standard 2.0. If you don't need to support .NET Framework, then you can target either .NET Standard 2.1 or .NET 6. It is recommended to target .NET 6 to gain access to new APIs, runtime, and language features.

Using the .NET CLI, running the following command creates a new class library:

```
dotnet new classlib -o MyLibrary
```

It creates a class library project with the target framework as .net6.0 or the latest available SDK on the developer machine.

If you examine the MyLibrary\MyLibrary.csproj file, it should look as in the following snippet. You will notice the target framework is set to net6.0:

```
<Project Sdk="Microsoft.NET.Sdk">
  <PropertyGroup>
    <TargetFramework>net6.0</TargetFramework>
    <ImplicitUsings>enable</ImplicitUsings>
    <Nullable>enable</Nullable>
  </PropertyGroup>
</Project>
```

You can force it to use a specific version of the target framework while creating a class library using the .NET CLI. The following command creates a class library targeting .NET Standard 2.0:

```
dotnet new classlib -o MyLibrary -f netstandard2.0
```

If you examine the MyLibrary\MyLibrary.csproj file, it looks as in the following snippet, where the target framework is netstandard2.0:

```
<Project Sdk="Microsoft.NET.Sdk">
  <PropertyGroup>
    <TargetFramework>netstandard2.0</TargetFramework>
  </PropertyGroup>
</Project>
```

If you create a library targeting .NET Standard 2.0, it can be accessed in an application built targeting .NET Core as well as .NET Framework.

Optionally, you can target multiple frameworks; for example, in the following code snippet, the library project is configured to target .NET 6.0 and .NET Standard 2.0:

```
<Project Sdk="Microsoft.NET.Sdk">
  <PropertyGroup>
    <TargetFrameworks>net6.0;netstandard2.0
      </TargetFrameworks>
  </PropertyGroup>
</Project>
```

When you configure your application to support multiple frameworks and build the project, you will notice it creates artifacts for each targeted framework version. Refer to the following screenshot:

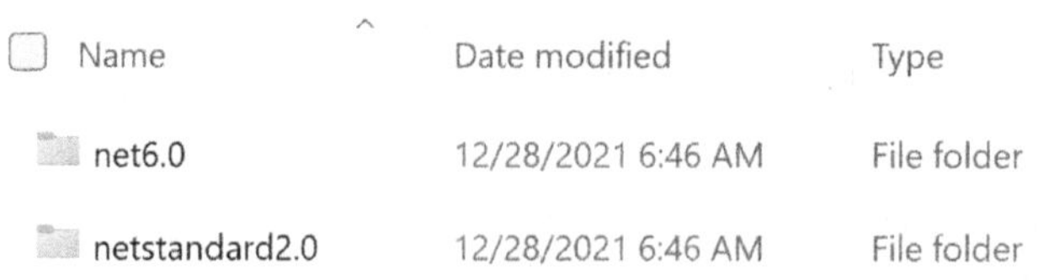

Name	Date modified	Type
net6.0	12/28/2021 6:46 AM	File folder
netstandard2.0	12/28/2021 6:46 AM	File folder

Figure 2.7 – Build artifacts targeting multiple frameworks

Let's summarize the information here:

- Use .NET Standard 2.0 to share code between .NET Framework and all other platforms.
- Use .NET Standard 2.1 to share code between Mono, Xamarin, and .NET Core 3.x.
- Use .NET 6 for code sharing moving forward.

In the next section, let's understand .NET 6's cross-platform capabilities and cloud application support.

Understanding .NET 6 cross-platform and cloud application support

.NET has many implementations. Each implementation contains runtimes, libraries, application frameworks (optional), and development tools. There are four .NET implementations:

- .NET Framework
- .NET 6
- **Universal Windows Platform (UWP)**
- Mono

And the set of API specifications common to all these implementations is .NET Standard.

Multiple .NET implementations enable you to create .NET applications targeting many operating systems. You can build .NET applications for the following:

.NET Implementations	Application Types
.NET Framework	WPF, Windows, and ASP.NET
.NET Core and .NET 6	Web, IoT apps, and REST-based API apps
Mono/Xamarin	Native Android, iOS, macOS, tvOS, watchOS
UWP	Windows application that can run on PCs, tablets, Xbox

Table 2.4 – .NET implementations

Let's understand more about .NET implementations:

- **.NET Framework** is the initial implementation of .NET. Using .NET Framework, you can develop Windows, WPF, web applications, and web and WCF services, targeting the Windows operating system. .NET Framework 4.5 and above implement .NET Standard, so libraries that are built targeting .NET Standard can be used in .NET Framework applications.

> **Note**
>
> .NET Framework 4.8 is the last version of .NET Framework and no new versions will be released in the future. Microsoft will continue to include it with Windows and support it with security and bug fixes. For new development, it is recommended to use .NET 6 or later.

- **UWP** is an implementation of .NET with which you can build touch-enabled Windows applications that can run on PCs, tablets, Xbox, and so on.

- **Mono** is an implementation of .NET. It is a small runtime that powers Xamarin to develop native Android, macOS, iOS, tvOS, and watchOS applications. It implements .NET Standard and libraries targeting .NET Standard can be used in applications built using Mono.

- **.NET 6** is an open source, cross-platform implementation of .NET with which you can build console, web, desktop, and cloud applications that can run on Windows, macOS, and Linux operating systems. .NET 6 is now the primary implementation of .NET, which is built on a single code base with a uniform set of capabilities and APIs that can be used by .NET applications.

The .NET 6 SDK, along with libraries and tools, also contains multiple runtimes, including the .NET runtime, the ASP.NET Core runtime, and .NET Desktop Runtime. To run .NET 6 applications, you can choose to install either the .NET 6 SDK or a respective platform and workload-specific runtime:

- **The .NET runtime** only contains components required to run console applications. To run web or desktop applications, you need to install the ASP.NET Core runtime and .NET Desktop Runtime separately. The .NET runtime is available on Linux, macOS, and Windows and supports the x86, x64, ARM32, and ARM64 processor architectures.

- **The ASP.NET Core runtime** enables you to run web/server applications and is available on Linux, macOS, and Windows for the x86, x64, ARM32, and ARM64 processor architectures.

- **.NET Desktop Runtime** enables you to run Windows-/WPF-based desktop applications on Windows. It is available for the x86 and x64 processor architectures.

The availability of .NET runtimes for multiple platforms makes .NET 6 cross-platform. On the target machine, you just need to install the runtime that is needed for your workload and run the application.

Now, let's explore the services offered by Azure that run .NET 6.

Cloud support

.NET 6 is supported by popular cloud service providers, including Azure, Google Cloud, and AWS. Let's understand a few services that can run .NET 6 applications in Azure:

- **Azure App Service** supports easily deploying and running ASP.NET Core 6 applications. Azure App Service offers you the chance to host .NET 6 applications on Linux or Windows platforms using the x86 or x64 processor architectures. For more information, you can refer to `https://docs.microsoft.com/en-in/azure/app-service/overview`.

- **Azure Functions** supports deploying and running serverless functions built on .NET 6. You can host Functions apps on Linux or Windows. For more information, you can refer to `https://docs.microsoft.com/en-us/azure/azure-functions/functions-overview`.

- **Docker** .NET 6 applications run on Docker containers. You can build independently deployable, highly scalable microservices that run on Docker containers. Official .NET Core Docker images are available at `https://hub.docker.com/_/microsoft-dotnet` for different combinations of .NET (SDK or runtime) and operating systems. Many Azure services support Docker containers, including Azure App Service, Azure Service Fabric, Azure Batch, Azure Container Instances, and **Azure Kubernetes Service** (**AKS**). For more information, you can refer to `https://docs.microsoft.com/en-us/dotnet/core/docker/introduction`.

With .NET 6, we can develop enterprise server applications or highly scalable microservices that can run in the cloud. We can develop mobile applications for iOS, Android, and Windows operating systems. .NET code and project files look similar and developers can reuse skills or code to develop different types of applications targeting different platforms.

Summary

In this chapter, we learned what .NET is and its core features. We learned about the application frameworks offered by .NET and the different deployment models it supports. Next, we learned about the core components, tools, and libraries offered by .NET and learned how to set up a development environment on a machine.

We also looked at the .NET CLI and created a sample application using the .NET CLI. Next, we learned what .NET Standard is and when to use .NET 6 and .NET Standard, and then concluded the chapter by discussing various .NET implementations, .NET 6 cross-platform support, and cloud support.

In the next chapter, we will learn what is new in C# 10.0.

Questions

1. .NET Core is which of the following?

    a. Open source

    b. Cross-platform

    c. Free

    d. All of the above

    Answer: d

2. The .NET Standard 2.0 library is supported by which of the following?

    a. .NET Framework 4.6.1 or later

    b. .NET Core 2.0 or later

    c. .NET 6

    d. Mono 5.4+ or later

    e. All of the above

    Answer: e

3. The .NET CLI driver that is mandatory to run CLI commands is which of the following?

   a. `net`

   b. `core`

   c. `dotnet`

   d. `none`

   Answer: c

4. The .NET SDK contains which of the following?

   a. The .NET CLI

   b. BCL

   c. The runtime

   d. All of the above

   Answer: d

Further reading

To learn more about .NET 6, you can refer to `https://docs.microsoft.com/en-us/dotnet/core/introduction`.

3
Introducing C# 10

C# is an elegant and type-safe object-oriented programming language that allows developers to build a wide range of secure and robust applications that run in the .NET ecosystem and is in the top 5 of the popular programming languages list published by GitHub.

C# was initially developed by Anders Hejlsberg at Microsoft as part of the .NET initiative. Since its first release in January 2002, there have been new features added consistently to the language to improve performance and productivity.

C# 10 released with .NET 6 comes with some cool new language features along with enhancements to the features released in earlier versions, which improve developer productivity. In this chapter, we will explore some of the new C# language features:

- Simplification of the using directives
- The record structs
- Improvements to the Lambda expressions
- Enhancements to interpolated strings
- Extended property patterns
- Additions to the caller argument attributes

By end of this chapter, you'll be familiar with the major new additions to C# 10. Also, this chapter will help us to upskill ourselves to build our next enterprise application in C#.

Technical requirements

You will need the following to understand the concepts of this chapter:

- Visual Studio 2022 version 17.0 Community Edition with the .NET 6.0 runtime

- A basic understanding of Microsoft .NET

The code used in this chapter can be found at `https://github.com/PacktPublishing/Enterprise-Application-Development-with-C-10-and-.NET-6-Second-Edition/tree/main/Chapter03`.

Simplification of the using directives

A top-level statement is a new feature introduced in C# 9.0, which makes it easy for developers to remove the ceremony code. The project templates that come with Visual Studio 2022 embrace the language changes introduced in C# such as top-level statements. For example, if you create a `Console` application, you will see the `Program.cs` file contains the code shown in the following snippet:

```
// See https://aka.ms/new-console-template for more //
information
Console.WriteLine("Hello, World!");
```

The preceding code came with a `console` application template that did not have the ceremony code such as class definition and the `main` method. This simplified the number of lines we could write by removing the redundant code.

The concepts of the `implicit` using directives and `global` using directives introduced in C# 10 reduce the repetition of the `using` statements in each CS file.

The global using directives

With the `global using` directives, we do not repeat the namespace `using` statements in all the `.cs` files. The `global` keyword is used to mark a `global using` directive as shown in the following code snippet:

```
global using System.Threading;
```

In the preceding code, we marked `System.Threading` as `global`. Now, we can reference the types under `System.Threading` by having the `using` directive at the start of the `.cs` file.

We can also create `global` aliases to the namespaces to resolve the namespace conflicts, as shown in the following code snippet:

```
global using SRS = System.Runtime.Serialization;
```

By defining this, we can refer to all the classes defined under `System.Runtime.Serialization` using the alias name, `SRS`. We can also define a `global using static` directive as shown here:

```
global using static System.Console;
```

With this, we can use all the `static` functions defined in the `System.Console` class directly without referring to the class name. For example, to write a line to the console, we can just call the `WriteLine` method without referring to the `Console` class name, as shown here:

```
WriteLine("Hello C# 10");
```

We can specify `global using` directives in any `.cs` file of the project. The only constraint is they should appear before any regular file-scoped using directives. The common practice seen among the developers is to create a `.cs` with the name `GlobalUsings.cs` and add the `global using` directive in that file. This will help to restrict the change to a single file when we need to add or remove a `global using` directive. The scope of the `global using` directives is the complication unit that is the current project.

The implicit using directives

In C#, we find a few framework namespaces, such as `System` and `System.Linq`, are present in almost all the classes. With C# 10, these commonly-used namespaces are implicitly added as `global` using directives. The namespaces added implicitly are based on the project target SDK and are documented here: `https://docs.microsoft.com/en-us/dotnet/core/project-sdk/overview#implicit-using-directives`.

In addition to these, if we wish to include any other namespace to be part of these implicit directives or remove any of the predefined namespaces, we can do so by adding `ItemGroup` to the `.csproj` file, as shown here:

```
<ItemGroup>
   <Using Include="System.Threading" />
   <Using Remove="System.IO" />
</ItemGroup>
```

In the previous snippet, we are including `System.Threading` and removing `System.IO` from the `implicit using` directives.

To completely remove the `implicit using` directives, we can uncheck the **Implicit global usings** option from the project properties under the **Build | General** tab, or by disabling the `ImplicitUsings` flag in the `.csproj` file as shown here:

```
<ImplicitUsings>disable</ImplicitUsings>
```

The simplification of `using` directives is another step toward removing the redundant ceremony code and making the content in the `.cs` files concise.

In the next section, we will explore the `record` structs introduced with C# 10.

The record structs

The *record types* introduced in C# 9 provide type declaration to create immutable reference types with synthesized methods for equality check and `ToString`. C# 10 brings us the *record structs*. In this section, we will see what `record struct` is and how it is different from `record class`.

We use the `record` keyword to declare `record class`, and we use the same `record` keyword to declare `record struct`, as shown in the following code:

```
public record struct Employee(string Name);
```

> **Note**
>
> In C# 9, to declare a `record` class, we don't explicitly use the `class` keyword. We simply specify `record` to declare it as shown here: `public record Shape(string Name);`
>
> Simply using the `record` keyword will continue to work in C# 10 to declare a `record` class, but it is recommended to specify `class` or `struct` explicitly for better readability.

`record struct` offers similar benefits to what `record class` offers, such as the following:

- Simplified declaration syntax
- Value equality
- Reference semantics

- Deconstruction

- Meaningful `ToString` output

Let's understand these by creating a sample `Console` application and defining an `EmployeeRecord` record struct. Add the following code to the `Program.cs` file, which is using the `EmployeeRecord` record struct defined in the previous code snippet:

```
using static System.Console;
 public record struct EmployeeRecord(string Name);
Employee employee1 = new EmployeeRecord("Suneel", "Kunani");
Employee employee2 = new EmployeeRecord("Suneel", "Kunani");
WriteLine(employee1.ToString());
WriteLine($"HashCode of s1 is :{ employee1.GetHashCode()}");
WriteLine($"HashCode of s2 is :{ employee2.GetHashCode()}");
WriteLine($"Is s1 equals s2 : { employee1 == employee2}");
//deconstruct the fields from the employee object
string firstName;
 (firstname, var lastname) = employee1;
Console.WriteLine($"firstname: {firstname},
lastname:{lastname}");
```

In the preceding code, we are creating two instances of the `EmployeeRecord` record struct with name field values using the simplified declaration syntax, then printing the hash code of the instance objects, and then checking the equality. Here, we are also deconstructing the fields from the `employee` object.

When we run the code, we see the output as shown in the following screenshot:

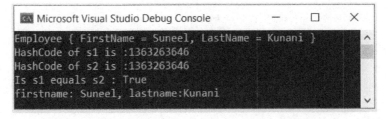

Figure 3.1 – Output of record struct example

When we look at the output, we observe that `ToString` is overridden to include the contents of the instance. As expected, the hash code of both instances is the same, as the field values are the same. In a regular struct, the hash code of the object is generated based on the first non-nullable field. In the `record` struct, the `GetHashCode` method is also overridden to include all the fields to generate the hash code.

The `record` struct synthesizes the implementation of the `IEquatable<T>` interface. It also implements the `==` and `!=` operators. The regular struct does not have these operators implemented by default. The regular struct has the `Equals` method inherited from `ValueType`, which uses reflection to do the equality check. So, the synthesized equality check in the `record` struct is more performant. The `record` struct also synthesizes the `Deconstruct` method to populate the fields out of the object. If you take a closer look at the deconstruction code, you will notice the mixed declaration of the variables. We have `lastName` being declared during deconstruction, whereas `firstName` was declared in the preceding statement. This mixed declaration of variables is only possible in C#10 and above.

When we disassemble the code in a disassembler tool such as ILSpy or Reflector, we see the generated code as shown in the following figure:

```csharp
public struct Employee : IEquatable<Employee>
{
    public string FirstName { get; set; }

    public string LastName { get; set; }

    public Employee(string FirstName, string LastName)
    {...}

    public override readonly string ToString()
    {...}

    private readonly bool PrintMembers(StringBuilder builder)
    {...}

    public static bool operator !=(Employee left, Employee right)
    {...}

    public static bool operator ==(Employee left, Employee right)
    {...}

    public override readonly int GetHashCode()
    {...}

    public override readonly bool Equals(object obj)
    {...}

    public readonly bool Equals(Employee other)
    {...}

    public readonly void Deconstruct(out string FirstName, out string LastName)
    {...}
}
```

Figure 3.2 – Generated code of the Employee class

> **Note**
>
> You can install ILSpy from `https://marketplace.visualstudio.com/items?itemName=SharpDevelopTeam.ILSpy`.

If we look closely at the Employee type definition, we can see all the plumbing synthesized by the C# compiler for the record struct type. From this, we can understand that the record struct is basically a struct that implements the IEquatable interface and overrides the GetHashCode and ToString methods. You can overwrite the ToString method to create your own string representation for the record type. Beginning with C# 10, you can also mark the ToString override as sealed, which prevents the compiler from synthesizing a ToString method or derived types from overriding it. Sealing the ToString method in the base record type ensures that the string representation is consistent across all derived types. The compiler also provides the Deconstruct method, which is used to deconstruct the record struct into its component properties. Unlike record classes, the record structs are mutable. To make a record struct immutable, we can add a readonly modifier to the declaration:

```
public readonly record struct Employee(string Name);
```

To change the fields of the readonly record struct, we can use the operator as shown here like with the record class:

```
Employee employee2 = employee1 with { LastName = string.Empty
};
```

In this section, we have learned about the record struct introduced in C# 10 and how it compares with the record class and regular struct. In the next section, let's learn about improvements to Lambda expressions.

Improvements to Lambda expressions

A Lambda expression is a way to represent an anonymous method. It allows us to define the method implementation inline.

A delegate type may be created from any Lambda expression. The types of a Lambda expression's parameters and return value determine the delegate type to which it can be transformed. A Lambda expression can be changed to an Action delegate type if it doesn't return a value; otherwise, it can be converted to one of the Func delegate types. In this section, we will learn about the improvements C# 10 brings to Lambda expressions.

Inferring the expression type

C# language compiler will now infer the expression type if the parameter's types are explicit and the return type can be inferred. For example, consider the following code snippet where we defined a Lambda expression to find the square of the given integer:

```
Var Square = (int x) => x * x;
```

In the preceding code, the parameter x type is specified as `int` and the return type is inferred as `int` from the expression. If we mouse-hover on `var` in Visual Studio, we can see the inferred type of the `Square` Lambda expression, as shown in the next screenshot, which uses the `Func` delegate:

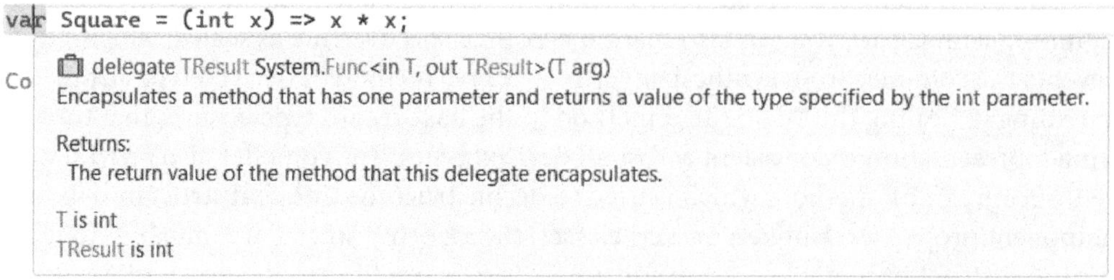

Figure 3.3 – Inferred type of Square expression

For the code shown here, the compiler will use the `Action` delegate, as the expression return type is `void`:

```
var SayHello = (string name) => Console.WriteLine($"Hello
{name}");
```

The inferred type will use `Func` or `Action` delegates if it is suitable. Otherwise, the compiler will synthesize a delegate type, for example, if the Lambda expression is taking a `ref` type, as shown in the following code snippet:

```
Var SayWelcome = (ref string name) => Console.
WriteLine($"Welcome {name}");
```

The synthesized type for the previous expression will be an anonymous delegate type.

The compiler will try to infer the return type based on the expression. Sometimes, it may not be possible to infer the type. We will get a compilation error if it is unable to infer the type information.

Return types for Lambda expressions

In situations where it is not possible for the compiler to infer the return type, we can specify explicitly in C# 10. Consider the following code snippet, where we have `record` classes of `Employee` and `Manager` inherited from a `Person` record class:

```
public record class Person();
public record class Employee() : Person();
public record class Manager() : Person();
```

```
var createExpression = (bool condition) => condition ? new
Employee() : new Manager();
```

The `createExpression` term in the preceding code snippet creates an instance of an `Employee` or `Manager` type based on the condition passed in. In this situation, the compiler cannot infer the return type, which will result in a compilation error. With C#10, we can now explicitly specify the return type for a Lambda expression as shown in the following code:

```
var createEmployee = Person (bool hasReportees) => condition ?
new Manager() : new Employee();
// Create the Person object based on condition
var manager = createEmployee(true);
```

The expression type inferred for the preceding code is `Func<bool, Person>`.

Adding attributes to Lambda expressions

Starting from C# 10, we can add attributes to the Lambda expressions and their parameters and return types. The following code snippet defines a Lambda expression to retrieve employees for the given ID:

```
var GetEmployeeById =  [Authorize] Employee ([FromRoute]int id)
=> { return new Employee { }; };
```

The `GetEmployeeeById` expression has the `[Authorize]` attribute and the `id` parameter is attributed with `[FromRoute]`.

Attributes on Lambda expressions don't have any effect when they are invoked, as the invocation is via the underlying delegate type. The attributes defined on Lambda expressions can be discovered via reflection.

The minimal API introduced with ASP.NET 6.0 is one of the driving factors behind these improvements. We will see the usage of this in *Chapter 10, Creating an ASP.NET Core 6 Web API*.

In this section, we have learned about the improvements to the Lambda expressions; in the next section, we will see improvements to interpolated strings.

Enhancements to interpolated strings

Almost every application will have some sort of text processing. In .NET, there are many ways available for string manipulation, such as the `string` primitive type, `StringBuilder`, `ToString` overrides on types, String concatenation, and `string.Format`, which provides functionality to build a string from a composite format string. `String.Format` takes a format string and format items as input and generates the formatted string as depicted in the following code:

```
string message = string.Format("{0}, {1}!", Greeting, Message);
```

In the previous code, the positions `{0}` and `{1}` in the format string will be filled with the `Greeting` and `Message` format items respectively passed in as arguments. To make it more friendly and readable, C# 6 added a new language syntax called **interpolated strings**, as shown in the following code snippet:

```
string Greeting = "Hello";
string Language = "C#";
int version = 10;
string message = $"{Greeting}, {Language}!";
string messageWithVersion = $"{Greeting}, {Language}
{version}!";
```

When interpolated strings syntax is used, the .NET compiler generates the code that is best suited for the interpolated string to produce the same result.

Use a disassembler such as ILSpy or SharpLab to look at the generated code for the previous code snippet; it will look something like the following code snippet:

```
String text = "Hello";
string text2 = "C#";
int num = 10;
string text3 = text + ", " + text2 + "!";
string text4 = string.Format("{0}, {1} {2}!", text, text2,
num);
```

> **Note**
>
> `https://sharplab.io/` is a .NET code playground that shows the intermediate results of code compilation.

For the `message` interpolated string, the code was generated using concatenation. For the second string, `messageWithVersion`, where a non-string literal is involved, the generated code uses `string.Format`.

The compiler did what was intended, but it had a few issues where the code was generated using `string.Format`:

- The compiler parsed the interpolated string to generate code with `string.Format`. The same string must be parsed by the .NET runtime also to find the literal positions.

- The argument type of the literals in the `string.Format` method is `Object`. So, any value type used in `string.Format` involves boxing.

- The overload of `string.Format` takes a maximum of three arguments. Beyond three is served by the overload that takes `params object[]`. So, more than three arguments require the instantiation of an array.

- Since `string.Format` accepts only the `Object` type, we cannot use `ref struct` types such as `Span<T>` and `ReadOnlySpan<char>`.

- Since `ToString` is called on the captured expression, multiple transient strings will be created.

All the shortcomings mentioned here will be addressed with C# 10 by generating code with a series of appends to the string builder. For the same code that we discussed, if you look at the generated code in C# 10, it uses `DefaultInterpolatedStringHandler` as shown in the following code snippet:

```
string Greeting = "Hello";
string Language = "C#";
int version = 10;
string message = Greeting + ", " + Language + "!";
DefaultInterpolatedStringHandler
defaultInterpolatedStringHandler = new
DefaultInterpolatedStringHandler(4, 3);
defaultInterpolatedStringHandler.AppendFormatted(Greeting);
defaultInterpolatedStringHandler.AppendLiteral(", ");
defaultInterpolatedStringHandler.AppendFormatted(Language);
defaultInterpolatedStringHandler.AppendLiteral(" ");
defaultInterpolatedStringHandler.AppendFormatted(version);
```

```
defaultInterpolatedStringHandler.AppendLiteral("!");
string messageWithVersion = defaultInterpolatedStringHandler.
ToStringAndClear();
```

For interpolated strings, instead of using `string.Format`, C# 10 compiler now uses **interpolated string handlers**. The built-in interpolated string handler in C# 10 is `DefaultInterpolatedStringHandler`. In the previously-generated code, `DefaultInterpolatedStringHandler` is constructed by passing in the two arguments, the number of characters in the literal portion of the interpolated string, and the number of positions in the string to be filled. `AppendLiteral` or `AppendFormatted` are called to append the literal or to append the formatted string, respectively. With the introduction of interpolated string handlers, the concerns discussed previously were addressed.

For the same interpolated string code written in earlier versions of C#, there will be an improvement in the performance in C# 10. We can also build our custom interpolated string handlers, which may be useful in situations when the data isn't going to be used as a string, or where conditional execution would be a logical fit for the target method.

In this section, we have learned about the improvements to the interpolated string, which gives us better performance over earlier versions. In the next section, let's learn about the extended property patterns.

Extended property patterns

Pattern matching is a way to check an object's value or the value of a property having a full or partial match to a sequence. This is supported in C# in the form of `if...else` and `switch...case` statements. In modern languages, especially in functional programming languages such as F#, there is advanced support for pattern matching. With C# 7.0, new pattern matching concepts were introduced. Pattern matching provides a different way to express conditions to have more human-readable code. Pattern matching is being extended with every major release of C# since its introduction in C# 7.

In this section, let's learn about the extended property pattern introduced in C# 10.

Consider the following code snippet:

```
Product product = new Product
{
    Name ="Men's Shirt",
    Price =10.0m,
    Location = new Address
```

```
    {
        Country ="USA",
        State ="NY"
    }
};
```

In this code snippet, we have an object of the `Product` type, which contains the location of the product origin. Prior to C# 10, if we wanted to check whether the country of origin of this product was the USA, we would do something similar to the following code snippet:

```
if (product is Product { Location: { Country: "USA" } })
    Console.WriteLine("USA");
```

With C# 10, we can access the extended properties to make it more readable, as shown in the following code snippet:

```
if (product is Product { Location.Country : "USA" })
    Console.WriteLine("USA");
```

In the preceding code, we are validating the `Country` property of `Location` using an extended property pattern.

In this section, we have learned about extended property patterns. Let's learn about the new addition to `caller` argument attributes in the next section.

Addition to the caller argument attributes

C# 5 first introduced `caller` argument attributes. They are `CallerMemberName`, `CallerFilePath`, and `CallerLineNumber`. These attributes make the compiler populate the method arguments in the generated code. They are used in various scenarios such as populating more data in the debug traces while firing an `OnNotifyPropertyChanged` event in the MVVM pattern. For example, consider the following code snippet, which defines a `Gift` model:

```
public class Gift : INotifyPropertyChanged
{
    private string _description;
    public string Description
    {
        get
```

```
    {
        return _description;
    }
    set
    {
        _description = value;
        OnPropertyRaised();
    }
}
public event PropertyChangedEventHandler
    PropertyChanged;
private void OnPropertyRaised([CallerMemberName] string
    propertyname="")
{
    if (PropertyChanged != null)
    {
        PropertyChanged(this, new
            PropertyChangedEventArgs(propertyname));
    }
}
}
```

In the preceding Gift class definition, the OnPropertyChanged method
is called every time the setter of the Description property is called. In the
OnProperyChanged method implementation, we have the propertyName argument
attributed with CallerMemberName. This will make the compiler generate a setter as
shown in the following code:

```
public string Description
{
    get { return _description;        }
    set
    {
        _description = value;
        OnPropertyRaised("Description");
    }
}
```

In this generated code, the argument to `OnProperyChanged` is auto-populated with the property name, `Description`, by the compiler. This is a handy feature for the developer that helps to write error-free code. The other two `caller` argument attributes, `CallerFilePath` and `CallerLineNumber`, populate the file path of the `caller` method and line number respectively.

`CallerArgumentExpression` is a new addition to these in C# 10. As the name suggests, the attribute makes the compiler auto-populate the argument expression. Let's build a simple argument validation helper class that does the `null` check for the parameters passed. Consider the following implementation of an `ArgumentValidation` class, which implements a helper method that throws `ArgumentException` if the argument value is `null`:

```
public static class ArgumentValidation
{
    public static void ThrowIfNull<T>(T value,
    [CallerArgumentExpression("value")] string expression =
      null) where T : class
    {
        if (value == null)
            Throw(expression);
    }
    private static void Throw(string expression)
        => throw new ArgumentException($"Argument
            {expression} must not be null");
}
```

In the `ThrowIfNull` method, we are performing the `null` check and throwing `ArgumentException` with the details including the parameter name, which is picked from `CallerArgumentExpression`. We can use the preceding helper class to perform the `null` check on the arguments passed to a method. For example, consider the following method, which adds the passed-in product to the cart:

```
public async Task<ProductDetailsViewModel> AddProductAsync
(ProductDetailsViewModel product)
{
    ArgumentValidation.ThrowIfNull(product);
    // Implementation to add the product to cart
}
```

In this method, we use the `ArgumentValidation` helper class to check the `null` condition of the `product` argument. The generated code for the call to the `ThrowIfNull` helper method will be `ArgumentValidation.ThrowIfNull(product, "product");`.

The compiler auto-populated the parameter name in the string argument. Caller arguments will be useful where we want to add more details to the traces, which will help in troubleshooting the issue.

Summary

In this chapter, we have learned about the major additions to the C# language features in version 10. We have seen how C# 10 simplifies the code written with `implicit` and `global` using directives. We have learned about `record` structs and how they compare with the `record` class introduced in C# 9. We have also learned about the improvements to Lambda expressions, expression type inference, and explicitly specifying the return type for the expression. We have also seen performance improvements in interpolated strings. We have also learned how to build throw helpers using the `CallerArgumentExpression` attribute.

With this chapter, we have gained the skills to leverage these new features of C# 10 features in the enterprise e-commerce application that we are going to build in the coming chapters. In addition to these, there are a few more small enhancements. You can refer to the C# language documentation to learn more here: `https://docs.microsoft.com/en-us/dotnet/csharp/whats-new/csharp-10`. We will be highlighting the new features of C# 10 and .NET 6 throughout this book while implementing different features of our e-commerce application.

In the upcoming part, we will learn about the cross-cutting concerns that form the building blocks of our e-commerce application.

Questions

After reading the chapter, you should be able to answer the following questions:

1. True or false? Record structs are mutable:

    a. True

    b. False

    Answer: a

2. Which keyword should you use to make a record struct immutable?

    a. A record struct is immutable by default.

    b. `readonly`.

    c. `finally`.

    d. `sealed`.

    Answer: b

3. True or false? A compiler will infer the type expressions in all the scenarios:

    a. True

    b. False

    Answer: b

4. In which version of C# were caller argument attributes first introduced?

    a. C# 9

    b. C# 8

    c. C# 5

    d. C# 7

    Answer: c

Part 2: Cross-Cutting Concerns

We have a skeletal structure of an enterprise application at the moment. While filling this skeleton with business and technical functionality, we will come across a lot of code and constructs that will be used across the layers. These are sometimes referred to as cross-cutting concerns. Examples of cross-cutting concerns include threading, collections, logging, caching, configuration, networking, and dependency injection. In this part, we will quickly recap these fundamentals from the point of view of .NET 6 and enterprise applications. In each of these chapters, we will be developing a class library for one of the cross-cutting concerns that will be integrated with the UI and service layer.

This part comprises the following chapters:

- *Chapter 4, Threading and Asynchronous Operations*
- *Chapter 5, Dependency Injection in .NET 6*
- *Chapter 6, Configuration in .NET 6*
- *Chapter 7, Logging in .NET 6*
- *Chapter 8, All You Need to Know about Caching*

4

Threading and Asynchronous Operations

So far, we have looked at various design principles, patterns, what is new in .NET 6, and architecture guidelines that we are going to use during this book. In this chapter, we will see how we can take advantage of asynchronous programming while building enterprise applications.

One of the key measures for any web application is *scalability* – that is, scaling to reduce the time taken to serve a request, increase the number of requests that a server can process, and increase the number of users an application can simultaneously serve without increasing the load time. For mobile/desktop apps, scaling can improve the responsiveness of the app, allowing users to perform various actions without freezing the screen.

The proper use of asynchronous programming techniques and parallel constructs can do wonders in improving these metrics, and the best thing for this in C# is the simplified syntax of the **Task Parallel Library** (**TPL**), async-await, with which we can write clean asynchronous code.

In this chapter, we will cover the following topics:

- Understanding the jargon
- Demystifying threads, lazy initialization, and `ThreadPool`
- Understanding locks, semaphores, and `SemaphoreSlim`
- Introducing tasks and parallels
- Introducing async-await
- Using concurrent collections for parallelism

Technical requirements

You will need a basic understanding of .NET Core, C#, and the basics of LINQ. The code examples for this chapter can be found here: `https://github.com/PacktPublishing/Enterprise-Application-Development-with-C-10-and-.NET-6-Second-Edition/tree/main/Chapter04`.

A few instructions for the code can be found here: `https://github.com/PacktPublishing/Enterprise-Application-Development-with-C-10-and-.NET-6-Second-Edition/tree/main/Enterprise%20Application`.

Understanding the jargon

Before we dive into the technicalities of threading and asynchronous operations, let's take a real-world example and build an analogy between multitasking in real life and parallel programming. Imagine that you are waiting in a queue in a restaurant to order food, and while waiting in the queue, you reply to an email. Then, having ordered the food and while waiting for it to arrive, you answered a phone call. In the restaurant, there are multiple counters where orders are being taken, and food is prepared by the chef while orders are being placed.

While you were waiting in line, you concurrently replied to an email. Similarly, while you were ordering, the restaurant was parallelly taking orders at many other counters. The chef is cooking parallelly while orders are being placed. Also, you were given a token to pick up your food from the pickup counter; however, depending upon the preparation time of your food, an order placed after yours may arrive at the pickup counter before yours.

When talking about parallel programming, some key terms will appear multiple times. This jargon is represented in the following figure:

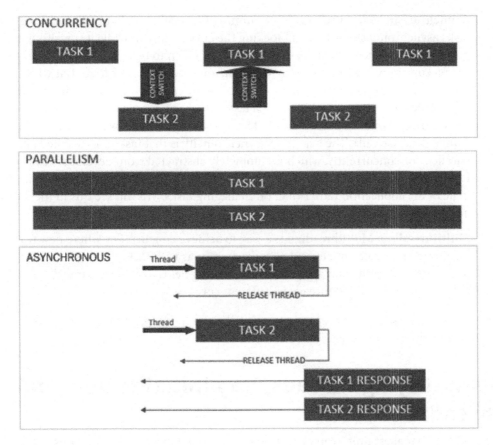

Figure 4.1 – Concurrency versus parallelism versus asynchronous

Let's cover each term:

- **Parallelism**: This entails multiple tasks being performed independently at the same time, as in the example of multiple restaurant orders being placed from different counters. In terms of enterprise applications, parallelism would be multiple threads/tasks being executed at the same time in a multicore CPU. However, a single-core CPU also supports parallelism through hyper-threading, which usually involves the logical division of a single core into more than one core, such as a hyper-threading-enabled dual-core CPU, which acts like a quad-core – that is, four cores.

- **Concurrency**: This entails doing many tasks at the same time, such as in our previous example of replying to an email while queuing for a restaurant counter, or the chef seasoning one dish and heating the pan for a second dish. In terms of enterprise applications, concurrency involves multiple threads sharing a core and, based on their time slicing, executing tasks and performing context switching.

- **Asynchronous**: Asynchronous programming is a technique that relies on executing tasks asynchronously instead of blocking the current thread while it is waiting. In our example, asynchronicity is waiting for your token to be called for you to go to the pickup counter while the chef is working on preparing your food. But while you're waiting, you have moved away from the ordering counter, thereby allowing other orders to be placed. This is like a task that executes asynchronously and frees up resources while waiting on an I/O task (for instance, while waiting on data from a database call). The beauty of asynchronicity is that tasks are executed either parallelly or concurrently, which is completely abstracted from developers by the framework. This lets the developer focus their development efforts on the business logic of the application rather than on managing tasks. We will see this in the *Tasks and parallels* section.

- **Multithreading**: Multithreading is a way to achieve concurrency where new threads are created manually and executed concurrently, as with `CLR ThreadPool`. In a multicore/multiprocessor system, multithreading helps to achieve parallelism by executing newly created threads in different cores.

Now that we understand the key terms in parallel programming, let's move on to look at how to create threads and the role of `ThreadPool` in .NET Core.

Demystifying threads, lazy initialization, and ThreadPool

A thread is the smallest unit in an operating system, and it executes instructions in the processor. A process is a bigger executing container, and the thread inside the process is the smallest unit to use processor time and execute instructions. The key thing to remember is that whenever your code needs to be executed in a process, it should be assigned to a thread. Each processor can only execute one instruction at a time; that's why, in a single-core system, at any point time, only one thread is being executed. There are scheduling algorithms that are used to allocate processor time to a thread. A thread typically has a stack (which keeps track of execution history), registers in which to store various variables, and counters to hold instructions that need to be executed.

A quick look at **Task Manager** will give us details regarding the number of physical and logical cores, and navigating to **Resource Monitor** will tell us about the CPU usage in each core. The following figure shows the details of a hyper-threading-enabled quad-core CPU that can execute eight threads in parallel at any point in time:

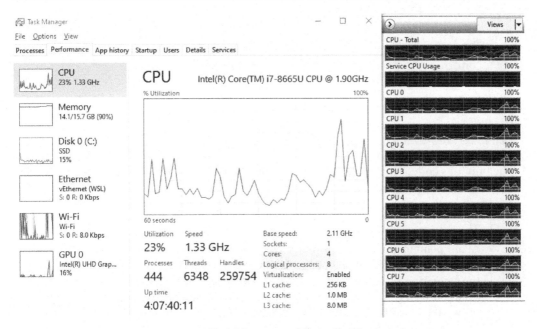

Figure 4.2 – Task Manager and Resource Monitor

A typical application in .NET Core has one single thread when it is started and can add more threads by manually creating them. A quick refresher on how this is done will be covered in the following sections.

Working with System.Threading.Thread

We can create new threads by creating an instance of System.Threading.Thread and passing a method delegate. Here is a simple example that simulates retrieving data from an API and loading a file from a disk:

```
Thread loadFileFromDisk = new Thread(LoadFileFromDisk);
void LoadFileFromDisk(object? obj)
{
    Thread.Sleep(2000);
    Console.WriteLine("data returned from API");
}
loadFileFromDisk.Start();
Thread fetchDataFromAPI = new Thread(FetchDataFromAPI);
void FetchDataFromAPI(object? obj)
```

```
{
    Thread.Sleep(2000);
    Console.WriteLine("File loaded from disk");
}
fetchDataFromAPI.Start("https://dummy/v1/api"); //Parameterized
method
Console.ReadLine();
```

In the previous code, `FetchDataFromAPI` and `LoadFileFromDisk` are the methods that would run on the new thread.

> **Tip**
>
> At any point in time, only one thread will be executing on each core – that is, only one thread is allotted CPU time. So, to achieve concurrency, the **Operating System (OS)** does a context switch when a thread that's been allocated CPU time is idle or if a high-priority thread arrives in the queue (there may be other reasons too, such as if a thread is waiting on a synchronization object or the allotted CPU time is reached).
>
> Since a thread that is switched out won't have completed its work, at some point, it will be assigned CPU time again. As such, the OS needs to save the state of the thread (its stack, its registers, and so on) and retrieve it again when the thread is allotted CPU time. Context switching is usually very expensive and one of the key areas of performance improvement.

All the properties and methods of the `Thread` class can be further reviewed at `https://docs.microsoft.com/en-us/dotnet/api/system.threading.thread?view=net-6.0`.

Although managing threads come with the advantage of having more control over how they are executed, it also comes with overheads in the form of the following:

- Managing the life cycle of threads, such as creating threads, recycling them, and context switching.

- Implementing concepts such as progress tracking/reporting for thread execution. Also, cancellation is quite complex and has limited support.

- Exceptions on threads need to be handled appropriately; otherwise, they may lead to the application crashing.

- Debugging, testing, and code maintenance can become a bit complex and, at times, can lead to performance issues if not handled correctly.

This is where the **Common Language Runtime (CLR)** ThreadPool comes into play, which is discussed in the next section.

ThreadPool

Threads can be created by making use of pools of threads managed by .NET Core, more commonly known as the CLR ThreadPool. The CLR ThreadPool is a set of worker threads that are loaded into your application along with the CLR and take care of the thread life cycle, including recycling threads, creating threads, and supporting better context switching. The CLR ThreadPool can be consumed by various APIs available in the System.Threading.ThreadPool class. Specifically, for scheduling an operation on a thread, there is the QueueUserWorkItem method, which takes a delegate of the method that needs to be scheduled. In the previous code, let's replace the code for creating a new thread with the following code, meaning the application will use ThreadPool:

```
ThreadPool.QueueUserWorkItem(FetchDataFromAPI);
```

As the name suggests, QueueUserWorkItem of the ThreadPool class does make use of queues, whereby any code that is supposed to be executed on the ThreadPool thread would be queued and then dequeued – that is, assigned to a worker thread in a **First-In, First-Out (FIFO)** manner.

The way ThreadPool is designed is that it has a global queue, and items are queued in it when we do the following:

- Call QueueUserWorkItem or a similar method of the ThreadPool class using a thread that is not part of the ThreadPool threads
- Call through the TPL

When a new thread is created in ThreadPool, it maintains its own local queue that checks the global queue and dequeues the work item in a FIFO manner; however, if the code executing on this thread creates another thread, such as a child thread, then that gets queued in the local queue as opposed to the global queue.

The order of execution for operations in the local queue of the worker thread is always **Last-In, First-Out (LIFO)**, and the reason for this is that the most recently created work item may still be hot in the cache and hence can be executed quickly. Also, we can say that at any point in time, there would be $n+1$ queues in ThreadPool, where n is the number of threads in ThreadPool – that is, n local queues – and 1 refers to the global queue.

A high-level representation of `ThreadPool` is shown in the following figure:

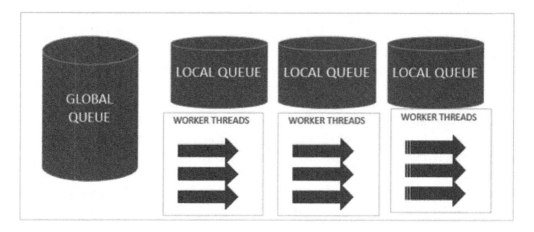

Figure 4.3 – ThreadPool high-level representation

Apart from `QueueUserWorkItem`, there are a lot of other properties/methods available for the `ThreadPool` class, such as these:

- `SetMinThreads`: Used to set the minimum worker and asynchronous I/O threads that `ThreadPool` will have when the program is started

- `SetMaxThreads`: Used to set the maximum worker and asynchronous I/O threads that `ThreadPool` will have, after which, new requests are queued

All the properties and methods of the `ThreadPool` class can be further reviewed at `https://docs.microsoft.com/en-us/dotnet/api/system.threading.threadpool?view=net-6.0`.

Although writing multithreaded code via `QueueUserWorkItem` of the `ThreadPool` thread simplifies life cycle management for threads, it has its own limitations:

- We cannot get a response from the work that is scheduled on the `ThreadPool` thread, hence the return type of the delegate is void.

- It is not easy to track the progress of the work that is scheduled on the `ThreadPool` thread, so something such as progress reporting isn't easy to achieve.

- It's not meant for long-running requests.

- `ThreadPool` threads are always background threads; so, unlike foreground threads, if a process is shut down, it will not wait for the `ThreadPool` threads to complete their work.

As there are limitations with `QueueUserWorkItem`, the `ThreadPool` threads can also be consumed through the TPL, which we will use in our enterprise application and is covered later in this chapter. In .NET Core, the TPL is the preferred approach to achieve concurrency/parallelism, as it overcomes all the limitations we have seen so far and eventually helps to achieve the goal of allowing your application to scale and be responsive.

Lazy initialization

The lazy initialization of a class is a pattern where the creation of an object is deferred until it is used for the first time. This pattern is based on the premise that as long as a class's properties are not being used, there is no advantage to initializing an object. Hence, this delays object creation and ultimately reduces the memory footprint of the application, improving performance. An example of this would be creating a database connection object only when you are about to retrieve data from a database. Lazy initialization is a good fit for classes that hold a lot of data and are potentially expensive to create. For instance, a class for loading all the products in an e-commerce application can be lazily initialized only when there is a need to list the products.

A typical implementation of such a class, as presented next, restricts the initialization of properties in constructors and has one or more methods that populate the properties of the class:

```
public class ImageFile
{
    string fileName;
    object loadImage;
    public ImageFile(string fileName)
    {
        this.fileName = fileName;
    }
    public object GetImage()
    {
        if (loadImage == null)
        {
            loadImage = File.ReadAllText(fileName);
        }
        return loadImage;
    }
}
```

Assuming this is a class used to load an image from a disk, there is no use in loading the image in the constructor because it cannot be consumed until the `Get Image` method is called. So, the lazy initialization pattern suggests that instead of initializing the `loadImage` object in the constructor, it should be initialized in `Get Image`, which means that the image is loaded into memory only when it is needed. This can also be achieved through properties, as shown here:

```
object loadImage;
public object LoadImage
{
    get
    {
        if (loadImage == null)
        {
            loadImage = File.ReadAllText(fileName);
        }
        return loadImage;
    }
}
```

As you can see, this is something that's typically done with cache objects and is also known as the **cache-aside pattern**, where we load an object in the cache when a specific object is being accessed for the first time. However, this implementation has a challenge in multithreaded code, where a call to disk can happen multiple times for the same file – that is, if two threads call the `LoadImage` method or property, it will lead to making a call to disk multiple times. So, there is a need for synchronization here through locks or some other mechanism, which obviously will add to the maintenance overhead, and the class implementation might become even more complex.

So, even though we can implement our own lazy load pattern, in C#, we have the `System.Lazy` class to handle such an implementation. One of the key advantages of using the `System.Lazy` class is that it is thread-safe.

The `System.Lazy` class provides multiple constructors to implement lazy initialization. Here are the two most common ways that we can make use of:

- Wrapping the class around `Lazy` and using the `Value` method of that object to retrieve data. This is typically used for classes that have initialization logic in constructors. Some sample code follows:

```
public class ImageFile
{
    string fileName;
    public object LoadImage { get; set; }
    public ImageFile(string fileName)
    {
        this.fileName = fileName;
        this.LoadImage = $"File {fileName}
         loaded from disk";
    }
}
```

While initializing this class, we will use the generic type of the `System.Lazy` class and pass the `ImageFile` class as its type and the object of `ImageFile` as a delegate:

```
Lazy<ImageFile> imageFile = new
 Lazy<ImageFile>(() => new ImageFile("test"));
var image = imageFile.Value.LoadImage;
```

Here, if you put a breakpoint in the `ImageFile` class's constructor, it would be hit only when the `Value` method of the `System.Lazy` class is called.

- For classes that have a method to load various parameters, we can pass the method to the `Lazy` class as a delegate. Taking the previous sample code and moving the file-retrieving logic to a separate method is shown here:

```
public class ImageFile
{
    string fileName;
    public object LoadImage { get; set; }
    public ImageFile(string fileName)
    {
        this.fileName = fileName;
```

```
        }
        public object LoadImageFromDisk()
        {
            this.LoadImage = $"File
            {this.fileName} loaded from disk";
            return LoadImage;
        }
    }
```

And while initializing this class, we pass a Lambda to the generic delegate, and that generic delegate is passed to initialize an object of the System.Lazy class, as shown in the following code:

```
        Func<object> imageFile = new Func<object>(()
        => { var obj = new ImageFile("test");
        return obj.LoadImageFromDisk(); });
        Lazy<object> lazyImage = new
        Lazy<object>(imageFile);
        var image = lazyImage.Value;
```

> **Note**
>
> A func in C# is a type of delegate that takes zero or more parameters and returns a value. More details can be found here: https://docs.microsoft.com/en-us/dotnet/api/system.func-1?view=net-6.0.

Both ways will delay the initializing of the object until the call to the Value method is made.

> **Note**
>
> One important thing that we need to note is that although Lazy objects are thread-safe, objects created through values aren't thread-safe. So, in this case, lazyImage is thread-safe, but image isn't. Hence, it needs to be synchronized in a multithreaded environment.

In general, lazy initialization is a good fit for caching classes and singleton classes and can be further extended for objects that are expensive to initialize.

All the properties of the `Lazy` class can be further reviewed at https://docs. microsoft.com/en-us/dotnet/api/system.lazy-1?view=net-6.0.

Although lazy initialization can be achieved by wrapping the underlying object with the `System.Lazy` class, there is also the `LazyInitializer` static class available in .NET that can be used for lazy initialization through its `EnsureInitialized` method.

It has a couple of constructors as mentioned in the MSDN documentation at https://docs.microsoft.com/en-us/dotnet/api/system.threading. lazyinitializer.ensureinitialized?view=net-6.0.

However, the idea is the same, in that it expects an object and a function to populate the object. Taking the previous example, if we had to use `LazyInitializer. EnsureInitialized` for lazy initialization, we would need to pass the instance of the object and the Lambda that creates the actual object to `LazyInitializer. EnsureInitialized`, as shown in the following code:

```
object image = null;
LazyInitializer.EnsureInitialized(ref image, () =>
    {
        var obj = new ImageFile("test");
        return obj.LoadImageFromDisk();
    });
```

Here, we are passing two parameters – one is the object that holds the value of the property of the `image` class, and the other is the function that creates an object of the `image` class and returns the image. So, this is as simple as calling the `Value` property of the `System.Lazy` property without having the overhead of initializing the object.

Clearly, a small added advantage of lazy initializing using `LazyInitializer` is that there aren't additional objects that aren't created, meaning a smaller memory footprint. On the other hand, `System.Lazy` provides much more readable code. So, if there are clear *space optimizations*, go with `LazyInitializer`; otherwise, use `System.Lazy` for much cleaner and more readable code.

Understanding locks, semaphores, and SemaphoreSlim

In the previous sections, we saw how we can use various APIs in .NET to achieve parallelism. However, when we are doing that, we need to take additional care with shared variables. Let's take the enterprise e-commerce application that we are building in this book. Think about the workflow of purchasing an item. Say that two users are planning to buy a product and only one item is available. Let's say that both users add the item to the cart and the first user places their order, and while the order is being processed through the payment gateway, the second user also tries to place their order.

In such cases, the second order should fail (assuming that the first order succeeded) because the quantity for the book is now zero; that would happen only if there was proper synchronization being applied to the quantity across threads. Also, if the first order fails in the payment gateway or the first user cancels their transaction, the second order should go through. So, what we are saying here is that the quantity should be locked while the first order is being processed and should be released only when the order is completed (ending in success or failure). Before we get into the handling mechanism, let's quickly recap what the critical section is.

The critical section and thread safety

The critical section is the part of an application that reads/writes variables that are used by multiple threads. We can think of these as the global variables that are used across the application and are modified in different places at different times or at the same time. In a multithreaded scenario, at any point in time, only one thread should be allowed to modify such variables, and only one thread should be allowed to enter the critical section.

If there are no such variables/sections in your application, it can be considered thread-safe. So, it's always advisable to identify variables in the application that are not thread-safe and handle them accordingly. To protect access to the critical section from non-thread-safe variables, there are various constructs available, known as **synchronization primitives** or **synchronization constructs**, which primarily fall into two categories:

- **Locking constructs**: These allow a thread to enter the critical section to protect access to the shared resources, and all other threads wait until the lock is freed by the acquired thread.

- **Signaling constructs**: These allow a thread to enter the critical section by signaling the availability of resources, as in a producer-consumer model, where a producer locks a resource and the consumer waits for a signal rather than polling.

Let's discuss a few synchronization primitives in the next section.

Introducing locks

A **lock** is a basic class that allows you to achieve synchronization in multithreaded code where any variable inside the lock block can be accessed by only one thread. In locks, the thread acquiring the lock needs to release the lock, and until then, any other thread trying to enter the lock goes into a wait state. A simple lock can be created, as shown in the following code:

```
object locker = new object();
lock (locker)
{
    quantity--;
}
```

The thread that is the first to execute this code will acquire the lock and release it after the completion of the code block. Locks can also be acquired using `Monitor.Enter` and `Monitor.Exit`, and in fact, using a lock compiler internally converts the thread to `Monitor.Enter` and `Monitor.Exit`. A few important points about locks follow:

- They should always be used on the reference type due to their thread affinity.

- They are very expensive in terms of performance, as they pause the threads that want to enter the critical section before allowing them to resume, which adds some lag.

- Double-checking the acquiring lock is also a good practice, similar to how it is done in the singleton implementation.

Locks do have some problems:

- You need to lock the shared data/object wherever it's being modified or enumerated. It's easy to miss critical sections in the application as *critical section* is more of a logical term. Compilers will not flag it if there aren't any locks around a critical section.

- If not handled correctly, you might end up in a deadlock.

- Scalability is a problem, as only one thread can access a lock at a time, while all other threads must wait.

> **Note**
>
> There is another important concept known as **atomicity**. An operation is atomic only if there isn't any way to read the intermediate state of a variable or to write the intermediate state to a variable. For example, if an integer's value is being modified from two to six, any thread reading this integer value will only see two or six; none of the threads will see the thread's intermediate state where the integer was only partially updated. Any code that is thread-safe automatically guarantees atomicity.
>
> Use concurrent collections, described in a later section, instead of locks, as concurrent collections internally handle locking critical sections.

Mutex (Windows only)

A **mutex** is also a type of lock, one that not only supports locking a resource within a process but also locking a resource across multiple processes. A mutex can be created using the `System.Threading.Mutex` class, and any thread that wants to enter the critical section needs to call the `WaitOne` method. Releasing a mutex happens through the `ReleaseMutex` method; so, we basically create an instance of the `System.Threading.Mutex` class and call `WaitOne`/`ReleaseMutex` to enter/exit the critical section, respectively. A couple of important points about mutexes follow:

- Mutexes have thread affinity, so a thread that calls `WaitOne` needs to call `ReleaseMutex`.

- A constructor of the `System.Threading.Mutex` class is available that accepts the name of a mutex, which allows sharing across processes using the name passed to the constructor.

Introducing semaphores and SemaphoreSlim

A **semaphore** is a non-exclusive lock that supports synchronization by allowing multiple threads to enter a critical section. However, unlike exclusive locks, a semaphore is used in scenarios where there is a need to restrict access to a pool of resources – for example, a database connection pool that allows a fixed number of connections between an application and a database.

Going back to our example of shopping for a product in an e-commerce application, if the available quantity of a product is 10, that means that 10 people can add this item to their shopping carts and place orders. If 11 orders are placed concurrently, 10 users should be allowed to place orders, and the 11th should be put on hold until the first 10 orders are completed.

In .NET, a semaphore can be created by creating an instance of the `System.Threading.Semaphore` class and passing two parameters:

- The initial number of active requests
- The total number of concurrently allowed requests

Here is a simple code snippet that creates a semaphore:

```
Semaphore quantity = new Semaphore(0, 10);
```

In this case, 0 means none of the requests has acquired the shared resource and a maximum of 10 concurrent requests are allowed. To acquire a shared resource, we need to call `WaitOne()`, and to release a resource, we need to call the `Release()` method.

To create semaphores, there is another lightweight class available in .NET, and that is `SemaphoreSlim`, the slim version, which usually relies on a concept called **spinning**. In this, whenever a shared resource needs to be locked, instead of locking the resource immediately, `SemaphoreSlim` uses a small loop that runs for a few microseconds so that it doesn't have to go through the costly process of blocking, context switching, and internal kernel transition (semaphores use Windows kernel semaphores to lock a resource). Eventually, `SemaphoreSlim` falls back to locking if the shared resource still needs to be locked.

Creating a `SemaphoreSlim` instance is almost the same as for semaphores; the only difference is that for locking, it has `WaitAsync` instead of `WaitOne`. There is also `CurrentCount` available, which tells us the number of locks acquired.

Some key facts about semaphores and `SemaphoreSlim` follow:

- As a semaphore is used to access a pool of resources, semaphores and `SemaphoreSlim` don't have thread affinity, and any thread can release a resource.
- The `Semaphore` class in .NET Core supports named semaphores. Named semaphores can be used to lock resources across processes; however, the `SemaphoreSlim` class does not support named semaphores.
- The `SemaphoreSlim` class, unlike `Semaphore`, supports asynchronous methods and cancellation, which means it can be used well with async-await methods. The async-await keyword helps in writing non-blocking asynchronous methods and is covered in the *Introducing async-await* section in this chapter.

Choosing the right synchronization constructs

There are other signaling constructs to cover; the following table gives you a high-level view of their usage and real-life examples of them:

Synchronization Construct	Type	Usage	Example
Lock/monitor	Locking construct	To lock a critical section by a single thread.	Any shared variable in the application.
Mutex (Windows only)	Locking construct	To lock a critical section by a single thread across processes or inter-process synchronization.	If only one instance of a process needs to be allowed, a cross-process mutex can be used.
Semaphore/SemaphoreSlim	Locking construct	To lock a pool of resources in an application or across a process or inter-process synchronization.	Database connection pool. From an e-commerce standpoint, this would be allowing the placing of x number of orders for a product concurrently, where x is the maximum available quantity of the product at that time.
AutoResetEvent	Signaling construct	Allows resource access to a single thread through a signal. The resource would be unavailable until a signal is resent. Usually used for resources that are available based on a condition for a single thread.	A price-matching algorithm such as one for a bidding process, where one bid can be completed based on a specific price.

Synchronization Construct	Type	Usage	Example
`ManualResetEvent/` `ManualResetEventSlim`	Signaling construct	Allows unblocking of all waiting threads through a signal until access to a resource is manually blocked by resetting `ManualResetEvent`.	An online platform that supports bidding x quantity for a particular item, and the bid that is placed can be less than or equal to x, and if a lower bid is placed, the item is open for further bidding until the sum of all the bids is equal to x.
Volatile	Locking construct	A locking mechanism that guarantees that writes are updated in main memory. Volatile is especially useful in multi-core systems where updating a variable is maintained briefly in the CPU cache before updating it back to the main memory.	

Table 4.1 – A synchronization constructs comparison

So far, we have covered the following:

- Various ways of multithreading using the `Thread` and `ThreadPool` classes and their limitations
- The importance of lazy initialization and how it helps in multithreaded environments
- The various synchronization constructs that are available in .NET

We will use these concepts in later chapters when we create some cross-cutting components.

In the next section, we will see how to overcome the limitations of `Thread` and `ThreadPool` through tasks and the use of the TPL.

Introducing tasks and parallels

We know that asynchronous programming helps our applications to scale and respond better, so implementing asynchronous applications should not be overhead for developers. `Thread` and `ThreadPool`, while helping to achieve asynchronicity, add a lot of overhead and come with limitations.

Hence, Microsoft came up with tasks that make it easier to develop asynchronous applications. In fact, most of the newer APIs in .NET 6 only support the asynchronous way of programming – for example, the **Universal Windows Platform** (**UWP**) doesn't even expose APIs to create threads without tasks. As such, understanding tasks and the TPL is fundamental to being able to write asynchronous programs using C#.

We will dive deep into these topics in this section, and later, we will see how the C# async-await keywords combined with the TPL simplify asynchronous programming.

Introduction to Task and the TPL

The idea behind asynchronous programming is that none of the threads should be waiting on an operation – that is, the framework should have the capability to wrap an operation into some abstraction and then resume once the operation is completed without blocking any threads. This abstraction is nothing but the `Task` class, which is exposed through `System.Threading.Tasks` and helps in writing asynchronous code in .NET.

The `Task` class simplifies wrapping any wait operation, whether it is data retrieved from a database, a file being loaded into memory from disk, or any highly CPU-intensive operation, and simplifies running it on a separate thread if needs be. It has the following important features:

- `Task` supports returning values from an operation once it is completed through its generic type, `Task<T>`.

- `Task` takes care of scheduling threads on `ThreadPool`, partitioning operations, and scheduling more than one thread from `ThreadPool` accordingly, all while abstracting the complexity of doing it.

- Reports completion supports cancellation through `CancellationToken` and progress reporting through `IProgress`.

- `Task` supports creating child tasks and manages relationships between child and parent tasks.

- Exceptions are propagated to the calling application, even for multi-hierarchical parent/child tasks.

- Most importantly, `Task` supports async-await, which helps in resuming the processing in a calling application/method once the operation in the task is completed.

The TPL is a group of APIs provided by .NET in `System.Threading.Tasks` and `System.Threading`, and it provides ways to create and manage tasks. Tasks can be created by creating an object of the `System.Threading.Tasks.Task` class and passing a block of code that needs to be executed on the task. We can create a task in multiple ways:

- You can create an object of the `Task` class and pass a Lambda expression. In this method, it needs to be started explicitly, as shown in the following code:

```
Task dataTask = new Task(() =>
   FetchDataFromAPI("https://foo.com/api"));
dataTask.Start();
```

- A task can also be created using `Task.Run`, as shown in the following code, which supports creating and starting the task without explicitly calling `Start()`:

```
Task dataTask = Task.Run(() => FetchDataFromAPI
("https://foo.com/api"));
```

- Another way to create a task is by using `Task.Factory.StartNew`:

```
Task dataTask = Task.Factory.StartNew(() =>
FetchDataFromAPI("https://foo.com/api"));
```

In all these methods, a `ThreadPool` thread is used to run the `FetchDataFromAPI` method and is referenced via the `dataTask` object, which is returned to the caller to track the completion of the operation/exception.

As this task would asynchronously execute on a `ThreadPool` thread, and as all `ThreadPool` threads are background threads, the application wouldn't wait for the `FetchDataFromAPI` method to complete. The TPL exposes a `Wait` method to wait on the completion of the task, such as `dataTask.Wait()`. Here is a code snippet from a small console application that uses a task:

```
Task t = Task.Factory.StartNew(() =>
             FetchDataFromAPI("https://foo.com"));
t.Wait();
```

```
void FetchDataFromAPI(string apiURL)
{

    Thread.Sleep(2000);
    Console.WriteLine("data returned from API");

}
```

In this snippet, we used a Lambda expression. However, it could be a delegate or action delegate (in the case of a parameter-less method), so something such as the following can also be used to create a task:

```
Task t = Task.Factory.StartNew(delegate {
FetchDataFromAPI("https://foo.com");});
```

Either way, you receive a reference to the Task object and handle it accordingly. If a method is returning a value, then we can use a generic version of the Task class and use the Result method to retrieve data from Task. For example, if FetchDataFromAPI returns a string, we can use Task<String>, as shown in the following snippet:

```
Task<string> t =
  Task.Factory.StartNew<string>(()
  => FetchDataFromAPI(""));
t.Wait();
Console.WriteLine(t.Result);
```

There are various additional parameters that each of these methods accepts, and a few important ones are as follows:

- Cancellation using an object of the CancellationToken class, generated using the CancellationTokenSource class.

- Control the behavior of task creation and execution through the TaskCreationOptions enum.

- Custom implementation of TaskScheduler to control how tasks are queued.

TaskCreationOptions is an enum in the TPL that tells TaskScheduler what kind of task we are creating. For example, we can create a long-running task, as follows:

```
Task<string> t = Task.Factory.StartNew<string>(() =>
FetchDataFromAPI(""), TaskCreationOptions.LongRunning);
```

Although this doesn't guarantee any faster output, it acts more like a hint to the scheduler to optimize itself. For example, the scheduler can spin up more threads if it sees a long-running task being scheduled. All the options for this enum can be found at `https://docs.microsoft.com/en-us/dotnet/api/system.threading.tasks.taskcreationoptions?view=net-6.0`.

`Task` also supports waiting on multiple tasks at the same time by creating and passing all the tasks as parameters to the following methods:

- `WaitAll`: Wait for the completion of all tasks and block the current thread. Not recommended for application development.

- `WhenAll`: Wait for the completion of all tasks without blocking the current thread. Usually used with async-await. Recommended for application development.

- `WaitAny`: Wait for the completion of one of the tasks and block the current thread until then. Not recommended for application development.

- `WhenAny`: Wait for the completion of one of the tasks without blocking the current thread. Usually used with async-await. Not recommended for application development.

Tasks, unlike threads, have comprehensive exception handling support. Let's see that in the next section.

Handling task exceptions

Exception handling in tasks is as simple as writing a `try` block around the task and then catching the exceptions, which are usually wrapped in `AggregateException`, as shown in the following code snippet:

```
try
{
    Task<string> t =
     Task.Factory.StartNew<string>(()
     => FetchDataFromAPI(""));
    t.Wait();
}
catch (AggregateException agex)
{
    //Handle exception
    Console.WriteLine(
```

```
                    agex.InnerException.Message);
    }
```

In the preceding code, `agex.InnerException` will give you the actual exception, as we are waiting on a single task. However, if we are waiting on multiple tasks, it would be the `InnerExceptions` collection that we could loop through. Also, it comes with a `Handle` callback method, which can be subscribed in a `catch` block, and the callback once triggered will have information about the exception.

As shown in the preceding code, for a task to propagate an exception, we need to call the `Wait` method or some other blocking construct such as `WhenAll` to trigger the `catch` block. However, under the hood, any exception to `Task` is actually held in the `Exception` property of the `Task` class, which is of the `AggregateException` type and can be observed for any underlying exceptions in the task.

Also, if a task is the parent of attached child tasks or nested tasks, or if you are waiting on multiple tasks, multiple exceptions can be thrown. To propagate all the exceptions back to the calling thread, the `Task` infrastructure wraps them in an `AggregateException` instance.

More details about handling exceptions can be found at `https://docs.microsoft.com/en-us/dotnet/standard/parallel-programming/exception-handling-task-parallel-library`.

Implementing task cancellation

.NET provides two primary classes to support the cancellation of a task:

- `CancellationTokenSource`: A class that creates a cancellation token and supports the cancellation of a token through the `Cancel` method
- `CancellationToken`: A structure that listens to cancellation and triggers a notification if a task is canceled

For canceling a task, there are two types of cancellation:

- One where a task is executed by mistake and needs to be canceled immediately
- Another where a task has started and needs to be stopped (aborted) midway

For the former, we can create a task that supports cancellation. We use the TPL APIs and pass the cancellation token to the constructor and call the `Cancel` method of the `CancellationTokenSource` class if the task needs to be canceled, as shown in the following code snippet:

```
cts = new CancellationTokenSource();
CancellationToken token = cts.Token;
Task dataFromAPI = Task.Factory.StartNew(()
 => FetchDataFromAPI(new List<string> {
    "https://foo.com",
    "https://foo1.com",}), token);
cts.Cancel();
```

All the .NET Core APIs that support asynchronous calling, such as `GetAsync` and `PostAsync` of the `HttpClient` class, have overloads to accept cancellation tokens. For the latter case (aborting a task), the decision is based on whether the operation that would be running supports cancellation or not. Assuming it supports cancellation, we can pass the cancellation token to the method and, inside the method call, check the `IsCancellationRequested` property of the cancellation token and handle it accordingly.

Let's create a simple console application that creates a task that does support cancellation. Here, we are creating a `FetchDataFromAPI` method that accepts a list of URLs and retrieves data from those URLs. This method also supports cancellation using `CancellationToken`. In the implementation, we loop through the list of URLs and continue until cancellation is requested or the loop completes all iterations:

```
static string FetchDataFromAPI(List<string>
 apiURL, CancellationToken token)
{
    Console.WriteLine("Task started");
    int counter = 0;
    foreach (string url in apiURL)
    {
        if (token.IsCancellationRequested)
        {
            throw new TaskCanceledException($"data
             from API returned up to iteration
              {counter}");
            //throw new
```

```
                               //OperationCanceledException($"data
                               //from API returned up to iteration
                               //{counter}");
                               // Alternate exception with same result
                               //break; // To handle manually
                        }
                        Thread.Sleep(1000);
                        Console.WriteLine($"data retrieved from
                         {url} for iteration {counter}");
                        counter++;
                }
                return $"data from API returned up to iteration
                 {counter}";
        }
```

Now, call FetchDataFromAPI with a list of four URLs from the main method, as shown in the following code. Here, we are creating CancellationToken using the Token property of the CancellationTokenSource class and passing it to the FetchDataFromAPI method. We are simulating a cancellation after 3 seconds so that FetchDataFromAPI will be canceled before the fourth URL is retrieved:

```
CancellationTokenSource cts = new CancellationTokenSource();
CancellationToken token = cts.Token;
Task<string> dataFromAPI;
try
{
    dataFromAPI = Task.Factory.StartNew<string>(() =>
     FetchDataFromAPI(new List<string> {
    "https://foo.com","https://foo1.com","https://foo2.com"
      ,"https://foo3.com", "https://foo4.com", }, token));
    Thread.Sleep(3000);
    cts.Cancel(); //Trigger cancel notification to
                     //cancellation token
    dataFromAPI.Wait(); // Wait for task completion
    Console.WriteLine(dataFromAPI.Result); // If task is
      //completed display message accordingly
}
```

```
catch (AggregateException agex)
{// Handle exception}
```

Once we run this code, we can see output for three URLs and then an exception/break (based on whichever line is commented out in the `FetchDataFromAPI` method).

In the preceding sample, we have simulated a long-running code block using a `for` loop and `Thread.Sleep`, canceled the task, and handled the code accordingly. However, there could be a scenario where the long-running code block may not support cancellation.

In those cases, we must write a wrapper method that accepts a cancellation token and have the wrapper internally call the long-running operation; then, in the main method, we call the wrapper code. The following snippet shows a wrapper method that makes use of `TaskCompletionSource`, which is another class in the TPL. It is used to convert non-task-based asynchronous methods (including even the ones based on asynchronous methods) to tasks through the `Task` property available in the class. In this case, we will pass the cancellation token to `TaskCompletionSource` so that its `Task` is updated accordingly:

```
static Task<string>
FetchDataFromAPIWithCancellation(List<string>
apiURL, CancellationToken cancellationToken)
{
    var tcs = new TaskCompletionSource<string>();
    tcs.TrySetCanceled(cancellationToken);
    // calling overload of long running operation
    // that doesn't support cancellation token
    var dataFromAPI = Task.Factory.StartNew(() =>
     FetchDataFromAPI(apiURL));
    // Wait for the first task to complete
    var outputTask = Task.WhenAny(dataFromAPI,
     tcs.Task);
    return outputTask.Result;
}
```

In this case, `CancellationToken` is tracked through the `Task` property of `TaskCompletionSource`, and we created another task to call our long-running operation (the one without cancellation token support), and whichever task finishes first is the one we return.

Of course, the `Main` method needs to be updated to call the wrapper, as shown here (the rest of the code remains the same):

```
dataFromAPI = Task.Factory.StartNew(() =>
FetchDataFromAPIWithCancellation(new
List<string>
    {
        "https://foo.com",
        "https://foo1.com",
        "https://foo2.com",
        "https://foo3.com",
        "https://foo4.com",
    }, token)).Result;
```

This doesn't cancel the underlying method but still allows the application to exit before the underlying operation is completed.

Task cancellation is a very useful mechanism that helps in reducing unwanted processing, either in tasks that haven't started yet or ones that have started but need to be stopped/aborted. Hence, all the asynchronous APIs in .NET do support cancellation.

Implementing continuations

In enterprise applications, most of the time, there will be a need to create multiple tasks, build a hierarchy of tasks, create dependent tasks, or create child/parent relationships between tasks. Task continuation can be used to define such child tasks/sub-tasks. It works like JavaScript promises and supports chaining tasks up to multiple levels. Just like promises, the subsequent task in a hierarchy executes after the first task, and this can be further chained to multiple levels.

There are various ways to achieve task continuation, but the most common way is to use the `ContinueWith` method of the `Task` class, as shown in the following example:

```
Task.Factory.StartNew(() => Task1(1)) // 1+2 = 3
            .ContinueWith(a => Task2(a.Result)) // 3*2 = 6
                .ContinueWith(b => Task3(b.Result))// 6-2=4
                    .ContinueWith(c => Console.WriteLine(c.
Result));
Console.ReadLine();
```

```
static int Task1(int a) => a + 2;
static int Task2(int a) => a * 2;
static int Task3(int a) => a - 2;
```

As you might have guessed, here the output would be 4, and each task executes once the preceding task's execution is completed.

ContinueWith accepts one important enum called TaskContinuationOptions, which supports continuation for different conditions. For example, we can pass TaskContinuationOptions.OnlyOnFaulted as a parameter to create a continuation task that executes when there is an exception in the preceding task or pass TaskContinuationOptions.AttachedToParent to create a continuation task that enforces a parent-child relationship and forces a parent task to complete execution only after the child task.

As with WhenAll and WhenAny, ContinueWith also comes with similar siblings, as follows:

- Task.Factory.ContinueWhenAll: This accepts multiple task references as parameters and creates a continuation when all the tasks are completed.

- Task.Factory.ContinueWhenAny: This accepts multiple task references as parameters and creates a continuation when one of the referenced tasks is completed.

Grasping task continuation is critical to understanding the under-the-hood workings of async-await, which we will discuss later in this chapter.

SynchronizationContext

SynchronizationContext is an abstract class available in System.Threading that helps in communication between threads. For example, updating a UI element from a parallel task requires the thread to rejoin the UI thread and resume execution. SynchronizationContext provides this abstraction primarily through the Post method of this class, which accepts a delegate to execute at a later stage. So, in the preceding example, if I need to update a UI element, I need to take SynchronizationContext of the UI thread, call its Post method, and pass the necessary data to update the UI element.

As SynchronizationContext is an abstract class, there are various derived types of it – for instance, Windows Forms has WindowsFormsSynchronizationContext and WPF has DispatcherSynchronizationContext.

The primary advantage of `SynchronizationContext` being an abstraction is that it can be helpful to queue a delegate, irrespective of the overridden implementation of the `Post` method.

TaskScheduler

When we created tasks using the various methods described earlier, we saw that a task gets *scheduled* on a `ThreadPool` thread, but the question arises of who or what does that. `System.Threading.Tasks.TaskScheduler` is the class available in the TPL that takes care of queueing and executing task delegates on a `ThreadPool` thread.

Of course, this is an abstract class, and the framework comes with two derived classes:

- `ThreadPoolTaskScheduler`
- `SynchronizationContextScheduler`

`TaskScheduler` exposes a `Default` property, which is by default set to `ThreadPoolTaskScheduler`. Hence, by default, all tasks are scheduled to `ThreadPool` threads; however, a GUI application typically uses `SynchronizationContextScheduler` so that tasks can successfully go back and update UI elements.

.NET Core comes with sophisticated derived types of the `TaskScheduler` and `SynchronizationContext` classes. However, they play a major role in async-await, and they help in debugging any deadlock-related issues quickly.

Note that looking at the internal workings of `TaskScheduler` and `SynchronizationContext` is beyond the scope of this book and is left to you to explore as an exercise.

Implementing data parallelism

Data parallelism is all about partitioning a source collection into multiple parallel executable tasks that perform the same operation parallelly. With the TPL, this is available in the `Parallel` static class, which exposes methods such as `For` and `ForEach` with multiple overloads to handle such execution.

Say you have a collection of a million numbers and you need to find the prime numbers. Data parallelism can come in handy here, as the collection can be split into ranges and evaluated for prime numbers. A typically parallel `for` loop is written, as shown in the following snippet:

```
List<int> numbers = Enumerable.Range(1,
  100000).ToList();
Parallel.For(numbers.First(), numbers.Last(), x
  => CalculatePrime(x));
```

However, a more realistic example would be something like an image processing application that needs to process each pixel in an image and reduce the brightness of each pixel by five points. Such operations can be hugely benefited by data parallelism, as each pixel is independent of the others and hence can be processed parallelly.

Similarly, there is a `ForEach` method in the `Parallel` static class, which can be used as follows:

```
Parallel.ForEach(numbers, x => CalculatePrime(x));
```

Some of the key advantages of data parallelism using `Parallel.For` and `Parallel.ForEach` are listed here:

- Good for canceling loops; they work similarly to `break` in a regular `for` loop. In `Parallel.For`, this is supported by passing `ParallelStateOptions` to the delegate and then calling `ParallelStateOptions.Break`. When `Break` is encountered by one of the tasks, the `LowestBreakIteration` property of the `ParallelStateOptions` class is set, and all the parallel tasks will iterate until this number is reached. `ParallelLoopResult`, which is the return type of `Parallel.For` and `Parallel.ForEach`, has the `IsCompleted` property, which states whether the loop executed prematurely.

- They also support stopping the loop immediately through `ParallelStateOptions.Stop`. Also, some of the constructors of `Parallel.For` and `Parallel.ForEach` accept cancellation tokens, which can also be used to simulate `ParallelStateOptions.Stop`; however, a loop should be wrapped within a `try...catch` block, as `OperationCanceledException` would be thrown.

- If one of the tasks throws an exception, all the tasks will complete their current iteration and then stop processing. As with tasks, `AggregateException` is thrown back.

- Degrees of parallelism are supported by passing `ParallelOptions` and setting `MaxDegreeOfParallelism`, which will control the number of cores that tasks can parallelly execute on.

- The custom partitioning of a source collection is supported through range partitioning or chunk partitioning.

- Supports thread-safe local variables that are scoped to a thread or partition.

- Nested `Parallel.For` loops are supported, and their synchronization is automatically handled without introducing any manual synchronization.

- If each iteration uses a shared variable, synchronization needs to be implemented explicitly. So, to get the most out of data parallelism, use it for operations that can execute independently for each iteration without depending on shared resources.

> **Tip**
> Data parallelism should be used carefully, as at times it is misused. It's like splitting 40 tasks among 4 people. If organizing this work (splitting and consolidating it) among 4 people represents much more work than just performing the overall work of the 40 tasks, then data parallelism isn't the right choice. For further reading, refer to `https://docs.microsoft.com/en-us/dotnet/standard/parallel-programming/data-parallelism-task-parallel-library`.

Using Parallel LINQ (PLINQ)

PLINQ is a parallel implementation of LINQ; this is a set of APIs available in the `ParallelEnumerable` class that enables the parallel execution of LINQ queries. The simplest way of making a LINQ query run parallelly is to embed the `AsParallel` method in the LINQ query. See the following code snippet, which calls a method that calculates the prime numbers between 1 and 1,000:

```
List<int> numbers = Enumerable.Range(1, 1000).ToList();
var resultList = numbers.AsParallel().Where(I => CalculatePrime
(i)).ToList();
```

Using LINQ query syntax, this would be as follows:

```
var primeNumbers = (from i in numbers.AsParallel()where
CalculatePrime(i) select i).ToList();
```

Internally, this query is split into multiple smaller queries that are parallelly executed on each processor, hence speeding up the query. The partitioned source needs to be merged back on the main thread so that the result (output collection) can be looped through for further processing/display.

Let's create a console application that prints all prime numbers between a given range, using PLINQ combined with `Parallel.For`. Add the following method, which takes a number and returns `true` if it's a prime number and `false` otherwise:

```
bool CalculatePrime(int num)
{
    bool isDivisible = false;
    for (int i = 2; i <= num / 2; i++)
    {
        if (num % i == 0)
        {
            isDivisible = true;
            break;
        }
    }
    if (!isDivisible && num != 1)
        return true;
    else
        return false;
}
```

Now, in the main method, add the following code, which creates a list of the first 100 numbers that we will loop through using PLINQ before passing it to the `CalculatePrime` method; then, we'll finally display the list of prime numbers using `Parallel.ForEach`:

```
List<int> numbers = Enumerable.Range(1, 100).ToList();
try
{
        var primeNumbers = (from number in
        numbers.AsParallel() where CalculatePrime(number) ==
        true select number).ToList();
    Parallel.ForEach(primeNumbers, (primeNumber) =>
    {
      Console.WriteLine(primeNumber);
    });
}
catch (AggregateException ex)
{
    Console.WriteLine(ex.InnerException.Message);
}
```

The output for this sample would be a list of prime numbers; however, you can see that the output will not be prime numbers in ascending order but in a random order, as the `CalculatePrime` method is called with multiple numbers parallelly.

A diagram of the internal working of the preceding code follows:

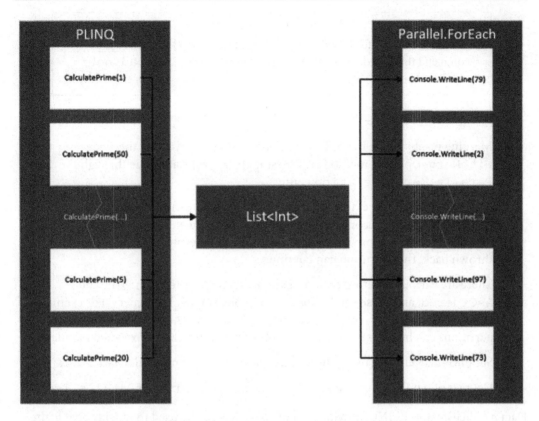

Figure 4.4 – PLINQ and Parallel.ForEach

PLINQ further provides a method to process the result of each partition/thread without the overhead of merging the result into a calling thread using `ForAll`, and the preceding code can be further optimized as follows:

```
(from i in numbers.AsParallel()
where CalculatePrime(i) == true
select i).ForAll((primeNumber) =>
    Console.WriteLine(primeNumber));
```

> **Tip**
> One of the best tools for playing around with LINQ/PLINQ is LINQPad; I recommend that you download it from `https://www.linqpad.net/Download.aspx`.

Some of the important things to remember for PLINQ are as follows:

- Merging results to the main thread can be configured by using the `WithMergeOption` method and passing the appropriate value through the `ParallelMergeOperation` enum.

- As with other parallel extensions, any exception is returned as `AggregateException`, and the execution of all the iterations stops immediately. Of course, if exceptions are swallowed within the delegate instead of them being thrown back, the execution can continue.

- There are various other extension methods, such as `AsSequential` and `AsOrdered`, and these can be combined in one single LINQ query. For example, based on that, `AsSequential` can be combined with `AsParallel` so that some partitions can be run sequentially and other partitions can be executed parallelly.

- Supports cancellation using the `WithCancellation` method.

- Degrees of parallelism are supported through `WithDegreeOfParallelism`.

Data parallelism and PLINQ provide a lot of APIs that can be used to quickly enable the parallel execution of code without adding any additional overhead to the application logic. However, there is a subtle difference between them, as explained in the preceding section, and they should be used differently accordingly.

> **Tip**
> PLINQ and the TPL together comprise parallel extensions.

In this section, we have used `Thread.Sleep` in many places, but that has primarily been to simulate long-running operations; however, it is never recommended that you use this in production.

In the next section, we will see how we can club tasks with async-await and use async-await in enterprise applications.

Introducing async-await

So far, we have discussed writing asynchronous code using tasks and how the TPL simplifies creating and managing tasks. However, tasks primarily rely on continuation, callbacks, or events to continue execution after the completion of a task.

In enterprise applications, managing such code would be difficult; any runtime exceptions would be difficult to debug if too many tasks were chained. That's where C# comes in with async-await, a language feature introduced in C# 5.0 that simplifies the writing of asynchronous code, makes it more readable and maintainable, improves exception handling, and makes things easy to debug. So, let's dive into async-await.

`async` is a keyword in C# that is used as a modifier and, when prefixed to any method (or Lambda), converts a method into a state machine, enabling the method to use the `await` keyword in its body.

`await` is a keyword in C# that is used as an operator and is followed by an expression that returns an awaitable object (usually a task). `await` can be used only inside a method that has an `async` modifier, and as soon as a caller encounters an `await` statement, control is returned and things are resumed; after `await`, the task is completed using continuations.

The task-based asynchronous pattern

The **Task-Based Asynchronous Pattern** (**TAP**) is a pattern used to implement asynchronous methods in which we make use of the `async` modifier and then use `await` on an asynchronous operation that is wrapped in a task (or any custom awaitable type that exposes `GetAwaiter()`). To put it simply, this pattern involves representing an asynchronous operation using a single method that has an `async` modifier and returns a task; any asynchronous operation is further awaited using `await`. The following is a sample code snippet that downloads a file asynchronously, which is implemented using the TAP:

```
0 references            1
static async Task Main(string[] args)
{
    // Call async method
    2 await DownloadFileAsync("https://github.com/Ravindra-a/largefile/blob/master/README.md",
        @$"{System.IO.Directory.GetCurrentDirectory()}\download.txt");
    5 Console.WriteLine("File downloaded!!");
    Console.ReadLine();
}

1 reference
private static async Task DownloadFileAsync(string url, string path)
{
    // Create a new web client object
    using WebClient webClient = new WebClient();
    webClient.Headers.Add("user-agent", "Mozilla/5.0 (Windows NT 10.0; WOW64)");
    3 byte[] data = await webClient.DownloadDataTaskAsync(url);
    // Write data in file.
    using var fileStream = File.OpenWrite(path);
    {
    4     await fileStream.WriteAsync(data, 0, data.Length);
    }
}
```

Figure 4.5 – A sample asynchronous method using async-await

In the preceding figure, control flows as follows (using the number labels in the figure):

1. The application starts execution with the Main method. Since Main is prefixed with the `async` method, it gets transformed into a type that implements a state machine. Execution continues until `await` is encountered at `await DownloadFileAsync`, and the thread is returned to the caller.

2. Before returning to the caller, a call to the `DownloadFileAsync` method is stored in a `Task` object, and a reference to the `Task` object is also preserved. The remaining code of the Main method is wrapped inside the continuation of this task.

3. A `ThreadPool` thread will start executing a `DownloadFileAsync` method, and it repeats the same steps – that is, it converts a method into a type that implements a state machine, continues execution until `await` is encountered, and then the task that is referenced is passed back; the remaining code is moved to the continuation of this task.

4. At some point, when the `DownloadDataTaskAsync` method is completed, the task continuation gets triggered and will execute the remaining code.

5. The process repeats until the task that has the reference of `DownloadFileAsync` completes and its continuation is executed, which is `Console.WriteLine("File downloaded!!")` in this case, and then the application exits.

At an approximate high level, the code would be transformed as shown here:

```
static void Main(string[] args)
{
    // Call async method
    // Create a new web client object
    using WebClient webClient = new WebClient();
    webClient.Headers.Add("user-agent", "Mozilla/5.0 (Windows NT 10.0; WOW64)");
    webClient.DownloadDataTaskAsync("https://github.com/Ravindra-a/largefile/blob/master/README.md").ContinueWith(dataTask =>
    {
        using var fileStream = File.OpenWrite(@$"{System.IO.Directory.GetCurrentDirectory()}\download.txt");
        {
            // Write data in file.
            fileStream.WriteAsync(dataTask.Result, 0, dataTask.Result.Length).ContinueWith(writeTask =>
            {
                Console.WriteLine("File downloaded!!");
            });
        }
    });
    Console.ReadLine();
}
```

Figure 4.6 – A transformed sample asynchronous method

Although this is an oversimplification of the under-the-hood workings of async-await, we can see the compiler doing a lot of heavy lifting, including generating a type that implements a state machine and continuing the execution using the state of the callback.

We have seen how simple it is to write async methods, and we will be writing many such methods in our enterprise application throughout the course of the book. However, async-await is not a silver bullet; it is not an answer to every application issue. We need to verify certain factors to make use of async-await. Let's see what the principles are for using async-await.

> **Note**
>
> The preceding code would change slightly if there was
> `SynchronizationContext`. For instance, in Windows Forms or WPF
> apps, continuation is posted on the current `SynchronizationContext`
> using the `Post` method of `SynchronizationContext` or
> `TaskScheduler.FromCurrentSynchronizationContext`. As
> per the standard naming convention, asynchronous methods are suffixed with
> the word `async` for readability purposes, but syntactically, it is not needed.

Principles of using async-await

As we start using async-await, there are certain practices that are recommended that will enable an application to take advantage of asynchronous principles. For example, for nested calls, we should use async-await all the way; do not use `.Result` and so on. Here are a few guidelines to help you use async-await effectively.

Chain async-await all the way

An asynchronous method implemented using async-await should be triggered from an async-await method so that it is properly awaited. If we try to call an asynchronous method from a synchronous method using the `Result` method or the `Wait` method of a task, it could lead to a deadlock.

Let's look at the following code snippet from a WPF application that downloads files from the network upon a button click. However, instead of awaiting a call to the asynchronous method, we are using the `Result` method of `Task`:

```
        private void Button_Click(object sender,
         RoutedEventArgs e)
        {

            var task =
            DownloadFileAsync("https://github.com/Ravindra-
            a/largefile/blob/master/README.md", @$"{System.
   IO.Directory.GetCurrentDirectory()}\download.txt");
            bool fileDownload = task.Result; // Or
                            //task.GetAwaiter().GetResult()
            if (fileDownload)
            {
                MessageBox.Show("file downloaded");
            }
```

```
        }
        private async Task<bool> DownloadFileAsync(string
        url, string path)
        {
            // Create a new web client object
            using WebClient webClient = new WebClient();
            // Add user-agent header to avoid forbidden
            // errors.
            webClient.Headers.Add("user-agent",
              "Mozilla/5.0 (Windows NT 10.0; WOW64)");
            byte[] data = await
              webClient.DownloadDataTaskAsync(url);
            // Write data in file.
            Using var fileStream = File.OpenWrite(path);
            {
                await fileStream.WriteAsync(data, 0,
                data.Length);
            }
            return true;
        }
```

In this method, the code after `await webClient.`
`DownloadDataTaskAsync(url);` will never execute, for the following reasons:

- As soon as await is encountered, the `Task` reference object captures `SynchronizationContext` in `TaskAwaitable` through the `GetAwaiter` method.

- Once the `async` operation is completed, the continuation of that `await` needs to execute on `SynchronizationContext` (through `SynchronizationContext.Post`).

- However, `SynchronizationContext` is already blocked because the call to `task.Result` on the click of a button is on the same `SynchronizationContext` and is waiting for `DownloadDataTaskAsync` to complete, hence it is causing a deadlock.

So, never block `async` methods; the best way to do `async` is all the way. So, in the preceding code, you would change the call to `await DownloadFileAsync` (and `async void` for button click – `await` needs a method to have an `async` modifier).

> **Note**
>
> The same code works fine in ASP.NET Core 6 applications
> without causing a deadlock because ASP.NET Core 6 doesn't have
> `SynchronizationContext`, and continuation executes on a
> `ThreadPool` thread without any involvement of a request context; however,
> blocking asynchronous calls is still not recommended, even in ASP.NET Core
> 6.

ConfigureAwait

In the preceding discussion, since we had the end-to-end application code, it was easier to find the cause of the deadlock. However, if we are developing a library with asynchronous methods that can be used in WPF, ASP.NET Core 6, or .NET Framework applications, we need to ensure that the asynchronous code within the library does not cause a deadlock, even though the caller may be consuming library methods through synchronous methods (`GetAwaiter().GetResult()`).

In such cases, `Task` provides a method called `ConfigureAwait` that accepts a Boolean value, which, when `true`, will use the original context of the caller and, when `false`, will resume operation after `await` without depending on the original context. In layman's terms, any code after `await` will execute independently, irrespective of the state of the context that initiated the request.

Use `ConfigureAwait(false)`, especially if you are implementing a library method, as it will avoid running a continuation on the original context. For library methods, it is a must to use `ConfigureAwait(false)`, as they should never depend on the calling/original context for the continuation. For example, the following code won't cause a deadlock:

```
    private void Button_Click(object sender,
RoutedEventArgs e)
    {
        string output = GetAsync().Result; //Blocking
          //code, ideally should cause deadlock.
        MessageBox.Show(output);
    }
//  Library code
public async Task<string> GetAsync()
    {
        var uri = new Uri("http://www.google.com");
        return await new HttpClient().
```

```
            GetStringAsync(uri).ConfigureAwait(false);
    }
```

By default, every `await` expression has `ConfigureAwait(true)`, so it's recommended to call `ConfigureAwait(false)` explicitly as much as possible. Apart from avoiding deadlocks, `ConfigureAwait(false)` also improves performance, as there is no marshaling of the original context.

This brings us to the question of whether there is a scenario that needs to use `ConfigureAwait(true)`. The answer is that there are scenarios where a custom `SynchronizationContext` is being built that needs to be used by a callback, and it is then recommended to use `ConfigureAwait(true)`, or at least not use `ConfigureAwait(false)`, as the default behavior of any task is the same as `ConfigureAwait(true)`.

CPU-bound versus I/O-bound

Always use async-await for I/O-bound work and the TPL for CPU-bound work to achieve asynchrony. I/O operations such as database calls, network calls, and filesystem calls can be wrapped in async-await asynchronous methods. However, a CPU-intensive operation such as calculating pi is better handled using the TPL.

Going back to our earlier discussion, the idea of asynchronous programming is to release `ThreadPool` threads instead of waiting on the completion of an operation. This can very easily be achieved when we represent outbound calls as tasks and use async-await.

However, for a CPU-intensive operation, a `ThreadPool` thread will continue to execute instructions on the worker thread (as it is a CPU-intensive operation and needs CPU time) and obviously cannot release that thread. This means that wrapping a CPU-intensive operation in async-await is not going to yield any benefit and is the same as running it synchronously. So, a better way to handle CPU-intensive operations is by using the TPL.

This does not mean we will stop using async-await the moment we encounter a CPU-intensive method. The recommended way is to still use async-await to manage CPU-bound operations along with the TPL and not break our first principle of using async-await all the way.

Here is a simple code snippet using async-await to manage CPU-bound work:

```
    private async Task CPUIOResult()
    {
        var doExpensiveCalculationTask = Task.Run(() =>
        DoExpensiveCalculation()); //Call a method
```

```
                 //that does CPU intense operation
            var downloadFileAsyncTask = DownloadFileAsync();
            await Task.WhenAll(doExpensiveCalculationTask,
             downloadFileAsyncTask);
        }
    private async Task DownloadFileAsync(string url, string path)
        {
            // Implementation
        }
        private float DoExpensiveCalculation()
        {
            //Implementation
        }
```

As seen in the preceding code, it's still possible to manage CPU-bound work with a mix of async-await and the TPL; it's up to the developer to assess all the possible options and write their code accordingly.

Avoid async void

Always make sure to have `Task` or `Task<T>` as the return type for an asynchronous method implemented using async-await instead of `void` if a method is not expected to return anything. The reason for this is that `Task` is a complex abstraction that handles many things for us, such as exception handling and task completion status. However, if an asynchronous method has an `async void` return type, it is like a fire-and-forget method, and any caller to this method won't be able to know the status of the operation, even if there is an exception.

That is because inside an `async void` method, as soon as an `await` expression is encountered, the call is returned to the caller without any reference to `Task`, so there is no reference to raise an exception for. For a UI application such as WPF, any exceptions on the `async void` method will crash the application; however, an exception for this is `async void` event handlers.

Another disadvantage with `async void` methods is the inability to write unit tests and assert them correctly. So, it's always recommended to use async `Task` exceptions as top-level event handlers (top-level is key here) because top-level events such as a button click or a mouse click are more of a one-way signal and are not used any differently in asynchronous code compared to their synchronous counterparts.

The same consideration needs to be taken in the case of `async` Lambdas, where we need to avoid passing them as an argument to a method that takes the `Action` type as its parameters. See the following example:

```
long elapsedTime = AsyncLambda(async() =>
{
    await Task.Delay(1000);
});
Console.WriteLine(elapsedTime);
Console.ReadLine();
static long AsyncLambda(Action a)
{
    Stopwatch sw = new Stopwatch();
    sw.Start();
    for (int i = 0; i < 10; i++)
    {
        a();
    }
    return sw.ElapsedMilliseconds;
}
```

Here, it's expected that the value of `elapsedTime` will be somewhere around 10,000. However, it's close to 100 for the same reason – that is, with `Action` being a delegate of the `void` return type, the call to `AsyncLambda` is returned immediately to the `Main` method (as with any `async void` method). This can be fixed by changing `AsyncLambda` as follows (or just by changing the parameter to `Func<Task>` and handling the wait on a () accordingly) and then forcing the caller to use `async` all the way:

```
async static Task<long> AsyncLambda(Func<Task> a)
{
    Stopwatch sw = new Stopwatch();
    sw.Start();
    for (int i = 0; i < 10; i++)
    {
        await a();
```

```
        }
        return sw.ElapsedMilliseconds;
    }
```

A word of caution – if there are methods in your application that accept the Action type parameters, it's recommended that you have an overload that accepts Func<Task> or Func<Task<T>>. Fortunately, the C# compiler automatically handles this and always calls the overload with Func<Task> as a parameter.

> **Tip**
> Use the Visual Studio 2022 Exception Helper feature to debug async exceptions that are rethrown by framework code.

Async streams with IAsyncEnumerable

We all know that foreach is used to loop over IEnumerable<T> or IEnumerator<T>. Let's look at the following code, in which we retrieve all employee IDs from a database and loop through each employee to print their ID:

```
static async Task Main(string[] args)
{
    var employeeTotal = await
    GetEmployeeIDAsync(5);
    foreach (int i in employeeTotal)
    {
        Console.WriteLine(i);
    }
}
```

The GetEmployeeIDAsync implementation is as follows:

```
static async Task<IEnumerable<int>>
GetEmployeeIDAsync(int input)
{
    int id = 0;
    List<int> tempID = new List<int>();
    for (int i = 0; i < input; i++) //Some async DB
        //iterator method like ReadNextAsync
    {
```

```
            await Task.Delay(1000); // simulate async
            id += i; // Hypothetically calculation
            tempID.Add(id);
        }
        return tempID;
    }
```

Here, you can see that we must use a temporary list until we have received all the records from the database, and finally, we return the list. However, if there is an iterator in our method, `yield` in C# is an obvious choice, as that helps in returning the results immediately and avoiding temporary variables. Now, say you used `yield`, as shown in the following code:

```
yield return id;
```

You would receive the following error upon compilation:

```
The body of 'Program.GetEmployeeIDAsync(int)' cannot be an
iterator block because 'Task<IEnumerable<int>>' is not an
iterator interface type
```

Hence, there is a need to be able to use `yield` with an `async` method and also loop through a collection to call an application asynchronously. That's where C# 8.0 came up with asynchronous streams through `IAsyncEnumerable`, which primarily enables you to return data immediately and asynchronously consume a collection. So, the preceding code can be changed as follows:

```
await foreach (int i in GetEmployeeIDAsync(5))
    {
        Console.WriteLine(i);
    }
static async IAsyncEnumerable<int>
 GetEmployeeIDAsync(int input)
{
    int id = 0;
    List<int> tempID = new List<int>();
    for (int i = 0; i < input; i++)
    {
        await Task.Delay(1000);
        id += i; // Hypothetically calculation
```

```
        yield return id;
    }
}
```

So, here you can see that once a method starts returning, `IAsyncEnumerable` loops can be iterated asynchronously, and this is helpful in many situations to write cleaner code.

ThreadPool starvation

Say you have an application with asynchronous code. However, you have noticed that periodically, during high loads, the response time for requests drastically increases. You research it further, but neither is the CPU of your server fully utilized nor is the memory of your process high, and it isn't a case of your database becoming a bottleneck either. In this case, your application is possibly causing what is known as `ThreadPool` starvation.

`ThreadPool` starvation is a state in which new threads keep being added to serve concurrent requests, and eventually, a point is reached where `ThreadPool` is unable to add more threads, and requests start seeing delayed response times or even start failing in the worst-case scenario. Even if `ThreadPool` can add threads at a rate of one or two per second, new requests may be coming at a higher rate (as in a burst load on a web application during the holiday season). Hence, there is a significant increase in the response time. There are multiple reasons why this can happen; a few of them are listed here:

- The consumption of more threads to speed up long-running CPU-bound work

- The calling of an `async` method in a `sync` method using `GetAwaiter()`. `GetResult()`

- The incorrect use of synchronization primitives, such as a thread holding a lock for a long time and other threads waiting to acquire it

In all the preceding points, the common thing is blocking code; so, the use of blocking code such as `Thread.Sleep` even for a short duration, something such as `GetAwaiter().GetResult()`, or trying to allocate more threads for a CPU-bound item increases the number of threads in `ThreadPool` and eventually leads to starvation.

`ThreadPool` starvation can be further diagnosed using tools such as **PerfView**, where you capture a trace for, say, 200 seconds, and verify the growth of threads in your process. If you see that your threads are growing at a rapid pace during peak load, then there is a possibility of starvation.

The best way to prevent ThreadPool starvation is to use async-await throughout the application and never block any async calls. Also, the throttling of newly created operations can help, as it restricts the number of items that can be queued at a time.

In this section, we discussed two important constructs, async-await and the TPL, which when combined make writing asynchronous code simpler. In the next section, we will learn about various data structures that are available in .NET 6 to support synchronization/thread safety without writing any additional code.

Using concurrent collections for parallelism

Collections classes are one of the most used types to encapsulate, retrieve, and modify enumerated sets of related data. Dictionary, list, queue, and array are some of the frequently used collection types, but they are not thread-safe. These collections are good if you access them from just one thread at a time.

A real-world environment would be multithreaded, and to make it thread-safe, you will have to implement various synchronization constructs, as described in an earlier section. To solve this problem, Microsoft came up with concurrent collection classes, such as ConcurrentQueue, ConcurrentBag, ConcurrentDictionary, and ConcurrentStack, which are thread-safe, as they internally implement synchronization. Let's look at them in detail in the following sections.

ConcurrentDictionary

Let's stimulate a multithreaded environment using a dictionary. Consider the t1 task as one operation from a client who is adding to the dictionary and the t2 task as a second operation from another client who is reading from the dictionary.

We add Thread.Sleep in each task to mimic a real-world scenario to ensure that one task doesn't complete before the other in this example. Let's consider an example console application with the following code snippet:

```
// Task t1 as one operation from a client who is adding to the
dictionary.
Dictionary<int, string> employeeDictionary = new
Dictionary<int, string>();
        Task t1 = Task.Factory.StartNew(() =>
        {
            for (int i = 0; i < 100; ++i)
```

```
    {
        employeeDictionary.TryAdd(i, "Employee"
        + i.ToString());
        Thread.Sleep(100);

    }
});
```

This is Task t2 as a second operation from another client who is reading from the dictionary:

```
Task t2 = Task.Factory.StartNew(() =>
{
    Thread.Sleep(500);
    foreach (var item in employeeDictionary)
    {
        Console.WriteLine(item.Key + "-" +
        item.Value);
        Thread.Sleep(100);
    }
});
```

Now, both tasks are executed at the same time, as shown in the following:

```
try
{
    Task.WaitAll(t1, t2); // Not recommended to
    //use in production application.
}
catch (AggregateException ex)
{
    Console.WriteLine(ex.Flatten().Message);
}
Console.ReadLine();
```

When you run this program, you will get the following exception, which states that you cannot modify and enumerate the collection at the same time:

Name	Value	Type
$exception	{"Collection was modified; enumeration operation may not execute."}	System. InvalidOperationException

Table 4.2 – The ConcurrentDictionary sample output

You may think now that we can add a lock to manage thread synchronization and avoid this exception in multithreaded scenarios for thread safety. I added a lock to the code wherever the dictionary is modified and enumerated to synchronize the threads. Here are the updated code snippets:

1. First, we have Task t1 as one operation from a client who is adding to the dictionary:

```
Dictionary<int, string> employeeDictionary = new
Dictionary<int, string>();
        Task t1 = Task.Factory.StartNew(() =>
        {
            for (int i = 0; i < 100; ++i)
            {
                //Lock the shared data
                lock (syncObject)
                {
                    employeeDictionary.TryAdd(i,
                        "Employee" + i.ToString());
                }
                Thread.Sleep(100);

            }
        });
```

2. Then, we have Task t2 as a second operation from another client who is reading from the dictionary:

```
        Task t2 = Task.Factory.StartNew(() =>
        {
            Thread.Sleep(500);
```

```
                //Lock the shared data
                lock (syncObject)
                {
                        foreach (var item in
                        employeeDictionary)
                        {
                                Console.WriteLine(item.Key +
                                "-" + item.Value);
                                Thread.Sleep(100);
                        }
                }
        });
```

3. Now, we have both tasks executed at the same time:

```
    try
        {
                Task.WaitAll(t1, t2); // Not
                //recommended to use in production
                //application.
        }
        catch (AggregateException ex)
        {
                Console.WriteLine(ex.Flatten()
                .Message);
        }
        Console.ReadLine();
```

When you run this code, you will not see any exceptions. However, locks have some issues, as mentioned earlier, so this code can be rewritten using concurrent collections. They internally use a multiple-thread synchronization technique that helps to scale well, prevent data corruption, and avoid all the problems with locks.

We can rewrite our code using ConcurrentDictionary, which is available in the System.Collections.Concurrent namespace. Replace Dictionary with ConcurrentDictionary in the sample code. You can also remove the reference to the System.Collections.Generic namespace, as Dictionary is not used now. Also, remove all the locks. The updated code is as follows, where we replace Dictionary with ConcurrentDictionary and remove the lock:

We have `Task t1` as one operation from a client who is adding to the dictionary, and an explicit lock is not needed with concurrent collections:

```
ConcurrentDictionary<int, string> employeeDictionary =
new ConcurrentDictionary<int, string>();
            Task t1 = Task.Factory.StartNew(() =>
            {
                for (int i = 0; i < 100; ++i)
                {
                    employeeDictionary.TryAdd(i,
                        "Employee"
                        + i.ToString());
                    Thread.Sleep(100);


                }
            });
```

4. Then, we have `Task t2` as a second operation from another client who is reading from the dictionary, and an explicit lock is not needed with concurrent collections:

```
            Task t2 = Task.Factory.StartNew(() =>
            {
                Thread.Sleep(500);
                foreach (var item in
                    employeeDictionary)
                {
                    Console.WriteLine(item.Key + "-" +
                        item.Value);
                    Thread.Sleep(100);
                }
            });
```

5. Now, both tasks are executed at the same time:

```
    try
            {
                Task.WaitAll(t1, t2);
            }
            catch (AggregateException ex) // You will
```

```
                    //not get Exception
              {
                  Console.WriteLine(ex.Flatten()
                    .Message);
              }
              Console.ReadLine();
```

When you run the program now, you will not get any exceptions, as all operations are thread-safe and atomic in ConcurrentDictionary. There is no overhead for the developer in implementing the locks and maintaining them as the project grows bigger. Here are some caveats with concurrent collections such as ConcurrentDictionary that you need to bear in mind:

- If two threads call AddOrUpdate, there's no guarantee which of the factory delegates will be called and even no guarantee that if a factory delegate produces an item, the item will be stored in the dictionary.

- The enumerator obtained by the GetEnumerator call is not a snapshot and may be modified during enumeration (which doesn't cause any exceptions).

- Key and value properties are snapshots of corresponding collections and may not correspond to the actual dictionary state.

We've looked at ConcurrentDictionary in detail; let's look at other concurrent collections in the next section.

Producer-consumer concurrent collections

In producer-consumer concurrent collections, one or more threads can produce tasks (adding to a queue, stack, or bag, for instance), and one or more other threads can consume tasks from the same collection (the queue, stack, or bag).

ConcurrentDictionary, which we saw in the previous section, is a general-purpose collection class where you add an item that you want and specify which item you want to read. Other concurrent collections are designed for specific problems:

- ConcurrentQueue is for scenarios where you want FIFO.

- ConcurrentStack is for scenarios where you want LIFO.

- ConcurrentBag is for scenarios where you want the same thread producing and consuming data stored in the bag and the order doesn't matter.

These three collections are also known as **producer-consumer collections**, where one or more threads can produce tasks and consume tasks from the same collection, as shown in the following figure:

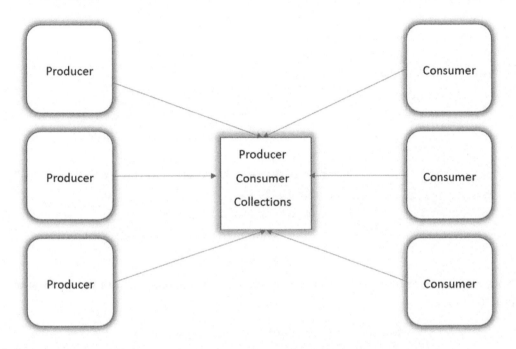

Figure 4.7 – A producer-consumer concurrent collection

All these three collections implement the `IProducerConsumerCollection<T>` interface, and the most important methods are `TryAdd` and `TryTake`, as shown here:

```
// Returns: true if the object was added successfully;
otherwise, false.
bool TryAdd(T item);
// Returns true if an object was removed and returned
successfully; otherwise, false.
bool TryTake([MaybeNullWhen(false)] out T item);
```

Let's take an example of a producer-consumer and simulate it using `ConcurrentQueue`:

- **Producer**: A client sending a request to a web service and the server storing a request in a queue
- **Consumer**: A worker thread pulling the request from the queue and processing it

The implementation is shown in the following code:

```
//Producer: Client sending request to web service and server
storing the request in queue.
ConcurrentQueue<string> concurrentQueue = new
ConcurrentQueue<string>();
        Task t1 = Task.Factory.StartNew(() =>
        {
            for (int i = 0; i < 10; ++i)
            {
                concurrentQueue.Enqueue("Web request "
                 + i);
                Console.WriteLine("Sending "+ "Web
                 request " + i);
                Thread.Sleep(100);
            }
        });
```

Now, we have `Consumer`, where a `Worker` thread pulls the request from the queue and processes it:

```
        Task t2 = Task.Factory.StartNew(() =>
        {
            while (true)
            {
                if (concurrentQueue.TryDequeue(out
                 string request))
                {
                    Console.WriteLine("Processing "+
                     request);
                }
                else
                {
                    Console.WriteLine("No request");
                }
            }
        });
```

Both producer and consumer tasks are executed at the same time successfully. Wait for all provided tasks to complete execution within the specified number of milliseconds. Refer to the following code snippet:

```
try
        {
                Task.WaitAll(new Task[] { t1, t2 }, 1000);
        }
        catch (AggregateException ex) // No exception
        {
                Console.WriteLine(ex.Flatten().Message);
        }
```

This is according to the method definition from Microsoft:

- concurrentQueue.Enqueue: This adds an object to the end of ConcurrentQueue<T>.

- concurrentQueue.TryDequeue: This tries to remove and return the object at the beginning of ConcurrentQueue.

When you run the program, you can see task t1 producing requests and task t2 polling and then consuming requests. We'll get into the details in a short while. We also said that these classes implement IProducerConsumerCollection<T>, so we are going to make three changes to the previous code:

- Replace ConcurrentQueue<string> with IProducerConsumerCollection<string>.

- Replace concurrentQueue.Enqueue with concurrentQueue.TryAdd.

- Replace concurrentQueue.TryDequeue with concurrentQueue.TryTake.

This is how the code looks now:

```
IProducerConsumerCollection<string> concurrentQueue = new
ConcurrentQueue<string>();
//Removed code for brevity.
Task t1 = Task.Factory.StartNew(() =>
        {
                for (int i = 0; i < 10; ++i)
```

```
                {
                        concurrentQueue.TryAdd("Web request " +
                        i);
    //Removed code for brevity.
    Task t2 = Task.Factory.StartNew(() =>
                {
                        while (true)
                        {
                                if (concurrentQueue.TryTake(out string
                                request))
    //Removed code for brevity.
```

Now, go ahead and run the program. You can see task t1 producing requests and task t2 polling and then consuming requests. You can see all 10 requests produced by task t1 and consumed by task t2. But there are two problems:

- The producer is producing at its own rate, the consumer is consuming at its own rate, and there is no synchronization.

- There is continuous indefinite polling from the consumer in task t2, which is not good for performance and CPU usage, as we can see by **No request** being printed when we don't get any request to process from concurrentQueue.TryTake.

This is where BlockingCollection<T> comes in handy.

The BlockingCollection<T> class

BlockingCollection<T> supports bounding and blocking. Bounding allows you to specify a maximum capacity for a collection. Controlling the maximum size of a collection helps to prevent producing threads from moving too far ahead of consuming threads. Multiple producing threads can add items to BlockingCollection<T> concurrently until the collection reaches its maximum size, after which they will be blocked until an item is removed by consumers.

Similarly, multiple consuming threads can remove items from a blocking collection concurrently till the collection becomes empty, after which they will be blocked until an item is added by producers. A producing thread can invoke the `CompleteAdding` method when no more items will be added and indicate that it has completed adding. This will help consumers to monitor the `IsCompleted` property to know that no more items will be added when the collection is empty.

When you create a `BlockingCollection<T>` class, along with the bounding capacity, you can also specify the type of concurrent collection to use depending upon the scenario. By default, the collection type is `ConcurrentQueue<T>` for `BlockingCollection<T>` when you don't specify the type.

Here is a sample code snippet:

```
BlockingCollection<string> blockingCollection = new
BlockingCollection<string>(new ConcurrentQueue<string>(),5);
        Task t1 = Task.Factory.StartNew(() =>
        {
            for (int i = 0; i < 10; ++i)
            {
                blockingCollection.TryAdd("Web request
                " + i);
                Console.WriteLine("Sending " + "Web
                request " + i);
                Thread.Sleep(100);
            }
            blockingCollection.CompleteAdding();
        });
```

Then, the consumer with the `Worker` thread pulls the item from the queue and processes it:

```
        Task t2 = Task.Factory.StartNew(() =>
        {
            while (!blockingCollection.IsCompleted)
            {
                if (blockingCollection.TryTake(out
                string request,100))
```

```
            {
                Console.WriteLine("Processing " +
                request);
            }
            else
            {
                Console.WriteLine("No request");
            }
        }
    });
```

Now, the producer and consumer thread are accessed concurrently.

There are a few points to consider in the code:

- The specified bounding of 5: `BlockingCollection<string>`
  `blockingCollection = new BlockingCollection<string>(new`
  `ConcurrentQueue<string>(),5);`.

- The producing thread invokes the `CompleteAdding` method when no more items
  will be added to indicate that it has completed adding: `blockingCollection.`
  `CompleteAdding();`.

- Consumers monitor the `IsCompleted` property to find out that no more items
  will be added when the collection is empty: `while (!blockingCollection.`
  `IsCompleted)`.

- Try to remove an item from `BlockingCollection<T>` in the specified time
  – for example, I have gone with 100 milliseconds: `if (blockingCollection.`
  `TryTake(out string request, 100))`.

This is the power of a blocking collection. Both the producer and consumer are decoupled,
they can be coded independently by different teams, and at runtime, they use a blocking
concurrent collection to share data with each other. Plus, at the same time, flow is
controlled with the bounding capacity so that the producer doesn't move too far ahead of
consumers.

> **Note**
>
> In addition to the `TryTake` method that we've seen, you can also use a `foreach` loop to remove items from a blocking collection. You can read about it here:
>
> `https://docs.microsoft.com/en-us/dotnet/standard/collections/thread-safe/how-to-use-foreach-to-remove`
>
> With blocking collections, there will be scenarios where the consumer will have to work with multiple collections and take or add items. The `TakeFromAny` and `AddToAny` methods will help you in this scenario. You can read further about these two methods here:
>
> `https://docs.microsoft.com/en-us/dotnet/api/system.collections.concurrent.blockingcollection-1.takefromany?view=net-6.0`
>
> `https://docs.microsoft.com/en-us/dotnet/api/system.collections.concurrent.blockingcollection-1.addtoany?view=net-6.0`

Summary

Wrapping up, writing, and maintaining clean asynchronous code is difficult. However, with the various constructs available in .NET and C#, developers can now write asynchronous code with less framework overhead and focus more on the business requirements.

In this chapter, we covered various ways to write scalable asynchronous code using the TPL, async-await, and concurrent collections, and we also covered the fundamentals of threads and `ThreadPool` in .NET to understand the framework internals and write cleaner code for enterprise applications. Now, we have a deeper understanding of multithreading and how to protect shared data in a multithreaded environment. We learned about creating tasks and implementing asynchronous functions using async-await, and finally, we learned about the concurrent collections available in .NET Core and their implementation in various concurrent scenarios.

In the next chapter, we will look into dependency injection in .NET 6 and how it plays a significant role in loosely coupling various low-level classes in enterprise applications.

Questions

1. In a multithreaded environment, which of the following data structures should you use to protect data from getting overwritten/corrupted?

   a. `async-await.`

   b. Tasks.

   c. Synchronization constructs such as locks.

   d. Data never gets corrupted.

   Answer : a

2. If you have a WPF application that retrieves data from a REST API, which of the following should you implement for better responsiveness?

   a. A concurrent collection

   b. `Parallel.For`

   c. `async-await` for the REST API calls

   Answer: c

3. Which of the following should be passed to cancel a task?

   a. `CancellationToken`

   b. `ConcurrentDictionary`

   c. `SemaphoreSlim`

   Answer: a

4. Which of the following is the recommended return type for an asynchronous method that uses async-await and does not return anything?

   a. `async void`

   b. `async Task`

   c. `async book`

   d. `async Task<bool>`

   Answer: b

Further reading

- https://www.packtpub.com/product/hands-on-parallel-programming-with-c-8-and-net-core-3/9781789132410

- https://devblogs.microsoft.com/dotnet/configureawait-faq/

- http://www.albahari.com/threading/

- *Dataflow (Task Parallel Library) | Microsoft Docs*: https://docs.microsoft.com/en-us/dotnet/standard/parallel-programming/dataflow-task-parallel-library

5
Dependency Injection in .NET 6

A big issue that an enterprise application can face is the complexity of wiring different elements together and managing their lifetimes. To address this, we use the **inversion of control (IoC)** principle, which recommends removing the dependency between objects. By delegating the flow of control, IoC makes the program extensible and increases the modularity. Events, callback delegates, the observer pattern, and **dependency injection (DI)** are some of the ways to achieve IoC.

In this chapter, we will learn about the following:

- What is DI?
- DI in ASP.NET Core 6
- Managing application services
- Using third-party containers

By the end of this chapter, you'll have a good idea about DI and how it's leveraged in .NET 6 applications, the types of scopes provided in ASP.NET Core 6, and how to leverage them in your projects.

Technical requirements

The code used in this chapter can be found here: `https://github.com/ PacktPublishing/Enterprise-Application-Development-with-C-10- and-.NET-6-Second-Edition/tree/main/Chapter05`.

What is DI?

DI is a technique in which an object receives objects that it depends on. The DI pattern fulfills the DI principle covered as part of the **single-responsibility principle, open-closed principle, Liskov substitution principle, interface segregation principle, and dependency inversion principle (SOLID)** design principles in *Chapter 1, Designing and Architecting the Enterprise Application*. With the use of DI, code will be more maintainable, readable, testable, and extensible.

DI is one of the most well-known methods to help achieve better maintainable code. DI has three entities involved, as shown in the following diagram:

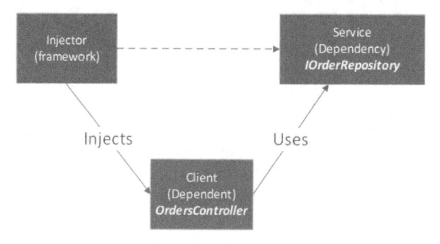

Figure 5.1 – DI relationship

The **Injector** creates an instance of **Service** and injects it into the **Client** object. The **Client** depends on the injected **Service** to perform its operations—for example, in the enterprise application that we are going to build, `IOrderRepository` is responsible for **create, read, update, and delete (CRUD)** operations on the `Order` entity. .NET IoC container (**Injector**) instantiates `IOrderRepository` (**Service**) and injects it into `OrderController` (client).

IoC container (also known as **DI Container**) is a framework for implementing automatic DI. In *Figure 5.1*, this is referred to as **Injector**. It is responsible for creating or referencing a dependency and injecting it into **Client**.

Now that we have learned what DI is, let's learn about the types of DI.

Types of DI

There are multiple ways a service can be injected into a dependency. Based on the way a service is injected into the client object, DI is categorized into three types, as outlined here:

- **Constructor injection**: Dependencies are injected through a constructor while instantiating the dependent. In the following example, the `IWeatherProvider` dependency is injected through the constructor parameter:

```
public class WeatherService
{
    private readonly IweatherProvider
        weatherProvider;
    public WeatherService(IWeatherProvider
        weatherProvider)
            => this.weatherProvider =
                weatherProvider;
    public WeatherForecast GetForecast(string
        location) =>
        this.weatherProvider.
            GetForecastOfLocation (location);
}
```

In the preceding example, `WeatherService` is dependent on `IWeatherProvider`, which is injected via a constructor parameter.

> **Note**
>
> For an implementation of the `WeatherProvider` service, refer to the sample code from GitHub, which can be found at the following link: `https://github.com/PacktPublishing/Enterprise-Application-Development-with-C-10-and-.NET-6-Second-Edition/blob/main/Chapter05/DITypes/Service/WeatherProvider.cs`.

Setter injection: In the case of setter injection, the dependent exposes a setter method or property that the injector uses to inject the dependency. This is also referred to as property injection. In the following example, the `IWeatherProvider` dependency is not set while initializing `WeatherService2`. It is set via the `WeatherProvider` property post object initialization:

```
public class WeatherService2
{
    private IWeatherProvider _weatherProvider;
    public IWeatherProvider WeatherProvider
    {
        get => _weatherProvider == null ?
                throw new
                    InvalidOperationException(
                    "WeatherService is not
                    initialized")
                : _weatherProvider;
        set => _weatherProvider = value;
    }
    public WeatherForecast GetForecast(string
        location) =>
        this.WeatherProvider.
            GetForecastOfLocation(location);
}
```

- **Method injection**: Another way to inject a dependency is by passing it as a method parameter. In this example, the `IWeatherProvider` dependency is injected as a method parameter wherever required.

In the following code snippet, the `IWeatherProvider` service is injected into `WeatherService` via the `GetForecast` method:

```
public class WeatherService
{
    public WeatherForecast GetForecast(
        string location, IWeatherProvider
        weatherProvider)
        {
```

```
        if(weatherProvider == null)
        {
            throw new ArgumentNullException(
                nameof(weatherProvider));
        }
        return weatherProvider.
            GetForecastOfLocation (location);
    }
}
```

Here are some suggestions to help in choosing the type of DI:

- Use constructor injection when the class has a dependency without which the functionality won't work.

- Use constructor injection when the dependency is used in multiple functions in the class.

- Use property injection when the dependency can change after the class is instantiated.

- Use method injection when the implementation of the dependency changes with every call.

In most cases, constructor injection will be used for clean and decoupled code, but depending on the need, we will also leverage method and property injection techniques.

We have now learned the concepts of DI. Let's dive into what .NET 6 offers to achieve DI.

DI in ASP.NET Core 6

.NET 6 comes with a built-in IoC container framework, which simplifies DI. This comes with the `Microsoft.Extensions.DependencyInjection` NuGet package and the ASP.NET Core 6 framework itself relies heavily on this. To support DI, a container needs to support three basic actions on objects/services, as outlined here:

- **Registering**: The container should have provisions to register dependencies. This will help to map the correct type to a class so that it can create the right dependency instance.

- **Resolving**: The container should resolve dependencies by creating a dependency object and injecting it into the dependent instance. IoC container manages the creation of registered objects by passing in all the required dependencies.

- **Disposing**: The container is responsible for managing the lifetime of dependencies created through it.

In .NET 6, the following terms are used:

- **Service**: Refers to a dependency managed by a container
- **Framework services**: Refers to services provided by .NET 6 Framework—for example, `IConfiguration`, `ILoggerFactory`, `IWebHostEnvironment`, and so on
- **Application services**: Refers to services that a developer creates to support application functionality—for example, the `IWeatherProvider` service that we used in the previous section

For the application to start, the ASP.NET Core 6 framework injects a few dependencies, which are referred to as **framework services**. When you create an ASP.NET Core 6 web application, `WebApplicationBuilder` is injected with the required framework services such as `IConfiguration` and `IWebHostEnvironment`. When you try printing the registered services, as shown in the following code snippet (refer to the code from `https://github.com/PacktPublishing/Enterprise-Application-Development-with-C-10-and-.NET-6-Second-Edition/blob/main/Chapter05/DITypes/Program.cs#L16`), we can list the framework services registered:

```
foreach(var i in builder.Services.AsEnumerable())
{
    Console.WriteLine($"{i.Lifetime} - {i.ServiceType.ToString()}");
}
```

In ASP.NET Core 6.0, the `IWebHostEnvironment` framework service is available from the `builder.Environment` property. Similarly, the configuration is available from the `builder.Configuration` property.

ASP.NET Core 6 Runtime instantiates all the required framework services and registers them with IoC container. Starting with ASP.NET Core 6, they are available through properties of `WebApplication` and `WebApplicationBuilder` in `Program.cs`. These framework services can be injected into controllers and other services through any of the DI types we discussed in the previous section.

Application services are services injected into the container by the developer. These services will be registered using the `Services` property of `WebApplicationBuilder`. The following code snippet shows how to register the `IWeatherProvider` application service with the container:

```
builder.Services.AddScoped<IWeatherProvider, WeatherProvider>();
```

In the next section, we will learn about the lifetime of these services and how they are managed.

> **Note**
>
> Refer to *Chapter 10, Creating an ASP.NET Core 6 Web API*, to learn about the code present in the `Program.cs` file.

Understanding service lifetimes

When you register a service with a specified lifetime, the container will automatically dispose of the object according to the lifetime specified. There are three types of lifetimes available to use with Microsoft DI Container, as outlined here:

- **Transient**: With this lifetime, an object is created every time it is requested from the service container. If the creation of a service is time-consuming, this may not be the right scope as it will add latency. The `AddTransient` extension method is used to register with this lifetime, as illustrated in the following code snippet:

    ```
    public static IServiceCollection AddTransient(this
        IServiceCollection services, Type serviceType);
    ```

    > **Note**
    > A transient lifetime is normally used for stateless, lightweight services.

- **Singleton**: A singleton lifetime allows the container to create an object only once per application life cycle, and we get the same object every time it is requested. An object is created when there is a first request to the service or when providing the implementation instance directly at the time of registration. Services registered as a singleton are disposed of when `ServiceProvider` is disposed of on application shutdown. The `AddSingleton` extension method is used to register with this lifetime, as illustrated in the following code snippet:

```
public static IServiceCollection AddSingleton(this
    IServiceCollection services, Type serviceType);
```

- **Scoped**: By using this lifetime, a service will be created only once in the client request scope. This is particularly used in ASP.NET Core 6 where an object instance is created once per **HyperText Transfer Protocol (HTTP)** request. Services such as **Entity Framework Core's (EF Core's)** `DbContext` are registered with a scoped lifetime. The `AddScoped` extension method is used to register with the scoped lifetime scope, as illustrated in the following code snippet:

```
public static IServiceCollection AddScoped(this
    IServiceCollection services, Type serviceType);
```

The lifetime type needs to be chosen wisely in application development. A service should not depend on a service that has a shorter life span than its own; for example, a service registered as a singleton should not depend on a service that is registered as transient. The following table shows which lifetimes can safely depend on which other lifetime scopes:

	Singleton	Scoped	Transient
Singleton	✓	✗	✗
Scoped	✓	✓	✗
Transient	✓	✓	✓

Table 5.1 – Lifetime dependency

As a developer, you need not worry about scope validation. Built-in scope validation is done in ASP.NET Core 6 when the environment is set to **Development**. In the case of misconfiguration, `InvalidOperationException` is thrown while building the application. This can be explicitly turned on by enabling `ValidateScopes` options for all environment configurations while registering `ServiceProvider`, as shown in the following code snippet. Here, while creating a host builder, `ValidateScopes` is set to `true` to turn on the scope validation:

```
builder.Host.UseDefaultServiceProvider(opt => { opt.ValidateScopes
= true; });
```

Let's create an ASP.NET Core 6 web application to understand the service lifetime. We will be creating different services and registering them with the singleton, scoped, and transient lifetime scopes and observing how they behave. Proceed as follows:

1. Create a new ASP.NET Core web application (**Model-View-Controller**, or **MVC**) and name it `DISampleWeb`.

2. Create a new project folder with the name `Services` and add three classes: `ScopedService`, `SingletonService`, and `TransientService`. Add the following code (all these services will be the same without any real code in them; we just register them with different lifetime scopes as per their name):

> **Note**
> In the following sample, the interface and the class are defined in a single file. This is done purely for demonstration purposes. Ideally, the interface and the class are to be defined in two different classes.

- `ScopedService.cs`: This class will be registered with the scoped lifetime scope, as illustrated in the following code snippet:

```
public interface IScopedService {      }
public class ScopedService : IScopedService {     }
```

- `SingletonService.cs`: This class will be registered with the singleton lifetime scope, as illustrated in the following code snippet:

```
public interface ISingletonService   {     }
public class SingletonService : ISingletonService {  }
```

- `TransientService.cs`: This class will be registered with the transient lifetime scope, as illustrated in the following code snippet:

```
public interface ITransientService   {    }
public class TransientService : ITransientService{    }
```

3. Now, register these services in `Program.cs` with `IServiceCollection`, as shown here:

```
//Register as Scoped
builder.Services.AddScoped<IScopedService,ScopedService>();
//Register as Singleton
builder.Services.
AddSingleton<ISingletonService,SingletonService>();
//Register as Transient
builder.Services.
AddTransient<ITransientService,TransientService>();
```

The collection of service descriptors, `IServiceCollection`, is exposed via the `Services` property of `WebApplicationBuilder`.

4. Now, add the `HomeViewModel` model class under the `Models` folder, which will be used to show data retrieved from the services registered previously. The following code snippet illustrates how to do this:

```
public class HomeViewModel
{
        public int Singleton { get; set; }
        public int Scoped { get; set; }
        public int Scoped2 { get; internal set; }
        public int Transient { get; set; }
        public int Transient2 { get; internal set; }
}
```

Since we registered `ScopedService`, `SingletonService`, and `TransientService` with ASP.NET Core 6 IoC container, we will get these services via constructor injection.

5. Now, we will add code to get these services in HomeController and Views to show data retrieved from these objects on the home page. Modify the home controller to get two instances of ScopedService and TransientService and set ViewModel with the object hash code of the service object. The solution structure is shown in the following screenshot:

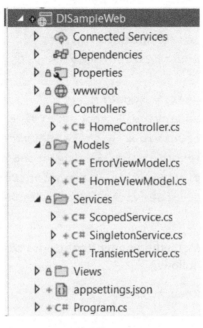

Figure 5.2 – Solution structure

Note

The GetHashCode method returns the hash code of the object. This will change per instance.

---

6. Modify the constructor of HomeController to accept the registered services and define private fields to reference service instances, as follows:

```
private readonly ILogger<HomeController> _logger;
private readonly IScopedService scopedService;
private readonly IScopedService scopedService2;
private readonly ISingletonService singletonService;
```

```
private readonly ITransientService transientService;
private readonly ITransientService transientService2;
public HomeController(ILogger<HomeController> logger,
IScopedService scopedService,
IScopedService scopedService2,
ISingletonService singletonService,
ITransientService transientService,
ITransientService transientService2)
{
    this._logger = logger;
    this.scopedService = scopedService;
    this.scopedService2 = scopedService2;
    this.singletonService = singletonService;
    this.transientService = transientService;
    this.transientService2 = transientService2;
}
```

7. Now, modify the Index method under HomeController to set
    HomeViewModel, as follows:

```
public IActionResult Index()
{
    var viewModel = new HomeViewModel
    {
        Scoped = scopedService.GetHashCode(),
        Scoped2 = scopedService2.GetHashCode(),
        Singleton = singletonService.GetHashCode(),
        Transient = transientService.GetHashCode(),
        Transient2 = transientService2.GetHashCode(),
    };
    return View(viewModel);
}
```

8. Next, modify `Index.cshtml` under the `~/Views/Home` folder to show `HomeViewModel` on the page, as follows:

```
@model HomeViewModel
@{
    ViewData["Title"] = "Home Page";
}
<h2 class="text-success">Singleton.</h2>
<p>
        <strong>ID:</strong> <code>@Model.Singleton
</code>
</p>
<h2 class="text-success">Scoped instance 1</h2>
<p>
        <strong>ID:</strong> <code>@Model.Scoped</code>
</p>
<h2 class="text-success">Scoped instance 2</h2>
<p>
        <strong>ID:</strong> <code>@Model.Scoped2</code>
</p>
<h2 class="text-success">Transient instance 1</h2>
<p>
        <strong>ID:</strong> <code>@Model.Transient</code>
</p>
<h2 class="text-success">Transient instance 2</h2>
<p>
        <strong>ID:</strong> <code>@Model.Transient2</code>
</p>
```

9. Now, run the application. You will see an output like this:

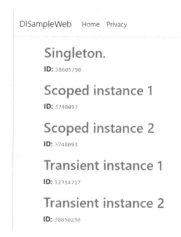

Figure 5.3 – Sample output on the first run

If we observe the output, the **identifiers (IDs)** displayed for both instances of ScopedService are the same. This is because only one object for IScopedService is created per request scope. Please note the IDs may be different when you run the code as they are generated at runtime.

The IDs of the transient service are different for both services. As we learned, this is because a new instance is created for every request to IoC container.

10. Now, refresh the page again. You'll see an output that looks something like this:

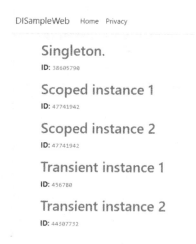

Figure 5.4 – Sample output on the second run

If we compare the outputs in both *Figure 5.3* and *Figure 5.4*, we will notice that the ID of SingletonService did not change—this is because only one object is created for a singleton object per lifetime of the application. Up until now, we have seen how the service lifetime is managed based on the registration. It is also important to understand when objects are to be disposed of. In the next section, we will learn about the disposal of services.

Disposal of services

As we learned earlier in this chapter, the disposal of objects is the responsibility of the IoC container framework. The container calls the Dispose method on those services that implement IDisposable. Services created by the container should never be disposed of by the developer explicitly. Similarly, developers are responsible for disposing of instances created by them.

Consider the following code snippet, where the SingletonService instance is registered with the singleton scope:

```
var _ disposableSingletonService= new
DisposableSingletonService();
// Registering an instance of a class with singleton lifetime
builder.Services.AddSingleton<IDisposableSingletonService>( _
disposableSingletonService);
```

> **Note**
>
> For a simple implementation of DisposableSingletonService, refer to the code at the following link: https://github. com/PacktPublishing/Enterprise-Application- Development-with-C-10-and-.NET-6-Second-Edition/ blob/main/Chapter05/DISampleWeb/Services/ DisposableSingletonService.cs.

In the preceding code snippet, we created an object of
`DisposableSingletonService` and registered it with IoC container. The service
instance is not created by the container. In this case, IoC Container does not dispose of the
object; it is the developer's responsibility to dispose of it. We can dispose of objects when
an `ApplicationStopping` event is fired from `IHostApplicationLifetime`,
which is exposed through the `Lifetime` property of `WebApplication`, as shown in
the following code snippet:

```
app.Lifetime.ApplicationStopping.Register(() => {
    _ disposableSingletonService.Dispose();
});
```

In the preceding code snippet, `IHostApplicationLifetime` is injected by the
runtime into `WebApplication`. This interface allows consumers to be notified of
`ApplicationStarted`, `ApplicationStopped`, and `ApplicationStopping`
application lifetime events. To dispose of the singleton object, we will call a Dispose()
method by registering to the `ApplicationStopping` lifetime event.

A new addition in .NET 6 to DI is the support of `IAsyncDisposable` for scopes. A new
`CreateAsyncScope` extension method is added to `IServiceProvider` to support
the creation of an asynchronous service scope, and an `AsyncServiceScope` wrapper
is added, which implements `IAsyncDisposable`. The following code disposes of the
scopes asynchronously:

```
// Refer AsyncDisposableScope sample code for the implementation
await using (var scope = provider.CreateAsyncScope())
{
    var foo = scope.ServiceProvider.
GetRequiredService<IWeatherProviderAsync>();
}
```

Going forward, if the dependency **service provider (SP)** supports this, it is recommended
to use `CreateAsyncScope` wherever you are creating scopes manually.

> **Note**
>
> Refer to the following Microsoft documentation to learn more about DI
> guidelines:
>
> https://docs.microsoft.com/en-us/dotnet/core/
> extensions/dependency-injection-guidelines

Up until now, we have looked at service lifetimes and how they are disposed of in .NET 6. In the next section, we will learn about managing application services.

Managing application services

In ASP.NET Core 6, when a request is received by `MvcMiddleware`, routing is used to select a controller and action method. `IControllerActivator` creates an instance of the controller and loads constructor arguments from DI Container.

In the *Understanding service lifetimes* section, we saw how application services are registered and how their lifetimes are managed. In the example, the services were injected through a constructor, which is known as constructor injection. In this section, we will see how to achieve method injection and go through different ways application services can be registered and accessed in ASP.NET Core 6 IoC container.

Accessing registered services via method injection

In the previous sections, we saw how the dependency service is injected into the controller constructor and the reference is stored in a local field that is used to call a method/ **application programming interface (API)** of the dependency.

Sometimes, we don't want the dependency service to be available in all actions of the controller. In such scenarios, the service can be injected via method injection. This is done by making a parameter with the `[FromServices]` attribute, as shown in the following example:

```
public IActionResult Index([FromServices] ISingletonService
singletonService2)
{
}
```

Minimal APIs introduced in ASP.NET Core 6 allow us to request DI services in route handlers without explicitly marking them with the `[FromServices]` attribute, as illustrated here:

```
app.MapGet("/", (ISingletonService service) => service.DoAction());
```

You might be wondering how the runtime differentiates injected services from other parameters. To achieve that, .NET6 introduced a new `IServiceProviderIsService` interface, which helps to identify that a given service type is registered in the DI container without creating an instance of it.

In the next section, we will see the registration of multiple instances for the same service type and how to access them.

Registering multiple instances

For a given interface, we can register multiple implementations with the IoC container.

> **Note**
> If more than one implementation is registered with the same service type, the last registration will take precedence over all previous registrations.

Consider the following service registration, where the IWeatherForecastService service is registered with two implementations—WeatherForecastService and WeatherForecastServiceV2:

```
services.AddScoped<IWeatherForecastService,
WeatherForecastService>();
services.AddScoped<IWeatherForecastService,
WeatherForecastServiceV2>();
```

Now, when there is a request for an instance of IWeatherForecastService from the controller, an instance of WeatherForecastServiceV2 will be served, as illustrated in the following code snippet:

```
private readonly IWeatherForecastService weatherForecastService;
public
WeatherForecastController(ILogger<WeatherForecastController>
logger, IWeatherForecastService weatherForecastService)
{
    _ logger = logger;
    this.weatherForecastService = weatherForecastService;
}
```

In the previous example, it might appear that the registration of WeatherForecastV2 is overwriting the previous registration of WeatherForecastService. However, ASP. NET Core 6 IoC container will have all registrations of IWeatherForecastService. To get all registrations, fetch the service as IEnumerable, as follows:

```
private readonly IEnumerable<IWeatherForecastService>
weatherForecastServices;
```

```
public WeatherForecastController(
ILogger<WeatherForecastController> logger,
IEnumerable<IWeatherForecastService> weatherForecastServices)
{
    _ logger = logger;
    this.weatherForecastServices = weatherForecastServices;
}
```

This may be useful in scenarios such as executing a **rules engine**, where we want to run through all rules before we process a request. A set of rules will be configured through the Services property of WebApplicationBuilder. So, in the future, when there is an addition of a rule or the removal of an existing rule, the change will only be to inject a new service into the Services property.

Using TryAdd

In this section, we will learn about how we can avoid accidentally overriding already registered services.

The TryAdd extension method registers services only when no registration exists for the same service. The TryAdd extension method is available for all lifetime scopes (TyrAddScoped, TryAddSingleton, and TryAddTransient).

With the service registration shown in the following code snippet, when there is a request for IWeatherForecastService, IoC container serves WeatherForecastService, not WeatherForecastServiceV2:

```
services.AddScoped<IWeatherForecastService,
WeatherForecastService>();
services.TryAddScoped<IWeatherForecastService,
WeatherForecastServiceV2>();
```

To overcome side effects that might occur with duplicate registrations, it is always recommended to use TryAdd extension methods to register a service.

Now, let's see how to replace an already registered service.

Replacing an existing registration

ASP.NET Core 6 IoC container provides a way to replace existing registrations. In the following example, IWeatherForecastService is initially registered with WeatherForecastService. It is then replaced with WeatherForecastServiceV2:

```
builder.Services.TryAddScoped<IWeatherForecastService,
WeatherForecastService>();
builder.Services.Replace(ServiceDescriptor.
Scoped<IWeatherForecastService, WeatherForecastServiceV2>());
```

As with the Replace instance of WeatherForecastServiceV2, an implementation is served to the constructor of WeatherForecastController. In the following code snippet, unlike in the *Registering multiple instances* section, we will only see one object in the weatherForecastService constructor variable:

```
public
WeatherForecastController(ILogger<WeatherForecastController>
logger, IEnumerable<IWeatherForecastService>
weatherForecastService)
{

    _ logger = logger;
    this.weatherForecastService = weatherForecastService;

}
```

Till now in this section, we have learned about registering and replacing services with the IoC container. There may be times when we need to delete current registrations. Consider a scenario where you wish to utilize services and registrations from a library but you don't have access to its source code. If you reimplement some of the interfaces from that library and reregister them with the container, you might see some unexpected behavior. In the next section, we will see how to remove a registered service.

Removing an existing registration

To remove an existing registration, ASP.Net Core 6 IoC container provides the Remove extension. You can use the RemoveAll method to remove all registrations related to a service, as seen in the following code snippet:

```
services.RemoveAll<IWeatherForecastService>();
```

In the following code snippet, the `Remove` method removes the registration of the `WeatherForecastService` implementation from the container:

```
//Removes the first registration of IWeatherForecastService
Builder.Services.Remove(ServiceDescriptor.
Scoped<IWeatherForecastService, WeatherForecastService>());
```

Up until now, we have seen how we work with complex services, but when it comes to generic open types, it will be difficult to register every generic constructed type. In the next section, we will learn how to deal with generic open-type services.

> **Note**
>
> To learn more about generic types, you can refer to the following website: `https://docs.microsoft.com/en-us/dotnet/csharp/language-reference/language-specification/types`.

Registering generics

This section will introduce you to dealing with generic-type services with DI.

In the case of generic types, it does not make sense to register the service for each type of implementation that is in use. ASP.NET Core 6 IoC container provides a way to simplify the registration of the generic type. One such type that is already provided by the framework itself is `ILogger`, as illustrated in the following code snippet:

```
Builder.Services.TryAdd(ServiceDescriptor.
Singleton(typeof(ILogger<>), typeof(Logger<>)));
```

> **Note**
>
> For your reference, you may visit the following link: `https://github.com/dotnet/runtime/blob/main/src/libraries/Microsoft.Extensions.Logging/src/LoggingBuilderExtensions.cs`.

Another use case for generics is with a generic repository pattern used with the data access layer.

With all the registrations we have, the `ConfigureServices` method can grow big and can no longer be readable. The next section will help you learn how to address that.

Extension methods for code readability

The pattern that is followed in the ASP.NET Core 6 framework to make code look more readable is to create an extension method with a logical grouping of service registrations. The following code tries to group and register notification-related services using an extension method. General practice is to use the `Microsoft.Extensions.DependencyInjection` namespace to define service registration extension methods. This will make the developer use all the functionality related to DI just by using the `Microsoft.Extensions.DependencyInjection` namespace.

In the following code snippet, notification-related services were registered with `AddNotificationServices`:

```
namespace Microsoft.Extensions.DependencyInjection
{
public static class
NotificationServicesServiceCollectionExtension
{
    public static IServiceCollection AddNotificationServices(this
IServiceCollection services)
    {
        services.TryAddScoped<INotificationService,
EmailNotificationService>();
        services.TryAddScoped<INotificationService,
SMSNotificationService>();
        return services;
    }
}
}
```

Now that the extension method is created, we can use the `AddNotificationServices` method to register notification services under `ConfigureServices`. This will make `ConfigureServices` become more readable. The code is illustrated here:

```
builder.Services.AddNotificationServices();
```

We have seen how to inject services into controllers and other classes. In the next section, we will learn how to inject services into views.

DI in Razor Pages

The purpose of views in MVC is to display data. Most of the time, data displayed in views is passed from the controller. Passing all required data from controllers is recommended considering the **separation of concerns (SoC)** principle, but there may be cases where we want to view specific services from pages such as localization and telemetry services. Using DI supported by Razor views, we can inject such services into views.

To learn about injecting services into views, let's modify the DISampleWeb application that we created in previous chapters. We will be modifying the DISampleWeb application to display additional content on the home page if a flight flag is set. Add the isFlightOn configuration, as shown in the following code snippet, to appsettings.json:

```
{
    "AllowedHosts": "*",
    "isFlightOn": "true"
}
```

Now, modify the index view under Home to display the content under Flight, as shown in the following code snippet:

```
@using Microsoft.Extensions.Configuration
@inject Iconfiguration Configuration
@{
    string isFlightOn = Configuration["isFlightOn"];
    if (string.Equals(isFlightOn, "true", StringComparison.
OrdinalIgnoreCase))
    {
        <h1>
         <strong>Flight content</strong>
        </h1>
    }
}
```

Here, the Iconfiguration service, which provides the functionality of reading the configuration file, is injected into the Razor view using the @inject keyword. The injected configuration service is used to get the configuration and display additional content based on the settings. We can inject any service registered with IserviceCollection into Razor views using the @inject keyword.

Up until now, we have seen how we can leverage the .NET 6 built-in IoC container. In the next section, we will learn about leveraging third-party containers.

Using third-party containers

Though the built-in container is sufficient for most of our scenarios, .NET 6 provides a way to integrate with third-party containers that can be leveraged if need be.

Let's have a closer look at how the framework wires up the services. When the `Startup` class is registered with `HostBuilder` in `Program.cs`, .NET Framework uses reflection to identify and call the `Configure` and `ConfigureServices` methods.

Here is a snippet from the `LoadMethods` method of the `StartupLoader` class in ASP. NET Core 6 (refer to the code from `https://github.com/dotnet/aspnetcore/blob/main/src/Hosting/Hosting/src/Internal/StartupLoader.cs`):

```
public static StartupMethods
LoadMethods(IServiceProvider hostingServiceProvider,
[DynamicallyAccessedMembers(StartupLinkerOptions.Accessibility)]
Type startupType, string environmentName, object? instance =
null)
{
    var configureMethod = FindConfigureDelegate(startupType,
environmentName);
    var servicesMethod =
FindConfigureServicesDelegate(startupType, environmentName);
    var configureContainerMethod =
FindConfigureContainerDelegate(startupType, environmentName);

    -----------------------

}
```

From the preceding code snippet, we can see that the first two methods, `FindConfigureDelegate` and `FindConfigureServicesDelegate`, are to find the `Configure` and `ConfigureServices` methods.

The last line is for `ConfigureContainer`. We can define a `ConfigureContainer` method in the `Startup` class to configure the services into a third-party container.

Here are some of the popular DI frameworks available for ASP.NET Core 6:

- **Unity**: Unity was initially built by Microsoft and is currently open sourced. This is one of the oldest DI containers for .NET. The documentation is available at the following link: `http://unitycontainer.org/`.

- **Autofac**: This is one of the most popular DI containers. It has comprehensive documentation available at the following link: `https://autofaccn.readthedocs.io/en/latest/index.html`.

- **Simple Injector**: This is one of the late entrants on the list. The documentation can be found at the following link: `https://simpleinjector.readthedocs.io/en/latest/index.html`.

- **Castle Windsor**: This is one of the oldest DI frameworks available for .NET. See its documentation at the following link: `http://www.castleproject.org/projects/windsor/`.

Though there are a few differences between these frameworks, there is generally feature parity. It is mostly the developer's experience that determines the choice of framework.

In the next section, let's see how to leverage the Autofac third-party IoC container.

Autofac IoC container

Autofac is one of the most popular IoC containers among the developer community. As with any other IoC container, it manages dependencies between classes so that applications remain easy to change as they grow in complexity and size. Let's learn how to use Autofac to register the same `WeatherProvider` service that we used earlier in this chapter. Proceed as follows:

1. Create a new project using the ASP.NET Core web API template and name it `AutofacSample`.

2. Add the `Autofac.Extensions.DependencyInjection` NuGet package reference to the `AutofacSample` project, as illustrated in the following screenshot:

Figure 5.5 – Adding the Autofac.Extensions.DependencyInjection NuGet package

3. We need to register `AutofacServiceProviderFactory` with `ConfigureHostBuilder` so that the runtime will use the Autofac IoC container. In `Program.cs`, register the Autofac SP factory, as shown in the following code snippet:

```
builder.Host.UseServiceProviderFactory(new
AutofacServiceProviderFactory());
```

4. Now, let's register the `IWeatherProvider` service that we used in the *Types of DI* section with the Autofac container. Call the `ConfigureContainer` method on the `ConfigureHostBuilder` property of `WebApplicationBuilder` in `Program.cs` to register `IWeatherProvider` with the `WeatherProvider` implementation, as follows:

```
builder.Host.ConfigureContainer<ContainerBuilder>(builder =>
{
    builder.RegisterType<WeatherProvider>()
                .As<IWeatherProvider>();
});
```

5. Similar to the default .NET IoC container, we get the `IWeatherForecast` service injected into the `WeatherForecastController` controller, as shown in the following code snippet:

```
public class WeatherForecastController : ControllerBase
{
        private readonly ILogger<WeatherForecastController>
 _logger;
        private readonly IWeatherProvider weatherProvider;
        public WeatherForecastController(
ILogger<WeatherForecastController> logger,
IWeatherProvider weatherProvider)
        {
            _logger = logger;
            this.weatherProvider = weatherProvider;
        }
        [HttpGet]
        public IEnumerable<WeatherForecast> Get()
```

```
        {
            return weatherProvider.GetForecast();
        }
    }
```

Now, when you run the project and navigate to the `https://localhost:7184/` `WeatherForecast` **Uniform Resource Identifier (URI)**, you will see the output in the browser, as follows:

```
[
  ▼ {
        "date": "2020-10-25T13:50:42.2369526+05:30",
        "temperatureC": 23,
        "temperatureF": 73,
        "summary": "Freezing"
    }
]
```

Figure 5.6 – Final output for the container

In the previous example, we have seen the use of the third-party Autofac IoC container in place of the default container provided by .NET 6.

Summary

This chapter introduced you to the concepts of DI, which helps to write loosely coupled, more testable, and more readable code. This chapter covered the types of DI and how they are supported in ASP.NET Core 6. We have also seen how object lifetime is managed with different types of registrations. This chapter also introduced you to some of the popular third-party IoC containers available to further explore. We will be using the concepts learned in this chapter to build our e-commerce application. In *Chapter 15*, *Testing*, we will also see how DI can help with testability.

As recommended in *Chapter 1*, *Designing and Architecting the Enterprise Application*, under the *Separation of concerns/single - responsibility architecture* section, we always try to have services registered via interfaces. This will help with changing the concrete implementation at any time without changing the client implementation.

In the next chapter, we will learn how to configure .NET 6 and understand the different configurations while learning how to build a custom one.

Questions

1. Which of the following is not a framework service?

   a. `IConfiguration`

   b. `IApplicationBuilder`

   c. `IWeatherService`

   d. `IWebHostEnvironment`

   Answer: c

2. True or false: DI is one of the mechanisms to achieve IoC.

   a. True

   b. False

   Answer: a

3. True or false: An injected service can depend on a service that has a shorter life span than its own.

   a. True

   b. False

   Answer: b

4. Which of the following is not a valid lifetime scope of ASP.NET Core 6 IoC container?

   a. Scoped

   b. Singleton

   c. Transient

   d. Dynamic

   Answer: d

6
Configuration in .NET 6

A configuration in .NET 6 comprises the default settings as well as the runtime settings for your application; a configuration is a very powerful feature. We can update settings such as feature flags to enable or disable features, dependent service endpoints, database connection strings, logging levels, and much more, and control application behavior at runtime without recompilation.

In this chapter, we will cover the following topics:

- Understanding configuration
- Leveraging built-in configuration providers
- Building a custom configuration provider

By the end of this chapter, you'll have a good grasp of configuration concepts, configuration providers, and how to leverage them in your projects, as well as being able to identify the configurations and configuration sources that are appropriate for your applications.

Technical requirements

You will need a basic understanding of .NET and Azure. The code for the chapter can be found here: `https://github.com/PacktPublishing/Enterprise-Application-Development-with-C-10-and-.NET-6-Second-Edition/tree/main/Chapter06`.

Understanding configuration

A configuration is generally stored as **name-value pairs** and can be grouped into a multi-level hierarchy. In the application startup file (`Program.cs`), you will get a default configuration provided by .NET 6. In addition, you can configure different built-in and custom configuration sources, and then read them using different configuration providers whenever you need them anywhere in an application:

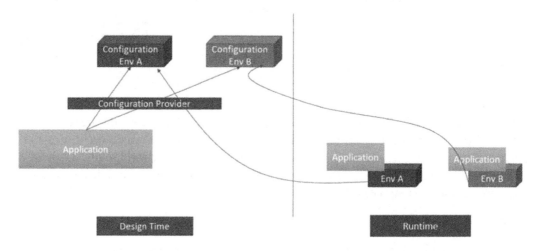

Figure 6.1 – Application and configuration

The preceding diagram shows a high-level relationship between an application, a configuration provider, and a configuration file. The application uses the configuration provider to read the configuration from the configuration source; the configuration can be environment-specific. **Env A** could be your development environment and **Env B** could be your production environment. At runtime, the application will read the right configurations based on the runtime context and environment where it's running.

In the next section, we will see how a default configuration works and how to add and read configurations from the `appsettings.json` file.

Default configuration

To understand how a default configuration works, let's create a new .NET 6 web API, set the project name as `TestConfiguration`, and open `Program.cs`. The following is a code snippet from the `Program.cs` file:

```
var builder = WebApplication.CreateBuilder(args);

// Add services to the container.

builder.Services.AddControllers();

builder.Services.AddEndpointsApiExplorer();
builder.Services.AddSwaggerGen();

var app = builder.Build();

// Configure the HTTP request pipeline.
if (app.Environment.IsDevelopment())
{
    app.UseSwagger();
    app.UseSwaggerUI();
}

app.UseHttpsRedirection();

app.UseAuthorization();

app.MapControllers();

app.Run();
```

From the preceding code, we see that `WebApplication.CreateBuilder` takes care of providing the default configuration for the application.

The loading of the configuration is done in the following order:

1. `MemoryConfigurationProvider`: This loads configurations from in-memory collection as configuration key-value pairs.

2. `ChainedConfigurationProvider`: This adds the host configuration and sets it as the first source. For more details on the host configuration, you can use this link: `https://docs.microsoft.com/en-us/aspnet/core/fundamentals/configuration/?view=aspnetcore-6.0`.

3. `JsonConfigurationProvider`: This loads the configurations from the `appsettings.json` file.

4. `JsonConfigurationProvider`: This loads the configurations from the `appsettings.Environment.json` file; `Environment` in `appsettings.Environment.json` can be set to refer to development, staging, or production.

5. `EnvironmentVariablesConfigurationProvider`: This loads environment variable configurations.

As mentioned at the beginning of this section, a configuration is specified as key-value pairs in sources. Configuration providers that are added later (in terms of order) override previous key-value pair settings. For example, if you have a `DbConnectionString` key in `MemoryConfigurationProvider` as well as in `JsonConfigurationProvider`, the value of the `DbConnectionString` key in `JsonConfigurationProvider` will override the key-value pair settings of `MemoryConfigurationProvider`.

When you debug the `Program.cs` code, you can see the default configuration provided by `CreateDefaultBuilder` being injected into the configuration as follows:

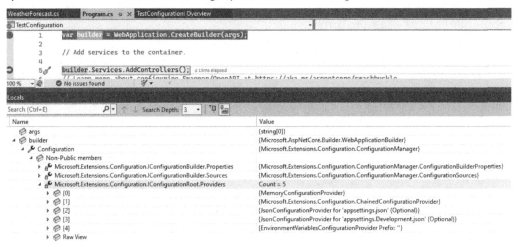

Figure 6.2 – Default configuration sources

Let's see how we can add the configurations required for our application in the next section.

Adding configurations

As we saw in the previous section, there are multiple configuration sources available. The appsettings.json file is what is most widely used in real-world projects to add the configuration required for an application unless it's a secret and cannot be stored as plain text.

Let's take a couple of common scenarios where we need configurations:

- If we need an ApplicationInsights instrumentation key to add application telemetry, which can be part of our configuration
- If we have dependent services that need to be invoked, which can be part of our configuration

These can change from environment to environment (the values differ between development environments and production environments).

You can add the following configurations to the appsettings.json file so that you can update it directly when there is a change and start consuming it without recompilation and deployment:

```
"ApplicationInsights": {
    "InstrumentationKey": "<Your instrumentation key>"
  }
"ApiConfigs": {
    "Service 1": {
      "Name": "<Your dependent service name 1>",
      "BaseUri": "<Service base uri>",
      "HttpTimeOutInSeconds": "<Time out value in
        seconds>",
      "ApiURLs": [
        {
          "EndpointName": "<End point 1>"
        },
        {
          "EndpointName": "<End point 2>"
        }
```

```
      ]
    },
    "Service 2": {
      "Name": "<Your dependent service name 2>",
      "BaseUri": "<Service base uri>",
      "HttpTimeOutInSeconds": "<Time out value in
       seconds>",
      "ApiURLs": [
        {
          "EndpointName": "<End point 1>"
        },
        {
          "EndpointName": "<End point 2>"
        }
      ]
    }
  }
}
```

From the preceding code, we see that we have added a key-value pair for the ApplicationInsights instrumentation key, where the key is the InstrumentationKey string, and the value is the actual instrumentation key that the application needs to instrument telemetry in ApplicationInsights. In the ApiConfigs section, we have added multiple key-value pairs in hierarchical order with the configuration required to invoke our dependent services.

In the next section, we will see how to read the configuration we have added.

Reading configurations

We have seen how we can add configurations to appsettings.json. In this section, we will see how we can read them inside our projects using the different options that are available.

The builder.Configuration object that you get in Program.cs provided by WebApplication.CreateBuilder implements the Microsoft.Extensions. Configuration.IConfiguration type, and you have the following options available to read in IConfiguration:

```
    // Summary:
    //     Gets or sets a configuration value.
```

```
// Parameters:
//   key:
//       The configuration key.
// Returns:
//       The configuration value.
string this[string key] { get; set; }


// Summary:
//Gets the immediate descendant configuration sub-
//sections.
// Returns:
//       The configuration sub-sections.
IEnumerable<IConfigurationSection> GetChildren();


// Summary:
//       Gets a configuration sub-section with the
//       specified key.
// Parameters:
//   key:
//       The key of the configuration section.
// Returns:
//The Microsoft.Extensions.Configuration
//.IConfigurationSection.
// Remarks:
//       This method will never return null. If
 // no matching sub-section is found with
//       the specified key, an empty
//Microsoft.Extensions.Configuration.IConfiguration
//       Section will be returned.
IConfigurationSection GetSection(string key);
```

Let's see how we can leverage these options from `Iconfiguration` to read the configurations that we added in the previous section, *Adding configurations*.

To read the `ApplicationInsights` instrumentation key from `appsettings.json`, we can use the `string this[string key] { get; set; }` option using the following code in `Program.cs`:

```
builder.
Configuration["ApplicationInsights:InstrumentationKey"];
```

To read `ApiConfigs`, we can use the following code. We can use a delimiter in the configuration keys for the configuration API to read the hierarchical configuration:

```
builder.Configuration["ApiConfigs:Service 1:Name"];
```

> **Note**
>
> Reading this way using a delimiter is error-prone and difficult to maintain. The preferred approach is to use the **options** pattern provided in ASP.NET Core. Instead of reading each key/setting value one by one, the options pattern uses classes, which will also give you strongly typed access to the related settings.

When configuration settings are isolated by scenarios into strongly typed classes, the application adheres to two important design principles:

- The **interface segregation principle (ISP)**, or encapsulation principle
- Separation of concerns

With ISP or encapsulation, you read the configuration through a well-defined interface or contract and depend only on the configuration settings you need. Also, if there is a huge configuration file, this will help in the separation of concerns, as different parts of the application won't be dependent on the same configuration, thus allowing them to be decoupled. Let's see how we can leverage the options pattern in our code.

You can create the following `ApiConfig` and `ApiUrl` classes and add them to your project:

```
public class ApiConfig
{
    public string Name { get; set; }

    public string BaseUri { get; set; }

    public int HttpTimeOutInSeconds { get; set; }
```

```
    public List<ApiUrl> ApiUrls { get; set; }
}
public class ApiUrl
{
    public string EndpointName { get; set; }
}
```

Add the following code in `Program.cs` to read the configuration using the `GetSection` method, and then call `Bind` to have the configuration bound to the strongly-typed class that we have:

```
List<ApiConfig> apiConfigs = new List<ApiConfig>();
builder.Configuration.GetSection("ApiConfigs").
Bind(apiConfigs);
```

`GetSection` will read the specific section from `appsettings.json` with the specified key. `Bind` will attempt to bind the given object instance to the configuration values by matching property names to the configuration keys. `GetSection(string sectionName)` will return `null` if the requested section does not exist. In real-world programs, please ensure that you add null checks.

In this section, we saw how we can add and read data from `appsettings.json` by using a configuration API. I also mentioned that we should use `appsettings.json` for plain text and not for secrets. In the next section, we will look at built-in configuration providers as well as how to add and read secrets using the Azure Key Vault configuration provider.

Leveraging built-in configuration providers

There are multiple configuration sources available other than `appsettings.json`, and .NET 6 provides several built-in configuration providers to read from them. The following are built-in providers available for .NET 6:

- The Azure Key Vault configuration provider reads configurations from Azure Key Vault.

- The file configuration provider reads configurations from INI, JSON, and XML files.

- The command-line configuration provider reads configuration from command-line parameters.

- The environment variable configuration provider reads configurations from environment variables.

- The memory configuration provider reads configurations from in-memory collections.

- The Azure App Configuration provider reads configuration from Azure App configuration.

- The key-per-file configuration provider reads configurations from a directory's files.

Let's see how we can leverage the Azure Key Vault configuration provider and the file configuration provider, as both are important and more widely used when compared to others.

> **Note**
>
> You can use the following link to learn about other configuration providers that we are not covering in detail here: `https://docs.microsoft.com/en-us/dotnet/core/extensions/configuration-providers`.

Azure Key Vault configuration provider

Azure Key Vault is a cloud-based service that provides a centralized configuration source for securely storing passwords, certificates, API keys, and other secrets. This helps to keep our application secured and compliant from a security breach. Let's see how we can create a key vault, add a secret to it, and access it from an application using the Azure Key Vault configuration provider.

Creating a key vault and adding secrets

In this section, we will use Azure Cloud Shell to create a key vault and add a secret. Azure Cloud Shell is browser-based and can be used to manage Azure resources. The following is the list of steps you need to take:

1. Sign in to the Azure portal using `https://portal.azure.com`. Select the Cloud Shell icon on the portal page:

Figure 6.3 – Azure Cloud Shell

2. You will get the option to select **Bash** or **PowerShell**. Choose **PowerShell**. You can change shells at any time:

Figure 6.4 – Azure Cloud Shell options – PowerShell and Bash

3. Create a resource group with the following command:

```
az group create --name "{RESOURCE GROUP NAME}" --location
{LOCATION}
```

The actual command I ran for this demonstration is this:

```
az group create --name "ConfigurationDemoVaultRG"
--location "East US"
```

{RESOURCE GROUP NAME} stands for the resource group name for the new resource group, and {LOCATION} stands for the Azure region (for your data center).

4. Create a key vault in the resource group with the following command:

```
az keyvault create --name {KEY VAULT NAME} --resource-
group "{RESOURCE GROUP NAME}" --location {LOCATION}
```

Here's the actual command I ran for this demonstration:

```
az keyvault create --name "TestKeyVaultForConfig"
--resource-group "ConfigurationDemoVaultRG" --location
"East US"
```

{KEY VAULT NAME} is the unique name for the new key vault.

{RESOURCE GROUP NAME} is the resource group name for the new resource group created in the prior step.

{LOCATION} is the Azure region (data center).

5. Create secrets in the key vault as name-value pairs with the following command:

```
az keyvault secret set --vault-name {KEY VAULT NAME}
--name "SecretName" --value "SecretValue"
```

Here's the actual command I ran for this demonstration:

```
az keyvault secret set --vault-name
"TestKeyVaultForConfig" --name "TestKey" --value
"TestValue"
```

{KEY VAULT NAME} is the same key vault name that you created in the prior step.

SecretName is the name of your secret.

SecretValue is the value of your secret.

We have now successfully created a key vault named TestKeyVaultForConfig and have added a secret with the key as TestKey and the value as TestValue using Azure Cloud Shell:

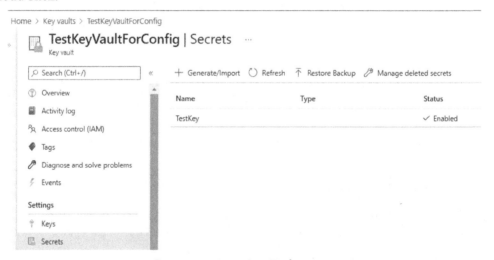

Figure 6.5 – Azure Key Vault secrets

You can also use the Azure **command-line interface (CLI)** to create and manage Azure resources. You can read more about the Azure CLI here: https://docs.microsoft. com/en-us/cli/azure/?view=azure-cli-latest.

In the next section, we will see how to give our application access to Key Vault.

Granting application access to Key Vault

In this section, let's see how our TestConfiguration web API can get access to Key Vault using the following steps:

1. Register the TestConfiguration application in **Azure Active Directory (AAD)** and create an identity. Sign in to the Azure portal using https://portal. azure.com.

2. Navigate to **Azure Active Directory | App Registrations**. Click on **New registration**:

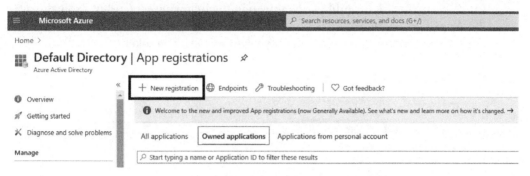

Figure 6.6 – AAD new application registration

3. Fill in the defaults and click on **Register**, as shown in the following screenshot, and note down the **Application (client) ID** value. This will be required later to access Key Vault:

Home > Default Directory | App registrations >

Register an application

* Name

The user-facing display name for this application (this can be changed later).

TestConfiguration

Supported account types

Who can use this application or access this API?

⦿ Accounts in this organizational directory only (Default Directory only - Single tenant)

◯ Accounts in any organizational directory (Any Azure AD directory - Multitenant)

◯ Accounts in any organizational directory (Any Azure AD directory - Multitenant) and personal Microsoft accounts (e.g. Skype, Xbox)

Help me choose...

Redirect URI (optional)

We'll return the authentication response to this URI after successfully authenticating the user. Providing this now is optional and it can be changed later, but a value is required for most authentication scenarios.

| Web ⌄ | e.g. https://myapp.com/auth |

By proceeding, you agree to the Microsoft Platform Policies ⌐

Register

Figure 6.7 – AAD registration completion

4. Click on **Certificates & secrets (1) | New client secret (2)** and enter a **Description (3)** value, then click on **Add (4)**, as shown in the following screenshot. Note down the **AppClientSecret** value showing under **New client secret**, which is what the application can use to prove its identity when requesting a token:

Figure 6.8 – AAD new application secret creation for its identity

5. Give the application access to Key Vault using an access policy. Search for the key vault you just created and select it:

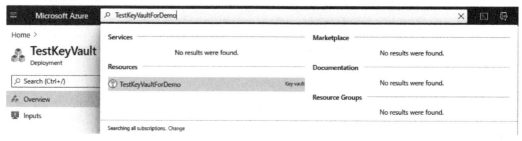

Figure 6.9 – Key vault search

6. In the key vault properties, select **Access policies** under **Settings** and click on **Add Access Policy**:

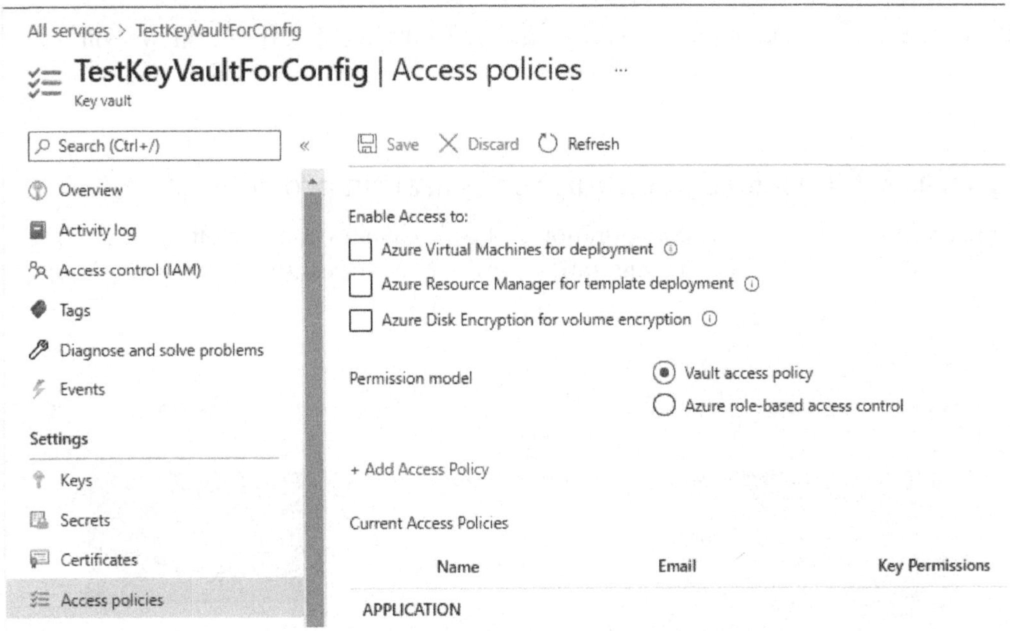

All services > TestKeyVaultForConfig

✓= TestKeyVaultForConfig | Access policies ⋯
Key vault

| 🔎 Search (Ctrl+/) | « | 🖫 Save ✕ Discard ⟲ Refresh |

🔘 Overview

🖥 Activity log

🔍 Access control (IAM)

🏷 Tags

🖉 Diagnose and solve problems

⚡ Events

Settings

🔑 Keys

🖫 Secrets

🖼 Certificates

✓= Access policies

Enable Access to:

☐ Azure Virtual Machines for deployment ⓘ

☐ Azure Resource Manager for template deployment ⓘ

☐ Azure Disk Encryption for volume encryption ⓘ

Permission model   ⦿ Vault access policy

                         ◯ Azure role-based access control

+ Add Access Policy

Current Access Policies

| Name | Email | Key Permissions |

APPLICATION

Figure 6.10 – Key Vault access policies

7. In the **Select principal** field, search for your application and select the required permissions for your application to access Key Vault, then click on **Add**:

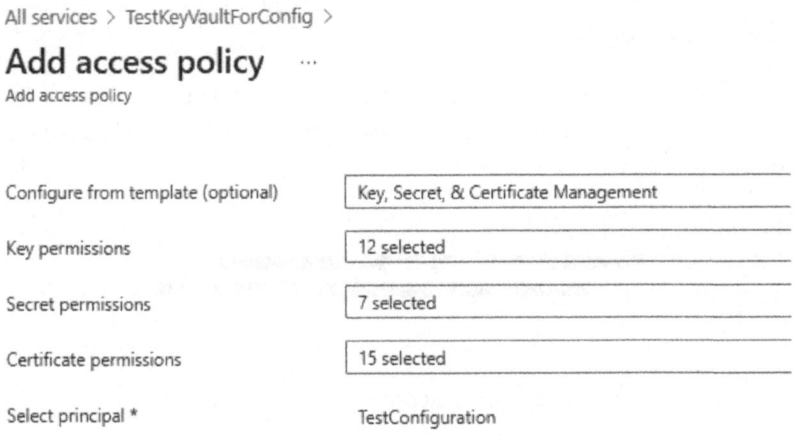

All services > TestKeyVaultForConfig >

Add access policy ⋯
Add access policy

| Configure from template (optional) | Key, Secret, & Certificate Management |

| Key permissions | 12 selected |

| Secret permissions | 7 selected |

| Certificate permissions | 15 selected |

| Select principal * | TestConfiguration |

Figure 6.11 – Add access policy

8.   After adding the policy, you must save it. This will complete the process of granting your application access to Key Vault.

We have now given our application access to Key Vault. In the next section, we will see how to access Key Vault from our application using the Azure Key Vault configuration provider.

Leveraging the Azure Key Vault configuration provider

In this section, we will make configuration and code changes in our application to leverage the Azure Key Vault configuration provider and access secrets from Key Vault, as follows:

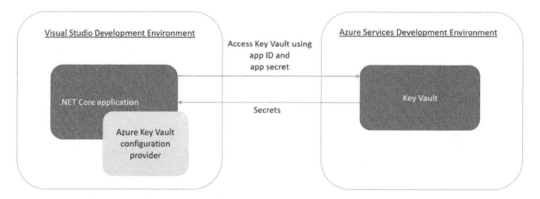

Figure 6.12 – Accessing Key Vault during development

The following is the list of changes:

1.   Add the key vault name, the AppClientId value that you noted down from *Figure 6.7*, and the AppClientSecret value that you noted down from AAD from *Figure 6.8* to the appsettings.json file in your TestConfiguration web API:

```
"KeyVault": {
  "Name": "TestKeyVaultForConfig",
  "AppClientId": "███████████████████████████",
  "AppClientSecret": "███████████████████████████"
}
```

Figure 6.13 – Key Vault section in appsettings.json

2. Install the following NuGet packages:

- `Microsoft.Azure.KeyVault`

- `Microsoft.Extensions.Configuration.AzureKeyVault`

- `Microsoft.Azure.Services.AppAuthentication`

3. Update `Program.cs` to leverage the Azure Key Vault configuration provider to use your key vault. The following code will add Azure Key Vault as another configuration source and get all configurations using the Azure Key Vault configuration provider:

```
using TestConfiguration;

var builder = WebApplication.CreateBuilder(args);

// Add services to the container.
builder.Services.AddControllers();

//Removed code for brevity
builder.Configuration.AddAzureKeyVault($"https://
{builder.Configuration["KeyVault:Name"]}.vault.azure.
net/",
builder.Configuration["KeyVault:AppClientId"],
builder.Configuration["KeyVault:AppClientSecret"]);

var app = builder.Build();

//Removed code for brevity
```

4. Update `WeatherForecastController.cs` to read the secret from Key Vault, as follows:

```
[ApiController]
[Route("[controller]")]
public class WeatherForecastController : ControllerBase
{
    private readonly ILogger<WeatherForecastController>
_logger;
    private readonly IConfiguration _configuration;
```

```
    public WeatherForecastController(ILogger<Weather
ForecastController> logger, IConfiguration configuration)
    {
        _logger = logger;
        _configuration = configuration;
    }
    [HttpGet]
    public IEnumerable<string> Get()
    {
        return new string[] { "TestKey",
        _configuration["TestKey"] };
    }
}
```

Include all references as per the code sample shared here. You can run the application and see the results:

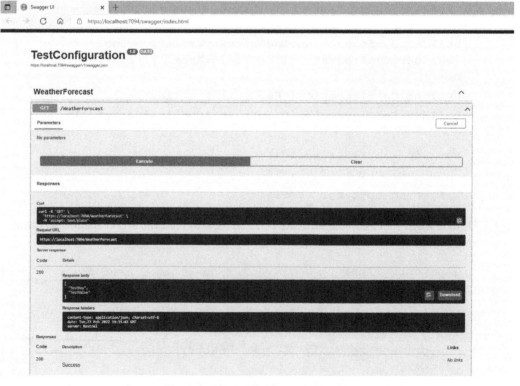

Figure 6.14 – Results from Key Vault

The application will be able to access the key vault using the Azure Key Vault configuration provider and fetch the secrets. It is very simple, as all the heavy lifting is done by .NET 6, and we just need to install the NuGet packages and add a few lines of code. However, you will now probably be thinking about how `AppClientId` and `AppClientSecret` have been added to the `appsettings.json` config file and about how this is not very secure. You are 100% correct.

We can fix this in two ways:

- One option is to encrypt and store these values in `appsettings.json`; they can then be read and decrypted in the code.

> **Reference**
>
> For safe storage of app secrets in development, please refer to `https://docs.microsoft.com/en-us/aspnet/core/security/app-secrets?view=aspnetcore-6.0&tabs=windows`.

- The other option is to use managed identities to access Azure resources, which allows the application to authenticate with Azure Key Vault using AAD authentication without credentials (the application ID and password/client secret).

Your application can be authenticated using its identity by any service that supports AAD authentication, such as Azure Key Vault, and this will help us in getting rid of credentials from code:

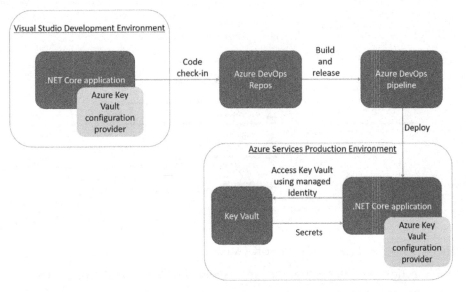

Figure 6.15 – Accessing Key Vault in production after deploying an application

> **Note**
>
> This is the best practice we follow for applications that are deployed to production. Managing credentials in code is a common challenge and keeping credentials safe and secure is an important security requirement. Managed identities for Azure resources in AAD help in solving this challenge. Managed identities provide Azure services with an automatically managed identity in AAD. You can use this identity to authenticate any service that supports AAD authentication, including Key Vault, without any credentials in your code.

You can read more about managed identities here: `https://docs.microsoft.com/en-us/azure/active-directory/managed-identities-azure-resources/overview`.

In this section, we saw how to create a key vault, how to add secrets to Key Vault, how to register our `TestConfiguration` web API in AAD, how to create a secret or identity, how to give the `TestConfiguration` web API access to Key Vault, and how to access Key Vault from our code using the Azure Key Vault configuration provider. You can also add Key Vault to your web application by using Visual Studio Connected Services, as described at `https://docs.microsoft.com/en-us/azure/key-vault/general/vs-key-vault-add-connected-service`:

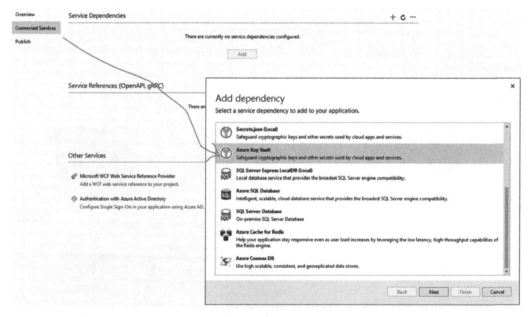

Figure 6.16 – Azure Key Vault as a connected service

In the next section, we will see how we can leverage the file configuration provider.

File configuration provider

The file configuration provider helps us to load a configuration from the filesystem. The JSON configuration provider and XML configuration provider derive their inheritance from the file configuration provider class and are used to read key-value pair configurations from JSON files and XML files, respectively. Let's see how we can add them to configuration sources as part of `CreateHostBuilder`.

JSON configuration provider

The JSON configuration provider can be configured using the following code in `Program.cs`:

```
//Removed code for brevity
builder.Configuration.AddJsonFile("AdditionalConfig.json",
                optional: true,
                reloadOnChange: true);
//Removed code for brevity
```

In this case, the JSON configuration provider will load the `AdditionalConfig.json` file, and three parameters to the `AddJsonFile` method provide us with options to specify the filename, whether the file is optional, and whether the file must be reloaded when any changes are made to the file.

The following is the `AdditionalConfig.json` sample file:

```
{   "TestKeyFromAdditionalConfigJSON":"TestValueFromAdditional
ConfigJSON"}
```

Then, we update `WeatherForecastController.cs` to read key-value pairs from the configurations loaded from the `AdditionalConfig.json` config file, as follows:

```
//Removed code for brevity
    [HttpGet]
    public Ienumerable<string> Get()
    {
        return new string[] {
          " TestKeyFromAdditionalConfigJSON",
          _configuration["TestKeyFromAdditionalConfigJSON"] };
    }
//Removed code for brevity
```

You can run the application and see the results. The application will be able to access the `AdditionalConfig.json` file and read the configuration. In the next section, we will look at the XML configuration provider.

XML configuration provider

We will add a new file to the project with the name `AdditionalXMLConfig.xml` and the required configurations. The XML configuration provider can then be configured using the following code in `Program.cs` to read from the file we added:

```
//Removed code for brevity
builder.Configuration.AddXmlFile("AdditionalXMLConfig.xml",
                optional: true,
                reloadOnChange: true);
//Removed code for brevity
```

In this case, the XML configuration provider will load the `AdditionalXMLConfig.xml` file and the three parameters provide us with options to specify the XML file, whether the file is optional or not, and whether the file must be reloaded when any changes are made.

The `AdditionalXMLConfig.xml` sample file is as follows:

```
<?xml version="1.0" encoding="utf-8" ?>
<configuration>
  <TestKeyFromAdditionalXMLConfig>TestValueFrom
AdditionalXMLConfig</TestKeyFromAdditionalXMLConfig>
</configuration>
```

Next, we update `WeatherForecastController.cs` to read key-value pairs from the configuration loaded from `AdditionalXMLConfig.xml` as follows:

```
    [HttpGet]
    public Ienumerable<string> Get()
    {
        return new string[] {
          "TestKeyFromAdditionalXMLConfig",
          _configuration["TestKeyFromAdditionalXMLConfig"] };
    }
```

You can run the application and see the results. The application will be able to access `AdditionalXMLConfig.xml` and read the configuration. With the JSON config file and the JSON configuration provider available in .NET 6, you don't need the XML config file and the XML configuration provider. That said, what we just covered is for folks who like XML files and open and close tags, for example.

In the next section, we will see why a custom configuration provider is required and how to build one.

Building a custom configuration provider

In the previous section, we looked at built-in or pre-existing configuration providers in .NET 6. There are scenarios where many systems maintain application configuration settings in a database. These could be managed by the admin from the portal or by the support engineer by running database scripts to create/update/delete application configuration settings as needed.

.NET 6 doesn't come with a built-in provider to read configurations from a database. Let's see how to build a custom configuration provider to read from a database with the following steps:

- **Implement configuration source**: To create an instance of the configuration provider
- **Implement configuration provider**: To load the configuration from the appropriate source
- **Implement configuration extension**: To add the configuration source to the configuration builder

Let's begin with the configuration source.

Configuration source

The responsibility of the configuration source is to create an instance of the configuration provider and return it to the source. It needs to inherit from the `IConfigurationSource` interface, which requires us to implement the `ConfigurationProvider Build(IConfigurationBuilder builder)` method.

Inside the `Build` method implementation, we need to create an instance of the custom configuration provider and return the same. There should also be the parameters needed to build the builder. In this case, as we are building a custom SQL configuration provider, the important parameters are the connection string and the SQL query. The following code snippet shows an example implementation of a `SqlConfigurationSource` class:

```
public class SqlConfigurationSource : IConfigurationSource
    {
        public string ConnectionString { get; set; }
        public string Query { get; set; }
        public SqlConfigurationSource(string
          connectionString, string query)
        {
            ConnectionString = connectionString;
            Query = query;
        }
        public IConfigurationProvider
         Build(IConfigurationBuilder builder)
        {
            return new SqlConfigurationProvider(this);
        }
    }
```

It is very simple and easy to implement this, as you can see. You get the parameters required to build the provider and create a new instance of the provider, then return the parameters. Let's see how we can build a SQL configuration provider in the next section.

Configuration provider

The responsibility of the configuration provider is to load the required configuration from the appropriate source and return the same. It needs to inherit from the `IConfigurationProvider` interface, which requires us to implement the `Load()` method. The configuration provider class can instead inherit from the `ConfigurationProvider` base class as it has already implemented all the methods in the `IConfigurationProvider` interface. This will help us save time as we don't need to implement unused methods and can, instead, implement just the `Load` method.

Inside the Load method implementation, we need to have the logic to fetch the configuration data from the source. In this case, we will execute a query to fetch the data from the SQL store. The following code snippet shows an example implementation of a SqlConfigurationProvider class:

```
public class SqlConfigurationProvider : ConfigurationProvider
    {
        public SqlConfigurationSource Source { get; }
        public SqlConfigurationProvider
          (SqlConfigurationSource source)
        {
            Source = source;
        }
        public override void Load()
        {
            try
            {
                // create a connection object
                SqlConnection sqlConnection = new
                  SqlConnection(Source.ConnectionString);
                // Create a command object
                SqlCommand sqlCommand = new
                  SqlCommand(Source.Query, sqlConnection);
                sqlConnection.Open();
                // Call ExecuteReader to return a
                // DataReader
                SqlDataReader salDataReader =
                  sqlCommand.ExecuteReader();
                while (salDataReader.Read())
                {
                    Data.Add(salDataReader.GetString(0),
                      salDataReader.GetString(1));
                }
                salDataReader.Close();
                sqlCommand.Dispose();
                sqlConnection.Close();
            }
```

```
        }
    }
```

Let's see how to build a configuration extension in the next section.

Configuration extension

As with other providers, we can use an extension method to add the configuration source to the configuration builder.

> **Note**
> Extension methods are static methods in which you can add methods to existing classes without modifying or recompiling the original class.

The following code snippet shows an example implementation of a `SqlConfigurationExtensions` class in the configuration builder:

```
public static class SqlConfigurationExtensions
    {
        public static IConfigurationBuilder
         AddSql(this IConfigurationBuilder
         configuration, string connectionString,
         string query)
        {
            configuration.Add(new
             SqlConfigurationSource(connectionString,
             query));
            return configuration;
        }
    }
```

The extension method will reduce the code in our application startup.

We can add bootstrapping code to `Program.cs` just as we added it for other configuration providers, as shown in the following code:

```
builder.Configuration.AddSql("Connectionstring","Query");
```

The following screenshot shows some sample configuration settings in a database. You can pass the appropriate connection string and SQL query in `config.AddSql()` and load the following configuration from the database. The SQL query may be a simple `select` statement to read all key-value pairs, as it is in the following screenshot:

```
USE [ECommerce]
GO

select * from ConfigurationSettings (NoLock)
```

100 %

Results   Messages

	Key	Value
1	TestSqlKey	TestValueFromSql

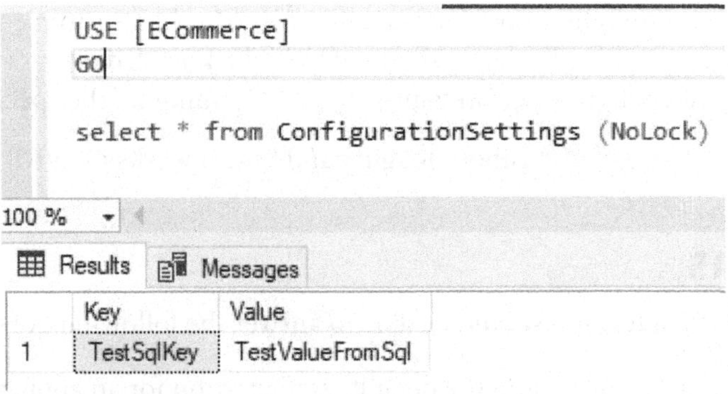

Figure 6.17 – Database configuration settings

Update `WeatherForecastController.cs` as follows to read key-value pairs from the configuration loaded from the SQL configuration provider:

```
[HttpGet]
public IEnumerable<string> Get()
{
    return new string[] { "TestSqlKey",
    _configuration["TestSqlKey"] };
}
}
```

You can run the application and see the results. The application will be able to access the SQL configuration and read the configuration.

This is an example of just one custom configuration provider. You may be able to think of different scenarios where you would build other different custom configuration providers, such as when reading from CSV files or reading encrypted values from JSON or XML files and decrypting them.

Summary

In this chapter, we saw how configuration works in .NET 6, how the default configuration is provided to the application, how to add key-value pair configurations in a hierarchical order, how to read a configuration, how to leverage the Azure Key Vault configuration provider and the file configuration provider, and how to build a custom configuration provider to read from a SQL database. You now have the knowledge that's needed to implement different configurations in your project depending on the specific needs.

In the next chapter, we will learn about logging and how it works in .NET 6.

Questions

After reading this chapter, you should be able to answer the following questions:

1. What takes care of providing the default configuration for an application in .NET 6?

    a. `CreateDefaultBuilder`

    b. `ChainedConfigurationProvider`

    c. `JsonConfigurationProvider`

    d. All of the above

    Answer: a

2. Which of the following is not correct?

    a. The Azure Key Vault configuration provider reads configurations from Azure Key Vault.

    b. The file configuration provider reads configurations from INI, JSON, and XML files.

    c. The command-line configuration provider reads configurations from a database.

    d. The memory configuration provider reads configurations from in-memory collections.

    Answer: c

3. Which interface is used to access a configuration at runtime and is injected via dependency injection?

   a. `IConfig`

   b. `IConfiguration`

   c. `IConfigurationSource`

   d. `IConfigurationProvider`

   Answer: b

4. Which provider/source is recommended for storing secrets in production?

   a. JSON from `appsettings.json`

   b. `FileConfiguration` from an XML file

   c. `AzureKeyVaultProvider` from `AzureKeyVault`

   d. The command-line configuration provider from the command line

   Answer: c

Further reading

- https://docs.microsoft.com/en-us/aspnet/core/blazor/fundamentals/configuration?view=aspnetcore-6.0

- https://docs.microsoft.com/en-us/aspnet/core/fundamentals/configuration/options?view=aspnetcore-6.0

7
Logging in .NET 6

Logging helps you to record your application's behavior for different data at runtime and you can control what you want to record and where you want to record it. Once the development of your feature is complete, you can unit test it thoroughly on a development PC, deploy it in a test environment for thorough integration testing, then deploy it in production, and finally, open it up for many users. The context in which your application is running (such as servers, data, and load) is different in test environments and production environments when you compare it with the development box, and you might face unexpected issues in the test and production environments in the initial days.

This is where logging plays a very important role in recording what happens during runtime when different components in the end-to-end flow perform their functions and interact with each other. With the log information available, we can debug production issues and build very useful insights. We will learn about logging best practices and the different logging providers available, such as Azure App Service logging and Application Insights logging, and will build a reusable logging library that can be used in different projects.

In this chapter, we will cover the following topics:

- Characteristics of good logging
- Understanding the available logging providers
- Working with Azure App Service
- Real-time telemetry in Application Insights
- Creating a .NET 6 logging class library

By the end of the chapter, you'll have a good idea about logging as well as some of the platform-level concepts from Azure App Service and Application Insights that can be applied when working on deployment.

Technical requirements

A basic understanding of Microsoft .NET and Azure is required.

The code for the chapter can be found here: `https://github.com/ PacktPublishing/Enterprise-Application-Development-with-C-10- and-.NET-6-Second-Edition/tree/main/Chapter07`.

Characteristics of good logging

Logging is implemented but the information in the logs is not useful for building insights or debugging production issues. How many times have you seen this issue?

That's where best practices come into the picture, to implement good logging in your application. Some of the characteristics of good logging are as follows:

- It should not affect the actual application performance.
- It should be accurate and complete.
- It should be leveraged for data analytics and learning about application usages, such as concurrent users, peak load time, and most/least used features.
- It should help us reproduce the issue reported for root cause analysis and minimize *unable to reproduce* instances.
- It should be distributed and easily accessible by everyone – development, product owner, and support.
- It should not contain protected or sensitive information, **personally identifiable information (PII)**, or duplicate or unnecessary logs.

In addition to these, it should capture some of the following key information:

- **Correlation ID**: A unique identifier for an issue that can be used to search in the log store.
- **Log level**: Information, warning, and error, for example.

- **Timestamp**: Time of the log entry (always use one agreed standard format, such as UTC or server time, and don't mix both).

- **Message**: Message to be logged. This could be an information or custom error message, an actual exception message, or a combination of a custom and actual error message.

- **Machine/server/instance name**: There could be multiple servers in the load balancer. This would help us with finding the server where the log occurred.

- **Assembly**: Name of the assembly where the log occurred.

What do you want to record? This is where log-level guidance comes into the picture:

Level	Guidance
Trace	Logs to understand the detailed trace of requests throughout the application, for example, API begin/end and so on
Debug	Logs to understand information that is useful for debugging an application, for example, an object and its variables/values in business logic and so on
Information	Logs to understand the general flow of the application, performance log entry, user action, and so on, for example, user login/out, when the service started/stopped, time taken by the API, and so on
Warning	Logs to understand unexpected behavior (not errors), for example, CPU spikes, retries, a transient exception in the code that you are catching and suppressing, and so on
Error	Logs to understand errors in a specific operation, for example, API failure, database command failure, and so on
Critical/Fatal	Logs to understand errors that are causing a system crash or the application to go down

Table 7.1

The log level is configurable and based on the level specified; it will be enabled from that specified level to all higher levels. For example, if you specify the log level as **Information** in your configuration, all log messages from **Information**, **Warning**, **Error**, and **Fatal** will be logged, and **Debug** and **Trace** messages will not be logged, as shown in the following table. If no log level is specified, logging defaults to the **Information** level:

Log Level Configured	What's logged and traced with each log level					
	Trace	Debug	Information	Warning	Error	Fatal
Trace	Included	Included	Included	Included	Included	Included
Debug		Included	Included	Included	Included	Included
Information			Included	Included	Included	Included
Warning				Included	Included	Included
Error					Included	Included
Fatal						Included

Table 7.2

Where do you want to record? This is where logging providers come into the picture. Let's look at them in the next section.

Understanding the available logging providers

.NET 6 supports multiple built-in logging providers as well as several third-party logging providers. APIs exposed by these providers help in writing log output to different sources, such as a file or event log supported by the providers. Your code can also enable multiple providers, which is a very common scenario when you are moving from one provider to another, where you can keep the old one, monitor the new one, and once you are good, you can retire the old provider. Let's discuss both types of providers in detail.

Built-in logging providers

All built-in logging providers are supported in the `Microsoft.Extensions.Logging` namespace. Let's have a look at some of them:

Providers	Description
Console	• Writes log output to the console window. • The logs are not persistent. • Suitable only for initial development and not for production.
Debug	• Writes log output to the debug window when a debugger is attached. • Debug provider uses the `System.Diagnostics.Debug` class to write log output. • The logs are not persistent. • Helpful during debugging.
EventSource/ **Event Tracing for Windows (ETW)**	• The EventSource provider writes to a cross-platform event source with the name `Microsoft-Extensions-Logging`. On Windows, the provider uses ETW. • In production, you will have multiple servers with a load balancer and each server will have its own event tracing. • Multiple tools for analyzing event tracing data and centralizing the data are available, with a need to choose the right one. • Limited **graphical user interface (GUI)** and **command-line interface (CLI)** availability.
EventLog	• Writes log output to the Windows event log. • This is for Windows only. • In production, you will have multiple servers with a load balancer and each server will have its own event log. You might have to log in to all the servers in person and search each one of them. • Windows logs have three important sections: **Application**: Application-related events are logged here. You can filter based on the log level, date and time, and source (application). **Security**: Microsoft Windows security events are logged here. **System**: System-/server-related events are logged here. • Not very user-friendly to search and filter when the number of events in the log grows big.

Providers	Description
Azure App Service Diagnostics	• Azure provides built-in diagnostics for Azure App Service. • Writes log output to text files in an Azure App Service app's filesystem (not recommended for the long term) and/or to Blob storage in an Azure Storage account. • The Azure app, once deployed, uses the following settings at runtime: **Application Logging (Filesystem)** or **Application Logging (Blob)** set on/off in the App Service logs for your Azure app Logging options set using `AzureFileLoggerOptions` or `AzureBlobLoggerOptions` in the code • Azure App Service has integration with Azure Monitor to send logs and from Azure Monitor, you can set up alerts, dashboards, and so on.
Application Insights	• Writes log output to Azure Application Insights. • Can be leveraged by applications and components running anywhere – Azure, AWS, your own on-premises servers, a mobile platform, and so on. • Can be leveraged by almost all application types – web applications, web services, Windows services, background services, JavaScript, and so on. • Monitors your applications live and provides metrics. • Monitors dependencies to help you identify issues with external services. • Has powerful tools and dashboards to help you analyze and troubleshoot issues. • Monitors and raises alerts based on logs.

Table 7.3

Third-party logging providers

While .NET 6 provides several powerful inbuilt logging providers, it also supports third-party logging providers. Let's look at them:

Providers	Description
Log4net	Writes log output to multiple targets, such as a database, Windows Event Log, files, and so on. Started way back in 2001 and configuration is a bit tedious work as there are several fields to update and the configuration section is quite long. It is part of Apache Logging Services and the status is dormant, which means there are no active volunteers to take care of code commit/review/release.
Logger	Writes log output from all tiers in your app to its backend and has a powerful analytics tool for visualization, as well as supporting queries to dig deep.
NLog	Writes log output to multiple targets, such as a database, Windows Event Log, files, and so on. Started way back in 2001 and the status is still active, with updates being made.
Serilog	Writes log output to files, the console, and elsewhere like all other providers. When it was launched in 2013, it provided structured logging out of the box; other providers adopted this later.

Table 7.4

Having taken a brief look at the multiple built-in and third-party providers, let's take a deeper look at Azure App Service and Application Insights in the next section.

Working with Azure App Service

In an **Infrastructure as a Service (IaaS)** hosting model, you have full control over the operating system and software installed on the machine. It is very similar to the on-premises deployments that many of us are used to. You can access the servers via remote desktop, go through IIS logs, Windows Event Viewer, or files. When you move to the **Platform as a Service (PaaS)** hosting model, Azure takes care of managing the instances completely. This helps in saving a considerable amount of time as your engineers don't have to spend time managing the servers to keep up to date with respect to the operating systems, infrastructure, and security updates.

In this section, we will see how to do extensive logging and monitoring when you deploy your app in an Azure App Service plan (one of the important PaaS offerings from Microsoft).

Enabling application logging in Azure App Service

To enable application logging, you need to perform the following steps:

1. **Installing the package**: Install the AzureAppServices package in any of your existing .NET 6 projects using the dotnet add <.csproj> package <Nuget package> -v <Version number> command, as shown:

Figure 7.1 – Installing a package from the CLI

You can get more details about .NET CLI commands from https://docs. microsoft.com/en-us/dotnet/core/tools/dotnet.

You can also right-click on **Dependencies** in your project and select **Manage NuGet Packages**. Search for the Microsoft.Extensions.Logging. AzureAppServices package and install it as shown in the following screenshot:

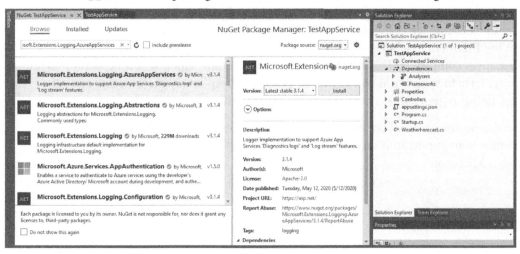

Figure 7.2 – Installing a package from the IDE

2. **Configuring the logger**: In the `Program.cs` file of your .NET 6 app, add the following highlighted code in the `CreateHostBuilder` method:

```
//Removed code for brevity
builder.Logging.AddAzureWebAppDiagnostics();
//Removed code for brevity
```

`CreateHostBuilder` does the default configuration for the app we are developing. Let's add a logging configuration here, which will also dynamically inject `_logger` (object creation happens using **dependency injection (DI)**, as explained in *Chapter 5, Dependency Injection in .NET 6*).

3. **Adding logging**: Add the following highlighted logging code to your methods in any of the controllers where core logic resides generally to test whether logging works:

```
[ApiController]
[Route("[controller]")]
public class WeatherForecastController : ControllerBase
  {
        private static readonly string[] Summaries =
new[]
        {
            "Freezing", "Bracing", "Chilly", "Cool",
"Mild", "Warm", "Balmy", "Hot", "Sweltering", "Scorching"
        };
        private readonly ILogger<WeatherForecast
Controller> _logger;
        public
WeatherForecastController(ILogger<WeatherForecast
Controller> logger)
        {
            _logger = logger;
        }
        [HttpGet]
        public IEnumerable<WeatherForecast> Get()
        {
            _logger.LogInformation("Logging Information
for testing");
            _logger.LogWarning("Logging Warning for
testing");
```

```
        _logger.LogError("Logging Error for
testing");
            var rng = new Random();
            return Enumerable.Range(1, 5).Select(index =>
new WeatherForecast
            {
                Date = DateTime.Now.AddDays(index),
                TemperatureC = rng.Next(-20, 55),
                Summary = Summaries[rng.Next(Summaries.
Length)]
            })
            .ToArray();
        }
    }
```

4. **Publishing your app**: Publish your app service to an Azure resource group with the name `TestAppServiceForLoggingDemo`. For more information on how to publish, refer to `https://docs.microsoft.com/en-us/visualstudio/ deployment/quickstart-deploy-to-azure?view=vs-2022`. For this example, we have leveraged the Windows-based App Service plan.

5. **Enabling logging**: Go to the Azure portal | **Your subscription** | **Resource Group** | **App service** where it is deployed, and select **App Service logs** under **Monitoring**. You can see different logging options, as shown:

Figure 7.3 – App Service logs default state

All logging options are turned off by default, as shown in the previous screenshot. Let's see what those options are:

- **Application Logging (Filesystem)**: Writes log messages from the application to the local filesystem on the web server. This will be enabled for 12 hours once you turn it on and will be disabled automatically after that. Therefore, this option is for temporary debugging purposes.

- **Application Logging (Blob)**: Writes log messages from the application to Blob storage for persistent logs for a configured retention period. Logging in blobs is for long-term debugging purposes. You would need a Blob storage container to write logs to. You can read more about Blob storage containers here: `https://docs.microsoft.com/en-us/azure/storage/blobs/storage-blobs-introduction`. Once you select **On**, you will get an option to create a new storage account or search for an existing storage account where you can write the logs. Click on **+ Storage account** and specify a name to create a new account, as shown in the following screenshot:

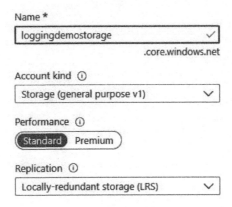

Figure 7.4 – Storage account configuration

- **Web server logging**: IIS logs on servers that give diagnostic information such as the HTTP method, resource URI, client IP, client port, user agent, and response code. You can store the logs in Blob storage or on the filesystem. In **Retention Period (Days)**, you can configure the number of days for which the logs should be retained.

- **Detailed error messages**: Detailed error messages for HTTP 400 responses from the server, which can help you determine why the server returned this error.

> **Note**
>
> For security reasons, we don't send detailed error pages to clients in production, but App Service can save this error in the filesystem each time an application error occurs that has HTTP code 400 or greater.

- **Failed request tracing**: Detailed information on failed requests, including IIS trace and so on. For each failed request, a folder is generated that contains the XML log file and the XSL stylesheet to view the log file.

The following screenshot shows how it will look when you turn it on and enable all the log options:

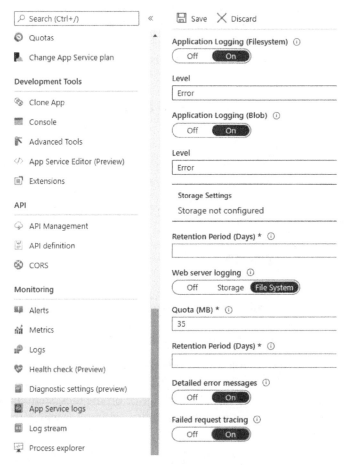

Figure 7.5 – App Service logs enabled

6. You can verify logs from any of the logging options we have enabled by browsing the site hosted on App Service and navigating to the page that hits the controller where logging is done. For example, let's check **Application Logging (Blob)** by accessing the Blob storage where we configured one of the logging options, as shown in the following screenshot:

Figure 7.6 – App Service logs from Blob storage

You can also see the logs in the log stream in real-time from the controller where we added test logs by navigating to **Log stream** under **Monitoring**:

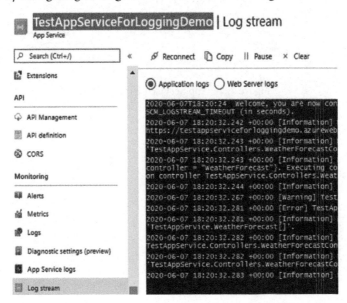

Figure 7.7 – App Service logs in Log stream

We saw how to enable different logs in Azure App Service and verified logs in **Application Logging (Blob)** and **Log stream**. In the next section, we will see how we can monitor and raise alerts.

Monitoring using metrics

You can monitor your App Service plan and app services using metrics in Azure Monitor.

Navigate to your App Service plan and check the overview, as shown in the following screenshot. You can see standard charts for CPU, memory, data in, data out, and so on:

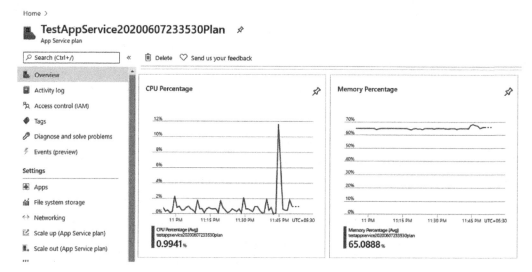

Figure 7.8 – App Service plan overview

Now, click on any of the charts, for example, the **CPU Percentage** chart. You will get the view shown in the following screenshot (the default duration is 1 hour):

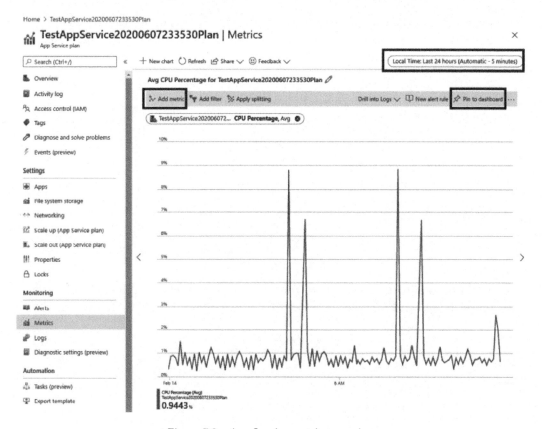

Figure 7.9 – App Service metrics overview

I have highlighted three important sections in the chart shown in the previous screenshot. Let's discuss them:

- **Local Time**: When you click on **Local Time**, you will get options as shown in the following screenshot. You can change the value of the time range for which this chart should represent:

Figure 7.10 – App Service metrics time range

- **Add metric**: When you click on **Add metric**, you will get the options shown in the following screenshot. You can select the metric you want the chart to display:

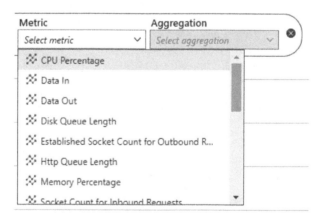

Figure 7.11 – App Service – Add metric

- **Pin to dashboard**: You can click on **Pin to dashboard** and add the chart to the dashboard so that you can see updates when you log in to the Azure portal.

When you click on the left portal menu, you can see **Dashboard**, and you can click on that to see all the pinned dashboards:

Figure 7.12 – Left portal menu option for Dashboard

In the next section, let's see how to enable real-time telemetry in Azure Application insights.

Real-time telemetry in Azure Application Insights

Application Insights is one of the best telemetry offerings provided by Microsoft Azure for developers and DevOps professionals as an extensible **application performance management (APM)** service to do the following:

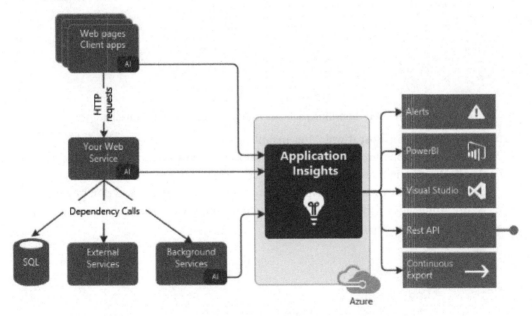

Figure 7.13 – Application Insights instrumentation for telemetry

Note
There is no impact on your app performance. Calls to Application Insights are non-blocking and sent in separate threads in batches.

Enabling application logging in Application Insights

The steps to enable application logging when using Application Insights are as follows:

1. **Installing the ApplicationInsights package**: Install the `Microsoft.ApplicationInsights.AspNetCore` package from **Tools | NuGet Package Manager | Package Manager Console** as shown, using the `Install-Package <Package name> -version <Version number>` command:

```
Package Manager Console                                                        ▾  ┬┬ ×
Package source:  All                    ▾  ⚙  Default project:  TestAppInsights        ▾  ⅀≣  ▪
PM> Install-Package Microsoft.ApplicationInsights.AspNetCore -Version 2.14.0               ▲
Restoring packages for E:\Learnings\.NetCore\TestAppService\TestAppInsights\TestAppInsights.csproj...
Installing NuGet package Microsoft.ApplicationInsights.AspNetCore 2.14.0.
Committing restore...
Writing assets file to disk. Path: E:\Learnings\.NetCore\TestAppService\TestAppInsights\obj\project.assets.json
Restored E:\Learnings\.NetCore\TestAppService\TestAppInsights\TestAppInsights.csproj (in 961 ms).
Successfully installed 'Microsoft.ApplicationInsights 2.14.0' to TestAppInsights
Successfully installed 'Microsoft.ApplicationInsights.AspNetCore 2.14.0' to TestAppInsights
Successfully installed 'Microsoft.ApplicationInsights.DependencyCollector 2.14.0' to TestAppInsights
Successfully installed 'Microsoft.ApplicationInsights.EventCounterCollector 2.14.0' to TestAppInsights
Successfully installed 'Microsoft.ApplicationInsights.PerfCounterCollector 2.14.0' to TestAppInsights
Successfully installed 'Microsoft.ApplicationInsights.WindowsServer 2.14.0' to TestAppInsights
Successfully installed 'Microsoft.ApplicationInsights.WindowsServer.TelemetryChannel 2.14.0' to TestAppInsights
Successfully installed 'Microsoft.AspNetCore.Hosting 1.0.2' to TestAppInsights
Successfully installed 'Microsoft.AspNetCore.Hosting.Abstractions 1.0.2' to TestAppInsights
Successfully installed 'Microsoft.AspNetCore.Hosting.Server.Abstractions 1.0.2' to TestAppInsights
Successfully installed 'Microsoft.AspNetCore.Http 1.0.2' to TestAppInsights
Successfully installed 'Microsoft.AspNetCore.Http.Abstractions 1.0.2' to TestAppInsights
Successfully installed 'Microsoft.AspNetCore.Http.Extensions 1.0.2' to TestAppInsights
Successfully installed 'Microsoft.AspNetCore.Http.Features 1.0.2' to TestAppInsights
100 %   ▾ ◂                                                                             ▸
```

Figure 7.14 - Installing packages from Package Manager Console

2. **App settings configuration**: After installing the package, you need to add a telemetry section and update the **instrumentation key (GUID)** of your Azure Application Insights resource in `appsettings.json` so that all telemetry data is written to your Azure Application Insights resource. If you don't have an Azure Application Insights resource, go ahead and create one, and then add it to `appsettings.json`:

```
{
    "Logging": {
      "LogLevel": {
        "Default": "Information",
        "Microsoft": "Warning",
        "Microsoft.Hosting.Lifetime": "Information"
```

```
        }
    },
    "Telemetry": {
        "InstrumentationKey": "Your AppInsights
    Instrumentation Key "
    }
```

3. **Enabling the ApplicationInsights telemetry**: In your `Program.cs` file, add the highlighted code:

```
string InstrumentationKey = builder.
Configuration["Telemetry:InstrumentationKey"];
// The following line enables Application Insights
telemetry collection.
builder.Services.
AddApplicationInsightsTelemetry(InstrumentationKey);
```

Now, you can build and run the application. Out of the box, you will get a lot of telemetry data.

Navigate to **Application Insights | Overview** and you can see any failed requests, the server response time, and server requests, as shown in the following screenshot:

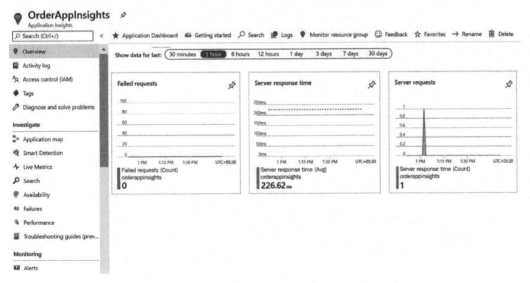

Figure 7.15 – Application Insights overview

You can navigate to **Application Insights | Live Metrics** for real-time performance counters, as shown in the following figure:

Figure 7.16 - Application Insights live metrics

You can navigate to **Application Insights | Metrics** to get different metrics and charts, as shown in the following figure:

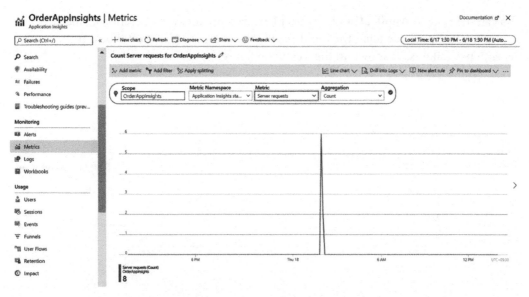

Figure 7.17 – Application Insights metrics

You can navigate to **Application Insights | Performance** and analyze operation duration, dependency response time, and so on, as shown in the following figure:

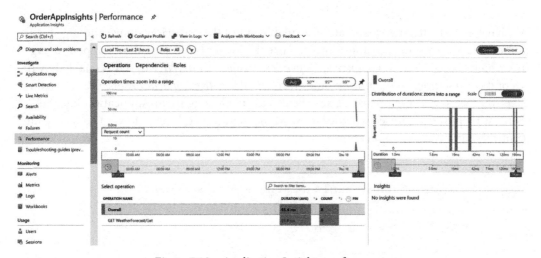

Figure 7.18 – Application Insights performance

You can navigate to **Application Insights | Failures** and analyze operations, failed requests, failed dependencies, the top three response codes, exception types, and dependency failures, as shown in the following figure:

Figure 7.19 – Application Insights failures

We have seen the telemetry and alerts available out of the box. How do we add logs for information, errors, or warnings? You can use the logger (object creation happens using DI, which was covered in *Chapter 5, Dependency Injection in .NET 6*). DI is enabled by the second (*App settings configuration*) and third (*Enabling the Application Insights telemetry*) steps that we saw in the preceding set of steps to enable logging in Application Insights. For testing purposes, to see whether it's working, you can add the following code to your controller and run the application:

```
[HttpGet]
        public IEnumerable<WeatherForecast> Get()
        {
    //Removed code for brevity


        _logger.LogWarning("Logging Warning for
            testing");
        _logger.LogError("Logging Error for testing");
        //Removed code for brevity
```

You can navigate to **Application Insights | Logs** and check traces, where you can see both the warnings and errors that were logged, as shown in the following figure:

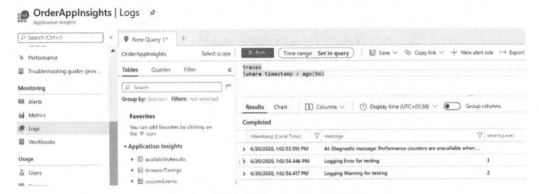

Figure 7.20 – Application Insights logs

Application Insights is very simple to use and a very powerful log provider. We saw the rich telemetry it provides out-of-the-box and added our own logs. In the next section, we will develop a custom logging class library. The default logger provided in .NET 6 is more than enough for your application telemetry. If you need custom metrics and events to be logged on top of what's provided by default in .NET 6, you can leverage the following custom logger library.

Creating a .NET 6 logging class library

We will create a class library (DLL) that will support Application Insights logging and can be extended to support logging to other sources if needed. Perform the following steps for this:

1. Create a new .NET 6 class library with the name `Logger`.

2. Install the `Microsoft.ApplicationInsights` package.

3. Create a new class called `ICustomLogger.cs` and add the following code:

```
using System;
using System.Collections.Generic;
namespace Logger
{
    public interface ICustomLogger
    {
        void Dependency(string dependencyTypeName,
```

```
        string dependencyName, string data,
        DateTimeOffset startTime, TimeSpan duration,
        bool success);
    void Error(string message, IDictionary<string,
        string> properties = null);
    void Event(string eventName,
    IDictionary<string, string> properties = null,
    IDictionary<string, double> metrics = null);
    void Metric(string name, long value,
        IDictionary<string, string> properties =
        null);
    void Exception(Exception exception,
        IDictionary<string, string> properties =
        null);
    void Information(string message,
        IDictionary<string, string> properties =
        null);
    void Request(string name, DateTimeOffset
        startTime, TimeSpan duration, string
        responseCode, bool success);
    void Verbose(string message,
        IDictionary<string, string> properties =
        null);
    void Warning(string message,
        IDictionary<string, string> properties =
        null);
    }
}
```

4. Create a new class called `AiLogger.cs` and add the following code to log custom events and metrics:

-   **Namespaces and Constructor**:

    ```
    using Microsoft.ApplicationInsights;
    using Microsoft.ApplicationInsights.DataContracts;
    using System;
    ```

```
using System.Collections.Generic;

namespace Logger
{
    public class AiLogger : ICustomLogger
    {
        private TelemetryClient client;

        public AiLogger(TelemetryClient client)
        {
            if (client is null)
            {
                throw new
ArgumentNullException(nameof(client));
            }
            this.client = client;
        }
```

- **Code to log warning, error, and exception**:

```
        public void Warning(string message,
IDictionary<string, string> properties = null)
        {
            this.client.TrackTrace(message,
SeverityLevel.Warning, properties);
        }
        public void Error(string message,
IDictionary<string, string> properties = null)
        {
            this.client.TrackTrace(message,
SeverityLevel.Error, properties);
        }
        public void Exception(Exception exception,
IDictionary<string, string> properties = null)
        {
```

```
        this.client.TrackException(exception,
properties);
        }
```

- **Code to log custom event, metric, information, request, and dependency**:

```
public void Event(string eventName, IDictionary<string,
string> properties = null, IDictionary<string, double>
metrics = null)
        {
            this.client.TrackEvent(eventName, properties,
metrics);
        }
        public void Metric(string name, long value,
IDictionary<string, string> properties = null)
        {
            this.client.TrackMetric(name, value,
properties);
        }

        public void Information(string message,
IDictionary<string, string> properties = null)
        {
            this.client.TrackTrace(message,
SeverityLevel.Information, properties);
        }

        public void Request(string name, DateTimeOffset
startTime, TimeSpan duration, string responseCode, bool
success)
        {
            this.client.TrackRequest(name, startTime,
duration, responseCode, success);
        }
    }

public void Dependency(string dependencyTypeName, string
dependencyName, string data, DateTimeOffset startTime,
TimeSpan duration, bool success)
```

```
        {              this.client.
TrackDependency(dependencyTypeName, dependencyName, data,
startTime, duration, success);
        }
```

AiLogger uses the TelemetryClient class, which sends telemetry to Azure Application Insights.

5. Build the library, and your custom .NET 6 logger is ready to consume events in your project.

In the upcoming chapters, we will be consuming the logging library as part of our enterprise application development. In the example provided for this chapter, you can see how we have dynamically injected this custom logger into the LoggerDemoService project.

Summary

In this chapter, we learned about the characteristics of good logging, the different logging providers available, such as the Azure App Service logging provider and the Azure Application Insights logging provider, and how to create a reusable logger library.

You now have the necessary knowledge of logging that will help you to implement a reusable logger or extend a current logger in your project, with the right level of logging and key information to debug issues and build analytics on production data.

In the next chapter, we will learn about various techniques to cache data in .NET 6 applications, as well as various caching components and the platforms available that can be integrated with a .NET application.

Questions

1. Which logs highlight when the current flow of execution has stopped due to a failure? These should indicate a failure in the current activity, not an application-wide failure:

    a. Warning

    b. Error

    c. Critical

    d. Information

    Answer : b

2. What can be leveraged by applications and components running anywhere, on Azure, AWS, your own on-premises servers, or a mobile platform, for logging?

    a. Application Insights

    b. Azure App Service

    c. EventLog

    d. Serilog

    Answer: a

3. What are the logging options available in Azure App Service?

    a. **Application Logging (Filesystem)** and **Application Logging (Blob)**

    b. **Web server logging** and **Detailed error messages**

    c. **Failed request tracing**

    d. All the above

    Answer: d

4. Application Insights is an extensible APM service to do which of the following?

    a. Monitor your live applications.

    b. Automatically detect performance anomalies.

    c. Include powerful analytics tools to help you diagnose issues.

    d. All the above.

    Answer: d

8
All You Need to Know about Caching

Caching is one of the key system design patterns that help in scaling any enterprise application along with improving response time. Any web application typically involves reading and writing data from and to a data store, which is usually a relational database such as SQL Server or a NoSQL database such as Cosmos DB. However, reading data from the database for every request is not efficient, especially when the data hasn't changed. This is because databases usually persist data to disk and it's a costly operation to load the data from disk and send it back to the browser client (or device in the case of mobile/desktop applications) or user. This is where caching comes into play.

Cache stores can be used as a primary source for retrieving data, falling back to the original data store only when the required data is not available in the cache, thus giving a faster response to the consuming application. When using caches this way, we also need to ensure that the cached data is expired/refreshed as and when the data in the original data store is updated.

In this chapter, we will learn about various techniques for caching data in .NET 6 applications as well as various caching components and the platforms available that can be integrated with a .NET 6 application. We will cover the following topics:

- Introduction to caching
- Understanding the components of caching
- Caching platforms
- Designing a cache abstraction layer using distributed caching

Technical requirements

A basic understanding of .NET Core, C#, Azure, and the .NET CLI is required. The code for the chapter can be found here: `https://github.com/PacktPublishing/ Enterprise-Application-Development-with-C-10-and-.NET-6- Second-Edition/tree/main/Chapter08`.

The instructions for the code examples can be found here: `https://github.com/ PacktPublishing/Enterprise-Application-Development-with-C-10- and-.NET-6-Second-Edition/tree/main/Enterprise%20Application`.

Introduction to caching

There are multiple ways to improve the performance of an application and caching is one of the key techniques used in enterprise applications. A **cache** is like a temporary data store, with a limited size and limited data, but has much faster data access compared to the original data source and usually holds only a subset of the data, the most frequently used data that does not change often.

A **cache store** could be as simple as the RAM of the computer that is used by the process during execution, or it could be something such as Redis, which uses both memory and disks to store data. The key thing here is that it is usually on hardware that has a lower access time compared to the original storage layer.

Caching can be implemented at every layer in the architecture so that data can be retrieved from the layer closest to the user. For example, in any web application, the moment a URL is typed in the browser and we press *Enter*, it goes through various web components that are involved in loading the web application, starting with the browser, proxies, and DNS, to the web server and database. Caching is something that can be applied at all these layers.

If data is cached in the browser, it can be loaded immediately. It can alternatively fall back to a higher layer if data is not available in the layer closest to the user, thus reducing the load on higher layers that are shared across multiple users, such as the application server and database tier.

The following figure depicts this discussion at a high level, where a request is flowing through various layers and is moved to a higher layer only when data is not available (represented by the dotted line) in the cache:

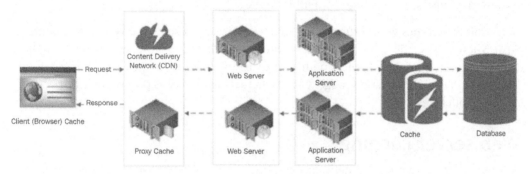

Figure 8.1 – Cache layers in a request flow

Let's discuss some of these layers in application architecture where data can be cached.

Client caching

Commonly requested data can be cached on the client side to avoid unnecessary round trips to the server. For example, Microsoft's Outlook app downloads the most recent emails from the server and keeps a copy of them on the client side, and then periodically syncs for new emails. If there is a need to search for an email that isn't already downloaded, it goes back to the server.

Similarly, browsers can cache various resources and responses from a web application based on certain headers, and subsequent requests for the same resource load from the browser cache. For example, all JavaScript files, image files, and CSS are usually cached on the browser for a certain period. Also, a response from an API can be cached by sending appropriate response headers. This is also known as **HTTP caching** or **response caching**, which is discussed in detail in a later section.

Content Delivery Network (CDN)

A **Content Delivery Network (CDN)** is a set of servers that are globally distributed and are usually used to serve static content such as HTML, CSS, and video. Whenever an application requests a resource, if the CDN is enabled, the system will first look to load the resource from the CDN server that is physically closest to the user. However, if it is not available on the CDN server, the resource is retrieved from the server and is cached in the CDN to serve subsequent requests. Netflix is one such great example that heavily relies on its custom-built CDN to deliver content to users.

Microsoft also comes with Azure CDN, which is primarily used to serve static content. Also, Microsoft's CDN gives an option to integrate with Azure Storage, which we will be using in our e-commerce application to serve various product images. Similarly, AWS has Amazon Cloudfront and Google Cloud offers Cloud CDN as part of their respective e-storage offerings.

Web server caching

Although CDNs are great for static content, they come with additional costs and maintenance overhead in terms of refreshing data from application servers. To overcome these limitations, applications can use web servers or reverse proxies to serve static content. A lightweight NGINX server is one such example that can be used to serve static content.

Web servers can also cache dynamic content, such as an API response coming from the application server. Web servers such as NGINX or IIS, when configured as a reverse proxy, can be further used to cache dynamic content, thereby reducing the load on the application server by serving requests from its cache.

> **Note**
> NGINX is an open source solution that is primarily known for its web server capabilities; however, it can also be used as a reverse proxy, for load balancing, and more. For further reading, please refer to `https://www.nginx.com/`.

Database caching

Increasingly, database servers cache certain components of a query; for example, SQL Server usually has cache execution plans and also has a data buffer to cache, and MongoDB keeps recently queried data in memory for faster retrieval. So, it is good to tweak these settings to improve the performance of the application.

> **Note**
>
> Database caching doesn't guarantee that subsequent execution of the same query executes with zero CPU consumption; that is, it is not practically free. The same query in subsequent requests executes at a faster pace.

Application caching

Application caching can be achieved by caching data retrieved from the storage layer within the application server. This is mostly done in the following two ways:

- Stored in the memory of the application server, also known as in-memory caching

- Stored in an external store, such as Redis or Memcached, that has a faster access time as compared to the underlying original data store

Application caching usually involves integrating extra code within the application logic to cache data. So, whenever a request for data is made, the application first looks in the cache. But if it's not available in the cache, the application will fall back to the original data store, such as a database. Usually, the size of the application cache is limited compared to the original data store, so internally, application caching platforms will employ various algorithms such as **Least Recently Used (LRU)** or **Least Frequently Used (LFU)** to clean up the data stored in the cache. We will discuss more about caching platforms in the *Caching platforms* section.

Another important point to consider for application caches is data invalidation, which is how frequently data needs to be expired or synced with the original data source. So, things such as cache expiry and various strategies to update the cache with the original data store (read-through, write-through) need to be considered. We will discuss more cache invalidation/refresh strategies in the *Cache access patterns* section.

Understanding the components of caching

Before we understand the various possible cache stores/platforms available in .NET 6 applications, we need to understand the various components of caching that are available in .NET 6 and how to use them in enterprise applications. Along the way, we will also cover various cache eviction strategies and techniques to keep the cache in sync with original data stores.

Response caching

Response caching is a caching technique supported by HTTP to cache the response to a request made using HTTP or HTTPS either on the client (for example, a browser) or an intermediate proxy server. From an implementation standpoint, this is controlled by setting the appropriate value for the `Cache-Control` header in both requests and responses. A typical `Cache-Control` header will look as follows:

```
Cache-Control:public,max-age=10
```

In this case, if the header is present in the response, the server is telling the client/proxy (public) that the client can cache the response for 10 seconds (`max-age=10`). However, the client can still override it and cache it for a shorter duration; that is, if both the request and response set the cache headers, the cache duration would be the minimum of both.

Along with `max-age`, as per the HTTP specification (`https://tools.ietf.org/html/rfc7234#section-5.2`), `Cache-Control` can additionally hold the following values:

- **Public**: The response can be cached anywhere – client/server/intermediate proxy server.

- **Private**: The response can be stored for a specific user but not in a shared cache server; for example, it can be stored in the client browser or application server.

- **No-cache**: The response cannot be cached.

Other headers that play a role in response caching are the following:

- **Age**: This is a response header indicating the duration for which an object is present in the cache (proxy/browser). The accepted value is an integer and represents the duration in seconds.

- **Vary**: This is the response header that, when received, tells the client the request header on which basis the responses are cached. The value of this header is one of the request headers and based on the value of that header, the client can decide whether to use a cached response or download data from the server. For example, if `Vary` is set to the `user-agent` value, responses are uniquely cached per `user-agent`.

The following screenshot shows response headers related to the cache for a sample request in Postman:

KEY	VALUE
Cache-Control ⓘ	public,max-age=50000
Transfer-Encoding ⓘ	chunked
Content-Type ⓘ	application/json; charset=utf-8
Vary ⓘ	user-agent
Server ⓘ	Microsoft-IIS/10.0
X-Powered-By ⓘ	ASP.NET
Date ⓘ	Sun, 21 Jun 2020 12:59:57 GMT

Figure 8.2 – Sample response with Cache-Control and Vary headers

The following sequence diagram shows a sample API built using ASP.NET Core 6 that has response caching middleware enabled:

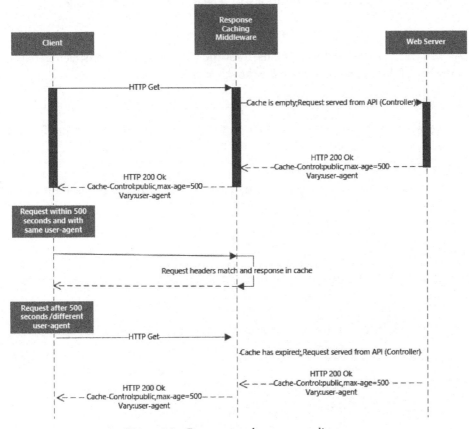

Figure 8.3 – Response cache sequence diagram

After creating a new ASP.NET Core 6 MVC/Web API application, or using an existing ASP.NET Core 6 MVC/Web API application, to configure response caching, the following code changes are required:

1. Add `builder.Services.AddResponseCaching()` to `Program.cs` and add the required middleware using `app.UseResponseCaching()`. This middleware holds the required logic to cache data. Ensure this middleware is injected before `app.UseEndpoints`.

2. Handle the response to set cache headers either through custom middleware or using the `ResponseCache` attribute.

> **Note**
>
> `UseCors` must be called before `UseResponseCaching` when using CORS middleware. For further information on this ordering, please refer to `https://github.com/dotnet/AspNetCore.Docs/blob/master/aspnetcore/fundamentals/middleware/index.md`.

The `ResponseCache` attribute can be used for the entire controller or specific methods in a controller, and it accepts the following key properties:

- `Duration`: A numeric value that sets the `max-age` value in the response header

- `ResponseCacheLocation`: An enum that takes three values – `Any`, `Client`, and `None` – and further sets the `Cache-Control` header to `public`, `private`, or `no-store`

- `VaryByHeader`: A string that controls cache behavior to cache based on a specific header

- `VaryByQueryKeys`: An array of strings that accepts key values on which basis data is cached

A typical method with the `ResponseCache` attribute looks like this:

```
[HttpGet]
[ResponseCache(Duration = 500, VaryByHeader =
  "user-agent", Location =
  ResponseCacheLocation.Any, VaryByQueryKeys =
  new[] { "Id" })]
public async Task<IActionResult>
  Get([FromQuery]int Id = 0)
```

This method would be cached for 500 seconds based on a unique user-agent header and Id value. If any of these values change, a response is served from the server, otherwise, it's served from the cache middleware.

As you can see here, we need to prefix the ResponseCache attribute to every controller/method. So, if the application has many controllers/methods, this could be a maintenance overhead since, in order to make any changes to the way data is cached (such as changing the Duration value), we need to apply the change at the controller/method level, and that's where cache profiles come into play.

So, instead of setting properties individually, we can group them and give them a name in Program.cs, and that name can be used in the ResponseCache attribute. So, for the preceding properties, we can create a cache profile by adding the code shown here in Program.cs:

```
builder.Services.AddControllers(options =>
{
    options.CacheProfiles.Add("Default",
      new CacheProfile {
        Duration = 500,
        VaryByHeader = "user-agent",
        Location = ResponseCacheLocation.Any,
        VaryByQueryKeys = new[] { "Id" } });
});
```

And on the controller, call this cache profile using CacheProfileName:

```
[ResponseCache(CacheProfileName = "Default")]
```

For an MVC application, CacheProfile can be configured in services.AddControllersWithViews().

Distributed caching

As we know, in a distributed system, the data store is split across multiple servers. Similarly, distributed caching is an extension of traditional caching in which cached data is stored in more than one server in a network. Before we get into distributed caching, here's a quick recap of the **CAP theorem**:

- **C** stands for consistency, meaning the data is consistent across all the nodes and each node has the same copy of the data.

- **A** stands for availability, meaning the system is available, and the failure of one node doesn't cause the system to go down.

- **P** stands for partition-tolerant, meaning the system doesn't go down even if the communication between nodes goes down.

As per the CAP theorem, any distributed system can only achieve two of the preceding principles, and as distributed systems must be partition-tolerant (P), we can only achieve either consistency (C) of data or high availability (A) of data.

So, distributed caching is a cache strategy in which data is stored in multiple servers/nodes/shards outside the application server. Since data is distributed across multiple servers, if one server goes down, another server can be used as a backup to retrieve data.

For example, if our system wanted to cache countries, states, and cities, and if there are three caching servers in a distributed caching system, hypothetically there is a possibility that one of the cache servers will cache countries, another one will cache states, and one will cache cities (of course, in a real-time application, data is split in a much more complex way).

Also, each server will additionally act as a backup for one or more entities. So, on a high level, one type of distributed cache system looks as shown:

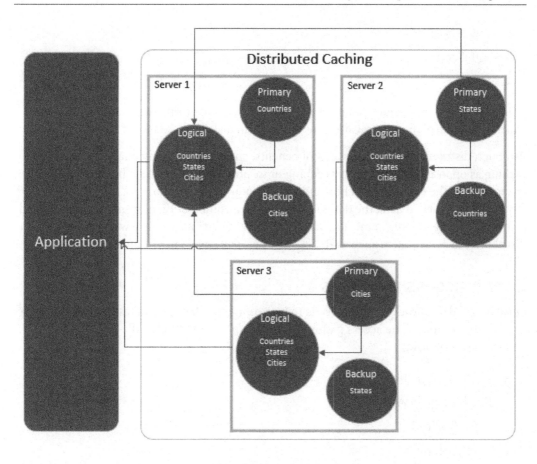

Figure 8.4 – Distributed caching high-level representation

As you can see, while reading data, it is read from the primary server, and if the primary server is not available, the caching system will fall back to the secondary server. Similarly, for writes, write operations are not complete until data is written to the primary as well as the secondary server. Until this operation is completed, read operations can be blocked, hence compromising the availability of the system. Another strategy for writes could be background synchronization, which will result in the eventual consistency of data, hence compromising the consistency of data until synchronization is completed. Going back to the CAP theorem, most distributed caching systems fall under the category of CP or AP.

The following are a few of the distributed caching providers that are integrated with .NET 6 applications:

- Redis Cache
- Memcached

- Couchbase

- SQL Server

- NCache

This can be further extended to any cluster orchestration platform, for example, **Terracotta**, which takes care of managing various nodes and can distribute data to all nodes.

Although distributed caching has a lot of benefits, one possible disadvantage of distributed caching as opposed to single-server caching or in-process caching could be the introduced latency due to the possible extra hop and serialization/deserialization. So, if applications rely heavily on cached data, the design can consider a combination of in-memory cache and distributed cache. However, most scenarios are covered by integrating a well-implemented distributed caching system such as Redis, which we will cover later in this chapter.

Cache access patterns

Once object data is cached, there needs to be a design in place that takes care of refreshing the cache. Multiple cache access patterns can be implemented to handle this. A few key patterns are as follows:

- Cache-aside pattern

- Read-through/write-through

- Refresh-ahead

- Write-behind

Let's discuss each in detail.

Cache-aside pattern

As the name suggests, in the cache-aside pattern, the cache store is kept alongside the data store. In this pattern, the application code checks for data availability in the cache store. If it's not available in the cache store, the data is retrieved from the underlying data store and is updated in the cache. Subsequent requests would again query the data in the cache and if the data is available in the cache, it will be served from the cache. The cache-aside pattern relies on the concept of lazy loading, discussed in *Chapter 4, Threading and Asynchronous Operations*, and populates as and when data is accessed for the first time; a subsequent request for the same entity would be loaded from cache.

The expiry of data in the cache store should be handled while updating the data in the original data store, and then subsequent reads will add the updated data to the cache again.

The following are the advantages of this pattern:

- Simplified implementation compared to the read-through/write-through patterns covered in the next section. As the cache isn't the primary data source in the application, we do not need additional classes to synchronize the cache store with the data store.

- As it relies on the lazy loading principle, the cache is populated only when any data is accessed at least once.

However, there are a few cons associated with this pattern:

- It leads to the possibility of a greater number of cache misses. Cache misses should always be minimal as they introduce latency in the application due to the additional hop.

- If cache expiry is missed during data updates, it can lead to stale data in the cache. This can occur if data is updated by a background/external process that doesn't have information on the caching system.

One way to mitigate issues with expiration is to set the **Time to Live** (**TTL**) for each entity so that objects are automatically expired after a certain period. However, the TTL duration needs to be carefully evaluated after monitoring the data refresh rate. Another common practice in the case of the cache-aside pattern is to prepopulate the cache store during the startup of the application as this helps in reducing the number of cache misses. Most enterprise applications usually implement a caching layer using the cache-aside pattern and prepopulate it with master data rather than transactional data.

Read-through/write-through

In read-through/write-through, the application directly reads/writes data from the cache store; that is, the application uses it as a primary store and the cache layer is responsible for loading the data in the cache and also for writing any updates from the cache store back to the original store.

When the application wants to read an entity, it will directly request it from the cache store. If that entity is available in the cache, a response is returned. However, if it isn't present in the cache, the caching layer requests it from the original data store, which is updated in the cache for future use, and then the response is returned from the cache layer.

When updating an entity, the following steps occur:

1. It is first updated in the cache.

2. The cache layer writes it back to the original data store.

The major advantages of this kind of system are as follows:

- Significant load reduction on the original data store, which is usually a database, as in most enterprise applications, all the calls would be served from the cache apart from calls from the cache layer to the data store.

- Simplified application code as it only interacts with one store, unlike the cache-aside pattern, which interacts with the cache store as well as a data store from within the application code.

A few disadvantages of this pattern are as follows:

- An additional mechanism is required to synchronize data between the cache and data store.

- Cache updating becomes a bit tricky as it involves additional complexity to refresh the cache store.

Refresh-ahead

The refresh-ahead strategy allows you to load data into the cache store asynchronously; that is, in this design, the application still talks directly to the cache store. However, the cache layer periodically refreshes the data before the data in the cache expires. The refresh happens asynchronously for the entries that were accessed most recently and are refreshed from the original store asynchronously before their expiration. This way, there won't be any latency in the application if any item cache is expired.

Write-behind

In the write-behind strategy, data is updated into the cache store first and asynchronously updated back to the data store, as opposed to the write-through strategy in which data is immediately updated to the data store. One of the key advantages of this strategy is reduced latency. However, as data is updated asynchronously (writing to the data store and cache store are two different transactions) to the data store, there should be a rollback mechanism implemented in case there is ever a failure.

Typically, this is much more complex to implement as opposed to write-through due to the additional handling needed to avoid any data loss during asynchronous updates, but it's still a good pattern to integrate if there is a requirement to have the cache store as the primary source.

All the patterns discussed up to now can be visualized at a high level as shown in the following figure:

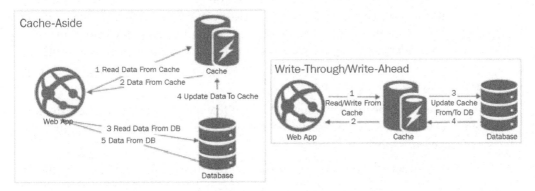

Figure 8.5 – Cache patterns

Up to now, we have seen various caching patterns and strategies. In the next section, we will discuss various cache providers and their integration with .NET 6 applications.

Caching platforms

.NET 6 supports multiple caching platforms. A few of the commonly used cache platforms are as follows:

- **In-memory cache**: In this, the cache data is stored inside the process memory. For example, if the application is hosted on IIS, the in-memory cache will consume memory from w3wp.exe.

- **Distributed cache**: Data is stored across multiple servers. The data stores that can be integrated with .NET 6 applications are SQL Server, Redis, and NCache.

In-memory cache

To configure memory caching, after creating a new ASP.NET Core 6 MVC/Web API application, or for an existing ASP.NET Core 6 MVC/Web API application, the following code changes are required:

1. Add `builder.Services.AddMemoryCache()` to `Program.cs`. The `MemoryCache` class is a built-in implementation of `IMemoryCache` in .NET 6 and would be available in any C# class via `IMemoryCache`. It is instantiated using constructor injection. Object creation happens using **Dependency Injection (DI)**, as covered in *Chapter 5, Dependency Injection in .NET 6*. So, to cache any entity to the memory cache, create a property of `IMemoryCache` and create an instance of `MemoryCache` using constructor injection.

2. `MemoryCache` exposes many methods, but a few important ones are `Get` (to get the value of a key), `Set` (to insert a key and its value), and `Remove` (to remove a key (cache expiration)).

3. While creating a cache object (using `Set` or other methods), the memory cache can be configured for various parameters using `MemoryCacheEntryOptions`. The following properties are supported:

    a. `SetAbsoluteExpiration`: The absolute **Time To Live (TTL)** for a cache entry can be set in `TimeSpan` or the exact date and time (`DateTime`) until which the cache is valid.

    b. `SetSlidingExpiration`: The inactive time for the cache after which the cache entry is removed from the cache. For example, a sliding expiration value of 5 seconds will wait for the cache entry to be inactive for 5 seconds. Sliding expiration should always be less than absolute expiration as the cache would expire after the absolute expiration duration has been reached irrespective of the sliding expiration duration.

    c. `SetPriority`: As cache size is limited while performing cache eviction (**Least Recently Used (LRU)**, **Least Frequently Used (LFU)**), the priority of the cache entry is also considered. `SetPriority` can be used to set the priority for a cache entry through a `CacheItemPriority` enum. Its default value is `CacheItemPriority.Normal`.

A simple Web API controller with memory cache integration as per the preceding steps will look like this:

```
public class WeatherForecastController : ControllerBase
{
    private IMemoryCache cache;
```

```csharp
    public WeatherForecastController(IMemoryCache
      cache)
    {
        this.cache = cache;
    }
    [HttpGet]
    public IActionResult Get()
    {
        DateTime? cacheEntry;
        if (!cache.TryGetValue("Weather",
          out cacheEntry))
        {
            cacheEntry = DateTime.Now;
            var cacheEntryOptions = new
              MemoryCacheEntryOptions()
                .SetSlidingExpiration(
                TimeSpan.FromSeconds(50))
                .SetAbsoluteExpiration(
                TimeSpan.FromSeconds(100))
                .SetPriority(
                CacheItemPriority.NeverRemove);
            cache.Set("Weather", cacheEntry,
              cacheEntryOptions);
        }
        cache.TryGetValue("Weather", out cacheEntry);
        var rng = new Random();
        return Ok(from temp in Enumerable.Range(1, 5)
            select new
            {
                Date = cacheEntry,
                TemperatureC = rng.Next(-20, 55),
                Summary = "Rainy day"
            });
    }
}
```

As you can see, this code is self-explanatory and has an API using an in-memory cache.

One additional method that is available in `MemoryCache` is the integration of a callback method that is available through `RegisterPostEvictionCallback`. This is an extension method in `MemoryCacheEntryOptions` that accepts a `PostEvictionDelegate` delegate and a callback is triggered during cache entry expiration. The signature of `PostEvictionDelegate` is as follows:

```
public delegate void PostEvictionDelegate(object key, object
value, EvictionReason reason, object state);
```

So, that means the callback that we pass to `RegisterPostEvictionCallback` should follow the same signature, and as you can see, all the input parameters are self-explanatory. So, let's add a callback method and update `cacheEntryOptions` as follows:

```
private void EvictionCallback(object key, object value,
EvictionReason reason, object state)
{
    Debug.WriteLine(reason);
}
cacheEntryOptions.
RegisterPostEvictionCallback(EvictionCallback);
```

The code map of the weather controller is shown in the following screenshot:

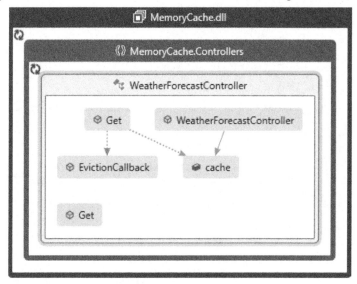

Figure 8.6 – Weather controller code map

Once we run this code, we can see that any subsequent calls to the controller after the absolute expiration of 50 seconds will trigger a callback and log the reason as `Expiration`. Once this is deployed to `AppService`, the callback is automatically triggered. Only for debugging purposes would we need to make another call.

Distributed cache

Having discussed in-memory cache, let's move on to the other cache platforms that can be configured for distributed caching. Distributed caching, just like distributed storage systems, distributes the cache data to multiple servers to primarily support scaling. In this section, we will look at the different types of distributed cache, starting with SQL.

SQL

Distributed caching can be implemented with various stores, one of them being SQL Server. The first step to using SQL Server for distributed caching is to create the required SQL table that will store cache entries. The entire setup for SQL as a distributed caching store involves the following steps:

1. Open a command line in the administrator prompt and run the following command to install the `dotnet-sql-cache` package globally:

   ```
   dotnet tool install --global dotnet-sql-cache
   ```

   This is how it appears:

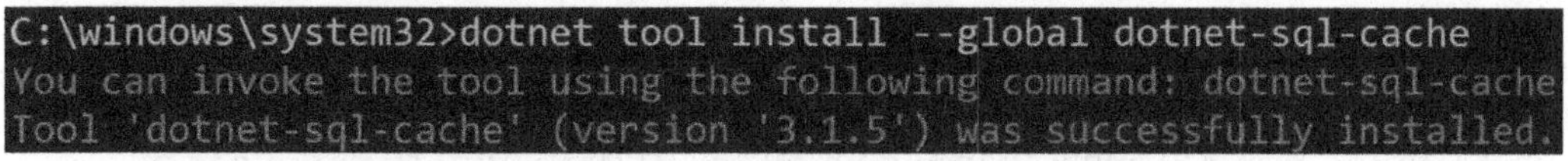

   ```
   C:\windows\system32>dotnet tool install --global dotnet-sql-cache
   You can invoke the tool using the following command: dotnet-sql-cache
   Tool 'dotnet-sql-cache' (version '3.1.5') was successfully installed.
   ```

   Figure 8.7 – Installing the sql-cache package using the .NET CLI

2. Create the required database (on-premises or using Azure SQL) and run the following command to create the table that stores cache data:

   ```
   dotnet sql-cache create "Data Source=.;Initial
   Catalog=DistributedCache;Integrated Security=true;" dbo
   cache
   ```

   In this command, we are passing the connection string of the database (update it accordingly when running it locally) as one parameter and the other is the name of the table (`cache` is the name of the table in the preceding snippet).

   ```
   C:\windows\system32>dotnet sql-cache create "Data Source=.;Initial Catalog=DistributedCache;Integrated Security
   =True;" dbo Cache
   Table and index were created successfully.
   ```

   Figure 8.8 – Creating a SQL table for distributed caching

3. Once the command has run successfully, if we open the SQL server in SSMS, we will see a table as shown in the following screenshot that has the columns and indexes required for optimization:

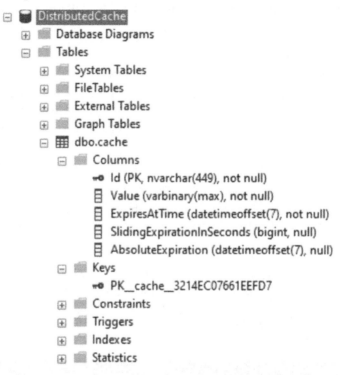

Figure 8.9 – Cache table in SQL distributed caching from SSMS

4. Create a Web API application and install NuGet Microsoft.Extensions. Caching.SqlServer (either through the **Package Manager Console (PMC)** or using the .NET CLI).

5. In Program.cs, add the following code:

```
builder.Services.AddDistributedSqlServerCache(options =>
{
    options.ConnectionString = "Data Source=.;Initial
    Catalog=DistributedCache;Integrated
    Security=true;";
    options.SchemaName = "dbo";
    options.TableName = "Cache";
});
```

6. To insert data into the cache, we need to make use of `IDistributedCache`, and the object will be created via constructor injection. So, clean up all the code in `WeatherForecastController` (the default controller created during the creation of the ASP.NET Core 6 Web API project) and add the following code (a Web API controller that has a `Get` method):

```
public class WeatherForecastController :
ControllerBase
    {
        private readonly IDistributedCache
          distributedCache;
        public WeatherForecastController(
          IDistributedCache distributedCache)
        {
            this.distributedCache = distributedCache;
        }
    }
```

7. Add the following `Get` method, which uses `distributedCache` and saves data to the cache store (SQL in this case):

```
[HttpGet]
public IActionResult Get()
    {
        DateTime? cacheEntry;
        if (distributedCache.Get("Weather") ==
          null)
        {
            cacheEntry = DateTime.Now;
            var cacheEntryOptions = new
              DistributedCacheEntryOptions()
                .SetSlidingExpiration(TimeSpan
                .FromSeconds(50))
                .SetAbsoluteExpiration(TimeSpan
                .FromSeconds(100));
            distributedCache.SetString("Weather",
              cacheEntry.ToString(),
              cacheEntryOptions);
```

```
    }
    var cachedDate =
      distributedCache.GetString("Weather");
    var rng = new Random();
    return Ok(from temp in Enumerable.Range(1,
      5)
              select new
              {
                  Date = cachedDate,
                  TemperatureC = rng.Next(-20,
                    55),
                  Summary = "Rainy day"
              });
    }
```

8. Run the application and we can see that the cache entry is getting stored in the SQL database, as shown in the following screenshot:

Figure 8.10 – Cache table in SQL distributed caching

As you can see, the code is very much like the `MemoryCache` code, except that we use `IDistributedCache` here to read/write data to cache and `DistributedCacheEntryOptions` for setting additional properties during cache entry creation.

A few recommendations for using SQL Server as a distributed caching store are as follows:

- SQL Server can be picked if the existing application does not support stores such as Redis. For example, an on-premises application that only integrates with SQL Server can easily extend SQL Server for caching purposes.

- The cache database should be different from the application database as using the same databases can cause bottlenecks and defeats the purpose of using a cache.

- The built-in implementation of `IDistributedCache` for SQL Server is `SqlServerCache` and does not support serializing a different schema for the caching table. Any customization has to be manually overridden by implementing `IDistributedCache` in a custom class.

Up until now, we have seen in-memory caching and distributed caching using SQL Server. In the next section, we will see how to use Redis (one of the recommended stores and a widely used store for caching) for distributed caching in .NET 6 applications.

Redis

Redis is an in-memory data store that is used for various purposes, such as databases, cache stores, and even as a message broker. The core data structure that Redis supports is key-value pairs where the value could be something as simple as a string, to a custom complex data type (nested classes). Redis works with an in-memory dataset and can also persist data to disk on a per-need basis. Redis also internally supports replication and automatic partitioning with Redis Cluster. With all these features available out of the box, it's an ideal store for distributed caching.

Azure provides a managed instance for Redis servers known as **Azure Cache for Redis**, and just like any other PaaS service, it is managed by Microsoft. This allows application developers to integrate it as is and leave the infrastructure overhead of maintaining, scaling, and upgrading the Redis server to Microsoft. Azure Cache for Redis can be used for distributed caching and can be easily integrated into .NET 6 applications using the following steps:

1. First, create an instance of Azure Cache for Redis as outlined at `https://docs.microsoft.com/en-in/azure/azure-cache-for-redis/quickstart-create-redis`. Navigate to **Access keys** and copy the value under **Primary connection string**, as shown in the following screenshot:

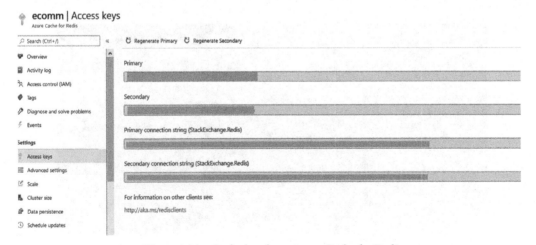

Figure 8.11 – Cache key from Azure Cache for Redis

2.   Create an ASP.NET Core 6 Web API application and install the NuGet `Microsoft.Extensions.Caching.StackExchangeRedis` package.

3.   In `Program.cs`, add the following code:

```
builder.Services.AddStackExchangeRedisCache(
    options =>
    {
        options.Configuration =
            "<Connection string copied in
                step 1>";
    });
```

4.   Update the default `WeatherForecastController` controller with the same code as shown in the previous *SQL* section.

5.   Run the application and we can see that data gets stored in the cache for 10 seconds. Any calls within 50 seconds to this API will retrieve data from the cache.

6.   Azure Cache for Redis also comes with a console that allows us to query the Redis server using Redis CLI commands. The console can be found in the Azure portal by navigating to the overview left menu of the Redis instance. Querying it for the `Weather` key will give us the results shown in the following screenshot:

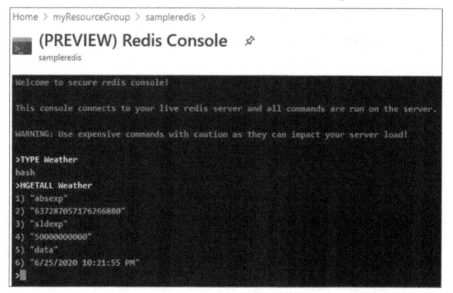

Figure 8.12 – Redis console

If we go with the Premium tier of Azure Cache for Redis, it also supports multiple shards to support higher volumes of data and geo-replication for high availability.

7. Additionally, to add/remove keys from the cache store, there are the `GetAsync` and `SetAsync` methods, which can be used to store more complex types or any type other than string. However, these methods return/accept `Task<byte[]>`, so the application needs to handle serialization/deserialization, which can be seen in the reusable caching library.

Redis is the most preferred cache store for enterprise applications, and in our e-commerce application, we will use Azure Cache for Redis as our cache store. Some additional information about Azure Cache for Redis can be found at `https://docs.microsoft.com/en-in/azure/azure-cache-for-redis/`.

Other providers

As you can see, distributed caching in .NET 6 applications is driven by `IDistributedCache`, and whichever store's implementation is injected in the `Program` class cache store is configured accordingly. Additionally, there are two more providers that .NET 6 has a built-in implementation for:

- **NCache**: This is a third-party cache store that is developed in .NET/.NET Core and has an implementation of `IDistributedCache`. NCache can be integrated like Redis or SQL. However, the NCache server needs to be configured locally for development and can be configured in IaaS using virtual machines or PaaS using app services.

- **Distributed memory cache** (`AddDistributedMemoryCache`): This is another built-in implementation of `IDistributedCache` and can be used similarly. It can be used for unit testing. Since it's not a distributed cache and uses process memory, it is not recommended for multiple application server scenarios. The only difference between `AddMemoryCache(IMemoryCache)` and `AddDistributedMemoryCache(IDistributedCache)` is that the latter one requires serialization to store complex data. So, if there is a type that cannot be serialized and needs to be cached, go with `IMemoryCache`, otherwise go with `IDistributedCache`.

In enterprise applications, `IDistributedCache` can address all the caching layer implementation, and a combination of in-memory cache for a development/testing environment and Redis for a production environment would be ideal. If your application is hosted on a single server, you can go with an in-memory cache but that's very rare for production applications, hence it is most recommended to go with distributed caching.

So, based on all the principles and patterns that we've discussed, we will design a cache abstraction layer to be used in an e-commerce application, which is discussed in the next section.

Designing a cache abstraction layer using distributed caching

In enterprise applications, it's always good to have a wrapper class on top of an underlying cache implementation as it abstracts the core logic of caching and can also be used as one single class that holds application-wide default cache entry options.

We will be implementing a cache wrapper class with an underlying store as Azure Cache for Redis using the `IDistributedCache` implementation. It's a .NET Standard 2.1 class library; the source code for this library is available in the `Packt.Ecommerce.Caching` project. Any class that wants to cache data should inject `IDistributedCacheService` using constructor injection and can call the following various methods:

- `AddOrUpdateCacheAsync<T>`: Adds or updates cache entries of type `T` asynchronously

- `AddOrUpdateCacheStringAsync`: Adds or updates cache entries of the string type asynchronously

- `GetCacheAsync<T>`: Gets cache entries of type `T` asynchronously

- `GetCacheStringAsync`: Gets cache entries of the string type asynchronously

- `RefreshCacheAsync`: Refreshes cache entries asynchronously

- `RemoveCacheAsync`: Removes cache entries asynchronously

`DistributedCacheService` is the wrapper class that inherits `IDistributedCacheService` and implements all the preceding methods. Additionally, `IDistributedCache` and `DistributedCacheEntryOptions` are configured in this class to use distributed caching.

For serialization and deserialization, we will use `System.Text.Json`, a custom `IEntitySerializer` interface, and the `EntitySerializer` class is created with the following methods:

- `SerializeEntityAsync<T>`: Serializes the specified object to a byte array asynchronously

- `DeserializeEntityAsync<T>`: Deserializes the specified stream asynchronously

The `IEntitySerializer` implementation is injected into the `DistributedCacheService` class using constructor injection and is used for serialization and deserialization.

> **Note**
>
> Please refer to the *Serialization performance comparison* article, which talks about benchmarking various serializers. You can find it at `https://maxondev.com/serialization-performance-comparison-c-net-formats-frameworks-xmldatacontractserializer-xmlserializer-binaryformatter-json-newtonsoft-servicestack-text/`.

The implementation of `DistributedCacheService` and `EntitySerializer` follows all the asynchronous principles discussed in *Chapter 4, Threading and Asynchronous Operations*, and the configuration as explained in *Chapter 6, Configuration in .NET 6*.

Finally, in an API/MVC application, perform these steps:

1. Install the NuGet `Microsoft.Extensions.Caching.StackExchangeRedis` package.

2. Configure caching by adding the following code snippet to `Program.cs`:

```
if (this.Configuration.
GetValue<bool>("AppSettings:UseRedis"))
{
    builder.Services.AddStackExchangeRedisCache(
      options =>
    {
        options.Configuration = this.Configuration
          .GetConnectionString("Redis");
    });
}
else
{
    services.AddDistributedMemoryCache();
}
```

3. From a configuration standpoint, two properties are added to `appsettings.`
    `json`, as shown here:

```
"ConnectionStrings": {
  //removed other values for brevity
  "Redis": "" //Azure Cache for Redis connection
             //string.
},
"AppSettings": {
  //removed other values for brevity
  "UseRedis": false //Flag to fallback to in memory
  //distributed caching, usually false for local
  //development.
},
```

Any class that wants to cache data needs to add a reference to the `Packt.Ecommerce.`
`Caching` project and inject `IDistributedCacheService`, and can call the
aforementioned methods to read/update/insert data in the cache store. The following is a
code snippet of a method using the cache service:

```
public class Country
  {
    public int Id { get; set; }
    public string Name { get; set; }
  }

    public async Task<Country> GetCountryAsync()
      {
        var country = await
        this.cacheService.GetAsync<Country>("Country"); //
cacheservice is of Type IDistributedCacheService and is
// injected using constructor injection.
        if (country == null)
          {
            country = await
              this.countryRepository.GetCountryAsync(); //
Retrieving data from database using Repository pattern.
            if (country != null)
              {
```

```
            await this.cacheService
              .AddOrUpdateAsync<Country>("Country",
              country, TimeSpan.FromMinutes(5));
          }
        }
      return country;
    }
```

Here, we are using the cache-aside pattern and checking for the Country key in the cache store first. If found, return it from the function, otherwise retrieve it from the database and insert it into the cache, and then return from the function. We will heavily use the cache service in *Chapter 10, Creating an ASP.NET Core 6 Web API*.

As you can see, we have used a few of the patterns that we discussed in earlier sections. There are also a few additional considerations discussed in the next section, which need to be kept in mind while designing the cache layer in an enterprise application.

Caching considerations

Having a cache layer is critical for improving performance and scalability in enterprise applications. Hence, the following are a few factors that need to be considered while developing the caching layer:

- If we are building a new application, then Azure Cache for Redis can be the starting point using the IDistributedCache implementation as it can easily be plumbed into the application with a few lines of code. However, this comes at a cost that needs to be evaluated.

- For an existing project, the current infrastructure plays a critical role and SQL can be the default choice if SQL Server is already being used as a data store. However, it's good to benchmark the performance of SQL against Redis, and a decision can be taken accordingly.

- Having a wrapper class on the underlying cache store is a good approach as it decouples the application from the cache store and makes the code more flexible and easily maintained in case of future changes in the cache store.

- The methods of `IMemoryCache` and `IDistributedCache` are not thread-safe. For example, say a thread queries a key from the cache and finds it isn't there in the cache, and falls back to the original data store. While data is retrieved from the original store if another thread queries the same key, it won't wait for the first thread to finish reading from the database. The second thread will also end up falling back to the database. So, thread safety needs to be handled explicitly, possibly in the wrapper class.

- Response caching should be implemented along with application caching for even more optimization.

- **Entity Tag (ETag)** response headers can be further used to improve the reusability of cached data. ETag is **Global Unique Identifier (GUID)**-generated while caching data on the server and is sent as a response header. This value is sent back to the server as part of the `If-None-Match` request header and if there is a match, the server returns `304` (no change) and the client can reuse the cached version of the data. For ETag, there is no built-in implementation on the server side, so a filter or middleware can be used to implement server-side logic.

- Although we used JSON serialization in our implementation, there are other formats, such as BSON or protocol buffers, that should be evaluated for serialization and deserialization.

Just like any other component in application development for caching, there is no one-size-fits-all solution. So, the preceding points should be evaluated and an appropriate caching solution implemented accordingly.

Summary

In this chapter, we learned about various caching techniques, patterns, and their benefits in improving application performance. Furthermore, we learned about HTTP caching, how response caching can be integrated into an API response, and further various available caching providers and their integration with .NET 6 applications. We also learned how to implement distributed caching using `IDistributedCache` and built a cache abstraction layer that will be used in subsequent chapters for caching requirements. Some of the key information and skills that we learned about along the way were why and when caching is needed and how to implement caching in .NET 6 applications.

In the next chapter, we will look at various data stores and providers in .NET 6 and their integration with .NET 6 applications.

Questions

1. Which of the following values for the `Cache-Control` header allows the response to be stored in any server (client/server/proxy)?

   a. `Private`

   b. `Public`

   c. `No-cache`

   Answer: b

2. In a multiple-application server scenario, which of the following caching platforms should we choose?

   a. Distributed caching

   b. In-memory caching

   Answer: a

3. True or false: In the cache-aside pattern, data is first updated in the cache store and then in the underlying data store.

   a. True

   b. False

   Answer: b

4. Which of the following caches is best suited to store static files and image files and supports geo-replication?

   a. Web server caching

   b. Application caching

   c. Content Delivery Network (CDN)

   Answer: c

Further reading

You can read more about caching here:

- `https://github.com/Alachisoft/NCache`
- `https://redis.io/`
- `https://aws.amazon.com/redis/`
- `https://docs.microsoft.com/en-us/azure/azure-cache-for-redis/cache-configure#redis-console`
- `Features (terracotta.org)`

Part 3: Developing Enterprise Applications

In this part, we will develop different layers of the application. We will start with the data layer and then develop the API and web layers. During the course of this development, we will integrate the libraries for cross-cutting concerns developed in *Part 2*.

This part comprises the following chapters:

- *Chapter 9, Working with Data in .NET 6*
- *Chapter 10, Creating an ASP.NET Core 6 Web API*
- *Chapter 11, Creating an ASP.NET Core 6 Web Application*

9
Working with Data in .NET 6

One of the essential components for any application is the ability to persist data to a permanent data store; some forethought in picking the right persistent store can help a system scale better in the future.

One of the common operations in any application is to log in to the system, perform some reads/updates, log off, and then come back later to see whether the changes were retained. Databases play a significant role in persisting these actions, which are typically called **user transactions**. Apart from transactional data, for monitoring and debugging purposes, an application may additionally need to store logging data and auditing data, such as who modified the date. An important step for designing any such application is to understand the requirements and design the database accordingly. It's also important to choose/design a database according to various data retention requirements and any data protection policies, such as the **General Data Protection Regulation (GDPR)**.

There can be multiple data providers for an application, such as a **Structured Query Language (SQL)** data provider, NoSQL data provider, and file data provider. In this chapter, we will discuss various data providers that can be used for storage and data handling in .NET 6. We will cover the following topics:

- Introduction to data
- Disk, files, and directories

- SQL, Azure Cosmos DB, and Azure Storage

- Working with EF Core

- Designing a Data Access service using Azure Cosmos DB

Technical requirements

A basic understanding of .NET Core, C#, Azure, and the .NET **command-line interface (CLI)** is required.

The code files for this chapter can be found at the following link: `https://github.com/PacktPublishing/Enterprise-Application-Development-with-C-10-and-.NET-6-Second-Edition/tree/main/Chapter08`.

The instructions for the code can be found here: `https://github.com/PacktPublishing/Enterprise-Application-Development-with-C-10-and-.NET-6-Second-Edition/tree/main/Enterprise%20Application`.

Introduction to data

Any web application, be it a content management system, social networking platform, or e-commerce application, needs to persist data to a permanent store so that users can retrieve, consume, and process data as needed. In *Chapter 8*, *All You Need to Know about Caching*, we discussed using cache stores; however, cache stores are temporary storage and data still needs to be persisted in permanent storage. So, we need a store that not only supports various **Create/Read/Update/Delete** (**CRUD**) operations on different entities but also supports high availability and recovers any data in case of an outage, that is, disaster recovery.

One of the key criteria for better system design is to have a data model designed at an early stage of the system. The data model should try to define all the possible entities that are required for the system to function and interact between various entities. Having a data model defined early on in the system design helps in identifying the right strategies on how to manage data and what data store can be used, and in deciding various replication/partition strategies.

Two commonly classified data stores are explained in the following sections.

Relational database management system (RDBMS)

Relational databases store data in tables. Each entity is defined as one or more tables and a database is defined using multiple tables. The process of segregating tables into multiple tables is called **normalization**. The relations between various tables are defined by foreign key constraints. Properties of entities are defined as columns, and multiple entities of the same type are stored as rows. Some commonly used relational databases are Microsoft SQL Server, MySQL, PostgresSQL, and Oracle.

A typical relational database to store employee information could possibly have an employee table defining various properties of employees, such as name, employee ID, and so on, and columns with employee ID as the primary key. Multiple employees are stored in separate rows in this table. Any properties of employees can further be normalized into a separate table; for example, an employee's projects can be stored in a separate table (as there can be more than one project), say, employeeproject, and can be linked to the employee table using the employee ID, as shown in the following diagram:

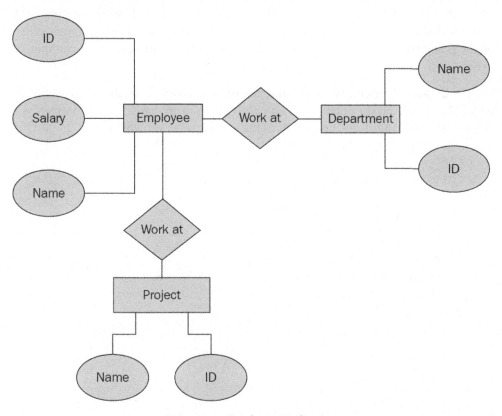

Figure 9.1 – Employee ER diagram

The following are a few key characteristics of the relational database:

- Relational databases are queried using SQL.

- Tables mostly have a well-defined schema and constraints and are less likely to change.

- All the transactions have **Atomicity/Consistency/Isolation/Durability (ACID)** properties, hence maintaining the data integrity and consistency.

- As data is normalized, redundancy is minimized.

- Relational databases usually support vertical scaling, that is, scaling up (they do support replication, but it is an expensive operation compared to replication in NoSQL databases).

NoSQL

Another kind of data store is NoSQL databases, which store data in an unstructured format where the data doesn't need to have a predefined schema. Most commonly, data is either stored as a key-value pair (such as in Redis), stored as a document (such as in MongoDB and CouchDB), or stored as a graph using a graph structure (for example, in Neo4j).

If we take the same employee example and persist it in a NoSQL database, such as MongoDB, we will end up storing it in something such as an `employee` collection, with each document storing all the properties of the employee, as shown here:

```
{
  "employee": [
    {
      "employeeid": 1,
      "name": "Ravindra",
      "salary": 100,
      "Projects": [
        {
          "id": 1,
                "name": "project1",
        },
        {

                "id": 2,
              "name": "project2",
```

```
            }
        ]
      }
    ]
}
```

The following are a few key characteristics of NoSQL databases:

- Entities do not necessarily need to support a fixed schema and, at any point in time, additional properties can be added.

- They are a good fit for unstructured data, for example, storing the location in a ride-sharing app.

- They can easily support horizontal scaling at a much lower cost compared to relational databases.

- Data is highly redundant; however, that gives a significant performance boost, as data is readily available without performing joins across tables.

Azure Cosmos DB is one such cloud-managed NoSQL database that we will use in our e-commerce application as a data store.

Let's look at the various storage options in detail in the next section.

SQL, Azure Cosmos DB, and Azure Storage

Earlier, we talked about the broader classification of data stores into RDBMSs and NoSQL. In this section, let's get into the details of some of the data providers available in the Microsoft ecosystem and their integration with .NET 6. There is a wide variety of providers, including SQL, Azure Cosmos DB, and Azure Storage, and the selection of data providers is completely driven by the application needs. However, in real life, application requirements evolve quite a bit, so the key is to abstract your data framework implementation with the business layer and **user interface** (**UI**), which further helps in evolving the design as required. With that, let's look at our first data provider, SQL, in the next section.

SQL Server

One of the dominant databases in the RDBMS market is Microsoft SQL Server, popularly known as SQL Server, which uses SQL to interact with the database. SQL Server supports all the RDBMS-based entities, such as tables, views, stored procedures, and indexes, and primarily works on the Windows environment. However, from SQL Server 2017 onward, it supports both Windows and Linux environments.

The primary component of SQL Server is its database engine, which takes care of processing queries and managing data in files. Apart from the database engine, SQL Server comes with various data management tools, such as the following:

- **SQL Server Management Studio (SSMS)**: To connect to SQL Server and perform operations such as creating a database, monitoring a database, querying databases, and backing up databases
- **SQL Server Integration Service (SSIS)**: For data integration and transformation
- **SQL Server Analysis Services (SSAS)**: For data analysis
- **SQL Server Reporting Services (SSRS)**: For reporting and visualization

To configure SQL Server on a local machine, we need to install one of the editions of SQL Server that installs the database engine and one or more preceding components. Installation typically involves downloading the installer and installing it either through the **graphical user interface (GUI)** or command line. For more details on installation, refer to `https://docs.microsoft.com/en-us/sql/database-engine/install-windows/install-sql-server?view=sql-server-ver15`.

> **Tip**
> There are also other editions of SQL Server such as the Developer edition and Express edition, which are lightweight and free and can be downloaded from `https://www.microsoft.com/en-in/sql-server/sql-server-downloads`.

Although on-premises, SQL Server has been widely used; there is always overhead to managing databases, upgrades, and so on, and that's where Microsoft has come up with Azure SQL, which is a fully managed **Platform as a Service (PaaS)** component that runs on the same database engine as on-premises SQL Server.

Azure SQL comes with the following variants:

- **Azure SQL Database (single database):** This is a managed database server that allows you to create a fully isolated database with dedicated resources.

- **Azure SQL Database (elastic pool):** Elastic pool allows you to run multiple single databases in a predefined pool of resources (in terms of CPU, memory, and **input/output (I/O)**) on a single server. It is ideal for businesses that have multiple databases with a mix of low and high usage. The advantage of using an elastic pool in such situations is that a database that needs more CPU usage can utilize it during high demand and release it when demand is low. The ideal situation to use an elastic pool is when there is a set of databases and their consumption is unpredictable. Anytime you see a database consistently consuming the same set of resources, it can be moved out of the elastic pool into a single database and vice versa.

- **Azure SQL Managed Instance:** This model provides a way for the seamless migration of on-premises SQL infrastructure to Azure SQL without re-architecting the on-premises applications and allows you to take advantage of PaaS. This is ideal for applications that have huge on-premises database infrastructure and need to migrate to the cloud without too much operational overhead.

- **SQL Server on VM (Windows/Linux):** SQL VMs come under the **Infrastructure as a Service (IaaS)** category and are very similar to on-premises SQL Server, except that VMs are on Azure instead of your local network.

> **Tip**
>
> It's recommended to install SSMS for performing various operations on SQL Server (on-premises or the cloud), as it supports all the database operations. There is also Azure Data Studio, which is lightweight and can connect to on-premise or cloud SQL Server and can be downloaded from `https://docs.microsoft.com/en-us/sql/azure-data-studio/download-azure-data-studio?view=sql-server-ver15`.

From a .NET 6 application standpoint, connecting to Azure SQL is the same as connecting to on-premises SQL Server. You can use ADO.NET, which we import using `System.Data.SqlClient` and then use the `SqlConnection` object to connect to SQL; then, use the `SqlCommand` object to execute the SQL query and the `SQLReader` class to return the values. Apart from this, we can use an **object-relational mapping (ORM)** such as **Entity Framework Core (EF Core)** to work with Azure SQL, which is discussed in the *Working with EF Core* section.

So, in this section, we have briefly covered Azure SQL. However, I would recommend reviewing all the functionality of Azure SQL here: `https://docs.microsoft.com/en-us/azure/azure-sql/`. For more samples please refer to `https://github.com/microsoft/sql-server-samples`.

With this, let's move on to Azure Cosmos DB, the database our e-commerce application will use as a persistent store.

Azure Cosmos DB

Azure Cosmos DB is a fully managed (PaaS) NoSQL, globally distributed, and highly scalable database. One of the key things about Azure Cosmos DB is its multi-modeled nature, which helps in passing data in various formats, such as JSON and BSON, using different API models, such as SQL, MongoDB, and Gremlin. Developers have the flexibility to query the database using the API they are comfortable with. For example, SQL developers can continue to query the database using SQL query syntax, MongoDB developers can continue to query the database using MongoDB syntax, and so on. Under the hood, Azure Cosmos DB stores the database in a format known as **atom-record-sequence** (**ARS**) and exposes data as an API depending on the mode selected during the creation of the database.

Another important thing about Azure Cosmos DB is its capability to automatically index all the data, independent of the API model that is used. All this happens without developers additionally creating an index, so enabling the faster retrieval of data.

Azure Cosmos DB supports the following APIs to perform operations on the database, which we choose while creating the database:

- **Core (SQL) API**: This is the default API that can be used to query the database; queries will have a syntax of SQL queries with I/O format in JSON. A typical query using the Core SQL API would look as follows: `SELECT * FROM product WHERE product.Name = ' Mastering enterprise application development Book'`.

- **MongoDB API**: This API is built on MongoDB's wire protocol to seamlessly integrate with MongoDB client SDKs, drivers, and tools. This API is ideal for applications that were already integrated with MongoDB and migrated to Azure Cosmos DB or are a right fit for teams that have developers that are used to the MongoDB query language. This most recent version of this API supports MongoDB server version 3.6, and a typical query connection between Azure Cosmos DB and the Mongo API will look as follows: `db.product.find({"Name": 'Mastering enterprise application development Book'})`. Just like MongoDB, data is represented in BSON.

- **Gremlin (graph) API**: This API supports using the Gremlin language to query and traverse data in graph format. This is ideal for situations where data can be represented in the form of a graph and can be queried through their relationships. A typical example can be a recommendation engine that can establish the relationship between two entities and come up with a recommendation.

Apart from these, there is the Cassandra API, which uses the **Cassandra Query Language (CQL)** to operate on databases, and then the Table API, which can be used by applications built on top of Azure Table storage as their data store.

As you can see, there are quite a number of APIs and more are getting added. Choosing the right API depends purely on the application requirements; however, the following few points can be used to narrow down the choice:

- If it's a new application, go with the Core (SQL) API.

- If it's an existing application built on NoSQL, choose the relevant API based on the underlying data store. For example, if the existing database is MongoDB, choose the Mongo API, and so on.

- For handling a specific scenario, such as establishing relationships between data, go with the Gremlin API.

For our enterprise application, since we are building this application from scratch, we will go with the Core (SQL) API as our API to interact with Azure Cosmos DB.

Let's create a simple console application to start with and perform a few operations on Azure Cosmos DB, and we will later reuse these concepts in building our Data Access service:

1. To start with, we need to have an Azure Cosmos DB account, so sign in to the Azure portal, click **Create resource**, and select **Databases | Azure Cosmos DB**.

2. This will open the **Create Azure Cosmos DB Account** page. Fill in the details as shown in the following screenshot and click **Review + create**. This is the page where we select the API we want to choose, which is the Core (SQL) API in our case:

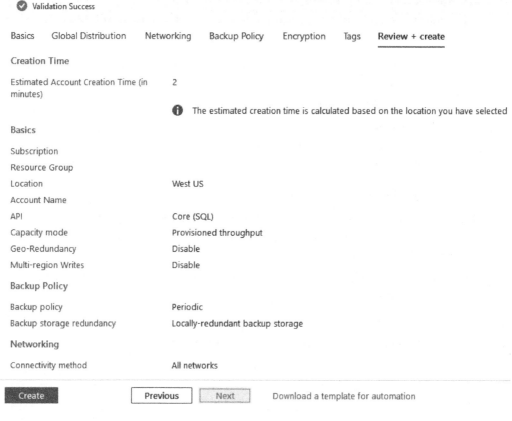

Figure 9.2 – Create Azure Cosmos DB Account page

3. Once the account is created, navigate to **Azure Cosmos DB Account | Keys**. Copy the **URI** and **PRIMARY KEY** values.

4. Open the command line and create a console application by using the following command:

```
dotnet new console --framework net6.0 --name
EcommerceSample
```

5. Navigate to the EcommerceSample folder and install the Azure Cosmos DB SDK using the following command:

```
dotnet add package Microsoft.Azure.Cosmos -s https://api.
nuget.org/v3/index.json
```

6. At this stage, we can open the folder in VS Code. Once we open the folder in VS Code, it will look as shown in the following screenshot:

Figure 9.3 – EcommerceSample in VS Code

7. Open Program.cs and add the following static variables to the Program class that will hold the **URI** and **PRIMARY KEY** values that were copied in *Step 3*:

```
string Uri = "YOUR URI HERE ";
string PrimaryKey = "YOUR PRIMARY KEY HERE";
```

8. Now, let's add code to create an object of the `CosmosClient` class and use that to create an Azure Cosmos DB database. Subsequently, this object will be used to communicate with our Azure Cosmos DB database. As `CosmosClient` implements `IDisposable`, we will create it inside a `using` block so that the object can be disposed of automatically after the `using` block. Once you run this code and navigate to **Azure Cosmos resource | Data Explorer** in the Azure portal, you can see that a database with the name `Ecommerce` will be created. As we have created our Azure Cosmos DB account using the Core (SQL) API, this database will support querying in SQL syntax:

```
using (CosmosClient cosmosClient = new CosmosClient(Uri,
  PrimaryKey))
{
  DatabaseResponse createDatabaseResponse
= await cosmosClient.CreateDatabaseIfNotExistsAsync
("ECommerce");
  Database database = createDatabaseResponse.Database;
}
```

9. Now, let's create a container that is analogous to a table in SQL by adding the following code after `createDatabaseResponse`. As we are using `CreateDatabaseIfNotExistsAsync` to create the database, running the same code will not cause any exceptions:

```
var containerProperties = new ContainerProperties
("Products", "/Name");
var createContainerResponse = await
database.CreateContainerIfNotExistsAsync(
containerProperties, 10000);
var productContainer = createContainerResponse.
Container;
```

Once we run this code, we can see in the Azure portal that a container with the name `Products` is created under the `Ecommerce` database:

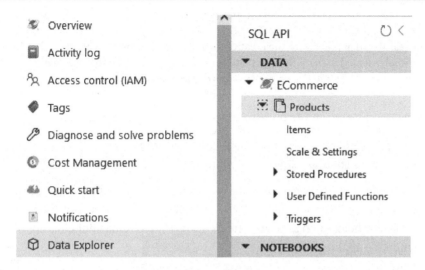

Figure 9.4 – Products container

A container is a unit in Azure Cosmos DB that is horizontally partitioned and replicated across multiple regions. In the preceding code, we have passed `ContainerProperties` while creating a container, and you can see that one of the values is `Name`, which is nothing but a partition key.

Partitioning is one of the key features of Azure Cosmos DB that segregates data within a container into multiple logical partitions based on the partition key, that is, all the items with the same partition key are part of the same logical partition. Using a partition key, Azure Cosmos DB achieves horizontal scaling of the database, therefore, satisfying the scalability and performance needs of the application.

Choosing a partition key is a key design decision, as it will significantly help the database to scale and better perform. Also, the partition key cannot be changed and has to be defined during the creation of the container. The following few points can be kept in mind when choosing the partition key:

- It should have a maximum number of unique values; the higher the number of unique values, the better the partitioning will be. For example, if we are creating a container for products, the product ID or name could be the partition key as these two attributes can uniquely identify most products. Under the hood, if a product name is chosen for the partition key and there are 100 products internally, it is represented by 100 logical containers in Azure Cosmos DB. Here, the product category can also be a partition key but, before choosing that as the partition key, we need to evaluate the sample data and decide based on the requirements.

- If there is no obvious unique choice, we can pick the most used field in the filtering query, so basically, a column that is very often used in the `where` clause.

Tip

In real-world applications, the creation of an Azure Cosmos DB account should be implemented using ARM templates or using Terraform so that templates can be easily integrated with **continuous deployment** (**CD**).

With this, let's add some data to our product container and query it:

1. We will add this entity based on the following sample JSON. Based on the product category, there could be different attributes.

    For example, if the product category is Books, there would be values in fields such as Authors and Format; however, if the category is Clothing, there would be values for fields such as Size and Color. This schema could be reused in our e-commerce application:

    ```
    {
        "Id": "Book.1",
        "Name": "Mastering enterprise application
            development Book",
        "Category": "Books",
        "Price": 100,
        "Quantity": 100,
        "CreatedDate": "20-02-2020T00:00:00Z",
        "ImageUrls": [],
        "Rating": [
          {"Stars": 5, "Percentage": 95},
          {"Stars": 4, "Percentage": 5}
        ],
        "Format": ["PDF","Hard Cover"],
        "Authors": ["Rishabh Verma","Neha Shrivastava",
            "Ravindra Akela","Bhupesh Guptha"],
        "Size": [],
        "Color": []
    }
    ```

2. Now, let's create **plain old CLR objects (POCOs)** that can be serialized to the preceding JSON. We would need two classes to represent them: one for the *product* and one for the *rating*, which is a child class of `Product`. One of the mandatory fields for any entity in Azure Cosmos DB with the Core (SQL) API is the `id` field, which is something like a primary key. So, it is necessary for our parent models to define the `id` field. These classes would look like the following:

```
public class Rating{
    public int Stars { get; set; }
    public int Percentage { get; set; }
}
public class Product{
    [JsonProperty(PropertyName = "id")]
    public string ProductId { get; set; }
    public string Name { get; set; }
    public string Category { get; set; }
    public int Price { get; set; }
    public int Quantity { get; set; }
    public DateTime CreatedDate { get; set; }
    public List<string>  ImageUrls { get; set; }
    public List<Rating> Rating { get; set; }
    public List<string> Format { get; set; }
    public List<string> Authors { get; set; }
    public List<int> Size { get; set; }
    public List<string> Color { get; set; }
}
```

3. Now, let's create the following object of the `Product` class and insert it into the database:

```
Product book = new Product()
{
    ProductId = "Book.1", Category = "Books", Price =
    100,
    Name = "Mastering enterprise application
    development Book",
    Rating = new List<Rating>() { new Rating { Stars =
    5, Percentage = 95 }, new Rating { Stars = 4,
```

```
    Percentage = 5 } },
    Format = new List<string>() { "PDF", "Hard Cover"
    },
    Authors = new List<string>() { "Suneel", "Arun",
      "Ravindra", "Bhupesh" }
};
```

4. Now, we will call the `CreateItemAsync` method using the
    `productContainer` object, as shown in the following code snippet. (There are
    other ways to retrieve records from the database, one of which is shown in the next
    point.) Also, we should ensure that an object with the same `ProductId` value isn't
    already present:

```
try
{
    // Check if item it exists.
    ItemResponse<Product> productBookResponse = await
      productContainer.ReadItemAsync<Product>(
      book.ProductId, new PartitionKey(book.Name));
}
catch (CosmosException ex) when (ex.StatusCode == System.
Net.HttpStatusCode.NotFound)
{
    ItemResponse<Product> productBookResponse = await
      productContainer.CreateItemAsync<Product>(book,
      new PartitionKey(book.Name));
    Console.WriteLine($"Created item
      {productBookResponse.Resource.ProductId}");
}
```

Once we run this code, data should be inserted into the `Ecommerce` database
under the `Products` container.

5. If we want to query this record other than the way mentioned in the previous point,
    we can use the following code to query the database. As you can see, the syntax is
    very similar to querying data from a SQL database:

```
string getAllProductsByBooksCAtegory = "SELECT * FROM p
WHERE p.Category = 'Books'";
QueryDefinition query = new
```

```
QueryDefinition(getAllProductsByBooksCAtegory);
FeedIterator<Product> iterator = productContainer.
GetItemQueryIterator<Product>(query);
while (iterator.HasMoreResults)
{
    FeedResponse<Product> result = await
      iterator.ReadNextAsync();
    foreach (Product product in result)
    {
        Console.WriteLine($"Book retrived -
        {product.Name}");
    }
}
```

Similarly, `ContainerClass` provides all the relevant methods that can be used for various CRUD operations. All those APIs can be found here: `https://docs.microsoft.com/en-us/dotnet/api/microsoft.azure.cosmos.container?view=azure-dotnet`.

With this foundation, we will design the data model required for our e-commerce application and the relevant data service layer to be consumed by various APIs. Up to now, we have seen SQL and NoSQL providers. Let's see what other options we have to persist data.

Azure Storage

Azure Storage is a highly available and scalable data store that supports storing data in various formats, including files. Primarily, Azure Storage supports the following four types of data:

- **Azure Table**: A NoSQL implementation that supports persisting schemaless data.

- **Azure Blob**: Blobs are unstructured data that are suitable for applications that have lots of files to upload, download, or stream.

- **Azure Queue**: This allows you to queue a message in any serializable format and can then be processed by a service. Queues are ideal for scenarios that have lots of service-to-service communication and act as a persistent layer for messages.

- **Azure Files/Azure Disk**: A data store for files and ideal for systems that are built on native file APIs.

The following are a few points that make Azure Storage one of the important components of application development:

- **High availability**: Data stored in Azure Storage gives out-of-the-box support for replication across data centers/regions, which further ensures that hardware failure in one region doesn't result in losing data.

- **Performance**: Out-of-the-box support for CDN integration that helps to cache and load data (especially static files) from locations (edge servers) closer to the user and further improves the performance. In addition to this, the storage type can be upgraded to premium storage, which takes advantage of SSDs to further speed up disk I/O and improve performance.

- **Fully managed**: Hardware is fully managed by Azure for any updates/maintenance.

- **Security**: All the data stored on disks is encrypted and access to the data in Azure Storage further supports private, public, and anonymous modes.

- **Pay as you go**: Just like all other Azure services, Azure Storage also supports a pay-as-you-go model based on the size of the data/operations.

Azure Storage accounts

Let's create a simple console application that uploads a file to Blob and downloads the file from Blob. To communicate with Azure Storage services, the prerequisite is to create an Azure Storage account that provides access to all Azure Storage services and gives us access to the data stored in Azure Storage over HTTP/HTTPS by a unique namespace to Azure Storage. To create an Azure Storage account, take the following steps:

1. Sign in to the Azure portal, click **Create resource**, and select **Storage Account**. This will open the **Create storage account** page. Fill in the details as shown in the following screenshot and click **Review + create**:

Create storage account

and redundant. Azure Storage includes Azure Blobs (objects), Azure Data Lake Storage Gen2, Azure Files, Azure Queues, and Azure Tables. The cost of your storage account depends on the usage and the options you choose below.
Learn more about Azure storage accounts ⬚

Project details

Select the subscription to manage deployed resources and costs. Use resource groups like folders to organize and manage all your resources.

Subscription *	▮▮▮▮▮▮▮▮ ∨
└─── Resource group *	ecommsample ∨
	Create new

Instance details

The default deployment model is Resource Manager, which supports the latest Azure features. You may choose to deploy using the classic deployment model instead. Choose classic deployment model

Storage account name * ⓘ	ecommercepackt ✓
Location *	(US) East US ∨
Performance ⓘ	◉ Standard ◯ Premium
Account kind ⓘ	StorageV2 (general purpose v2) ∨
Replication ⓘ	Read-access geo-redundant storage (RA-GRS) ∨

[Review + create]   [< Previous]   [Next : Networking >]

Figure 9.5 – Creating an Azure Storage account

There are two important properties **Account Kind** and **Replication** for Standard tier. For **Account Kind,** we have the following possible values:

- **StorageV2 (general purpose v2)**: The latest version of the account type, which gives access to all storage types, such as files, blobs, and queues. This is preferable for newly created storage accounts.

- **Storage (general purpose v1)**: An older version of the account type, which gives access to all storage types, such as files, blobs, and queues.

- **BlobStorage**: An account type that only supports blob storage.

The other is **Replication**, which supports replication of the storage data across data centers/regions. Possible values are shown in the following screenshot:

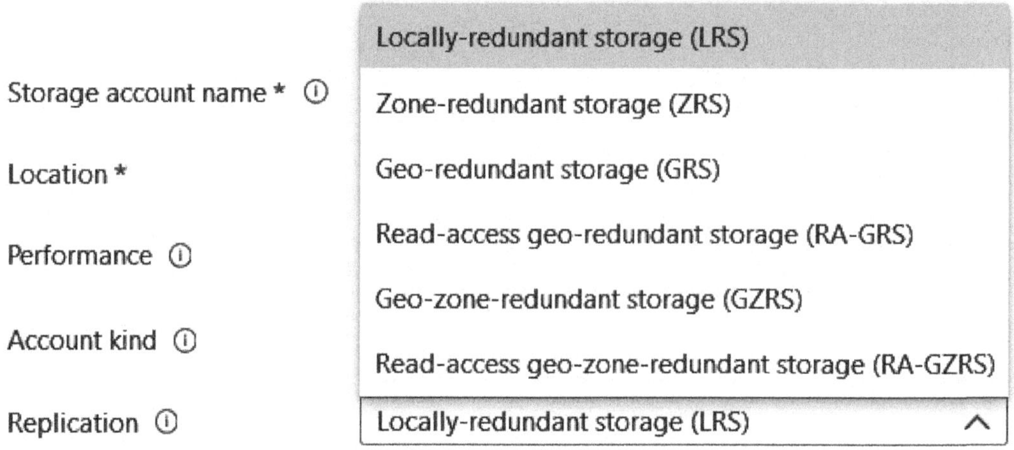

Storage account name * ⓘ

Location *

Performance ⓘ

Account kind ⓘ

Replication ⓘ

Locally-redundant storage (LRS)
Zone-redundant storage (ZRS)
Geo-redundant storage (GRS)
Read-access geo-redundant storage (RA-GRS)
Geo-zone-redundant storage (GZRS)
Read-access geo-zone-redundant storage (RA-GZRS)
Locally-redundant storage (LRS)   ∧

Figure 9.6 – Replication options in an Azure Storage account

2. Once the account is created, navigate to **Storage Account | Keys**. Copy the **Connection String** value.

3. Create a new .NET 6 console application and install the `Azure.Storage.Blobs` NuGet package.

4. To upload content to Azure Storage, we need to first create a container. We will make use of the `Azure.Storage.Blobs.BlobContainerClient` class and its `CreateIfNotExistsAsync` method to create the container if it doesn't exist. With this, update the `Program` class, as shown in the following code snippet:

```
string connectionString = «CONNECTION_STRING";
string containerName = «fileuploadsample";
string blobFileName = «sample.png";
// Upload file to blob
BlobContainerClient containerClient = new
BlobContainerClient(connectionString,
containerName);
await containerClient.CreateIfNotExistsAsync(
  PublicAccessType.None);//Making blob private.
```

5. Next, we need to upload the file to the container for which we will make use of `Azure.Storage.Blobs.BlobClient`, which takes the connection string, container name, and blob name as input parameters. For this sample, we are uploading a local `sample.png` file to the blob, which we will read using the `FileStream` class, and pass it to the `UploadAsync` method of the `Azure.Storage.Blobs.BlobClient` class. Add the following code snippet after container creation in the `Main` method:

```
BlobClient blobClient = new BlobClient(connectionString,
containerName, blobFileName);
using FileStream fileStream = File.
OpenRead(blobFileName); // blobFileName is relative path
of the file.
await blobClient.UploadAsync(fileStream, true);
fileStream.Close();
Console.WriteLine(blobClient.Uri.ToString());
```

Running the sample at this stage will upload the file to the blob and display the blob URL in the command line. However, if we try to access the URL, it won't be accessible as the blob created is private. To access private blobs, we need to generate a **shared access signature (SAS)** and pass it as a query string parameter. For that, add the following code after the uploading code in the `Main` method:

```
BlobSasBuilder sasBuilder = new BlobSasBuilder()
{
    BlobContainerName = containerClient.Name,
    Resource = "b", // c for container
    BlobName = blobClient.Name
};
sasBuilder.ExpiresOn = DateTimeOffset.UtcNow.AddHours(1);
// Setting expiry time of the SAS link to 1 hour
sasBuilder.SetPermissions(BlobContainerSasPermissions.
Read);
if (blobClient.CanGenerateSasUri)
{
    Uri blobSasUri =
        blobClient.GenerateSasUri(sasBuilder);
    Console.WriteLine(blobSasUri.ToString());
}
Console.ReadLine();
```

Here, we are using the `Azure.Storage.Sas.BlobSasBuilder` class to configure various parameters, such as permissions and the expiry time, to generate a SAS URI for the uploaded file. Finally, the output of the preceding code is shown in the following figure:

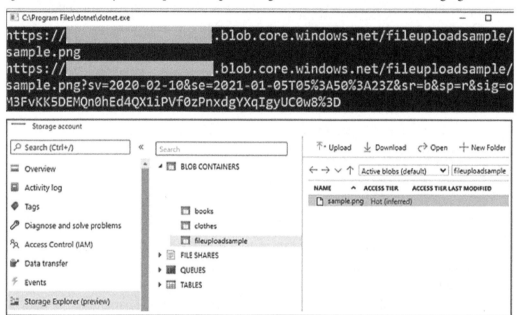

Figure 9.7 – Blob upload output and Storage Explorer

This is a small sample that makes use of Azure Storage for a file upload. This can be further enhanced as an API, which can eventually be used for file upload and download scenarios. For our e-commerce application, we will use Azure Blob to store the images of the products.

> **Note**
>
> For more advanced concepts on Azure Storage and samples, refer to the following links:
>
> `https://docs.microsoft.com/en-us/azure/storage/common/storage-account-overview`
>
> `https://github.com/Azure/azure-sdk-for-net/tree/master/sdk/storage/Azure.Storage.Blobs/samples`

In this section, we have discussed various data providers available in .NET 6. However, one important library that simplifies persisting data is EF. Let's see how to integrate EF in .NET 6 applications.

Working with EF Core

EF Core is an ORM that is recommended for any ASP.NET Core 6 application that uses a relational database as the data store. Earlier, we saw how in ADO.NET, we must create `Connection`, `Command`, and `Reader` objects. EF simplifies this process by providing abstraction and allowing developers to write application code, and like any other ORM, EF helps in performing various operations on databases using the object model paradigm.

Configuring EF Core is as simple as installing the required NuGet packages, injecting the required services in the `Program` class, and then using them wherever required. As part of this process, one of the key classes that needs to be defined is the database context, and that needs to inherit the `Microsoft.EntityFrameworkCore.DbContext` class. Let's see how we do that along with the remaining EF Core configuration.

Configuration and querying

The `DbContext` class in EF Core holds all the required abstraction for our application to communicate with the database, so a key setup that needs to be part of integrating EF Core is to define our application-specific context class. This class will primarily hold all the SQL tables/views in the form of public property of the `DbSet` type, as shown in the following code:

```
public virtual DbSet<Employee> Employees { get; set; }
```

Here, `Employee` is the POCO class representing tables in our database. The application context class should have the parameterized constructor that accepts `DbContextOptions` or `DbContextOptions<T>` and passes it to the base class.

Let's create a simple web application based on Razor Pages and SQLite, and read data using EF Core. For this sample, we will take a simple employee database that holds employee details with the following data model using SQLite:

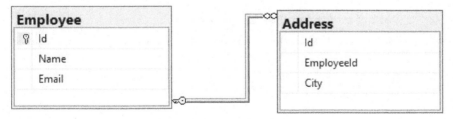

Figure 9.8 – Employee database model

If you haven't worked in Razor Pages before, do not worry about that; it's a page-based framework that can be used to build data-driven applications in ASP.NET Core 6 and is covered in *Chapter 11, Creating an ASP.NET Core 6 Web Application*.

Now, let's now create our application as mentioned in the following steps:

1. Create a new Razor Pages application using the following command from the command line, which will create a new Razor Pages application inside the EmployeeEF folder:

    ```
    dotnet new webapp --framework net6.0 --name EmployeeEF
    ```

2. Navigate to the EmployeeEF folder and open it in Visual Studio Code, and then install the following NuGet packages:

    *   Microsoft.EntityFrameworkCore.Sqlite

    *   Microsoft.EntityFrameworkCore.Design

    The former package is the EF Core provider for SQLite and the latter one is to be used to create a database based on C# POCOs using EF Core migrations.

3. Now, add the Models folder and add the necessary POCO classes as follows. These classes represent the database schema from *Figure 9.8*:

    ```
    public class Address
    {
     public int AddressId { get; set; }
     public int EmployeeId { get; set; }
     public string City { get; set; }
     public Employee Employee { get; set; }
    }
    public class Employee
    {
     public int EmployeeId { get; set; }
     public string Name { get; set; }
     public string Email { get; set; }
     public ICollection<Address> Address { get; set; }
    }
    ```

4. Here, all the columns in the database table are represented as a property with relevant data types. For relationships such as a foreign key, a property of the child type is created (known as **navigation properties**) and the type of the property is represented by ICollection, while another property of the parent class type is created in the child class. For example, in the preceding code, this is represented in the public Icollection<Address> Addresses and public Employee Employee properties, which define the foreign key constraint between the Employee and Address tables. Any property named ID or <class name>ID (EmployeeID) is automatically considered a primary key. Constraints can be further defined using the Fluent API during OnModelCreating or using annotations in System.ComponentModel.DataAnnotations. For more examples and details on model creation, refer to https://docs.microsoft.com/en-us/ef/core/modeling.

5. Add a class that inherits from Microsoft.EntityFrameworkCore.DbContext and name it EmployeeContext. Add the following code that defines our database context:

```
public class EmployeeContext : DbContext
{
    public DbSet<Employee> Employees { get; set;}
    public DbSet<Address> Addresses { get; set;}
    public EmployeeContext (DbContextOptions
    <EmployeeContext> options)
        : base(options)
    {}
    protected override void OnModelCreating
    (ModelBuilder modelBuilder)
    {
        modelBuilder.Entity<Employee>().ToTable
        ("Employee");
        modelBuilder.Entity<Address>().ToTable
        ("Address");
    }
}
```

6. Add the connection string in `appsettings.json`. As we are using SQLite, specifying the filename in the data source should be good enough. However, this will change as per the provider:

```
"ConnectionStrings": {
  "EmployeeContext": "Data Source=Employee.db"
}
```

7. Now, inject the database context class in the `Program` class so that it is available across the application. Here, we additionally pass connection strings and configure any additional options such as a retry policy and query logging:

```
builder.Services.AddDbContext<EmployeeContext>(options =>
{
  options.UseSqlite(builder.Configuration.
GetConnectionString("EmployeeContext"));
});
```

We are almost done with the EF Core setup. So now, let's create some sample data that can be used to seed the database.

8. For that, we will create an extension method on our database context and call it during startup. Create a `DbContextExtension` static class and add the following code to it. This code does nothing but add a few records to the database:

```
public static void SeedData(this EmployeeContext
context)
{
    SeedEmployees(context);
}
private static void SeedEmployees(EmployeeContext
context)
{
    if (context.Employees.Any())
    {
        return;
    }
    var employees = new Employee[]
    {
        new Employee{EmployeeId = 1, Name =
        "Sample1", Email="Sample@sample.com"},
```

```
        new Employee{EmployeeId = 2, Name =
        "Sample2", Email="Sample2@sample.com"},
        new Employee{EmployeeId = 3, Name =
        "Sample3", Email="Sample3@sample.com"}
      };
    context.Employees.AddRange(employees);
    var adresses = new Address[]
    {
      new Address{AddressId = 1, City = "City1",
      EmployeeId = 1},
      new Address{AddressId = 2, City = "City2",
      EmployeeId = 1},
      new Address{AddressId = 3, City = "City1",
      EmployeeId = 2},
    };
    context.Addresses.AddRange(adresses);
    context.SaveChanges();
}
```

9. Open the `Program` class and add the following code that seeds data during application startup. Since this is for a development environment, we can check whether the environment is a development one and add it. As we are checking what's on the employee table before inserting, multiple runs of the application will not overwrite the data:

```
using (var serviceScope = ((IApplicationBuilder)app).
ApplicationServices?.GetService<IServiceScopeFactory>()?.
CreateScope())
    {
    using (var context =
      serviceScope?.ServiceProvider
      .GetRequiredService<EmployeeContext>())
    {
      context?.SeedData();
    }
  }
```

10. Now, run `dotnet build` in the VS Code terminal and fix any build errors. To generate a database from our models and populate the database, we need to install `dotnet-ef` either locally or globally and run the migration commands, as follows, in the VS Code terminal, which would generate the `Migrations` folder and then the `Employee.db` file, which is our SQLite database:

```
dotnet tool install --global dotnet-ef --ignore-failed-
sources //Installing dotnet ef.
dotnet ef migrations add InitialCreate //Generate DB
migrations.
dotnet ef database update //Update database.
```

11. Now, to read the `Employee` table, navigate to `Index.cshtml.cs` and paste the following code. Here, we are injecting `EmployeeContext` and then reading data from the employee table:

```
public class IndexModel : PageModel
    {
        private readonly EmployeeContext context;
        public IndexModel(EmployeeContext context)
        {
            this.context = context;
        }
        public Ilist<Employee> Employees { get; set;
        }
        public async Task OnGetAsync()
        {
            this.Employees = await this.context.
            Employees.Include(x => x.Address).
            AsNoTracking().ToListAsync();
        }
    }
```

12. Update `Index.cshtml` with the following code, which loops through the employee records populated in the `Employees` property of `IndexModel` and displays them:

```
<table class="table">
<tbody>
    @foreach (var item in Model.Employees)
```

```
{<tr>
        <td>@Html.DisplayFor(modelItem =>
        item.EmployeeId)</td>
        <td>@Html.DisplayFor(modelItem =>
        item.Name)</td>
        <td>@Html.DisplayFor(modelItem =>
        item.Email)</td>
        <td>
            @foreach (var address in item.Address)
            {
                @Html.DisplayFor(modelItem =>
                address.City) @Html.DisplayName("
                ")
            }
        </td>
    </tr>
    }
</tbody>
</table>
```

Once we run this code, we can see the following output in the browser:

EmployeeEF   Home   Privacy

Welcome

Learn about building Web apps with ASP.NET Core.

1	Sample1	Sample@sample.com	City1 City2
2	Sample2	Sample2@sample.com	City1
3	Sample3	Sample3@sample.com	

Figure 9.9 – Employee app output

Similarly, there are additional methods available in the DbContext class, such as Add(), Remove(), and Find(), to perform various CRUD operations, and methods such as FromSqlRaw() to execute raw SQL queries or stored procedures.

This is a very simple example, and its main purpose is to show the capabilities of EF Core for real-world applications. We can use a repository pattern with a generic repository holding all the CRUD methods and specific repositories to perform specialized queries on a table. Additionally, a unit of work pattern can be used for transactions.

Code first versus database first

In the previous sample, we have newly created POCOs and generated a database out of them; this style of generating a database from POCOs is known as a **code-first approach**. As the definition suggests, we have our POCOs defined first and then the database is generated.

However, many times, especially during a migration scenario or in cases where there is a dedicated database team, we would need to generate POCOs out of database tables. EF Core supports such scenarios through the **database-first approach**, where models and the application database context class are generated from an existing database.

This process of generating POCOs from database models is known as **scaffolding**. In this approach, we can either use the .NET CLI or the Package Manager Console in Visual Studio and use the `Scaffold-DbContext` command, which accepts various parameters, such as a database connection string and the name of the application database context class, and then generates all the required classes needed for EF Core.

The rest of the configuration remains the same as in the code-first approach. A sample scaffolding command with various parameters will look like the following:

```
Scaffold-DbContext "Data Source=.;Initial Catalog=Employee.
DB;Trusted_Connection=True;" Microsoft.EntityFrameworkCore.
SqlServer -Namespace Api.Data.Models -ContextNamespaceApi.
Data -ContextDir Api.Data/Abstraction -Context EmployeeContext
-Force
```

In this command, we are reading a database, `Employee.DB`, generating all the models inside `Namespace Api.Data.Models`, generating context inside `Api.Data/Abstraction`, and naming the context `EmployeeContext`. In database-first, the relationship between classes is defined using the Fluent API as opposed to annotations.

One thing here is every time we run this command, all the POCOs will be overwritten along with the application context class. Secondly, this command generates a context class with the `protected override void OnConfiguring(DbContextOptions-Builder optionsBuilder)` method in it. This method is needed only if the context class needs to maintain the connection string and other EF Core options. However, in most real-world applications, the connection string is maintained in `appsettings.json` and EF Core is configured in the `Program` class, so this method can be deleted.

This means there is a cleanup involved after each time we scaffold, and a better way to avoid any customization is to create a partial class for our application database context and do all the customization there, such as adding specific models for stored procedures or defining any application-specific constraints. This way, any time we scaffold an application, customization won't be overwritten, which still allows us to auto-generate classes from a database.

Choosing the database-first approach or code-first approach is completely up to the development team, as both approaches have pros and cons and there isn't any specific feature that is available in one but not in the other.

> **Note**
> Scaffold-DbContext supports multiple parameters; for example, you can specify a schema for generating POCOs for a schema. For further reading, please refer to https://docs.microsoft.com/en-us/ef/core/managing-schemas/scaffolding?tabs=dotnet-core-cli.

With this understanding, let's create the Data Access service that we will use in our enterprise application in the next section.

Designing a Data Access service using Azure Cosmos DB

As NoSQL databases are all about fast access and high scalability, the schema for NoSQL is denormalized and so there is a high possibility of data redundancy. Let's map our requirements from *Chapter 1, Designing and Architecting the Enterprise Application,* to various entities. A quick refresher of various services from the architecture is shown in the following figure:

Figure 9.10 – Services in an e-commerce application

For easier understanding, we will represent entities in JSON before moving on to POCOs:

- **User container**: This container will hold all user profile information, such as the name and address. For this container, the `Email` field is used as a partition key:

```
{
    "Id": "1",
    "Name": "John",
    "Email": "John@xyz.com",
    "Address":[{"Address1":"Gachibowli","City":
        "Hyderabad","Country":"India"}],
    "PhoneNumber":12345
}
```

- **Product container**: The product container will be used to browse through the products and hold relevant fields to support searching by category and sorting by arrival date. The schema would be the one we used in our previous example, and the `Name` field is used as a partition key.

- **Order container**: The order container will store all historic orders along with their status for a particular user. This container will hold the shopping cart with the relevant status and update the status once the order is placed. For this container, the `Id` field is used as a partition key:

```
{
    "Id": "1",
    "UserId": "1",
    "Products": [{"Id":"1","Name":
        "T-Shirt","Quantity": 1,"Price": 10}],
    "OrderStatus" : "Processed",
    "OrderPlacedDate" : "20-02-2020T00:00:00Z",
    "ShippingAddress": {"Address1":"Gachibowli",
        "City":"Hyderabad","Country":"India"},
    "TrackingId": 1,
    "DeliveryDate":"28-02-2020T00:00:00Z"
}
```

- **Invoice container**: The invoice container will hold all the information related to the invoice for a particular order. For this container, the `Id` field is used as a partition key:

```
{
    "Id": "1",
    "OrderId": "1",
    "PaymentMode": "Credit Card",
    "ShippingAddress": {"Address1":"Gachibowli",
        "City":"Hyderabad","Country":"India"},
    "SoldBy": {"SellerName": "Seller1",  "Email":
        "seller@ecommerce.com", "Phone": "98765432"},
    "Products": [{"Id":"1", "Name": "T-Shirt",
        "Quantity": 1, "Price": 10}]
}
```

A combination of `Product` and `Order` is shown in the following screenshot:

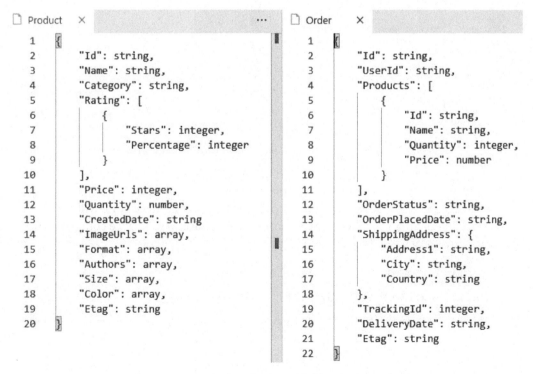

Figure 9.11 – E-commerce database model's Product and Order schema

As you can see, all *1:N* relationships are handled by embedding the child item as an array. Similarly, the `Invoice` and `User` entities schema is as shown in the following screenshot:

```
 Invoice    ×                        ...        User      ×
 1  v {                                          1  {
 2      "Id": string,                            2      "Id": string,
 3      "OrderId": string,                       3      "Name": string,
 4      "PaymentMode": string,                   4      "Email": string,
 5  v   "ShippingAddress": {                      5      "Address": [
 6          "Address1": string,                  6          {
 7          "City": string,                      7              "Address1": string,
 8          "Country": string                    8              "City": string,
 9      },                                        9              "Country": string
10  v   "SoldBy": {                              10          }
11          "SellerName": string,               11      ],
12          "Email": string,                    12      "PhoneNumber": integer,
13          "Phone": integer                    13      "Etag": string
14      },                                       14  }
15  v   "Products": [
16  v       {
17              "Id": string,
18              "Name": string,
19              "Quantity": integer,
20              "Price": number
21          }
22      ],
23      "Etag": string
24  }
```

Figure 9.12 – E-commerce database model's Invoice and User schema

In our enterprise application, `https://github.com/PacktPublishing/Enterprise-Application-Development-with-C-10-and-.NET-6-Second-Edition/tree/main/Enterprise%20Application`, we will have one service interacting with the Azure Cosmos DB database. This service comprises the following three projects, which are explained next:

- `Packt.Ecommerce.Data.Models`

- `Packt.Ecommerce.DataStore`

- `Packt.Ecommerce.DataAccess`

The first project is `Packt.Ecommerce.Data.Models`, which is a .NET Standard 2.1 library and comprises all of our POCOs to communicate with the database. As discussed earlier, all the POCOs will have a common `id` property and the other properties described in the JSON schema in the previous section.

> **Tip**
> If sample JSON is available, we can make use of JSON in C# class generation tools.

`Packt.Ecommerce.DataStore` is a .NET Standard 2.1 library and is the repository layer that holds a generic repository and entity-specific repositories. An important class in this project is `BaseRepository`, which has the following methods, and each method calls the respective method of the `CosmosClient` class:

- `GetAsync(string filterCriteria)`: This method gets records from a container based on `filterCriteria`. If `filterCriteria` is empty, all the records from that container are retrieved.

- `GetByIdAsync(string id, string partitionKey)`: This method helps in retrieving any record from a container by its ID and partition key.

- `AddAsync(Tentity entity, string partitionKey)`: This method allows us to insert a record into a container.

- `ModifyAsync(Tentity entity, string partitionKey)`: This method allows us to UPSERT (modify if a record is present, otherwise, insert) a record in a container.

- `RemoveAsync(string id, string partitionKey)`: This method allows the deletion of a record from a container.

Since, in Azure Cosmos DB, each record is uniquely identified by a combination of ID and partition key, all these methods accept a partition key along with `id`. Since this is a generic repository, the signature of the class would be the following, which allows us to pass any POCO for our application and perform CRUD operations on the corresponding container:

```
public class BaseRepository<TEntity> : IBaseRepository<TEntity>
where TEntity : class
```

All these methods would require an object of `Microsoft.Azure.Cosmos.Continer` for which we create a `readonly` private member, which is initialized in the constructor of the class, as follows:

```
private readonly Container container;
public BaseRepository(CosmosClient cosmosClient,
string databaseName, string containerName)
{
    if (cosmosClient == null)
    {
        throw new Exception("Cosmos client is
          null");
    }
    this.container = cosmosClient.GetContainer
    (databaseName, containerName);
}
```

Now, `CosmosClient` would be plumbed into the system through dependency injection and would be configured in the `static` class. As a best practice, it is recommended to have only one instance of `CosmosClient` in the lifetime of the application to better reuse connections, so we will be configuring it in our ASP.NET Core 6 dependency injection container as a singleton. We will come to this in a bit.

Coming back to the repository layer, `BaseRepository` is additionally inherited in the following concrete classes, with each repository representing a corresponding container:

- `ProductRepository`
- `UserRepository`
- `OrderRepository`
- `InvoiceRepository`

Taking the example of `ProductRepository`, it will have the following implementation, where we pass the singleton instance of `CosmosClient` and additional properties using the `IOptions` pattern:

```
public class ProductRepository :
BaseRepository<Product>, IProductRepository
{
```

```
    private readonly IOptions<DatabaseSettingsOptions>
    databaseSettings;
    public ProductRepository(CosmosClient,
    IOptions<DatabaseSettingsOptions>
    databaseSettingsOption)
        : base(cosmosClient, databaseSettingsOption.
          Value.DataBaseName, "Products")
    {
        this.databaseSettings = databaseSettingsOption;
    }
}
```

All the other repositories will follow a similar structure. Each repository will implement its own interface to support dependency injection.

Note

These repositories will evolve as and when we progress with our application implementation.

The next project is `Packt.Ecommerce.DataAccess`, which is a Web API project targeting .NET 6 and will primarily have all the controllers to expose our repositories. Each repository would be a *1:1* mapping with the corresponding controller. So, for example, there would be `ProductsController` exposing `ProductRepository` methods as a REST API. All the controllers will use constructor injection to instantiate their corresponding repositories. One important thing in `Packt.Ecommerce.DataAccess` is the configuration of the Azure Cosmos DB database. The design of various controllers would be very similar to the design of the `Packt.Ecommerce.Product` Web API, which is discussed in *Chapter 10, Creating an ASP.NET Core 6 Web API.*

To start with, we will have a corresponding section in `appsettings.json`, which is shown as follows:

```
"CosmosDB": {
  "DataBaseName": "Ecommerce",
  "AccountEndPoint": "",
  "AuthKey": ""
}
```

> **Note**
>
> For the local development environment, we will use **Manage User Secrets**, as explained here: https://docs.microsoft.com/en-us/aspnet/core/security/app-secrets?view=aspnetcore-6.0. We will set the following values:
>
> ```
> {
>
>    "CosmosDB:AccountEndPoint": "", //Cosmos DB End
> Point
>
>    "CosmosDB:AuthKey": "" //Cosmos DB Auth key
>
> }
> ```
>
> However, once the service is deployed, it should make use of Azure Key Vault, as explained in *Chapter 6, Configuration in .NET 6*.

We will define an extension class that will hold the dependency injection mapping. A snippet of that is shown here:

```
public static class RepositoryExtensions
{
    public static IServiceCollection
    AddRepositories(this IServiceCollection services)
    {
        services.AddScoped<IproductRepository,
        ProductRepository>();
        return services;
    }
}
```

Similarly, all the repositories would be mapped. Then, we will configure this in the `Program` class, along with Azure Cosmos DB configuration, by adding the following code:

```
builder.Services.AddOptions();
builder.Services.Configure<DatabaseSettingsOptions>(builder.
Configuration.GetSection("CosmosDB"));
string accountEndPoint = builder.Configuration.
GetValue<string>("CosmosDB:AccountEndPoint");
string authKey = builder.Configuration.
```

```
GetValue<string>("CosmosDB:AuthKey");
builder.Services.AddSingleton(s => new
CosmosClient(accountEndPoint, authKey));
builder.Services.AddRepositories();
```

Once we are done with the configuration, this service is ready for consumption in other services, such as `Products`, `Orders`, and `Invoice`. This library will have all the necessary REST APIs to perform CRUD operations on various entities.

This concludes the creation of a Data Access service that performs CRUD operations on various entities, and all the operations are exposed as APIs. This service will be called from all the other services that we will develop in *Chapter 10, Creating an ASP.NET Core 6 Web API*.

Summary

In this chapter, we learned about various persistent options that are available in .NET 6, from APIs to work with files and directories to databases such as Microsoft SQL Server and Azure Cosmos DB.

We also learned about ORMs, their importance, and how EF Core can be used to build a persistence layer while working with Microsoft SQL Server. Along the way, we built a data access layer for our e-commerce application using the Azure Cosmos DB SDK. Some of the key takeaways are the design decisions we took between SQL versus NoSQL, and how we can abstract a data layer with application logic and a UI layer that will help you to build scalable enterprise applications.

In the next chapter, we will look at the foundation of RESTful APIs and the internals of the ASP.NET Core 6 Web API, and further build various RESTful services for e-commerce applications.

Questions

1. Say you are migrating an existing web application to use EF Core; however, there isn't any change in the database schema and an existing one can be used as-is. What is the preferable mode to use EF Core?

   a. Database-first

   b. Code-first

   c. Both

   Answer: a

2. If we are building a recommendation system for our e-commerce application and we are using Azure Cosmos DB, what API is best recommended in this scenario?

    a. The Core (SQL) API

    b. The Mongo API

    c. The Cassandra API

    d. The Gremlin (graph) API

    Answer: d

3. I created a container in SQL API-based databases to store user profile information and defined `Email` as the partition key. My system has 100 unique emails. How many logical partitions will my container have?

    a. 1.

    b. 0.

    c. 100.

    d. Azure Cosmos DB does not support logical partitions.

    Answer: c

Further reading

A few links to understand the topics of this chapter further are provided as follows:

- `https://docs.microsoft.com/en-us/ef/core/saving/transactions`

- `https://docs.microsoft.com/en-us/ef/core/performance/advanced-performance-topics`

- `https://docs.microsoft.com/en-us/aspnet/core/security/gdpr?view=aspnetcore-6.0`

- `https://aws.amazon.com/products/databases/`

10
Creating an ASP.NET Core 6 Web API

In recent times, web services have become an important part of web application development. With ever-changing requirements and increased business complexity, it is very important to loosely couple various components/layers involved in web application development, and there is nothing better than decoupling the **user interface** (**UI**) part of the application with the core business logic. This is where the simplicity of web services using a RESTful approach (where **REST** stands for **REpresentational State Transfer**) helps us to develop scalable web applications.

In this chapter, we will learn how to build RESTful services using an ASP.NET Core web **application programming interface** (**API**), and along the way, we will build all the required APIs for our e-commerce application.

We'll be covering the following topics in detail:

- Introduction to REST
- Understanding the internals of an ASP.NET Core 6 web API
- Handling requests using controllers and actions
- Integration with the data layer
- Understanding **Google Remote Procedure Call (gRPC)**

Technical requirements

For this chapter, you will require a basic knowledge of C#, .NET Core, web APIs, **HyperText Transfer Protocol (HTTP)**, Azure, **dependency injection (DI)**, Postman, and the .NET **command-line interface (CLI)**.

The code for this chapter can be found here: `https://github.com/PacktPublishing/Enterprise-Application-Development-with-C-10-and-.NET-6-Second-Edition/tree/main/Chapter10/TestApi`.

For more code examples, refer to the following link: `https://github.com/PacktPublishing/Enterprise-Application-Development-with-C-10-and-.NET-6-Second-Edition/tree/main/Enterprise%20Application`.

Introduction to REST

REST is an architectural guideline for building a web service. Primarily, it defines a set of constraints that can be followed while designing a web service. One of the key principal REST approaches recommends that APIs should be designed around resources and should be media- and protocol-agnostic. The underlying implementation of the API is independent of the client consuming the API.

Considering an example of our e-commerce application, let's say we are searching for a product on the UI using a product's search field. There should be an API that is created for products, and here, products are nothing but a resource in the context of an e-commerce application. The **Uniform Resource Identifier (URI)** for that API could be something like this, which clearly states that we are trying to perform a GET operation on product entities:

```
GET http://ecommerce.packt.com/products
```

The response of the API should be independent of the client that is calling the API—that is, in this case, we are using a browser to load a list of products on the product search page. However, the same API can be consumed in a mobile application as well without any changes. Secondly, in this case, in order to retrieve product information internally, an application may be using one or more physical data stores; however, that complexity is hidden from the client application, and the API is exposed to the client as a single business entity—products. Although REST principles do not dictate the protocol to be HTTP, the majority of RESTful services are built over HTTP. Some key design principles/constraints/rules of HTTP-based RESTful APIs are outlined here:

- Identify the business entities of the system and design APIs around those resources. In the case of our e-commerce application, all our APIs would be around resources such as products, orders, payments, and users.

- REST APIs should have a uniform interface that assists in making them independent of the client. As all the APIs need to be resource-oriented, each resource is uniquely identified by a URI; additionally, various operations on resources are uniquely identified by HTTP verbs such as GET, POST, PUT, PATCH, and DELETE. For example, GET (http://ecommerce.packt.com/products/1) should be used to retrieve a product with an **identifier (ID)** of 1. Similarly, DELETE (http://ecommerce.packt.com/products/1) should be used to delete a product.

- As HTTP is stateless, REST dictates a number of things for RESTful APIs. What this means is that APIs should be atomic and conclude the processing of a request within the same call. Any subsequent request, even from the same client (same **Internet Protocol (IP)** address), is treated as a new request. For example, if an API accepts an authentication token, it should accept authentication for each request. One major advantage of statelessness is the scalability that servers can eventually achieve, as a client can make an API call to any of the available servers and still receive the same response.

- Apart from sending back a response, APIs should make use of HTTP status codes and response headers to send any additional information to the client. For example, if a response can be cached, an API should send the relevant response headers to the client so that it can be cached. **Response caching**, discussed in *Chapter 8, All You Need to Know about Caching*, is based on these headers. Another example is where an API should return the relevant HTTP status codes in the event of both success and failure scenarios—that is, 1xx for information, 2xx for success, 3xx for redirection, 4xx for client errors, and 5xx for server errors.

- APIs should give information about the resource such that clients should be easily able to discover it without any prior information relating to the resource—that is, there should follow the principle of **Hypermedia as the Engine of Application State (HATEOAS)**. For example, if there is an API to create a product, once a product is created, the API should respond with the URI of that resource so that the client can use that to retrieve the product later.

Refer to the following response for an API that retrieves a list of all products (GET /products) and has information to retrieve further details regarding each product:

```
{
"Products": [
{
"Id": "1",
"Name": "Men's T-Shirt",
"Category": "Clothing"
"Uri": "http://ecommerce.packt.com/products/1"
}
{
"Id": "2",
"Name": "Mastering enterprise application development
Book",
"Category": "books"
"Uri": "http://ecommerce.packt.com/products/2"
}
]
}
```

The preceding example is one way to implement the *HATEOAS* principle, but it can be designed in a more descriptive way, such as a response containing information about accepted HTTP verbs and relationships.

The REST maturity model

These are various guidelines that an API should follow in order for it to be RESTful. However, not all the principles need to be followed to make it perfectly RESTFUL; it's more important that an API should fulfill the business goal rather than being 100% REST-compliant. Leonard Richardson, an expert on RESTful API design, came up with the following model to categorize the maturity of an API:

- **Level 0—The Swamp of Plain Old XML (POX)**: Any API that has a single POST URI to perform all operations will fall under this category. An example would be a **Simple Object Access Protocol (SOAP)**-based web service that has a single URI, and all operations are segregated based on the SOAP envelope.

- **Level 1—Resources**: All resources are URI-driven, and APIs that have a dedicated URI pattern per resource fall under this maturity model.

- **Level 2—HTTP verbs**: Apart from a separate URI for each resource, each URI has a separate action based on the HTTP verb. As discussed earlier, a product API that supports GET and DELETE using the same URI with different HTTP verbs falls under this maturity model. Most enterprise application RESTful APIs fall under this category.

- **Level 3—HATEOAS**: APIs that are designed with all additional discovery information (the URI for the resources; various operations that the resource supports) fall under this maturity model. Very few APIs are compliant with this maturity level; however, as discussed earlier, it's important that our APIs fulfill the business objective and are as compliant as possible with RESTful principles, rather than 100% compliant but not fulfilling the business objective.

The following diagram illustrates Richardson's maturity model:

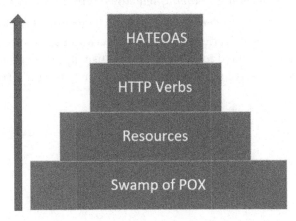

Figure 10.1 – Richardson's maturity model

Up to now, we have discussed various principles of REST architecture. In the next section, let's get into using an ASP.NET Core web API for which we will create various RESTful services in our e-commerce application.

Understanding the internals of an ASP.NET Core 6 web API

ASP.NET Core is a unified framework that runs on top of .NET Core and is used to develop web applications (MVC/Razor), RESTful services (web API), and—most recently—web assembly-based client applications (Blazor apps). The fundamental design of ASP.NET Core applications is based on the **Model-View-Controller** (**MVC**) pattern, which divides code into three primary categories, as follows:

- **Model**: This is a **plain old CLR object** (**POCO**) class that holds the data and is used to pass data between various layers of the application. Layers include passing data between the *repository* class and the *service* class or passing information back and forth between the *client* and *server*. The model primarily represents the resource state or the domain model of the application and contains information that you have requested.

  For example, if we wanted to store user profile information, this can be represented by the UserInformation POCO class and can contain all the profile information. This will be further used to pass between repositories and service classes and can also be serialized into **JavaScript Object Notation** (**JSON**)/**Extensible Markup Language** (**XML**) before being sent back to the client. In enterprise applications, we will encounter different types of models while creating models for our e-commerce application in the *Integration with the data layer* section.

- **View**: These are the pages that represent UIs. All our models retrieved from controllers are bound to various **HyperText Markup Language** (**HTML**) controls on views and are presented to users. Views are usually common in MVC/Razor applications; for web API applications, the process ends with serializing models as a response.

- **Controller**: These are a set of classes that receive all requests, perform all the required processing, populate the model, and then send it back to the client. In enterprise applications, they typically make use of service classes to handle the business logic, and repositories to communicate with the underlying data store. With the unified approach in ASP.NET core, both MVC/Razor applications and web API applications use the same `Microsoft.AspNetCore.Mvc.ControllerBase` class to define controllers.

So, in a web application developed using ASP.NET Core, whenever a request comes from a client (browser, mobile apps, and similar sources), it goes through the ASP.NET Core request pipeline and reaches a controller that interacts with the data store to populate models/view-models and send them back either as a response in the form of JSON/XML or to a view to further bind the response and present it to the user.

As you can see, there is a clear **separation of concerns (SOC)** where a controller is not aware of any UI aspect and performs the business logic in the current context and responds via models; views, on the other hand, receive models and use them to present them to the user in HTML pages. This SOC easily helps to unit test the application, as well as maintain and scale it as needed. MVC patterns are not only applicable to web applications and can be used for any application that requires an SOC.

As the focus of this chapter is to build RESTful services, we will focus on an ASP.NET Core web API in this chapter and discuss ASP.NET MVC and Razor Pages in *Chapter 11, Creating an ASP.NET Core 6 Web Application*.

To develop RESTful services, many frameworks are available, but here are a few advantages of going with ASP.NET Core on .NET 6:

- **Cross-platform support**: Unlike ASP.NET, which used to be part of the .NET Framework (which is coupled with the Windows operating system), ASP.NET Core is now part of the application, thereby eliminating platform dependency and making it compatible with all platforms.

- **Highly customizable request pipelines**: Use middlewares and support to inject various out-of-the-box modules, such as logging and configuration.

- **Out-of-the-box HTTP server implementation**: This can listen to HTTP requests and forward them to controllers. The server implementation includes cross-platform servers such as Kestrel and platform-specific servers such as `IIS` and `HTTP.sys`.

> **Note**
>
> By default, Kestrel is the HTTP server used in ASP.NET Core templates;
> however, that can be overridden as required.

- **Strong tooling support**: This comes in the form of **Visual Studio Code (VS Code)**, Visual Studio, and the DOTNET CLI, along with project templates, which means developers can start working on implementing the business logic with very little setup.

- **Open sourced**: Finally, the entire framework is open sourced and is available at `https://github.com/aspnet/AspNetCore`.

So, we now know why we picked ASP.NET Core as our framework to develop RESTful services. Let's now look into some key components that assist in the execution of the request and create a sample web API by using the following command:

```
dotnet new webapi -o TestApi
```

Once the preceding command is successfully executed, let's navigate to the `TestApi` folder and open it in VS Code to see the various files that are generated, as shown in the following screenshot:

Figure 10.2 – Test web API project in VS Code

Here, you can see a `Program` class used to bootstrap the application, and settings files, such as `appsettings.json`, that are used to run a web API project, and there is also `WeatherForecast`, which is a model class used in the controller class. Let's examine each of the components of `TESTAPI` in the following sections.

The Program class

The Program class is used to bootstrap web API projects in ASP.NET Core 6. Let's look at the activities performed by this class in the following steps:

1. The Program class is the entry point for our web API, and it tells ASP.NET Core to begin execution whenever someone executes the web API project. Primarily, this is the class that is used to bootstrap the application. Unlike earlier versions of ASP.NET Core applications, by default we don't have a Startup class—that is, the Program class has everything that we need—and to keep the code minimal, we further rely on C# 10's top-level statements and global using statements.

2. Since this is the entry point, we need to ensure all components such as the web server, routing, and configuration, get initialized and loaded, and that is what the CreateBuilder method of the WebApplication class helps with. It primarily creates an object of WebApplicationBuilder, which can be used to configure the HTTP request pipeline.

3. WebApplicationBuilder is inherited from the IApplicationBuilder interface, which is nothing but the **host** for our application. Earlier, we discussed the fact that ASP.NET Core comes with an inbuilt HTTP server implementation and various middlewares to plug in, and that Host is nothing more than an object that encapsulates these components, such as the HTTP server defaulted to Kestrel, all the middleware components, and any additional services—such as logging—that are injected. Finally, the Build() method is called to run actions and initialize the Host object. The Run() method is called to keep the Host object running.

Now that we have the Host object loaded with all the default components and it is up and running, let's examine whether we can inject additional ASP.NET Core classes/application-specific classes (repositories, services, options) and middlewares. Consider the following points:

*   This WebApplicationBuilder object is used to inject any ASP.NET Core-provided services so that applications can use those services. A few common services that enterprise applications can inject are shown in the following code snippet:

    ```
    var builder = WebApplication.CreateBuilder(args);
    builder.Services.AddAuthentication() // To enable
    //authentication.
    builder.Services.AddControllers(); // To enable
    //controllers like web API.
    builder.Services.AddControllersWithViews(); // To
    ```

```
//enable controller with views.
builder.Services.AddDistributedMemoryCache(); // To
enable distributed caching.
// App insights.
string appinsightsInstrumentationKey = builder.Configura-
tion.GetValue<string>("ApplicationSettings:Instrumenta-
tionKey");
builder.Services.AddApplicationInsightsTelemetry(appIn-
sightInstrumentKey); // To enable application insights
//telemetry.
```

Apart from services provided by ASP.NET Core, we can also inject any custom services specific to our application—for example, `ProductService` can be mapped to `IProductService` and can be made available for the entire application. Primarily, this is the place we can use to plumb anything into the DI container, as explained in *Chapter 5, Dependency Injection in .NET 6.*

Additionally, all services, including ASP.NET Core services and custom services, can be plumbed into the application and are available as extension methods of `IServiceCollection`.

- Next, we have an object of the `WebApplication` class that can be used to integrate all the middlewares required to be applied to the request pipeline. This object primarily controls how applications respond to HTTP requests—that is, how applications should respond to exceptions, how they should respond to static files, or how URI routing should happen. All can be configured using this object.

Additionally, any specific handling on a request pipeline—such as calling a custom middleware or adding specific response headers, or even defining a specific endpoint—can be injected using the `WebApplication` object. So, apart from what we saw earlier, the following code snippet shows a few common additional configurations that can be integrated using the `WebApplication` object:

```
var app = builder.Build();
// Endpoint that responds to /subscribe route.
app.UseEndpoints(endpoints =>
{
endpoints.MapGet("/subscribe", async context =>
```

```
{
    await context.Response.WriteAsync("subscribed");
});
});
// removing any unwanted headers.
app.Use(async (context, next) =>
{
context.Response.Headers.Remove("X-Powered-By");
context.Response.Headers.Remove("Server");
await next().ConfigureAwait(false);
});
```

Here, `app.UseEndpoints` is configuring a response for a URI that matches `/subscribe`. `app.UseEndPoints` works alongside routing rules and is explained in the *Handling requests using controllers and actions* section, while `app.Use`, on the other hand, is used to add an inline middleware. In this case, we are removing `X-Powered-By` and `Server` response headers from the response.

Since ASP.NET Core 6 supports something called **Minimal API**, the `Program` class alone can be used to build a fully working API; however, for enterprise applications, it is good to segregate APIs for easier maintenance and better readability, hence in our enterprise applications, we will be using APIs with the controller, which is supported by `MapControllers` middleware and is configured by calling `app.MapControllers()`.

To sum up, the `Program` class plays a vital role in bootstrapping the application and then customizing application services and HTTP request/response pipelines as needed.

Let's now see how middlewares help in customizing the HTTP request/response pipeline.

Note

ASP.NET Core 6 still supports using the `Startup` class, and the `Configure` and `ConfigureServices` methods can be used as-is.

Understanding middleware

We have been referring to middleware for a while now, so let's understand what middlewares are and how we can we build one and use it in our enterprise application. Middlewares are classes that intercept incoming requests, perform some processing on the requests, and then hand them over to the next middleware or skip them as required. Middlewares are bidirectional, hence all middlewares intercept both requests and responses. Let's assume that an API retrieves product information and, in the process, it goes through various middlewares. Representing them in pictorial form would look something like this:

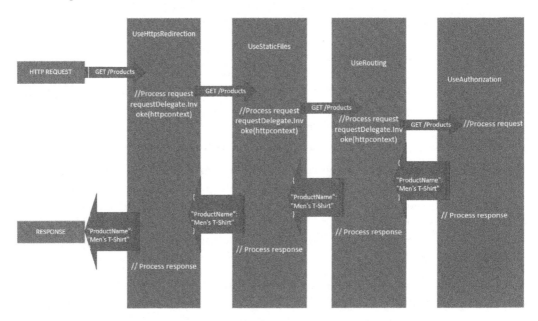

Figure 10.3 – Middleware processing

Each middleware has an instance of `Microsoft.AspNetCore.Http.RequestDelegate`. As a result of using this, the middleware invokes the next middleware. So, flows would typically process the request as per some processing logic that you want the middleware to perform on the request and then invoke `RequestDelegate` to hand the request over to the next middleware in the pipeline.

If we take an analogy from manufacturing, it would be like an assembly line in a manufacturing process, where parts are added/modified from workstation to workstation until a final product is produced. In the previous diagram, let's consider each middleware as a workstation, so it will be going through the following steps:

> **Note**
> The following explanation of each middleware is just a hypothetical explanation for our understanding; the internal workings of these middlewares differ slightly from what is explained here. More details can be found here:
> `https://docs.microsoft.com/en-us/dotnet/api/`
> `microsoft.aspnetcore.builder?view=aspnetcore-`
> `3.1&viewFallbackFrom=aspnetcore-6.0.`

1. `UseHttpsRedirection`: An HTTP request arrives for `GET/Products` and is inspected for the protocol. If the request is via HTTP, a redirect is sent back through the HTTP status code; if the request is on HTTPS, it's handed over to the next middleware.

2. `UseStaticFiles`: If the request is for a static file (usually detected based on the extension—the **Multipurpose Media Extensions** (**MIME**) type), this middleware processes the request and sends the response back, or else hands the request on to the next middleware. Here, as you can see, if the request is for a static file, the rest of the pipeline is not even executed as this middleware can process the complete request, thereby reducing the load on the server for any unwanted processing and also reducing the response time. This process is also known as **short-circuiting**, which every middleware can support.

3. `UseRouting`: The request is inspected further, and the controller/action that can process the request is identified. If there isn't any match, this middleware usually responds with a `404` HTTP status code.

4. `UseAuthorization`: Here, if the controller/action needs to be available for authenticated users, then this middleware will look for any valid token in the header and respond accordingly.

Once the controller gets the data from services/repositories, the response goes through the same middlewares in reverse order—that is, `UseAuthorization` first, followed by `UseHttpsRedirection`—and the response is processed as needed.

As mentioned earlier, all middlewares are installed using the `Program` class and are configured using the object of the `WebApplication` class. The order of middleware execution would precisely follow the way it is configured in the `Program` class.

Armed with this understanding, let's create a middleware that will be used to handle exceptions across the RESTful services of our e-commerce application, so instead of adding `try...catch` blocks in the code, we will create a middleware that gets installed at the beginning of the request pipeline and then catches any exceptions throughout.

Building a custom middleware

As the middleware is going to be reused across all RESTful services, we will add the middleware to the `Packt.Ecommerce.Common` project inside the `Middlewares` folder.

Let's first create a POCO class that represents the response in case of errors. This model will typically hold an error message, a **unique ID (UID)** to search in our log store application insights, and an inner exception (if needed). In production environments, an inner exception should not be exposed; however, for development environments, we can send the inner exception for debugging purposes, and we will control this behavior inside our middleware logic using a configuration flag. So, on this basis, add a class file named `ExceptionResponse` inside the `Models` folder of the `Packt.Ecommerce.Common` project and add the following code to it:

```
public class ExceptionResponse
{
    public string ErrorMessage { get; set; }
    public string CorrelationIdentifier { get; set; }
    public string InnerException { get; set; }
}
```

Now, create another POCO class that can hold the configuration to toggle the behavior of sending an inner exception in our response. This class will be populated using the `Options` pattern, which was discussed in *Chapter 6, Configuration in .NET 6*. Since it needs to hold only one setting, it will have one property. Add a class file named `ApplicationSettings` in the `Options` folder and then add the following code to it:

```
public class ApplicationSettings
{
    public bool IncludeExceptionStackInResponse { get; set; }
}
```

This class will be extended further for any configuration that will be common across all our APIs.

Navigate to the `Middlewares` folder and create a class named `ErrorHandlingMid-dleware`. As we discussed, one of the key properties in any middleware is a property of the `RequestDelegate` type. Additionally, we will add a property for `ILogger` to log the exception to our logging provider, and finally, we will add a property of the `bool` `includeExceptionDetailsInResponse` type to hold a flag that controls masking the inner exception. With this, here's what the `ErrorHandlingMiddleware` class will look like:

```
public class ErrorHandlingMiddleware
{
private readonly RequestDelegate requestDelegate;
private readonly ILogger logger;
private readonly bool includeExceptionDetailsInResponse;
}
```

Add a parameterized constructor where we inject `RequestDelegate` and `ILogger` for our logging provider and `IOptions<ApplicationSettings>` for configuration and assign them to the properties created earlier. Here, again, we are relying on the constructor injection of ASP.NET Core to instantiate the respective objects. With this, here's what the constructor of `ErrorHandlingMiddleWare` will look like:

```
public ErrorHandlingMiddleware(RequestDelegate,
ILogger<ErrorHandlingMiddleware> logger,
IOptions<ApplicationSettings> applicationSettings)
{
    NotNullValidator.ThrowIfNull(applicationSettings,
      nameof(applicationSettings));
    this.requestDelegate = requestDelegate;
    this.logger = logger;
    this.includeExceptionDetailsInResponse =
applicationSettings.Value.IncludeExceptionStackInResponse;
}
```

Finally, add an `InvokeAsync` method that will have the logic to process the request and then call the next middleware using `RequestDelegate`. Since this is an exception-handling middleware as part of our logic, all we are going to do is wrap the request in a `try...catch` block. In the `catch` block, we will log it to the respective logging provider using `ILogger`, and finally send an object, `ExceptionResponse`, back as the response. With this, here's what `InvokeAsync` will look like:

```
public async Task InvokeAsync(HttpContext context)
{
    try
    {
        if (this.requestDelegate != null)
        {
            // invoking next middleware.
            this.requestDelegate.Invoke(context)
              .ConfigureAwait(false);
        }
    }
    catch (Exception innerException)
    {
        this.logger.LogCritical(1001, innerException,
          "Exception captured in error handling
            middleware"); // logging.
        ExceptionResponse currentException = new
          ExceptionResponse()
        {

            ErrorMessage = Constants.ErrorMiddlewareLog,
          // Exception captured in error handling middleware
            CorrelationIdentifier =
              System.Diagnostics.Activity.Current?.RootId,
        };
        if (this.includeExceptionDetailsInResponse)
        {
            currentException.InnerException =
              $"{innerException.Message}
                {innerException.StackTrace}";
```

```
        }
        context.Response.StatusCode =
           StatusCodes.Status500InternalServerError;
        context.Response.ContentType = "application/json";
    await context.Response.WriteAsync(JsonSerializer.
Serialize(innerException)).ConfigureAwait(false);
        }
    }
}
```

Now, we can inject this middleware into the `Program` class with the following code:

```
app.UseMiddleware<GlobalExceptionHandlingMiddleware>();
```

Since this is an exception handler, it is recommended to configure it as early as possible in the `Program` class so that any exceptions in all subsequent middlewares are caught. Additionally, we need to ensure that we map the `ApplicationSettings` class to a configuration, so add the following code to the `Program` class:

```
Builder.Services.Configure<ApplicationSettings>(this.
Configuration.GetSection("ApplicationSettings"));
```

Add the relevant section to `appsettings.json`, as follows:

```
"ApplicationSettings": {
    "IncludeExceptionStackInResponse": true
  }
```

Now, if there is an error in any of our APIs, the response will look like the one shown in the following code snippet:

```
{
"ErrorMessage": "Exception captured in error handling
middleware",
"CorrelationIdentifier": "03410a51b0475843936943d3ae04240c ",
"InnerException": "No connection could be made because
the target machine actively refused it.    at System.Net.
Http.ConnectHelper.ConnectAsync(String host, Int32 port,
CancellationToken cancellationToken)\r\n   at System.Net.
Http.HttpConnectionPool.ConnectAsync(HttpRequestMessage
request, Boolean allowHttp2, CancellationToken
cancellationToken)\r\n   at System.Net.Http.HttpConnectionPool.
CreateHttp11ConnectionAsync(HttpRequestMessage request,
```

```
CancellationToken cancellationToken)\r\n   at System.Net.Http.
HttpConnectionPool.GetHttpConnectionAsync(HttpRequestMessage
request, CancellationToken cancellationToken)\
r\n   at System.Net.Http.HttpConnectionPool.
SendWithRetryAsync(HttpRequestMessage request, Boolean
doRequestAuth, CancellationToken cancellationToken)\r\n   at
System.Net.Http.RedirectHandler.SendAsync(HttpRequestMessage
request, CancellationToken cancellationToken)\r\n   at System.
Net.Http.DiagnosticsHandler.SendAsync(HttpRequestMessage
request, CancellationToken cancellationToken)\r\n   at
Microsoft.Extensions.Http.Logging.LoggingHttpMessageHandler.
SendAsync(HttpRequestMessage request, CancellationToken
cancellationToken)\r\n   at Microsoft.Extensions.Http.Logging.
LoggingScopeHttpMessageHandler.SendAsync(HttpRequestMessage
request, CancellationToken cancellationToken)\r\n   at System.
Net.Http.HttpClient.FinishSendAsyncBuffered(Task`1 sendTask,
HttpRequestMessage request, CancellationTokenSource cts,
Boolean disposeCts, CancellationToken callerToken, Int64
timeoutTime)\r\n   at Packt.Ecommerce.Product.Services.
ProductsService.GetProductsAsync(String filterCriteria) in
src\\platform-apis\\services\\Packt.Ecommerce.Product\\
Services\\ProductsService.cs:line 82\r\n   at Packt.Ecommerce.
Product.Controllers.ProductsController.GetProductsAsync(String
filterCriteria) in src\\platform-apis\\services\\Packt.
Ecommerce.Product\\Controllers\\ProductsController.cs:line
46\r\n   at Microsoft.AspNetCore.Mvc.Infrastructure.
ActionMethodExecutor.TaskOfIActionResultExecutor.
Execute(IActionResultTypeMapper mapper, ObjectMethodExecutor
executor, Object controller, Object[] arguments)\
r\n   at Microsoft.AspNetCore.Mvc.Infrastructure.
ControllerActionInvoker.<InvokeActionMethodAsync>g__
Logged|12_1(ControllerActionInvoker invoker)\
r\n   at Microsoft.AspNetCore.Mvc.Infrastructure.
ControllerActionInvoker.<InvokeNextActionFilterAsync>g__
Awaited|10_0(ControllerActionInvoker invoker, Task
lastTask, State next, Scope scope, Object state, Boolean
isCompleted)\r\n   at Microsoft.AspNetCore.Mvc.Infrastructure.
ControllerActionInvoker.Rethrow(ActionExecutedContextSealed
context)\r\n   at Microsoft.AspNetCore.Mvc.
Infrastructure.ControllerActionInvoker.Next(State& next,
Scope& scope, Object& state, Boolean& isCompleted)\
r\n   at Microsoft.AspNetCore.Mvc.Infrastructure.
ControllerActionInvoker.<InvokeInnerFilterAsync>g__
Awaited|13_0(ControllerActionInvoker invoker, Task
lastTask, State next, Scope scope, Object state,
```

```
Boolean isCompleted)\r\n   at Microsoft.AspNetCore.Mvc.
Infrastructure.ResourceInvoker.<InvokeFilterPipelineAsync>g__
Awaited|19_0(ResourceInvoker invoker, Task lastTask, State
next, Scope scope, Object state, Boolean isCompleted)\
r\n   at Microsoft.AspNetCore.Mvc.Infrastructure.
ResourceInvoker.<InvokeAsync>g__Logged|17_1(ResourceInvoker
invoker)\r\n   at Microsoft.AspNetCore.Routing.
EndpointMiddleware.<Invoke>g__AwaitRequestTask|6_0(Endpoint
endpoint, Task requestTask, ILogger logger)\r\n   at
Microsoft.AspNetCore.Authorization.AuthorizationMiddleware.
Invoke(HttpContext context)\r\n   at Packt.Ecommerce.Common.
Middlewares.ErrorHandlingMiddleware.InvokeAsync(HttpContext
context) in src\\platform-apis\\core\\Packt.Ecommerce.Common\\
Middlewares\\ErrorHandlingMiddleware.cs:line 65"
}
```

From the preceding code snippet, we can take `CorrelationIdentifier`, which is `03410a51b0475843936943d3ae04240c`, search the value in our logging provider, **Application Insights**, and we can ascertain additional information regarding the exception, as shown in the following screenshot:

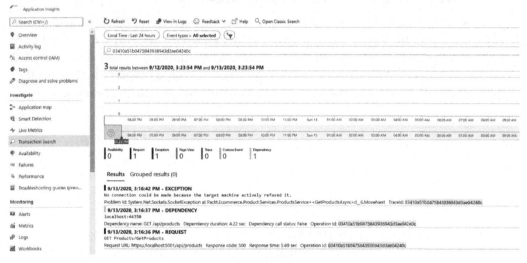

Figure 10.4 – Tracing CorrelationIdentifier in Application Insights

`CorrelationIdentifier` is extremely helpful in production environments where there is no inner exception.

This concludes our discussion regarding middleware. In the next section, let's look at what **controllers** and **actions** are and how they help in handling requests.

Handling requests using controllers and actions

Controllers are the fundamental blocks for handling requests for designing RESTful servicers using an ASP.NET Core web API. These are the primary classes that hold the logic to process requests, which includes retrieving data from a database, inserting a record into a database, and so on. Controllers are classes where we define methods to process requests. These methods usually include validating the input, talking to a data store, applying business logic (in enterprise applications, controllers will also call service classes), and—finally—serializing the response and sending it back to the client using HTTP protocols in JSON/XML form.

All these methods that hold the logic to process requests are known as **actions**. All requests received by the HTTP server are handed over to action methods using a routing engine. However, a routing engine transfers requests to actions based on certain rules that can be defined in a request pipeline. These rules are what we define in routing. Let's see how a URI for handling requests is mapped to a particular action in a controller.

Understanding ASP.NET Core routing

Up to now, we have seen that any HTTP request goes through the middleware and is finally handed over to the controller or an endpoint defined in the `configure` method, but who is responsible for this handover to a controller/endpoint, and how does ASP.NET Core know which controller and method inside the controller to trigger? That is what the routing engine is for, and this was injected when adding the following middlewares:

```
app.UseRouting();
app.UseEndpoints(endpoints =>
{
    endpoints.MapControllers();
});
```

Here, `app.UseRouting()` injects `Microsoft.AspNetCore.Routing.EndpointRoutingMiddleware`, which is used to make all routing decisions based on the URI. The primary job of this middleware is to set the instance of the `Microsoft.AspNetCore.Http.Endpoint` method with the value of the action that needs to be executed for a particular URI.

For example, if we are trying to get the details of a product according to its ID and have a product controller that has the `GetProductById` method to fulfill this request, when we make an API call to the `api/products/1` URI, putting a breakpoint in a middleware after `EndpointRoutingMiddleware` shows you that an instance of the `Endpoint` class is available with information regarding the action that matches the URI and should be executed. We can see this in the following screenshot:

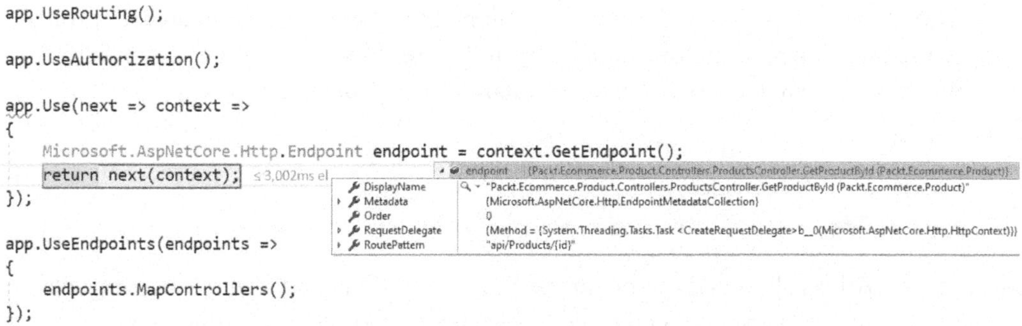

```
app.UseRouting();

app.UseAuthorization();

app.Use(next => context =>
{
    Microsoft.AspNetCore.Http.Endpoint endpoint = context.GetEndpoint();
    return next(context);
});

app.UseEndpoints(endpoints =>
{
    endpoints.MapControllers();
});
```

endpoint	{Packt.Ecommerce.Product.Controllers.ProductsController.GetProductById (Packt.Ecommerce.Product)}	
♪ DisplayName	Q → "Packt.Ecommerce.Product.Controllers.ProductsController.GetProductById (Packt.Ecommerce.Product)"	
♪ Metadata	{Microsoft.AspNetCore.Http.EndpointMetadataCollection}	
♪ Order	0	
♪ RequestDelegate	{Method = {System.Threading.Tasks.Task <CreateRequestDelegate>b__0(Microsoft.AspNetCore.Http.HttpContext)}}	
♪ RoutePattern	"api/Products/{id}"	

Figure 10.5 – Routing middlewares

This object would be null if there wasn't any matching controller/action. Internally, `EndpointRoutingMiddleware` uses the URI, query string parameters, and HTTP verbs and request headers to find the correct match.

Once the correct action method is identified, it's the job of `app.UseEndPoints` to hand over control to the action method identified by the `Endpoint` object and execute it. `UseEndPoints` injects `Microsoft.AspNetCore.Routing.EndpointMiddleware` to execute the appropriate method to fulfill a request. One important aspect of populating an appropriate `EndPoint` object is the various URIs that are configured inside `UseEndPoints` that can be achieved through the static extension methods available in ASP.NET Core. For example, if we want to configure just controllers, we can use `MapControllers` extension methods, which add endpoints for all actions in controllers for `UseRouting` to match further. If we are building RESTful APIs, it is recommended to use `MapControllers` extensions. However, there are many such extension methods for the following extensions that are commonly used:

- **MapGet/MapPost**: These are extension methods that can match specific patterns for GET/POST verbs and execute the request. They accept two parameters, one being the pattern of the URI and the second being the request delegate that can be used to execute when the pattern is matched. For example, the following code can be used to match the `/aboutus` route and respond with the text `Welcome to default products route`:

```
endpoints.MapGet("/aboutus", async context =>
{
```

```
await context.Response.WriteAsync("Welcome to default
products route");
});
```

- MapRazorPages: This extension method is used if we are using Razor Pages and need to route to appropriate pages based on routes.

- MapControllerRoute: This extension method can be used to match controllers with a specific pattern; for example, the following code can be seen in the ASP.NET Core MVC template, which matches methods based on a pattern:

```
endpoints.MapControllerRoute(
name: "default",
pattern: "{controller=Home}/{action=Index}/{id?}");
```

The request URI is split based on the forward slash (/) and is matched to the controller, action method, and ID. So, if you wanted to match a method in a controller, you need to pass the controller name (ASP.NET Core automatically suffixes the controller keyword) and method name in the URI.

Optionally, the ID can be passed as a parameter to that method. For example, if I have GetProducts in ProductsController, you would be calling it using the absolute URI, products/GetProducts. This kind of routing is known as **conventional routing** and is a good fit for UI-based web applications, and so can be seen in the ASP.NET Core MVC template.

This concludes our discussion of the basics of routing; there are many such extension methods available in ASP.NET Core that can be plumbed into the request pipeline based on application requirements. Now, let's look at attribute-based routing, a routing technique recommended for RESTful services built using ASP.NET Core.

> **Note**
> Another important aspect of routing, as with any other middleware sequence, is that injection is very important, and UseRouting should be called before UseEndpoints.

Attribute-based routing

For RESTful services, conventional routing contravenes a few REST principles, especially the principle that states that the operation on entities performed by the action method should be based on HTTP verbs; so, ideally, in order to get products, the URI should be GET api/products.

This is where attribute-based routing comes into play, in which routes are defined using attributes either at the controller level or at the action method level, or both. This is achieved using the Microsoft.AspNetCore.Mvc.Route attribute, which takes a string value as an input parameter and is used to map the controller and action. Let's take an example of ProductsController, which has the following code:

```
[Route("api/[controller]")]
[ApiController]
public class ProductsController : ControllerBase
{
    [HttpGet]
    [Route("{id}")]
    public IActionResult GetProductById(int id)
    {
        return Ok($"Product {id}");
    }
    [HttpGet]
    public IActionResult GetProducts()
    {
        return Ok("Products");
    }
}
```

Here, in the Route attribute at the controller level, we are passing the value api/[controller], which means that any URI matching api/products is mapped to this controller, where products is the name of the controller. Using the controller keyword inside square brackets is a specific way of telling ASP.NET Core to map the controller name automatically to the route.

However, if you want to stick to a specific name irrespective of the controller name, this can be used without square brackets. As a best practice, it is recommended to decouple controller names with routes. Hence, for our e-commerce application, we will go with exact values in routes—that is, ProductsController will have a route prefix of [Route("api/products")].

The Route attribute can also be added to action methods and can be used to additionally identify specific methods uniquely. Here, we are also passing a string that can be used to identify the method. For example, [Route("GetProductById/{id}")] would be matched to the api/products/GetProductById/1 URI, and the value inside the curly brackets is a dynamic value that can be passed as a parameter to the action method and matched with the parameter name.

What this means is that in the preceding code, there is an ID parameter, and the value inside the curly brackets should also be named ID so that ASP.NET Core can map values from the URI to the method parameter. Hence, for the api/products/1 URI, the ID parameter in the GetProductById method will have a value of 1 if the route attribute looks like this: [Route("{id}")].

Finally, the HTTP verb is represented by attributes such as [HttpGet], which will be used to map the HTTP verb from the URI to the method. The following table shows various examples and possible matches, assuming that ProductsController has [Route("api/products")]:

URI	Matching Method Signature
GET api/products	[HttpGet] public IActionResult GetProducts()
GET api/products/1	[HttpGet] [Route("{id}")] public IActionResult GetProducts(int id)
POST api/products	[HttpPost] public IActionResult CreateProduct(Product product)
PUT api/products/1	[HttpPut] [Route("{id}")] public IActionResult UpdateProduct(int id, Product product)
DELETE api/products/1	[HttpDelete] [Route("{id}")] public IActionResult DeleteProduct(int id)

Table 10.1

As you can see, the name of the method is immaterial here and so is not part of the URI matching unless it is specified in the `Route` attribute.

> **Note**
>
> One important aspect is that the web API supports the reading of parameters from various locations within a request, be it in the request body, header, query string, or URI. The following documentation covers the various options available: `https://docs.microsoft.com/en-us/aspnet/core/web-api/?view=aspnetcore-6.0#binding-source-parameter-inference`.

A summary of an entire API routing in ASP.NET Core could be represented as follows:

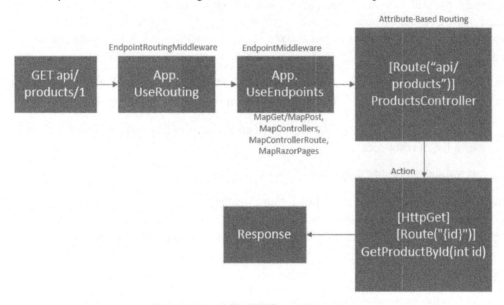

Figure 10.6 – ASP.NET Core API routing

Attribute-based routing is more RESTful, and we will follow this kind of routing in our e-commerce services. Now, let's look at the various helper classes available in ASP.NET Core that can be used to simplify the building of RESTful services.

> **Tip**
>
> The `{id}` expression in routing is known as a **routing constraint**, and ASP.NET Core comes with a varied set of such routing constraints that can also be found here: `https://docs.microsoft.com/en-us/aspnet/core/fundamentals/routing?view=aspnetcore-6.0#route-constraint-reference`.

The ControllerBase class, the ApiController attribute, and the ActionResult class

If we go back to any of the controllers created hitherto, you can see that all the controllers are inherited from the `ControllerBase` class. In ASP.NET Core, `ControllerBase` is an abstract class that provides various helper methods that assist in handling requests and responses. For example, if I wanted to send an HTTP status code `400` (bad request), there is a `BadRequest` helper method in `ControllerBase` that can be used to send an HTTP status code of `400`; otherwise, we have to manually create an object and populate it with the HTTP status code `400`. There are many such helper methods in `ControllerBase` that are available out of the box; however, not every API controller needs to be inherited from the `ControllerBase` class. All helper methods from the `ControllerBase` class are mentioned here: `https://docs.microsoft.com/en-us/dotnet/api/microsoft.aspnetcore.mvc.controllerbase?view=aspnetcore-3.1&viewFallbackFrom=aspnetcore-6.0`.

This brings us to a discussion as to what the return type of our controller methods should be because there could be at least two possible responses for any API in general, as follows:

- A successful response with a 2xx status code that possibly responds with a resource or a list of resources

- A validation failure case with a 4xx status code

To handle such scenarios, we need to create a generic type that can be used to send different response types, and this is where ASP.NET Core's `IActionResult` and `ActionResult` types come into play, providing us with derived response types for various scenarios. A few important response types that `IActionResult` supports are listed here:

- `OkObjectResult`: This is a response type that sets the HTTP status code to `200` and adds the resource to the body of the response containing the details of the resource. This type is ideal for all APIs that respond with a resource or a list of resources—for example, get products.

- `NotFoundResult`: This is a response type that sets the HTTP status code to `404` and has an empty body. This can be used if a particular resource is not found. However, in the case of a resource not found, we will use `NoContentResult` (`204`), as `404` will also be used for an API not found.

- `BadRequestResult`: This is a response type that sets the HTTP status code to `400` and contains an error message in the response body. This is ideal for any validation failures.

- `CreatedAtActionResult`: This is a response type that sets the HTTP status code to `201` and can add the newly created resource URI to the response. This is ideal for APIs that create resources.

All these response types are inherited from `IActionResult`, and there are methods available in the `ControllerBase` class that can create these objects; so, `IActionResult`, along with `ControllerBase`, would solve most of the business requirements, and this is what we will have as the return type for all our API controller methods.

The final important class available in ASP.NET Core that comes in handy is the `ApiController` class, which can be added as an attribute to the controller class or to an assembly, and adds the following behaviors to our controllers:

- It disables conventional routing and makes attribute-based routing mandatory.

- It validates models automatically, so we don't need to explicitly call `ModelState.IsValid` in every method. This behavior is very useful in the case of insert/update methods.

- It facilitates automatic parameter mapping from the body/route/header/query strings. What this means is that we don't specify whether a parameter of an API is going to be part of the body or route. For example, in the following code snippet, we don't need to explicitly say that the ID parameter is going to be part of the route as `ApiController` automatically uses something known as **inference rules** and a prefix in the ID with `[FromRoute]`:

```
[Route("{id}")]
public IActionResult GetProductById(int id)
{
    return Ok($"Product {id}");
}
```

- Similarly, in the following code snippet, `ApiController` will automatically add `[FromBody]` based on the inference rules:

```
public IActionResult CreateProduct(Product product)
{
//
}
```

- A couple of other behaviors that `ApiController` adds are inferring request content to multipart/form data and more detailed error responses, as per `https://tools.ietf.org/html/rfc7807`.

So, all in all, `ControllerBase`, `ApiController`, and `ActionResult` provide various helper methods and behaviors, thereby providing developers with all the tools needed to write RESTful APIs and allowing them to focus on business logic while writing APIs using ASP.NET Core.

With this foundation, let's design various APIs for our e-commerce application in the next section.

Integration with the data layer

The response from our APIs may or may not look like our domain models. Instead, their structure can resemble the fields that the UI or Views need to bind; hence, it is recommended to create a separate set of POCO classes that integrate with our UI. These POCOs are known as **Data Transfer Objects (DTOs)**.

In this section, we will implement our DTOs' domain logic integrating with the data layer and integrate the cache services discussed in *Chapter 8, All You Need to Know about Caching*, using the Cache-Aside pattern, and then—finally—implement the required RESTful APIs using controllers and actions. Along the way, we will use the `HTTPClient` factory for our service-to-service communication, and the `AutoMapper` library for mapping domain models to DTOs.

We will pick a product service that is part of `Packt.Ecommerce.Product`, a web API project using .NET 6, and discuss its implementation in detail. By the end of this section, we will have implemented the projects highlighted in the following screenshot:

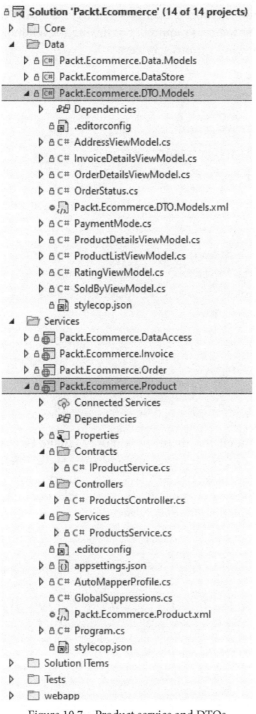

Figure 10.7 – Product service and DTOs

A similar implementation is replicated across all RESTful services with slight modifications in business logic, as required, but the high-level implementation remains the same across the following various services:

- `Packt.Ecommerce.DataAccess`
- `Packt.Ecommerce.Invoice`
- `Packt.Ecommerce.Order`
- `Packt.Ecommerce.Payment`
- `Packt.Ecommerce.UserManagement`

To start with, we will have the corresponding section in `appsettings.json`, which is shown as follows:

```
"ApplicationSettings": {
"UseRedisCache": false, // For in-memory
"IncludeExceptionStackInResponse": true,
"DataStoreEndpoint": "",
"InstrumentationKey": ""
},
"ConnectionStrings": {
"Redis": ""
}
```

For the local development environment, we will use **Manage User Secrets** (as explained at `https://docs.microsoft.com/en-us/aspnet/core/security/app-secrets?view=aspnetcore-6.0&tabs=windows`) and set the following values. However, once the service is deployed, it will make use of Azure Key Vault, as explained in *Chapter 6, Configuration in .NET 6*:

```
{
   "ApplicationSettings:InstrumentationKey": "", //relevant
                                                 //key
   "ConnectionStrings:Redis": "" //connection string
}
```

Let's begin by creating DTOs for the Products API.

Creating DTOs

The key requirements in terms of product services are to provide the ability to search for products, view additional details relating to the products, and then proceed with the purchase. Since a listing of products can have limited details, let's create a POCO (all DTOs are created in the `Packt.Ecommerce.DTO.Models` project) and name it `ProductListViewModel`. This class will have all the properties that we want to show on the product's list page, and it should look like this:

```
public class ProductListViewModel
{
        [JsonProperty(PropertyName = "id")]
        public string Id { get; set; }
        public string Name { get; set; }
        public int Price { get; set; }
        public Uri ImageUrl { get; set; }
        public double AverageRating { get; set; }
}
```

As you can see, these are minimum fields that are usually displayed on any e-commerce application. Hence, we will go with these fields, but the idea is to extend as the application evolves. Here, the `Id` and `Name` properties are important properties as those will be used to query the database once the user wants to retrieve all further details regarding the product. We are annotating the `Id` property with the `JsonProperty(PropertyName = "id")` attribute to ensure that the property name remains as `Id` during serialization and deserialization. This is important because, in our Cosmos DB instance, we are using `Id` as the key for most of the containers. Let's now create another POCO that represents the details of a product, as shown in the following code snippet:

```
public class ProductDetailsViewModel
{
        [Required]
        public string Id { get; set; }
        [Required]
        public string Name { get; set; }
        [Required]
        public string Category { get; set; }
        [Required]
        [Range(0, 9999)]
        public int Price { get; set; }
```

```
        [Required]
        [Range(0, 999, ErrorMessage = "Large quantity,
         please reach out to support to process request.")]
        public int Quantity { get; set; }
        public DateTime CreatedDate { get; set; }
        public List<string> ImageUrls { get; set; }
        public List<RatingViewModel> Rating { get; set; }
        public List<string> Format { get; set; }
        public List<string> Authors { get; set; }
        public List<int> Size { get; set; }
        public List<string> Color { get; set; }
        public string Etag { get; set; }
}
public class RatingViewModel
{
        public int Stars { get; set; }
        public int Percentage { get; set; }
}
```

So, in this DTO, apart from Id and Name, one of the important properties is Etag, which will be used for entity tracking to avoid concurrent overwrites on an entity. For example, if two users access a product and user A updates it before user B, using Etag, we can stop user B from overwriting user A's changes and force user B to take the latest copy of the product prior to updating. The AddProductAsync(ProductDetailsViewModel product) method in https://github.com/PacktPublishing/Enterprise-Application-Development-with-C-10-and-.NET-6-Second-Edition/tree/main/Enterprise%20Application/src/platform-apis/services/Packt.Ecommerce.Product/Controllers follows this pattern.

Another important aspect is that we are using ASP.NET Core's built-in validation attributes on our model to define all constraints on the models. Primarily, we will be using the [Required] attribute and any relevant attributes, as per https://docs.microsoft.com/en-us/aspnet/core/mvc/models/validation?view=aspnetcore-6.0#built-in-attributes.

All the DTOs would be part of the Packt.Ecommerce.DTO.Models project as they will be reused in our ASP.NET MVC application, which will be used to build the UI of our e-commerce application. Now, let's look at the contracts needed for the Products service.

Service-class contracts

Add a `Contracts` folder to `Packt.Ecommerce.Product` and create a contract/interface of a product's service class, for which we will refer to our requirements and define methods as needed. To start with, it will have all the methods to perform **create, read, update, and delete (CRUD)** operations on products based on that interface, and these will look like this:

```
public interface IProductService
    {
        Task<IEnumerable<ProductListViewModel>>
            GetProductsAsync(string filterCriteria = null);
        Task<ProductDetailsViewModel>
            GetProductByIdAsync(string productId,
                string productName);
        Task<ProductDetailsViewModel>
            AddProductAsync(ProductDetailsViewModel product);
        Task<HttpResponseMessage>
            UpdateProductAsync(ProductDetailsViewModel
                product);
        Task<HttpResponseMessage> DeleteProductAsync(
            string productId, string productName);
    }
```

Here, you can see that we are returning `Task` in all methods, thereby sticking to our asynchronous approach discussed in *Chapter 4, Threading and Asynchronous Operations*.

The mapper class using AutoMapper

The next thing that we will need is a way to transform our domain models to DTOs, and here, we will use a well-known library called `AutoMapper` (please refer to `https://docs.automapper.org/en/stable/Getting-started.html` for more details) to configure and add the following packages:

- `Automapper`
- `AutoMapper.Extensions.Microsoft.DependencyInjection`

To configure `AutoMapper`, we need to define a class that inherits from `AutoMapper.Profile` and then defines the mapping between various domain models and DTOs. Let's add an `AutoMapperProfile` class to the `Packt.Ecommerce.Product` project, as follows:

```
public class AutoMapperProfile : Profile
{

    public AutoMapperProfile()
    {
    }
}
```

`AutoMapper` comes with many inbuilt methods for mapping, one of these being `CreateMap`, which accepts source and destination classes and maps them based on the same property names. Any property that does not have the same name can be manually mapped using the `ForMember` method. Since `ProductDetailsViewModel` has a one-to-one mapping with our domain model, `CreateMap` should be good enough for their mapping. For `ProductListViewModel`, we have an additional field, `AverageRating`, for which we wanted to calculate the average of all the ratings given for a particular product. To keep it simple, we will use the `Average` method from `Linq` and then map it to the average rating. For modularization, we will have this in a separate method, `MapEntity`, which looks like this:

```
private void MapEntity()
{
        this.CreateMap<Data.Models.Product,
          DTO.Models.ProductDetailsViewModel>();
        this.CreateMap<Data.Models.Rating,
          DTO.Models.RatingViewModel>();
        this.CreateMap<Data.Models.Product,
          DTO.Models.ProductListViewModel>()
            .ForMember(x => x.AverageRating, o =>
              o.MapFrom(a => a.Rating != null ?
                a.Rating.Average(y => y.Stars) : 0));
}
```

Now, modify the constructor to call this method. Refer to `https://github.com/PacktPublishing/Enterprise-Application-Development-with-C-10-and-.NET-6-Second-Edition/blob/main/Enterprise%20Application/src/platform-apis/services/Packt.Ecommerce.Product/AutoMapperProfile.cs` for the complete implementation.

The final step involved in setting up `AutoMapper` is to inject it as one of the services, for which we will use the `WebApplicationBuilder` object of the `Program` class, using the following line of code:

```
Builder.Services.AddAutoMapper(typeof(AutoMapperProfile));
```

As explained earlier, this will inject the `AutoMapper` library into our API, and this will then allow us to inject `AutoMapper` into various services and controllers. Let's now look at the configuration of the `HttpClient` factory, which is used for calling the data access service.

HttpClient factory for service-to-service calls

To retrieve data, we must call APIs exposed by our data access service defined in `Packt.Ecommerce.DataAccess`. For this, we need a resilient library that can effectively use the available sockets, allowing us to define a circuit breaker as well as retry/timeout policies. `IHttpClientFactory` is ideal for such scenarios.

> **Note**
>
> One common issue with `HttpClient` is the potential `SocketException` error, which happens as `HttpClient` leaves the **Transmission Control Protocol** (**TCP**) connection open even after the object has been disposed of, and the recommendation is to create `HttpClient` as a static/singleton—which has its own overheads—while connecting to multiple services. These issues are summarized at `https://softwareengineering.stackexchange.com/questions/330364/should-we-create-a-new-single-instance-of-httpclient-for-all-requests`, and these are all now addressed by `IhttpClientFactory`.

To configure `IHttpClientFactory`, perform the following steps:

1. Install `Microsoft.Extensions.Http`.

2. We will be configuring `IHttpClientFactory` using typed clients, so add a `Services` folder and a `ProductsService` class and inherit them from `IProductService`. For now, leave the implementation empty. Now, map `IProductService` and `ProductsService` in the `Program` class using the following code:

```
builder.Services.AddHttpClient<IProductService,
ProductsService>()
        .SetHandlerLifetime(TimeSpan.FromMinutes(5))
        .AddPolicyHandler(RetryPolicy()) // Retry
                                         // policy.
        .AddPolicyHandler(CircuitBreakerPolicy());
        // Circuit breakerpolicy
```

Here, we are defining the timeout for `HttpClient` used by `ProductsService` as 5 minutes and additionally configuring a policy for retries and a circuit breaker.

Implementing a circuit-breaker policy

To define these policies, we will use a library called `Polly` (refer to `https://github.com/App-vNext/Polly` for the official documentation), which gives out-of-the-box resiliency and fault-handling capabilities. Install the `Microsoft.Extensions.Http.Polly` package and then add the following static method to the `Program` class that defines our circuit-breaker policy:

```
static IAsyncPolicy<HttpResponseMessage> CircuitBreakerPolicy()
{
    return HttpPolicyExtensions
        .HandleTransientHttpError()
        .CircuitBreakerAsync(5, TimeSpan.FromSeconds(30));
}
```

Here, we are saying that the circuit would be opened if there are 5 failures within 30 seconds. A circuit breaker assists in avoiding unnecessary HTTP calls where there is a critical failure that cannot be fixed with a retry.

Implementing a retry policy

Now, let's add our retry policy, which is a bit smarter compared with the standard retries that retire within a specified timeframe. So, we define a policy that will affect a retry and HTTP service calls on five occasions, and each retry would have a time difference in seconds at a rate of power of two. The code is illustrated here:

To add some randomness in terms of the time variation, we will use a Random class of C# to generate a random number and add it to the time gap. This random generation will be as shown in the following code:

```
private static IAsyncPolicy<HttpResponseMessage> RetryPolicy()
{
    Random random = new Random();
    var retryPolicy = HttpPolicyExtensions
        .HandleTransientHttpError()
        .OrResult(msg => msg.StatusCode ==
            System.Net.HttpStatusCode.NotFound)
        .WaitAndRetryAsync(
        5,
        retry => TimeSpan.FromSeconds(Math.Pow(2, retry))
        + TimeSpan.FromMilliseconds(random.Next(0, 100)));
    return retryPolicy;
}
```

Here, retry is an integer that increments by one with every retry. With this, add a static method to the Program class that has the preceding logic.

This completes our HTTPClient factory configuration, and ProductsService can use constructor injection to instantiate IHttpClientFactory, which can be further used to create HttpClient.

With all this configuration, we can now implement our service class. Let's look at that in the next section.

Implementing service classes

Let's now implement `ProductsService`, starting by defining various properties that we have now built and instantiating them using constructor injections, as shown in the following code block:

```
private readonly IOptions<ApplicationSettings>
applicationSettings;
private readonly HttpClient httpClient;
private readonly IMapper autoMapper;
private readonly IDistributedCacheService cacheService;
public ProductsService(IHttpClientFactory httpClientFactory,
IOptions<ApplicationSettings> applicationSettings, IMapper
autoMapper, IDistributedCacheService cacheService)
{
    NotNullValidator.ThrowIfNull(applicationSettings,
      nameof(applicationSettings));
    IHttpClientFactory httpclientFactory =
      httpClientFactory;
    this.applicationSettings = applicationSettings;
    this.httpClient = httpclientFactory.CreateClient();
    this.autoMapper = autoMapper;
    this.cacheService = cacheService;
}
```

All our services are going to use the same exception-handling middleware we defined in this chapter, so during service-to-service calls, if there is a failure in another service, the response would be of the `ExceptionResponse` type. Hence, let's create a private method, so deserialize the `ExceptionResponse` class and raise it accordingly. This is required because `HttpClient` would represent success or failure while using the `IsSuccessStatusCode` and `StatusCode` properties, so if there is an exception, we need to check `IsSuccessStatusCode` and rethrow it. Let's call this method `ThrowServiceToServiceErrors` and refer to the following code snippet:

```
private async Task
ThrowServiceToServiceErrors(HttpResponseMessage response)
{
```

```
    var exceptionReponse = await response.Content.
ReadFromJsonAsync<ExceptionResponse>().ConfigureAwait(false);
    throw new Exception(exceptionReponse.InnerException);
}
```

Let's now implement the GetProductsAsync method, in which we will use CacheService to retrieve data from the cache, and if it is not available in the cache, we will call the data access service using HttpClient, and finally map the Product domain's model to a DTO and return it asynchronously. The code will look like this:

```
public async Task<IEnumerable<ProductListViewModel>>
GetProductsAsync(string filterCriteria = null)
{
    var products = await this.cacheService
      .GetCacheAsync<IEnumerable<Packt.Ecommerce
      .Data.Models.Product>>($"products{filterCriteria}")
      .ConfigureAwait(false);
    if (products == null)
    {
        using var productRequest = new
          HttpRequestMessage(HttpMethod.Get,
          $"{this.applicationSettings.Value
           .DataStoreEndpoint}api/products
           ?filterCriteria={filterCriteria}");
        var productResponse = await this.httpClient
         .SendAsync(productRequest).ConfigureAwait(false);
        if (!productResponse.IsSuccessStatusCode)
        {
            await this.ThrowServiceToServiceErrors(
              productResponse).ConfigureAwait(false);
        }
        products = await productResponse.Content
          .ReadFromJsonAsync<IEnumerable<Packt
          .Ecommerce.Data.Models.Product>>()
          .ConfigureAwait(false);
        if (products.Any())
        {
            await this.cacheService.AddOrUpdateCacheAsync
```

```
                    <IEnumerable<Packt.Ecommerce.Data.Models
                .Product>>($"products{filterCriteria}",
                products).ConfigureAwait(false);
            }
        }
        var productList = this.autoMapper.Map<List
            <ProductListViewModel>>(products);
        return productList;
    }
}
```

We will follow a similar pattern and implement `AddProductAsync`, `UpdateProductAsync`, `GetProductByIdAsync`, and `DeleteProductAsync`. The only difference in each of these methods would be to use the relevant `HttpClient` method and handle them accordingly. Now that we have our service implemented, let's implement our controller.

Implementing action methods in the controller

Let's first inject the service created in the previous section into the ASP.NET Core 6 DI container so that we can use constructor injection to create an object of `ProductsService`. We will do this in the `Program` class using the following code:

```
builder.Services.AddScoped<IProductService, ProductsService>();
```

Also, ensure that all the required framework components—such as `ApplicationSettings`, `CacheService`, and `AutoMapper`—are configured.

Add a controller to the `Controllers` folder and name it `ProductsController` with the default route as `api/products`, and then add an `IProductService` property and inject it using constructor injection. The controller should implement five action methods, each calling one of the service methods, and use various out-of-the-box helper methods and attributes discussed in *The ControllerBase class, the ApiController attribute, and the ActionResult class* section of this chapter. The methods for retrieving specific products and creating a new product are shown in the following code block:

```
[HttpGet]
[Route("{id}")]
public async Task<IActionResult> GetProductById(string id,
[FromQuery] [Required] string name)
```

```csharp
{
    // FromQuery supports reading parameters from query
    // string, here the value of the query string parameter
    // 'name' will be mapped to name parameter.
    var product = await
        this.productService.GetProductByIdAsync(id,
        name).ConfigureAwait(false);
    if (product != null)
    {
        return this.Ok(product);
    }
    else
    {
        return this.NoContent();
    }
}
[HttpPost]
public async Task<IActionResult>
AddProductAsync(ProductDetailsViewModel product)
{
    // Product null check is to avoid null attribute
    // validation error.
    if (product == null || product.Etag != null)
    {
        return this.BadRequest();
    }
    var result = await this.productService
        .AddProductAsync(product).ConfigureAwait(false);
    return this.CreatedAtAction(nameof(
        this.GetProductById), new { id = result.Id, name =
        result.Name }, result); // HATEOS principle
}
```

The method implementation is self-explanatory and based purely on the fundamentals discussed in the *Handling requests using controllers and actions* section of this chapter. Similarly, we will implement all the other methods (`Delete`, `Update`, and `Get` all products) by calling the corresponding service method and returning the relevant `ActionResult`. With that, we will have APIs shown in the following table to handle various scenarios related to the product entity:

API	Description
`GET api/products`	Retrieve all products
`GET api/products/Cloth?name=T-Shirt`	Retrieve product details where the ID is Cloth and the name is T-Shirt
`POST api/products`	Create a product
`PUT api/products`	Update a product
`DELETE api/products/Cloth?name=T-Shirt`	Delete all products where the ID is Cloth and the name is T-Shirt
`GET api/products?filterCriteria=e.id='Cloth' and e.Price=987`	Retrieve all products where the ID is Cloth and the price is 987

Table 10.2

> **Tip**
>
> Another common scenario with APIs is to have an API that supports file upload/download. The upload scenario is achieved by passing `IFormFile` as an input parameter to the API. This serializes the uploaded file and can also save on the server. Similarly, for file downloading, `FileContentResult` is available and can stream files to any client. This is left to you as an activity to explore further.

For the testing API, we will use Postman (`https://www.postman.com/downloads/`). All Postman collections can be found under the `Solution Items` folder file, `Mastering enterprise application development Book.postman_collection.json`. To import a collection once Postman has been installed, perform the following steps:

1. Open Postman, and then click on **File**.

2. Click **Import | Upload files**, navigate to the location of the `Mastering enterprise application development Book.postman_collection.json` file and then click on **Import**.

A successful import will show the collection in the **Collections** menu of Postman, as depicted in the following screenshot:

Figure 10.8 – Collections in Postman

This completes our `Products` RESTful service implementation. All the other services mentioned at the beginning of this section are implemented in a similar way, where each of them is an individual web API project and handles the relevant domain logic for that entity.

Understanding gRPC

As per `grpc.io`, gRPC is a high-performance, open source universal RPC framework. Originally developed by Google, gRPC uses HTTP/2 for transport and a **Protocol Buffer (protobuf)** as the interface description language. gRPC is a contract-based binary communication system, and it is available across multiple ecosystems. The following diagram from gRPC's official documentation (`https://grpc.io`) illustrates client-server interaction using gRPC:

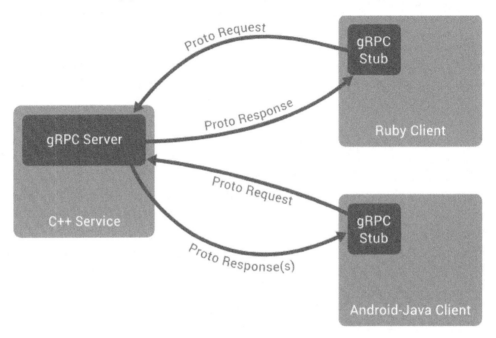

Figure 10.9 – gRPC client-server interaction

As with many distributed systems, gRPC is based on the idea of defining a service and specifying an interface with methods that can be invoked remotely, along with contracts. In gRPC, the server implements the interface and runs the gRPC server to handle client calls. The client side has the stub, which provides the same interface as defined by the server. The client calls the stub in the same way as it invokes methods in any other local object to invoke a method on the server.

By default, data contracts use **protocol buffers (protobufs)** to serialize the data from and to the client. Protobufs are defined in a text file with a `.proto` extension. In a protobuf, the data is structured as a logical record of the information contained in fields. In the upcoming section, we will learn about how to define a protobuf in Visual Studio for a .NET 6 application.

> **Note**
>
> Refer to the official documentation to learn more about gRPC: `https://grpc.io`. To learn more about protobufs, refer to `https://developers.google.com/protocol-buffers/docs/overview`.

Given the benefits of high performance, language-agnostic implementation, and reduced network usage associated with the protobuf of gRPC, many teams are exploring the use of gRPC in their endeavors to build microservices.

In the next section, we will learn how to build a gRPC server and client in .NET 6.

Building a gRPC server in .NET

After making its first appearance in .NET Core 3.0, gRPC has become a first-class citizen in the .NET ecosystem. Fully managed gRPC implementation is now available in .NET. Using Visual Studio 2022 and .NET 6, we can create gRPC server and client applications easily. Let's create a gRPC service using the gRPC service template in Visual Studio, shown in the following screenshot, and name it `gRPCDemoService`:

Figure 10.10 – gRPC Visual Studio 2022 project template

This will create a solution with a sample gRPC service named `GreetService`. Let's now understand the solution created with the template. The solution created will have a package reference to `Grpc.AspNetCore`. This will have the libraries required to host the gRPC service and a code generator for the `.proto` files. This solution will have a proto file created for `GreetService` under the `Protos` solution folder. The following code defines the `Greeter` service:

```
service Greeter {
  // Sends a greeting
  rpc SayHello (HelloRequest) returns (HelloReply);
}
```

The Greeter service has only one method named SayHello, which takes the input parameter as HelloRequest and returns a message of the HelloReply type. HelloRequest and HelloReply messages are defined in the same proto file, as shown in the following code snippet:

```
message HelloRequest {
   string name = 1;
}
message HelloReply {
   string message = 1;
}
```

HelloRequest has one field named name, and HelloReply has one field named message. The number next to the field shows the ordinal position of the field in the buffer. The proto files are compiled with the Protobuf compiler to generate stub classes with all the plumbing required. We can specify the kind of stub classes to generate from the properties of the proto file. Since this is a server, it will have the configuration set to **Server only**.

Now, let's look at the GreetService implementation. This will appear as shown in the following code snippet:

```
public class GreeterService : Greeter.GreeterBase
{
    private readonly ILogger<GreeterService> _logger;
    public GreeterService(ILogger<GreeterService> logger)
    {
        _logger = logger;
    }
    public override Task<HelloReply> SayHello(
      HelloRequest request, ServerCallContext context)
    {
        return Task.FromResult(new HelloReply
        {
            Message = "Hello " + request.Name
        });
    }
}
```

GreetService inherits from Greeter.GreeterBase, which is generated by the protobuf compiler. The SayHello method is overridden to provide the implementation so as to return a greeting to the caller by constructing HelloReply, as defined in the proto file.

To expose gRPC services in a .NET 6 application, all the required gRPC services are to be added to the service collection by calling AddGrpc in the Program class. The GreeterService gRPC service is exposed by calling MapGrpcService, as illustrated in the following code snippet:

```
app.MapGrpcService<GreeterService>();
```

That is everything that is required to expose a gRPC service in a .NET 6 application. In the next section, we will implement a .NET 6 client to consume GreeterService.

Building a gRPC client in .NET

As specified at the start of this *Understanding gRPC* section, .NET 6 has very good tooling for building a gRPC client as well. In this section, we will be building a gRPC client in a console application. Here are the steps to follow for you to accomplish this:

1. Create a .NET 6 console application and name it gRPCDemoClient.

2. Now, right-click on the project and click on the **Add | Service reference...** menu items. This will open the **Connected Services** tab, as shown in the following screenshot:

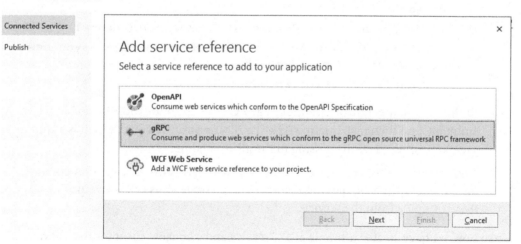

Figure 10.11 – gRPC Connected Services tab

3. Select **gRPC** in the **Add service reference** dialog, and then click on **Next**.

4. In the **Add new gRPC service reference** dialog, as shown in the following screenshot, select the **File** option, then select the `greet.proto` file from `gRPCDemoService`, and then click on the **Finish** button. This will add the proto file link to the project and marks the protobuf compiler to generate `Client` stub classes:

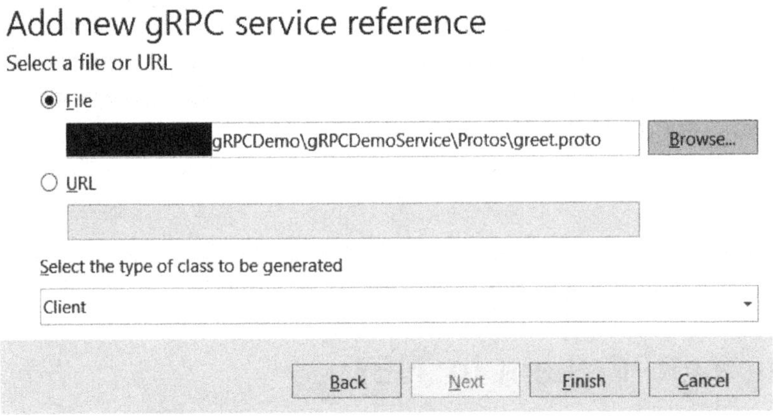

Figure 10.12 – Adding a gRPC service reference

This will also add the required `Google.Protobuf`, `Grpc.Net.ClientFactory`, and `Grpc.Tools` NuGet packages to the project.

5. Now, add the following code to the `Program` class of the `gRPCDemoClient` project:

```
var channel = GrpcChannel.ForAddress("https://
localhost:5001");
var client = new Greeter.GreeterClient(channel);
HelloReply response = await client.SayHelloAsync(new
HelloRequest { Name="Suneel" });
Console.WriteLine(response.Message);
```

In this code snippet, we are creating a gRPC channel to the `gRPCDemoService` endpoint, and then instantiating `Greeter.GreeterClient`, which is a stub to `gRPCDemoService`, by passing in the gRPC channel.

6. Now, to invoke the service, we just need to call the `SayHelloAsync` method on the stub by passing the `HelloRequest` message. This call will return `HelloReply` from the service.

Up to now, we have created a simple gRPC service and a console client for that service. In the next section, we will learn about `grpcurl`, which is a generic client to test gRPC services.

Testing gRPC services

To test or invoke a REST service, we use tools such as Postman or Fiddler. `grpcurl` is a command-line utility that helps us to interact with gRPC services. Using `grpcurl`, we can test gRPC services without building client apps. `grpcurl` is available for download from `https://github.com/fullstorydev/grpcurl`.

Once `grpcurl` is downloaded, we can call `GreeterService` using the following command:

```
grpcurl -d "{\"name\": \"World\"}" localhost:5001 greet.
Greeter/SayHello
```

> **Note**
>
> Currently, gRPC applications can only be hosted in Azure App Service and
> **Internet Information Services (IIS)**, hence we did not leverage gRPC in the
> demo e-commerce application that is hosted on Azure App Service. However,
> there is a version of the e-commerce application in this chapter demo, where
> obtaining a product according to its ID is exposed as a gRPC endpoint in a self-
> hosted service.

Summary

In this chapter, we covered the basic principles of REST and also designed enterprise-level RESTful services for our e-commerce application.

Along the way, we got to grips with the various web API internals of an ASP.NET Core 6 web API—including routing and sample middleware—and became familiar with tools for testing our services, while learning how to handle requests using a controller and its actions, which we also learned to build. Also, we saw how to create and test basic gRPC client and server applications in .NET 6. You should now be able to confidently build RESTful services using an ASP.NET Core 6 web API.

In the next chapter, we will go through the fundamentals of ASP.NET MVC, build our UI layer using ASP.NET MVC, and integrate it with our APIs.

Questions

1. Which of the following HTTP verbs is recommended for creating a resource?

   a. GET

   b. POST

   c. DELETE

   d. PUT

   Answer: b

2. Which of the following HTTP status codes represents No Content?

   a. 200

   b. 201

   c. 202

   d. 204

   Answer: d

3. Which of the following middlewares is used to configure routing?

   a. UseDeveloperExceptionPage()

   b. UseHttpsRedirection()

   c. UseRouting()

   d. UseAuthorization()

   Answer: c

4. If a controller is annotated with the [ApiController] attribute, do I need to class ModelState.IsValid explicitly in each action method?

   a. Yes—model validation isn't part of the ApiController attribute, hence you need to call ModelState.Valid in each action method.

   b. No—model validation is handled as part of the ApiController attribute, hence ModelState.Valid is triggered automatically for all action items.

   Answer: b

Further reading

- `https://docs.microsoft.com/en-us/dotnet/architecture/`
  `microservices/implement-resilient-applications/`
  `use-httpclientfactory-to-implement-resilient-http-requests`

- `https://docs.microsoft.com/en-us/aspnet/core/signalr/`
  `introduction?view=aspnetcore-6.0`

- `https://docs.microsoft.com/en-us/aspnet/core/tutorials/`
  `web-api-help-pages-using-swagger?view=aspnetcore-6.0`

- `https://docs.microsoft.com/en-us/aspnet/core/`
  `grpc/?view=aspnetcore-6.0`

- `https://docs.microsoft.com/en-us/odata/overview`

11

Creating an ASP. NET Core 6 Web Application

Up until now, we have built all the core components of the application, such as the data access layer and service layer, and all these components are primarily server-side components, also known as **backend components**.

In this chapter, we will build the presentation layer/**user interface (UI)** for our e-commerce application, which is also known as the **client-side component**. The UI is the face of the application; having a good presentation layer not only helps with keeping users engaged in the application but also encourages users to come back to the application. This is especially the case with enterprise applications, where a good presentation layer helps users to navigate through the application easily and helps them in performing various day-to-day activities that are dependent on the application with ease.

We will focus on understanding ASP.NET Core MVC and developing a web application using ASP.NET Core MVC. Primarily, we will cover the following topics:

- Introduction to frontend web development
- Integrating APIs with the service layer

- Creating the controller and actions

- Creating a UI using ASP.NET Core MVC

- Understanding Blazor

Technical requirements

For this chapter, you need a basic knowledge of C#, .NET Core, HTML, and CSS. The code examples for the chapter can be found here: `https://github.com/PacktPublishing/Enterprise-Application-Development-with-C-10-and-.NET-6-Second-Edition/tree/main/Chapter11/RazorSample`.

You can find more code examples here: `https://github.com/PacktPublishing/Enterprise-Application-Development-with-C-10-and-.NET-6-Second-Edition/tree/main/Enterprise%20Application`.

Introduction to frontend web development

The presentation layer is all about code that a browser can render and display to the user. Whenever a page gets loaded in a browser, it creates a hierarchy of various elements, such as textboxes and labels, that are present on the page. This hierarchy is known as the **Document Object Model (DOM)**.

A good frontend is all about the ability to manipulate the DOM as needed, and there are many technologies/libraries that support manipulating the DOM and loading data dynamically using the de facto language of the web, JavaScript. Be it jQuery (which simplifies the use of JavaScript), full-blown client-side frameworks such as Angular, React, or Vue (which support complete client-side rendering), or ASP.NET Core frameworks such as ASP.NET Core MVC, Razor Pages, or Blazor, it all boils down to handling the three major building blocks of the web: HTML, CSS, and JavaScript. Let's look into these three building blocks:

- **Hypertext Markup Language (HTML)**: HTML, as the full form states, is a markup language that browsers can understand and display the contents. It primarily consists of a series of tags, which are known as **HTML elements**, and allows developers to define the structure of the page. For example, if you want to create a form that needs to allow the user to enter their first name and last name, it can be defined by using input HTML elements.

- **Cascading Style Sheets (CSS)**: The presentation layer is all about presenting data in a way that makes a web application more appealing to users and ensures that the application is usable, irrespective of the device/resolution that a user tries to load the application in. This is where CSS plays a critical role in defining how the content is displayed on the browser. It controls various things, such as the styling of the pages, the theme of the application, and the color palette, and, more importantly, makes them responsive so that users have the same experience using the application, be it loaded on a mobile or a desktop.

The good thing about modern web development is we don't need to write everything from scratch and many libraries are available that can be picked and used as they are, in the application. We will be using one such library for an e-commerce application, which is explained in the *Creating a UI using ASP.NET Core MVC* section.

- **JavaScript**: JavaScript is a scripting language that helps in performing various advanced dynamic operations, for example, validating input text entered in a form or things such as enabling/disabling HTML elements conditionally or retrieving data from an API. JavaScript gives more power to web pages and adds many programming features that a developer can use to perform advanced operations on the client side. Just like HTML and CSS, all browsers can understand JavaScript, which forms an important part of the presentation layer. All these components can be linked to each other, as shown in the following diagram:

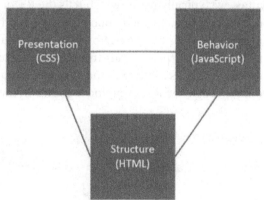

Figure 11.1 – HTML, CSS, and JavaScript

> **Note**
> HTML, CSS, and JavaScript all go hand in hand and play an important role in developing client-side/frontend applications and would require dedicated books to explain fully. Some related links can be found in the *Further reading* section.

Now that we understand the importance of HTML, CSS, and JavaScript, we need to know how we can use them to build the presentation layer of a web application so that it can support multiple browsers and devices with different resolutions and is able to manage the state (HTTP being stateless).

One technique could be to create all the HTML pages and host them on a web server; however, while this works well with static sites and also involves building everything from the ground up, if we want the content to be more dynamic and want a rich UI, we need to use technologies that can generate the HTML pages dynamically and provide seamless support to interact with the backend. Let's look, in the next section, at various technologies that can be used to generate dynamic HTML.

Razor syntax

Before we start understanding the various possible frameworks provided by ASP.NET Core, let's first understand what the Razor syntax is. It is a markup syntax to embed server-side components into HTML. We can use the Razor syntax to bind any dynamic data for display or send it back to the server from a view/page for further processing. The Razor syntax is primarily written in Razor files/Razor view pages, which are nothing more than files used by C# to generate dynamic HTML. They go with the `.cshtml` extension and support the Razor syntax. The Razor syntax is processed by an engine called the **view engine**, and the default view engine is known as the **Razor engine**.

To embed the Razor syntax, we typically use @, which tells the Razor engine to parse and generate HTML out of the engine. @ can be followed by any C# built-in methods to generate HTML. For example, `<b>@DateTime.Now</b>` can be used to display the current date and time in a Razor view/page. Apart from this, just like C#, the Razor syntax also supports code blocks and controls structures and variables, among other things. Some sample Razor syntax going through the Razor engine is shown in the following figure:

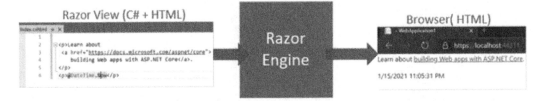

Figure 11.2 – Razor syntax

The Razor syntax also supports defining HTML controls; for example, to define a textbox, we can use the following Razor syntax:

```
<input asp-for=' FirstName ' />
```

The preceding code is known as an `input` tag helper and the Razor syntax takes care of what is known as **directive** tag helpers to bind data to an HTML control and generate rich, dynamic HTML. Let's discuss this briefly:

- **Directives**: Under the hood, each Razor view/page is parsed by the Razor engine, and a C# class is used to generate dynamic HTML and then send it back to the browser. Directives can be used to control the behavior of this class, which further controls the dynamic HTML that is generated.

  For example, the `@using` directive can be used to include any namespaces in the Razor view/page, or the `@code` directive can be used to include any C# members.

  One of the most used directives is `@model`, which allows you to bind a model to a view, which helps in validating the type of view as well as helps with IntelliSense. This process of binding views to a specific class/model is known as **strongly typing** views. We will be strongly typing all our views in our e-commerce application, which we will see in the *Creating a UI using ASP.NET Core MVC* section.

- **Tag helpers**: If you used ASP.NET MVC before ASP.NET Core, you would have come across HTML helpers, which are classes that help to bind data and generate HTML controls.

  However, with ASP.NET Core, we have tag helpers, which help us to bind data to an HTML control. The benefit of tag helpers over HTML helpers is that tag helpers use the same syntax as HTML with additional attributes assigned to the standard HTML controls that can be generated from dynamic data. For example, to generate an HTML textbox control, typically, we write the following code:

  ```
  <input type='text' id='Name' name='Name' value='
  Mastering enterprise application development Book'>
  ```

  Using tag helpers, this would be rewritten as shown in the following code, where `@Name` is the property of the model that the view is strongly typed to:

  ```
  <input type='text' asp-for='@Name'>
  ```

So, as you can see, it's all about writing HTML but taking advantage of Razor markup to generate dynamic HTML. ASP.NET Core comes with many built-in tag helpers, and more details about them can be found here: `https://docs.microsoft.com/en-us/aspnet/core/mvc/views/tag-helpers/built-in/?view=aspnetcore-6.0`.

It is not required to know about/remember every tag helper, and we will use this reference documentation as and when we develop our application UI.

> **Note**
>
> Since Razor syntax is markup, it's not necessary to know all the syntax. The following link can be used as a reference for Razor syntax: `https://docs.microsoft.com/en-us/aspnet/core/mvc/views/razor?view=aspnetcore-6.0`.

With this, let's look into the various options in ASP.NET Core as well as other common frameworks to develop the presentation layer.

Exploring Razor Pages

Razor Pages is the default way to implement a web application using ASP.NET Core. Razor Pages relies on the concept of having a Razor file that can serve requests directly and an optional C# file associated with that Razor file for any additional processing. A typical Razor application can be created with the following command:

```
dotnet new webapp --framework net6.0 -o RazorSample
```

As you can see, the project has Razor pages and their corresponding C# files. On opening any Razor view, we see a directive called `@page`, which helps in browsing the page. So, for example, `/index` will be routed to `index.cshtml`. It's important that all Razor pages have the `@page` directive at the top of the page and are placed in the `Pages` folder, as the ASP.NET Core runtime looks for all the Razor pages in this folder.

A Razor page can be further associated with a C# class, also known as a `PageModel` class, by using another directive called `@model`. The following is the code for the `index.cshtml` page:

```
@page
@model IndexModel
@{
    ViewData["Title"] = "Home page";
}
<form method="post">
    <div class="text-center">
        <select asp-for="WeekDaySelected"
          asp-items="Model.WeekDay"></select>
        <button type=Submit name="Submit">Submit</button>
        <br>
        <h3>@ViewData["Message"]</h3>
```

```
          </div>
   </form>
```

The PageModel class is nothing more than a C# class that can have specific methods for GET and POST calls so that data on the Razor page can be dynamically fetched, say, from an API. This class needs to be inherited by Microsoft.AspNetCore.Mvc.RazorPages.PageModel and is a standard C# class. PageModel for index.cshtml, which is part of index.cshtml.cs, is shown in the following code:

```
public class IndexModel : PageModel
{
    public IndexModel(ILogger<IndexModel> logger)
    {
    }
    public List<SelectListItem> WeekDay { get; set; }
    public void OnGet()
    {
        this.WeekDay = new List<SelectListItem>();
        this.WeekDay.Add(new SelectListItem
                    {
                            Value = 'Monday',
                            Text =  'Monday'
                    });
        this.WeekDay.Add(new SelectListItem
                    {
                            Value = 'Tuesday',
                            Text =  'Tuesday'
                    });

    }
}
```

Here, you can see that we are populating additional data that was used on the Razor page via the OnGet method, which is also known as a PageModel handler and can be used for the initialization of the Razor page. Like OnGet, we can add an OnPost handler that can be used to submit data back from the Razor page to PageModel and further the process.

The `OnPost` method will automatically bind all the properties in the `PageModel` class if they meet the following two conditions:

- The property is annotated with the `BindProperty` attribute.

- The Razor page has an HTML control with the same name as the property.

So, for example, if we wanted to bind the value of the `select` control in the preceding code, we need to first add a property to the `PageModel` class, as shown in the following code:

```
[BindProperty]
public string WeekDaySelected { get; set; }
```

Then, use the property name for the `select` control, as shown here, and Razor Pages will automatically bind the selected value to this property:

```
<select asp-for='WeekDaySelected' asp-items='Model.WeekDay'></
select>
```

We can use an asynchronous naming convention for the `OnGet` and `OnPost` methods so that they can be named as `OnGetAsync`/`OnPostAsync` if we are using asynchronous programming.

Razor Pages also supports calling methods based on the verb. The pattern for the method name should follow the `OnPost[handler]`/`OnPost[handler]Async` convention, where `[handler]` is the value set on the `asp-page-handler` attribute of any tag helper.

For example, the following code will call the `OnPostDelete`/`OnPostDeleteAsync` method from the corresponding `PageModel` class:

```
<input type='submit' asp-page-handler='Delete' value='Delete'
/>s
```

For the services configuration part, Razor Pages can be configured using the `AddRazorPages` method in the `Program` class by adding the service to the ASP.NET Core **dependency injection (DI)** container. Furthermore, `MapRazorPages` middleware needs to be injected for the Razor pages endpoint in the `Program` class, as shown in the following code. This is done so that all the Razor pages can be requested using the name of the page:

```
app.MapRazorPages();
```

This completes a simple Razor page application setup; we saw another sample in *Chapter 9, Working with Data in .NET 6*, that used Razor Pages to retrieve data from a database using **Entity Framework Core** (**EF Core**).

Razor Pages is the easiest form of developing web applications in ASP.NET Core; however, for a more structured form of developing web applications that can handle complex features, we can go with ASP.NET Core MVC. Let's explore developing web apps using ASP.NET Core MVC in the next section.

Exploring the ASP.NET Core MVC website

As the name suggests, ASP.NET Core MVC is based on the MVC pattern discussed in *Chapter 10, Creating an ASP.NET Core 6 Web API*, and is a framework in ASP.NET Core to build web applications. We saw in *Chapter 10, Creating an ASP.NET Core 6 Web API*, that the ASP.NET Core Web API also uses the MVC pattern; however, ASP.NET Core MVC also supports views to display data. The underlying design pattern is the same, where we have a model to hold data, a controller to transfer the data, and views to render and display the data.

ASP.NET Core MVC supports all the features that were discussed in *Chapter 10, Creating an ASP.NET Core 6 Web API*, such as routing, DI, model binding, and model validation, and uses the same bootstrapping technique of using the `Program` class. Like the Web API, .NET 6 application services and middlewares are configured in the `Program` class.

One of the key differences with MVC is the additional loading of views for which, instead of `AddControllers`, we need to use `AddControllersWithViews` in the `Program` class. An example is shown in the following figure:

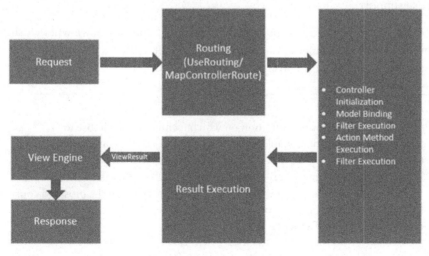

Figure 11.3 – MVC request life cycle

AddControllersWithViews primarily takes care of loading the views and handling the data sent by the controller, but most importantly, it takes care of configuring the Razor engine service that is used to process the Razor syntax in views and generate dynamic HTML.

Controller actions in ASP.NET Core MVC need to be routed based on the action name passed in the URL, so on the routing part, instead of calling MapController, we configure MapControllerRoute and pass a pattern to it. So, the default routing configuration in the UseEndpoints middleware looks as in the following code snippet:

```
app.UseEndpoints(endpoints =>
{
endpoints.MapControllerRoute(
name: 'default',
pattern: '{controller=Products}/{action=Index}/{id?}');
});
```

Here, in the pattern, we are telling the middleware that the first part of the URL should be a controller name, followed by the action name and an optional id parameter. If nothing is passed in the URL, the default route is the Index action method of ProductsController. So, primarily, this is the convention-based routing we discussed in *Chapter 10, Creating an ASP.NET Core 6 Web API*.

Just like Razor Pages, views in ASP.NET Core MVC applications support the Razor syntax and allow strongly typed views; that is, a view can be bound to a model for type checking, and model properties can be associated with HTML controls with compile-time IntelliSense support.

Since ASP.NET Core MVC gives more structure to the application, we will be using ASP.NET Core MVC for our presentation layer development, and it is discussed in detail while implementing the presentation layer in subsequent sections.

> **Note**
>
> There is always a common question on which technology to choose for frontend development. The following link has some recommendations around this topic: https://docs.microsoft.com/en-us/dotnet/architecture/modern-web-apps-azure/choose-between-traditional-web-and-single-page-apps. All the pros and cons should be evaluated before choosing the frontend technology as there are no one-size-fits-all requirements.

With this foundation, let's move on to the next section, where we will start integrating the backend APIs developed up until now with our presentation layer.

Integrating APIs with the service layer

In this section, we will be developing the `Packt.Ecommerce.Web` ASP.NET Core MVC application, which is created by adding the `ASP.NET Core web application (Model-View-Controller)` template. As we have already developed various APIs needed for the presentation layer, we will first build a wrapper class that will be used to communicate with these APIs.

This is a single wrapper class that will be used to communicate with various APIs, so let's create the contract for this class. For simplicity, we will limit the requirements to the most important workflow in our e-commerce application, and that will be as follows:

- The landing page retrieves all products in the system and allows users to search/filter the products.

- View the details of the products, add them to the cart, and be able to add more products to the cart.

- Complete the order and see the invoice.

To follow a more structured approach, we will segregate various classes and interfaces into separate folders. Let's see how in the following steps:

1. To start with, let's add a `Contracts` folder to the `Packt.Ecommerce.Web` project and add an interface with the name `IECommerceService`. This interface will have the following methods:

```
// Method to retrieve all products and filter.
Task<IEnumerable<ProductListViewModel>>
GetProductsAsync(string filterCriteria = null);
// Method to get details of specific product.
Task<ProductDetailsViewModel> GetProductByIdAsync(string
productId, string productName);
// Method to create and order, this method is primarily
used to create a cart which is nothing but an order with
order status as 'Cart'.
Task<OrderDetailsViewModel>
CreateOrUpdateOrder(OrderDetailsViewModel order);
// Method to retrieve order by ID, also used to retrieve
cart/order before checkout.
```

```
Task<OrderDetailsViewModel> GetOrderByIdAsync(string
orderId);
        Task<InvoiceDetailsViewModel>
GetInvoiceByIdAsync(string invoiceId);
// Method to submit cart and create invoice.
Task<InvoiceDetailsViewModel>
SubmitOrder(OrderDetailsViewModel order);
// Method to retrieve invoice details by Id.
Task<InvoiceDetailsViewModel> GetInvoiceByIdAsync(string
invoiceId);
```

2. Now, let's add a folder called `Services` and add a class called `EcommerceService`. This class will inherit `IECommerceService` and implement all the methods.

3. As we need to call various APIs, we need to make use of the **HttpClient factory**, as mentioned in *Chapter 10, Creating an ASP.NET Core 6 Web API*. All the API URLs are maintained in the application settings, so we will also populate `Packt.Ecommerce.Common.Options.ApplicationSettings` using the `options` pattern.

The `Program` class will have the following services configured for our MVC application:

- `AddControllersWithViews`: This will inject the necessary services for ASP.NET Core MVC to use controllers and views.

- `ApplicationSettings`: This will configure the `ApplicationSettings` class using the `IOptions` pattern with the following code:

```
builder.Services.Configure<ApplicationSettings>(this.
Configuration.GetSection('ApplicationSettings'));
```

- `AddHttpClient`: This will inject `System.Net.Http.IHttpClientFactory` and related classes that will allow us to create an `HttpClient` object. Additionally, we will configure the retry policy and circuit break policy, as discussed in *Chapter 10, Creating an ASP.NET Core 6 Web API*.

- Mapping `EcommerceService` to `IECommerceService` using the .NET Core DI container.

4. Configure the app insights using the following code:

```
string appinsightsInstrumentationKey = this.Configuration.
GetValue<string>('AppSettings:InstrumentationKey');

if (!string.
IsNullOrWhiteSpace(appinsightsInstrumentationKey))
        {
                builder.Services.AddLogging(logging =>
                {
logging.AddApplicationInsights(
                appinsightsInstrumentationKey);
                });
                builder.Services
                .AddApplicationInsightsTelemetry
                (appinsightsInstrumentationKey);
        }
```

Moving on to the middleware, we will be injecting the following middleware using the `Program` class, apart from the default routing middleware:

- `UseStatusCodePagesWithReExecute`: This middleware is used to redirect to a custom page other than for the 500 error code. We will add a method in `ProductController` in the next section that will be executed and loads the relevant view based on the error code. This middleware takes a string as an input parameter, which is nothing more than the route that should be executed in the case of an error, and to pass an error code, it allows a placeholder of {0}. So, the middleware configuration would look as follows:

```
app.UseStatusCodePagesWithReExecute('/Products/Error/
{0}');
```

- **Error handling**: As for the presentation layer, unlike with the API, we need to redirect users to a custom page that, in the case of runtime failures, has relevant information, such as a user-friendly failure message and a relevant logging ID that can be used to retrieve the actual failure at a later stage. However, in the case of a development environment, we can show the complete error along with the stack. So, we will configure two middlewares as shown in the following code:

```
{
if (env.IsDevelopment())
        app.UseDeveloperExceptionPage();
```

```
    }
    else
    {

        app.UseExceptionHandler('/Products/Error/500');

    }
```

Here, we can see that for the development environment, we are using the `UseDeveloperExceptionPage` middleware, which will load the full exception stack trace, whereas, for non-development environments, we are using the `UseExceptionHandler` middleware, which takes the path of the error action method that needs to be executed. Additionally, here, we don't need our custom error handling middleware, as the ASP.NET Core middleware takes care of logging detailed errors to the logging provider, which is Application Insights in our case.

- `UseStaticFiles`: To allow various static files, such as CSS, JavaScript, images, and any other static files, we don't need to go through the entire request pipeline, and that is where this middleware comes into play, which allows serving static files and supports short-circuiting the rest of the pipeline for static files.

Coming back to the `EcommerceService` class, let's first define the local variables and the constructor of this class, which will inject the `HTTPClient` factory and `ApplicationSettings` using the following code:

```
private readonly HttpClient httpClient;
private readonly ApplicationSettings applicationSettings;
public ECommerceService(IHttpClientFactory httpClientFactory,
IOptions<ApplicationSettings> applicationSettings)
{
NotNullValidator.ThrowIfNull(applicationSettings,
nameof(applicationSettings));
IHttpClientFactory httpclientFactory = httpClientFactory;
this.httpClient = httpclientFactory.CreateClient();
this.applicationSettings = applicationSettings.Value;
}
```

Now, to implement methods as per our `IECommerceService` interface, we will use the following steps for the Get APIs:

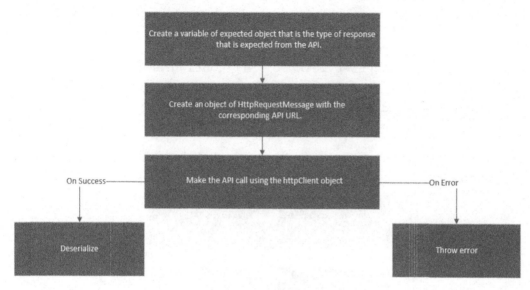

Figure 11.4 – Get call to API

Based on the steps in the preceding figure, the implementation of `GetProductsAsync`, which is primarily used to retrieve products for the landing page and apply any filters while doing a product search, will look as shown in the following code:

```
public async Task<IEnumerable<ProductListViewModel>>
GetProductsAsync(string filterCriteria = null)
{
    IEnumerable<ProductListViewModel> products = new
List<ProductListViewModel>();
    using var productRequest = new
      HttpRequestMessage(HttpMethod.Get,
        $'{this.applicationSettings.ProductsApiEndpoint}
        ?filterCriteria={filterCriteria}');
    var productResponse = await this.httpClient.SendAsync(
      productRequest).ConfigureAwait(false);
    if (!productResponse.IsSuccessStatusCode)
    {        await this.ThrowServiceToServiceErrors(
            productResponse).ConfigureAwait(false);
    }
```

```
    if (productResponse.StatusCode !=
      System.Net.HttpStatusCode.NoContent)
    {
        products = await productResponse.Content
          .ReadFromJsonAsync<Ienumerable
          <ProductListViewModel>>().ConfigureAwait(false);
    }
    return products;
}
```

For the POST/PUT APIs, we will have similar steps with slight modifications, as shown in the following figure:

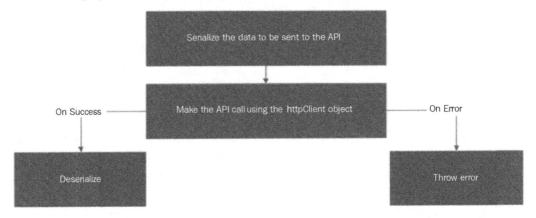

Figure 11.5 – Post call to API

Based on this, the strategy implementation of CreateOrUpdateOrder, which is primarily used to create the shopping cart, will look as shown in the following code:

```
public async Task<OrderDetailsViewModel>
CreateOrUpdateOrder(OrderDetailsViewModel order)
{
    NotNullValidator.ThrowIfNull(order, nameof(order));
    using var orderRequest = new
      StringContent(JsonSerializer.Serialize(order),
      Encoding.UTF8, ContentType);
    var orderResponse = await this.httpClient.PostAsync(new
      Uri($'{this.applicationSettings.OrdersApiEndpoint}'),
      orderRequest).ConfigureAwait(false);
```

```
        if (!orderResponse.IsSuccessStatusCode)
        {
            await this.ThrowServiceToServiceErrors(
              orderResponse).ConfigureAwait(false);
        }
        var createdOrder = await orderResponse.Content
          .ReadFromJsonAsync<OrderDetailsViewModel>()
          .ConfigureAwait(false);
        return createdOrder;
    }
```

Similarly, we will implement GetProductByIdAsync, GetOrderByIdAsync, GetInvoiceByIdAsync, and SubmitOrder using one of the preceding strategies and using the relevant API endpoints.

Now, let's create the controllers and action methods that will talk to EcommerceService and load the relevant views.

Creating the controller and actions

We have already seen that routing takes care of mapping the request URI to an action method in a controller, so let's further understand how the action methods then load the respective views. As you will have noticed, all the views in the ASP.NET Core MVC project are part of the Views folder, and when the action method execution is completed, it simply looks for Views/<ControllerName>/<Action>.cshtml.

For example, an action method mapping to the Products/Index route will load the Views/Products/Index.cshtml view. This is handled by calling the Microsoft.AspNetCore.Mvc.Controller.View method at the end of every action method.

There are additional overloads and helper methods that can override this behavior and route to a different view as needed. Before we talk about these helper methods, just like the Web API, each action method in the MVC controller can also return `IActionResult`, which means we can make use of helper methods to redirect to a view. In ASP.NET Core MVC, every controller is inherited by a base class, `Microsoft.AspNetCore.Mvc.Controller`, which comes with a few helper methods, and loading a view via an action method is handled by the following helper methods in the `Microsoft.AspNetCore.Mvc.Controller` class:

- `View`: This method has multiple overloads and primarily loads the view from the folder under `Views` based on the controller name. For example, calling this method in `ProductsController` can load any `.cshtml` file from the `Views/Products` folder. Additionally, it can take the name of the view, which can be loaded if required, and supports passing an object that can be retrieved in views by strongly typing the view.

- `RedirectToAction`: Although the `View` method handles most scenarios, there would be scenarios where we need to call another action method within the same controller or another controller, which is where `RedirectToAction` helps. This method comes with various overloads and allows us to specify the name of the action method, controller method, and object that the action method can receive as route values.

In short, to load the views and pass data from controllers, we will be passing respective models to the `View` method and, as required, we will use `RedirectToAction` whenever there is a need to call another action method.

Now, the question is how to handle data retrieval (`GET` calls) versus data submission (`POST` calls), and in ASP.NET Core MVC, all the action methods support annotating with HTTP verbs using the `HttpGet` and `HttpPost` attributes. The following are a few rules that can be used to annotate methods:

- If we want to retrieve data, then the action method is annotated using `HttpGet`.

- If we want to submit data to an action method, it should be annotated using `HttpPost` with the relevant object as the input parameter to that action method.

Typically, methods that need to send data from a controller to a view should be annotated with `[HttpGet]`, and methods that need to receive data from a view for further submission to the database should be annotated using `[HttpPost]`.

Now, let's move on to adding the required controllers and implementing them. When we add `Packt.Ecommerce.Web`, it creates a `Controllers` folder with `HomeController` created by default, which we need to delete. Then we need to add the three controllers by right-clicking on the `Controllers` folder, then selecting **Add | Controller | MVC Controller | Empty**, and naming them `ProductsController`, `CartController`, and `OrdersController`.

All these controllers will have the following two common properties, one for logging and one for calling methods of `EcommerceService`. They are further initialized using constructor injection as follows:

```
private readonly ILogger<ProductsController> logger;
private readonly IECommerceService eCommerceService;
```

Let's now discuss what is defined in each of these controllers:

- `ProductsController`: This controller will contain the `public async Task<IActionResult> Index(string searchString, string category)` action method to load the default view for listing all the products, which further supports filtering. There will be another method, `public async Task<IActionResult> Details(string productId, string productName)`, that takes the ID and name of the product and loads the details of the specified product. As both these methods are used for retrieving, they will be annotated using `[HttpGet]`. Additionally, this controller will have the `Error` method, as discussed earlier. Since it can receive an error code as an input parameter from the `UseStatusCodePagesWithReExecute` middleware, we will have simple logic to load the views accordingly:

```
[Route('/Products/Error/{code:int}')]
public IActionResult Error(int code)
{
    if (code == 404)
    {
        return
            this.View('~/Views/Shared/NotFound.cshtml');
    }
    else
```

```
    {
        return
        this.View('~/Views/Shared/Error.cshtml', new
        ErrorViewModel { CorrelationId =
        Activity.Current?.RootId ??
        this.HttpContext.TraceIdentifier });
    }
}
```

- `CartController`: This controller contains the `public async Task<IActionResult> Index(ProductListViewModel product)` action method to add a product to the cart, where we will create an order with the order status set to `'Cart'`, as this needs to receive data and further pass it to the API, which will be annotated with `[HttpPost]`. For simplicity, this is left anonymous but can be restricted for the logged-in users. Once the order is created, this method will make use of the `RedirectToAction` helper method and redirects to the `public async Task<IActionResult> Index(string orderId)` action method within this controller, which further loads the cart with all the products and the checkout form. This method can also be used to directly navigate to the shopping cart.

- `OrdersController`: This is the last controller in the flow, which contains the `public async Task<IActionResult> Create(OrderDetailsViewModel order)` action method to submit the order after filling in the payment details. This method updates the status of the order to `Submitted`, then creates an invoice for the order, and finally, redirects to another action method, `public async Task<IActionResult> Index(string invoiceId)`, which loads the final invoice of the order and completes the transaction.

The following diagram represents the flow between various methods across controllers to complete the shopping workflow:

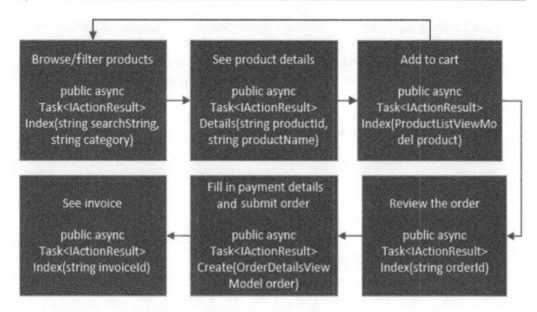

Figure 11.6 – Flow between controller action methods

With this knowledge, let's design the views in the next section.

Creating a UI using ASP.NET Core MVC

Up until now, we have defined a service to communicate with backend APIs and further defined controllers that will pass the data to views using models. Now, let's build various views that will render the data and present it to users.

To begin with, let's see the various components that are involved in rendering the views:

- The Views folder: All views are part of this folder, with each controller-specific view segregated by a subfolder, and finally, each action method is represented by a .cshtml file.

  To add a view, we can right-click on the action method and click **Add View**, which will automatically create a folder (if it isn't already present) with the name of the controller and add the view. Additionally, while doing this, we can specify the model that the view would be bound to.

- The Layout page: This is a common requirement in a web application where we have a common section across the application, such as a header with a menu or left navigation. To have a modular structure for our pages and to avoid any repetition, ASP.Net Core MVC comes with a layout page that is typically named _Layout. cshtml and is part of the Views/Shared folder. This page can be used as a parent page for all the views in our MVC project. A typical layout page looks like the one shown in the following code:

```
<!DOCTYPE html>
<html lang='en'>
<head>
    <meta charset='utf-8'>
    <meta name='viewport' content='width=device-width,
     initial-scale=1'>
    <meta http-equiv='x-ua-compatible'
     content='ie=edge'>
    <title>Ecommerce Packt</title>
</head>
<body class='hold-transition sidebar-mini layout-top-
nav'>
        <!-- Navbar -->
        <!-- Main content -->
        @RenderBody()
</body>
</html>
```

Here, you can see that it allows us to define the skeleton layout of the application, and then finally, there is a Razor method called @RenderBody(), which actually loads the child view. To specify a layout page in any view, we can use the following syntax, which adds _Layout.cshtml as a parent page to the view:

```
@{
    Layout = '~/Views/Shared/__Layout.cshtml';
}
```

However, there is no need to repeat this code in all the views, and that's where _ ViewStart.cshtml comes in handy. Let's see how it helps in reusing some of the code across views:

- `_ViewStart.cshtml`: This is a generic view that is located directly under the `Views` folder and is used by the Razor engine to execute any code that needs to be executed before the code in the view. So, typically, this is used to define the layout page and so, the preceding code can be added to this file so that it gets applied across the application.

- `_ViewImports.cshtml`: This is another page that can be used to import any common directives or namespaces across the application. Just like `_ViewStart`, this is also located directly under the root folder; however, both `_ViewStart` and `_ViewImport` can be in one (or more than one) folder and they are executed hierarchically starting from the one in the root views folder to the lower-level one in any subfolders. To enable client-side telemetry using Application Insights, we inject `JavaScriptSnippet` as shown in the following code. We learned about injecting dependent services into views in *Chapter 5, Dependency Injection in .NET 6*. In the following code, `JavaScriptSnippet` is injected into the view:

```
@inject Microsoft.ApplicationInsights.AspNetCore.
JavaScriptSnippet JavaScriptSnippet
```

- `wwwroot`: This is the root folder of the application, and all the static resources, such as JavaScript, CSS, and any image files, are placed here. This can further hold any HTML plugins that we want to use in our application. As we have already configured the `UseStaticFiles` middleware in our application, content from the folder can be directly served without any processing. The default template of ASP.NET Core MVC comes with a segregation of folders based on their type; for example, all JavaScript files are placed inside a `js` folder, CSS files are placed in a `css` folder, and so on. We will stick to that folder structure for our application.

> **Note**
>
> The process of automatically generating views by right-clicking on the action method and using built-in templates is known as **scaffolding** and can be used if are you new to the Razor syntax. However, creating a view using scaffolding or manually placing it inside the respective folder and strongly typing it results in the same behavior.

Setting up AdminLTE, the layout page, and views

An important thing for getting the same look and feel across an application is to choose the right styling framework. Doing that not only gives a consistent layout but also simplifies the responsive design, which helps in rendering the pages correctly in various resolutions. The ASP.NET Core MVC project template that we are using for `Packt.Ecommerce.Web` comes out of the box with Bootstrap as its styling framework. We will further extend this to a theme known as `AdminLTE`, which comes with some interesting layouts and dashboards that can be plugged into our presentation layer.

Let's perform the following steps to integrate `AdminLTE` into our application:

1. Download the most recent version of `AdminLTE` from here: `https://github.com/ColorlibHQ/AdminLTE/releases`.

2. Extract the ZIP file downloaded in the previous step and navigate to `AdminLTE-3.0.5\dist\css`. Copy `adminlte.min.css` and paste it inside the `wwwroot/css` folder of `Packt.Ecommerce.Web`.

3. Navigate to `AdminLTE-3.0.5\dist\js`. Copy `adminlte.min.js` and paste it inside the `wwwroot/js` folder of `Packt.Ecommerce.Web`.

4. Navigate to `AdminLTE-3.0.5\dist\img`. Copy the required images and paste them inside the `wwwroot/img` folder of `Packt.Ecommerce.Web`.

5. Copy the `AdminLTE-3.0.5\plugins` folder and paste it inside the `wwwroot` folder of `Packt.Ecommerce.Web`.

More information about `AdminLTE` can be found at `https://adminlte.io/docs/2.4/installation`.

Now, navigate to the `Views/_Layout.cshtml` page and remove all the existing code and replace it with the code from `Packt.Ecommerce.Web\Views\Shared\_Layout.cshtml`. On a high level, the layout is divided into the following:

*   A header with navigation to the home page on the left side
*   A search box in the header and a dropdown with search categories in the center
*   The shopping cart in the header on the right side
*   A breadcrumb trail to display the navigation
*   A section to render the child view using `@RenderBody()`

A couple of other key things that are needed to complete the integration of the `AdminLTE` template are as follows:

- Add the following styles defined in the `<head>` tag:

```
<link rel='stylesheet' href='~/plugins/fontawesome-free/
css/all.min.css'>
<link rel='stylesheet' href='~/css/adminlte.min.css'>
```

- Add the following JavaScript files just before the end of the `<body>` tag:

```
<!-- REQUIRED SCRIPTS (Order shouldn't matter)-->
<!-- jQuery -->
<script src='~/plugins/jquery/jquery.min.js'></script>
<!-- Bootstrap 4 -->
<script src='~/plugins/bootstrap/js/bootstrap.bundle.min.
js'></script>
<!-- AdminLTE App -->
<script src='~/js/adminlte.min.js'></script>
```

With this, we have the `AdminLTE` theme integrated into our application. To render the JavaScript required to enable the client telemetry using Application Insights, add the following code inside the `head` tag of `_Layout.cshtml`:

```
@Html.Raw(JavaScriptSnippet.FullScript)
```

The previous code injects the JavaScript required to send telemetry data from views along with the instrumentation key. Unlike the server side or the client side, the instrumentation key is exposed. Anyone can see the instrumentation key from the browser developer tools. But, this is how client-side telemetry is set up. At this point, the risk of this is that unwanted data can be pushed by a malicious user or attacker as the instrumentation key has write-only access. If you wish to make the client-side telemetry more secure, you can expose a secure REST API from your service and log the telemetry events from there. You will learn more about Application Insights features in *Chapter 14, Health and Diagnostics*.

Now, the application layout is ready. Let's now move on to defining various views in the application.

Creating the Products/Index view

This view will be used to list all the products available on our e-commerce application and is strongly typed with the `IEnumerable<Packt.Ecommerce.DTO.Models.ProductListViewModel>` model. It uses the `Index` action method of `ProductsController` to retrieve data.

In this view, we will use a simple Razor `@foreach (var item in Model)` loop and for each product, we will display an image of the product, its name, and its price. A sample of this view looks as shown in the following screenshot:

Figure 11.7 – Products view

Here, you can see that there is a search bar and a category dropdown coming from the layout page. Clicking on the product image will navigate to the `Products/Details` view. To support this navigation, we will make use of `AnchorTagHelper` and pass the product ID and name to the `Details` action method of `ProductsController` to further load the details of the product in the `Products/Details` view.

Creating the Products/Details view

This view will load the details of the product based on the product ID and the name passed from the `Products/Index` view. We will be using a sample page from AdminLTE as shown here: `https://adminlte.io/themes/dev/AdminLTE/pages/examples/e_commerce.html`.

This page will be strongly typed with `Packt.Ecommerce.DTO.Models.ProductDetailsViewModel` and will display all the details of the product. A sample of this page is shown in the following screenshot:

Figure 11.8 – Product details view

As you can see, there is an **Add to Cart** button here; clicking on it will create the cart for the user and add the item to that cart. Since the cart in our case is nothing but an order, with the status of the order set to `'Cart'`, this will call the `Index` action method of `CartController` to create the cart.

To pass data back to the action method, we will take the help of `FormTagHelper`, which allows us to wrap the page in an HTML form and specify the action and controller that the page can be submitted to using the following code:

```
<form asp-action='Index' asp-controller='Cart'>
```

With this code, once the **Add to Cart** button is clicked, which is of the `Submit` type, the page gets submitted to the `Index` action method of `CartController` to further save it to the database. However, we still need to pass the product details back to the `Index` action method and, for that, we will take the help of `InputTagHelper` and create hidden fields for all the values that need to be passed back to the action method.

The most important thing here is that the name of the hidden variable should match the name of the property in the model, so we will be adding the following code inside the form to pass the product values back to the controller:

```
<input asp-for='Id' type='hidden'>
<input asp-for='Name' type='hidden'>
<input asp-for='Price' type='hidden'>
<input asp-for='ImageUrls[0]' type='hidden'>
```

ASP.NET Core MVC's model binding system reads these values and creates the product object needed for the `Index` method of `CartController`, which further calls the backend system to create the order.

Creating the Cart/Index view

This view will load the cart details and will have a checkout form to fill in all the details and complete the order. Here, we can navigate back to the home page to add more products or complete the order.

This view is strongly typed with `Packt.Ecommerce.DTO.Models.OrderDetailsViewModel` and loads data using the `Index` action method of `OrdersController`. Here, we are using the Bootstrap checkout form example from `https://getbootstrap.com/docs/4.5/examples/checkout/`.

This form makes use of model validations and HTML attributes to perform validation on the required fields, and we are taking the help of ASP.NET Core MVC tag helpers and a few HTML helpers to render the form. A sample property with model validations would be as shown in the following code:

```
public class AddressViewModel
{
        [Required(ErrorMessage = 'Address is required')]
```

```
        public string Address1 { get; set; }
        [Required(ErrorMessage = 'City is required')]
        public string City { get; set; }
        [Required(ErrorMessage = 'Country is required')]
        public string Country { get; set; }
    }
```

This model is used in `https://github.com/PacktPublishing/Enterprise-Application-Development-with-C-10-and-.NET-6-Second-Edition/blob/main/Enterprise%20Application/src/platform-apis/data/Packt.Ecommerce.DTO.Models/OrderDetailsViewModel.cs` and triggers necessary validations while placing an order.

As this form also needs to be submitted, the entire form is wrapped in `FormTagHelper`, as shown in the following code:

```
<form asp-action='Create' asp-controller='Orders'>
```

To show these validations on the UI, add the following scripts to `_layout.cshtml` just after all the other scripts we added earlier:

```
<script src='~/lib/jquery-validation/dist/jquery.validate.min.
js'></script>
<script src='~/lib/jquery-validation-unobtrusive/jquery.
validate.unobtrusive.min.js'></script>
```

To display an error message, we can make use of a validation message tag helper, as shown in the following code snippet. On the server side, this can be further evaluated using `ModelState.IsValid`:

```
<input asp-for='ShippingAddress.Address1' class='form-control'
placeholder='1234 Main St'/>
<span asp-validation-for='ShippingAddress.Address1'
class='text-danger'></span>
```

A sample of this page would be as shown in the following screenshot:

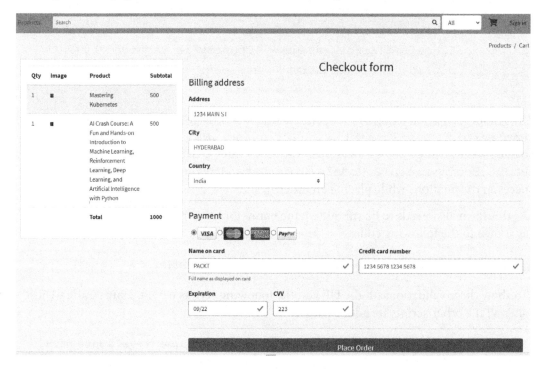

Figure 11.9 – Cart and checkout page

We will use `InputTagHelper` as hidden fields and textboxes to pass any additional information back to the action method. The good thing about textboxes is if the `id` attribute of the textbox matches the property name, that data is automatically passed back to the action method and ASP.NET Core MVC's model binding system will take care of mapping it to the required object, which, in this case, is of the `Packt.Ecommerce.DTO.Models.OrderDetailsViewModel` type, which finally submits the order, generates invoices, and redirects to the `Orders/Index` action method.

> **Note**
>
> In the preceding screenshot, although we have a checkout form that includes payment information in production applications, we would be integrating with a third-party payment gateway and, usually, this entire form sits on the payment gateway side of the application for various security reasons. `https://stripe.com/docs/api` and `https://razorpay.com/docs/payment-gateway/server-integration/dot-net/` are a couple of such third-party providers that help in payment gateway integration.

Creating the Orders/Index view

Finally, we will have the view to see the invoice of the order, which is a simple read-only view that displays invoice information sent from the `Index` action method of `OrdersController`. A sample of this page is shown in the following screenshot:

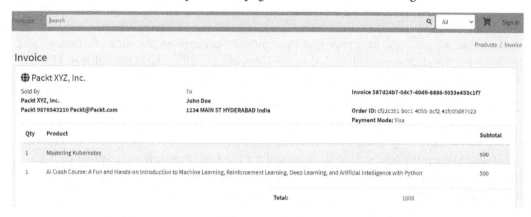

Figure 11.10 – Final invoice

This completes the integration of various views and, as you have seen, we have limited the views to the most important flow in the e-commerce application. However, you can further add more features using the same principles.

Understanding Blazor

Blazor is a new framework available from .NET Core 3.1 onward to develop the frontend layer of the application. It's one of the alternatives to MVC and Razor Pages and the application model is very much close to SPA; however, instead of JavaScript, we can write the logic in C# and Razor syntax.

All the code that is written in Blazor is placed in something called a **Razor component**, which allows you to write the HTML as well as the C# parts of the code to build any web page. A Razor component comes with an extension of `.Razor` and is used to represent the application; be it the entire web page or a small dialog popup, everything is created as a component in Blazor applications. A typical Razor component looks like the one in the following code snippet:

```
@page '/counter'
<h1>Counter</h1>
<p>Current count: @currentCount</p>
<button class='btn btn-primary' @onclick='IncrementCount'>Click
me</button>
```

```
@code {
    private int currentCount = 0;
    private void IncrementCount()
    {        currentCount++;        }
}
```

In this code, we are creating a page that increments a counter on the click of a button, and the logic for the click event is handled in the C# code, which updates the value in HTML. This page can be accessed using the `/counter` relative URL.

The major difference between Blazor and other MVC/Razor Pages is that unlike the request-response model, where every request is sent to the server and HTML is sent back to the browser, Blazor packages all the components (just like SPA) and loads them on the client-side. When the application is requested for the first time, any subsequent calls to the server are to retrieve/submit any API data or to update the DOM. Blazor supports the following two hosting models:

- **Blazor WebAssembly (WASM)**: WASM is low-level instructions that can be run on modern browsers, which further helps to run code written in high-level languages such as C# on a browser without any additional plugins. The Blazor WASM hosting model makes use of the open web standards given by WASM and runs the C# code of any Blazor WASM application in a sandbox environment on a browser. At a high level, all the Blazor components are compiled into .NET assemblies and are downloaded to the browser, and WASM loads the .NET Core runtime and loads all the assemblies. It further uses JavaScript interop to refresh the DOM; the only calls to the server would be any backend APIs. The architecture is shown in the following figure:

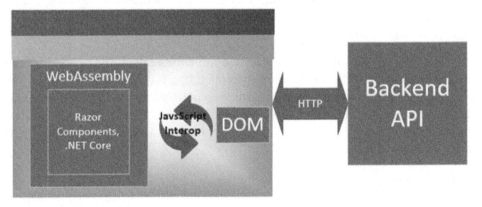

Figure 11.11 – Blazor WASM hosting

- **Blazor Server**: In the Blazor Server hosting model, the Blazor application is hosted on a web server where the compilation happens, and then the client makes use of SignalR to receive the updates from the server. To keep the connection alive, Blazor creates a JavaScript file called `blazor.server.js` and uses SignalR to receive all the DOM updates, and this further means that every user interaction will have a server call (although very light). The architecture is shown in the following figure:

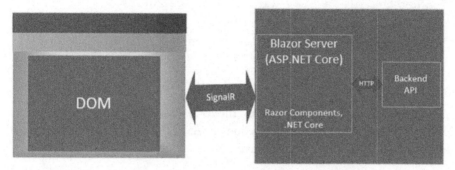

Figure 11.12 – Blazor Server hosting

.NET 6 comes with full tooling support for both hosting models, with their own project templates, and has its pros and cons, which are further explained here: `https://docs.microsoft.com/en-us/aspnet/core/blazor/hosting-models?view=aspnetcore-6.0`.

Let's now create a frontend application as per the following steps using a Blazor Server application, which allows us to add/modify product details for our e-commerce application:

1. Add a new Blazor Server application called `Packt.Ecommerce.Blazorweb` to the enterprise solution and add the `Products.razor`, `AddProduct.Razor`, and `EditProduct.razor` Razor components to the `Pages` folder.

2. This project contains the `Program` class, which is exactly like any other ASP.NET Core application with a few additional Blazor services. `_Host.cshtml` is the root of the application and an initial call to the application is received by this page and is responded to with HTML. This page further references the `blazor.server.js` script file for the SignalR connection. Another important component is the `App.Razor` component, which takes care of routing based on the URL. In Blazor, any component that needs to be mapped to a specific URL will have the `@page` directive at the beginning of the component, which specifies the relative URL of the application. `App.Razor` intercepts the URLs and routes them to the specified component. All Razor components are part of a `Pages` folder, and the `Data` folder comes with a sample model and a service that is used in the `FetchData.razor` component.

3. Let's add the following code to NavMenu.razor to add the Products navigation to the left menu. At this stage, if you run the application, you should be able to see the left menu with the Products navigation; however, it will not navigate to any page:

```
<li class='nav-item px-3'>
<NavLink class='nav-link' href='products'>
  <span class='oi oi-list-rich' aria-
  hidden='true'></span> Products
</NavLink>
</li>
```

4. As we are going to retrieve data from the API, we need to inject HTTPClient into our Program class, just as how it's done in ASP.NET Core applications. So, add the following code to the Program class:

```
builder.Services.AddHttpClient("Products", client =>
{
    client.BaseAddress = new Uri(builder.Configura-
tion["ApplicationSettings:ProductsApiEndpoint"]);
});
```

5. Add the following setting of ApplicationSettings:ProductsApiEndpoint to appsettings.json:

```
'ApplicationSettings': {
  'ProductsApiEndpoint':
  'https://localhost:7256/api/products/'
},
```

6. Since we are going to bind the products data, let's add Packt.Ecommerce.DTO.Models as a project reference to Packt.Ecommerce.Blazorweb. In the Pages folder, add the following code to the Products.razor page inside the @code block in which we are creating a HttpClient object using IHttpClientFactory, which will be injected in the next step, and retrieving the products data in the OnInitializedAsync method:

```
private List<ProductListViewModel> products;
protected override async Task OnInitializedAsync()
    {
        var client = Factory.CreateClient('Products');
```

```
            var result = await
                client.GetAsync('').ConfigureAwait(false);
            result.EnsureSuccessStatusCode();
            products = new List<ProductListViewModel>();
            products = await
                result.Content.ReadFromJsonAsync
                <List<ProductListViewModel>>()
                .ConfigureAwait(false);
        }
```

7. Next, add the following code at the beginning of the `Products.Razor` page (outside the `@code` block). Here, we set the relative route for this component via the `@page` directive to `/products`. Next, we inject `IHttpClientFactory` and the other required namespaces, then add the HTML part that renders the list of products. As you can see, it's a mixture of HTML and Razor syntax:

```
@page '/products'
@inject IHttpClientFactory Factory
@using System.Net.Http.Json;@using Packt.Ecommerce.DTO.
Models;
<h1>Products</h1>
<div>    <a class='btn btn-info' href='addproduct'><i
class='oi oi-plus'></i> Add Product</a> </div>
@if (products == null)
{ <p><em>Loading...</em></p> }
else { <table class='table'><thead><tr>
                <th>Id</th><th>Name</th>
                <th>Price</th><th>Quantity</th>
                <th>ImageUrls</th><th></th>
            </tr></thead><tbody>
            @foreach (var product in products)
            {<tr>
                <td>@product.Id</td>
                <td>@product.Name</td>
                <td>@product.Price</td>
                <td>@product.Quantity</td>
                <td><img
                    src='@product.ImageUrls[0]'
```

```
                          class='product-image w-10
                          col-3' alt='Product' /></td>
                    <td><a class='btn btn-info'
                          href='editproduct/
                          @product.Id/@product.Name'>
                          <i class='oi oi-pencil'>
                          </i></a></td></tr>
              }
        </tbody></table> }
```

At this point, if you run the application, you should see the output shown in the
following screenshot:

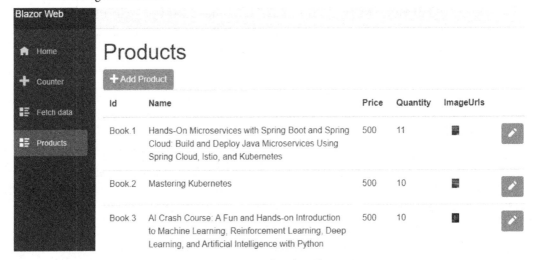

Figure 11.13 – Product list Blazor UI

8. Next, let's create the Add/Edit pages in which we will make use of Blazor forms.
    Some of the important tooling/components that are available for forms are the
    following.

    A Blazor form is created using an out-of-the-box template in Blazor known as
    EditForm, and it can be bound directly to any C# object using a model property.
    A typical EditForm looks as in the following code snippet. Here, we are defining
    to call the OnSubmit method when the form is submitted. Let's add this to
    AddProduct.razor:

```
<EditForm Model='@product' OnSubmit='@OnSubmit'>
</EditForm>
```

Here, `product` is the object of the model that we want to use, which in our case is `Packt.Ecommerce.DTO.Models.ProductDetailsViewModel`. To bind data to any control, we can use a mix of HTML and Razor syntax, as shown in the following code. Here, we are binding the `Name` property of the product object to a textbox and, similarly, the `Category` property to the dropdown. Once you enter any value in the textbox or select a value in the dropdown, it is automatically available in these properties to pass it back to any backend API or database. Let's add all the required properties to the HTML element in a similar manner:

```
<InputText id='category' @bind-Value='product.Name'></
InputText>
<InputSelect @bind-Value='product.Category'>
<option selected disabled value='-1'> Choose Category</
option>
<option value='Clothing'>Clothing</option>
<option value='Books'>Books</option>
</InputSelect>
```

Blazor forms support data validation using data annotations, so any model that we want to bind to the UI can have data annotations, and Blazor applies those validations out of the box to the controls that the property is bound to. To apply validations, we add the `DataAnnotationsValidator` component and can use the `ValidationSummary` component to show a summary of all the validation failures. You can find more details at `https://docs.microsoft.com/en-us/aspnet/core/blazor/forms-validation?view=aspnetcore-6.0`. We can further use the `ValidationMessage` component at the control level, as shown in the following code snippet:

```
<DataAnnotationsValidator />
<ValidationSummary />
<InputNumber id='quantity' @bind-Value='product.
Quantity'></InputNumber>
<ValidationMessage For='@(() => product.Quantity)' />
```

9. In the `code` component, add an object of `ProductDetailsViewModel` and name it as the product, that is, as defined in the `Model` attribute of `EditForm`, and further implement the `OnSubmit` method.

The entire code for `AddProduct.Razor` and `EditProduct.Razor` can be found in the GitHub repository, and once we run the application, we can see the following page:

Add Product

- Large quantity, please reach out to support to process request.

Product Name :   C# 9 and .NET 5

Product Category :   Books   ∨

Product Price :   500

Product Quantity :   -1

Large quantity. please reach out to
support to process request.

Image URL :   http://microsoft.com

Format :

Authors :

Size :

Colors :

Add Product

Figure 11.14 – The Add Product Blazor UI

This is a basic sample for building the frontend using Blazor that performs list, create, and update operations. However, there are many concepts in Blazor that can be further explored at `https://docs.microsoft.com/en-us/aspnet/core/blazor/?view=aspnetcore-6.0`.

Summary

In this chapter, we understood various aspects of the presentation layer and UI design. Along with this, we also learned various skills in developing the presentation layer using ASP.NET Core MVC and Razor Pages, and then, finally, we implemented the presentation layer for our enterprise application using ASP.NET Core MVC and Blazor.

With these skills, you should be able to build the presentation layer using ASP.NET Core MVC, Razor Pages, and Blazor, and integrate it with the backend API.

In the next chapter, we will see how to integrate authentication in our system across various layers of the application.

Questions

1. Which one of the following is a recommended page to define the left-side navigation that needs to appear throughout the web application?

   a. `_ViewStart.cshtml`

   b. `_ViewImports.cshtml`

   c. `_Layout.cshtml`

   d. `Error.cshtml`

   Answer: c

2. Which of the following pages can be used to configure the `Layout` page for the entire application?

   a. `_ViewStart.cshtml`

   b. `_ViewImports.cshtml`

   c. `_Layout.cshtml`

   d. `Error.cshtml`

   Answer: a

3. Which of the following special characters is used to write Razor syntax in a `.cshtml` page?

   a. @

   b. #

   c. `<% %>`

   d. None of the above

   Answer: a

4. Which method will be called on a button click in the following tag helper code in a Razor page application?

    ```
    <input type='submit' asp-page-handler='Delete'
    value='Delete' />
    ```

    a. `OnGet()`

    b. `onDelete()`

    c. `OnPostDelete()`

    d. `OnDeleteAsync()`

    Answer: c

Further reading

- https://www.packtpub.com/web-development/html5-and-css3-building-responsive-websites

- https://www.packtpub.com/product/bootstrap-for-asp-net-mvc-second-edition/9781785889479

- https://developer.mozilla.org/en-US/docs/WebAssembly

- https://docs.microsoft.com/en-us/aspnet/core/razor-pages/?view=aspnetcore-6.0

- https://docs.microsoft.com/en-us/aspnet/core/mvc/views/partial?view=aspnetcore-6.0

- https://developer.mozilla.org/en-US/docs/Learn/Accessibility

Part 4: Security

This part discusses the security aspects of programming, including authentication, authorization, and cryptography, and explains how both the web and service layers will need to be secured in any enterprise application.

This part comprises the following chapters:

12
Understanding Authentication

So far, we have built the **user interface** (UI) and service layer of our e-commerce application. In this chapter, we will learn how to secure it. Our e-commerce application should be able to uniquely identify a user and respond to that user's requests. A commonly used pattern for establishing user identity involves the provision of a username and password. These are then verified against the user's profile data, which is stored in a database or an application. If it matches, a cookie or token with the user's identity is generated and stored in the client's browser so that, for subsequent requests, a cookie/token is sent to the server and validated to service requests.

Authentication is a process in which you identify a user or a program accessing protected areas of your application. For instance, in our e-commerce application, a user can navigate through different pages and browse the products that are displayed. However, to place an order or view past orders, users need to provide a username and a password to identify themselves. If the user is new, they should create these to continue.

In this chapter, we will learn about the features offered by ASP.NET Core related to authentication and understand various methods to implement authentication. In this chapter, we will cover the following topics:

- Understanding the elements of authentication
- Introduction to ASP.NET Core Identity
- Understanding OAuth 2.0
- Introduction to **Azure Active Directory (Azure AD)**
- Introduction to Windows Authentication
- Understanding best practices to secure client and server applications

Technical requirements

For this chapter, you need basic knowledge of Azure, **Entity Framework (EF)**, Azure AD B2C, and an active Azure subscription with a contributor role. If you don't have one, you can sign up for a free account at `https://azure.microsoft.com/en-in/free/`. Visual Studio 2022 is used to illustrate a few examples. You can download it from `https://visualstudio.microsoft.com`.

Understanding the elements of authentication in .NET 6

Authentication in ASP.NET Core is handled by authentication middleware, which uses registered authentication handlers to perform authentication. Registered authentication handlers and their associated configurations are called **authentication schemes**.

The following list describes the core elements of an authentication framework:

- **Authentication scheme**: This defines the type and behavior of the authentication to be used to authenticate, challenge, and forbid. Authentication schemes are registered as authentication services in the application startup code in `Program.cs`. They comprise an authentication handler and have options to configure this handler. You can register multiple authentication schemes to authenticate, challenge, and forbid actions. Alternatively, you can specify authentication schemes in the authorization policies that you configure. The following is a sample code to register an `OpenIdConnect` authentication scheme:

```
services.AddAuthentication(OpenIdConnectDefaults.
AuthenticationScheme)
```

```
.AddMicrosoftIdentityWebApp(this.Configuration.
GetSection("AzureAdB2C"));
```

In the preceding code snippet, the authentication service is registered to use the `OpenIdConnect` authentication scheme with the Microsoft identity platform. Additionally, the necessary settings specified in the configuration file, in the `AzureAdB2C` section, are used to initialize the authentication options.

More details regarding `OpenIdConnect` and `AzureAdB2C` will be covered in the *Introduction to Azure AD* section of this chapter.

- **Authentication handler**: Authentication handlers are responsible for authenticating a user. Based on the authentication scheme, they either construct an authentication ticket (usually, this is a token/cookie with the user's identity) or reject a request if authentication is unsuccessful.

- **Authenticate**: This method is responsible for constructing an authentication ticket with the user identity. For example, a cookie authentication scheme constructs a cookie, while a **JavaScript Object Notation (JSON) Web Token (JWT)** bearer scheme constructs a token.

- **Challenge**: This method is invoked by authorization when an unauthenticated user requests a resource that requires authentication. Based on the configured scheme, the user is then asked to authenticate.

- **Forbid**: This method is invoked by authorization when an authenticated user tries to access a resource to which they are not permitted.

Now, let's understand how to add authentication using the ASP.NET Core Identity framework.

Introduction to ASP.NET Core Identity

ASP.NET Core Identity is a membership-based system that provides an easy way to add login and user management features to your application. It offers UIs and **application programming interfaces (APIs)** to create new user accounts, provide email confirmation, manage user profile data, manage passwords (such as changing or resetting passwords), perform logins, logouts, and more, and enable **multi-factor authentication (MFA)**. Also, it allows you to integrate with external login providers such as Microsoft Account, Google, Facebook, Twitter, and many other social websites. This is so that users can use their existing accounts to sign up instead of having to create new ones, thus enhancing the user experience.

By default, ASP.NET Core Identity stores user information such as usernames, passwords, and more in a SQL Server database using an EF Code-First approach. Additionally, it allows you to customize table/column names and capture additional user data such as the user's date of birth, phone number, and more. You can also customize it to save data in a different persistent store such as Azure Table Storage or a NoSQL database. It also provides an API to customize password hashing, password validation, and more.

In the next section, we will learn how to create a simple web application and configure it to use ASP.NET Core Identity for authentication.

Sample implementation

In Visual Studio 2022, create a new project, select the **ASP.NET Core Web Application** template, provide your project details to continue, and change **Authentication type**. You will find the following list of options to choose from:

- **None**: Choose this if no authentication is required for your application.
- **Individual Accounts**: Choose this if you use a local store or SQL database to manage user identities.
- **Microsoft Identity Platform**: Choose this if you wish to authenticate users against Azure AD or Azure AD B2C.
- **Windows**: Choose this if your application is only available on an intranet.

For this sample implementation, we will use a local store to save user data. Select **Individual Accounts**, and click on **Create** to create the project, as illustrated in the following screenshot:

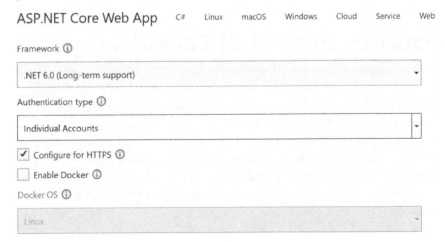

Figure 12.1 – Authentication type

Alternatively, you can use the `dotnet` **command-line interface (CLI)** to create a new web application that is configured with *individual accounts* as an authentication option and `SQLite` as the database store, as follows:

```
dotnet new webapp --auth Individual -o AuthSample
```

To configure a SQL database as a store, run the following command, making sure you apply migrations to create the necessary tables in the database:

```
dotnet new webapp --auth Individual -uld -o AuthSample
```

Now, run the following command to build and run the application:

```
dotnet run --project ./AuthSample/AuthSample.csproj
```

You should see output similar to the following:

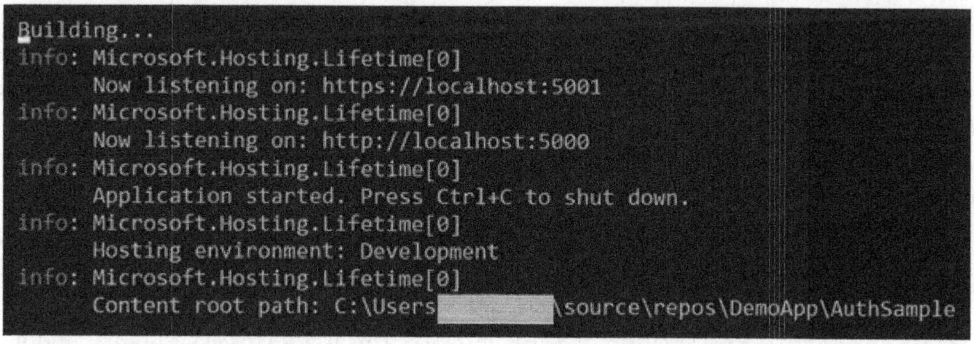

Figure 12.2 – The dotnet run command output for reference

In the preceding screenshot, notice the logs from the console and the **Uniform Resource Locators** (**URLs**) with ports at which the application is accessible.

Now that your application is up and running, open the URL in the browser and click on **Register**. Provide the required details, and click on the **Register** button. You might see the following error message the first time you try this:

A database operation failed while processing the request.

SqlException: Cannot open database "aspnet-AuthSample-53bc9b9d-9d6a-45d4-8429-2a2761773502" requested by the login. The login failed. Login failed for user

Applying existing migrations may resolve this issue

There are migrations that have not been applied to the following database(s):

ApplicationDbContext

- 00000000000000_CreateIdentitySchema

[Apply Migrations]

In Visual Studio, you can use the Package Manager Console to apply pending migrations to the database:

PM> Update-Database

Alternatively, you can apply pending migrations from a command prompt at your project directory:

> dotnet ef database update

Figure 12.3 – A runtime exception due to missing migrations

You can click on **Apply Migrations** to run migrations and refresh the page, which should fix the problem. Alternatively, open the project in Visual Studio, and in the package manager console, run `Update-Database` to apply the migrations and rerun the application. Now, you should be able to register and log in to the application. Next, let's examine a project structure that has been created for us.

Under **Dependencies Packages**, you will notice the following NuGet packages:

- `Microsoft.AspNetCore.Identity.UI`: This is a Razor class library, and it contains the entire identity UI with which you can navigate from a browser—for example, `/Identity/Account/Register` or `/Identity/Account/Login`.

- `Microsoft.AspNetCore.Identity.EntityFrameworkCore`: This is used by ASP.NET Core Identity to interact with the database store.

- `Microsoft.EntityFrameworkCore.SqlServer`: This is a library that is used to interact with SQLDB.

The packages can be seen in the following screenshot:

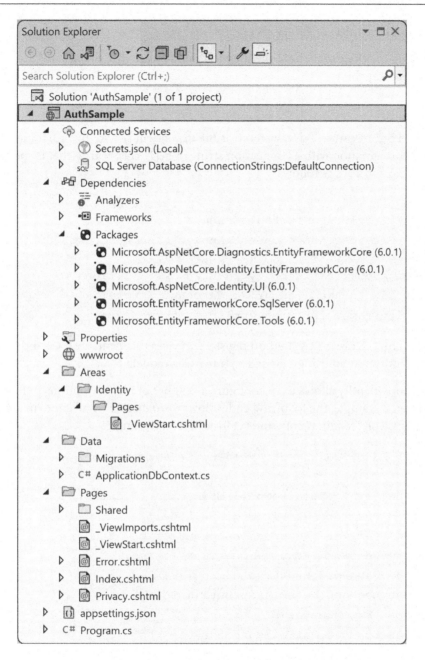

Figure 12.4 – The Solution Explorer view of the AuthSample project

Now, let's examine the code of `Program.cs`.

The following code registers the authentication middleware that enables the authentication capability:

```
app.UseAuthentication();
```

`ApplicationDbContext` is registered as the dependent service by providing an `options` configuration with a connection string of `sql database` that is specified in `appsettings.json`, as follows:

```
var connectionString = builder.Configuration.
GetConnectionString("DefaultConnection");
builder.Services.AddDbContext<ApplicationDbContext>(options =>
options.UseSqlServer(connectionString));
services.AddDefaultIdentity<IdentityUser>(options =>
options.SignIn.RequireConfirmedAccount = true)
.AddEntityFrameworkStores<ApplicationDbContext>();
```

The `AddDefaultIdentity` method registers services that generate a UI and configures a default identity system using `IdentityUser` as a model.

ASP.NET Core Identity allows us to configure a number of identity options to meet our needs—for example, the following code allows us to disable email confirmations, configure password requirements, and set lock timeout settings:

```
services.AddDefaultIdentity<IdentityUser>(options =>
{
  options.SignIn.RequireConfirmedAccount = false;
  options.Password.RequireDigit = true;
  options.Password.RequireNonAlphanumeric = true;
  options.Password.RequireUppercase = true;
  options.Password.RequiredLength = 8;
  options.Lockout.DefaultLockoutTimeSpan =
  TimeSpan.FromMinutes(5);
  options.Lockout.MaxFailedAccessAttempts = 5;
})
.AddEntityFrameworkStores<ApplicationDbContext>();
```

For more details, you can refer to `https://docs.microsoft.com/en-us/aspnet/core/security/authentication/identity?view=aspnetcore-6.0`.

Scaffolding

To further customize the UI and any other settings, you can selectively add source code contained in the Razor class library. Then, you can modify the generated source code to suit your needs. To scaffold, in Solution Explorer, right-click on **Project | Add | New Scaffolded Item | Identity | Add**.

This will open a window where you can select the files that you want to override, as illustrated in the following screenshot:

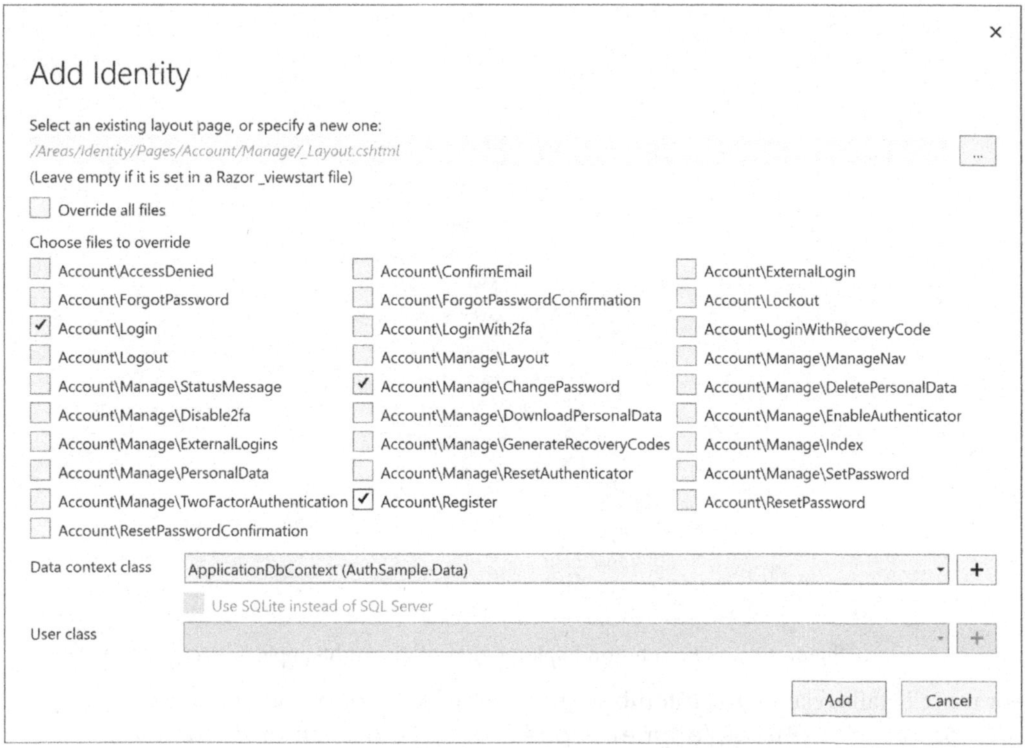

Figure 12.5 – Dialog to override the identity modules

You can select to override all files or only choose those files that you want to customize. Choose your data context class and click on **Add** to add the source code to your project. This will add files under the `Identity` folder—both Razor and the corresponding C# files will be added. The following screenshot illustrates the files that have been added based on the selection:

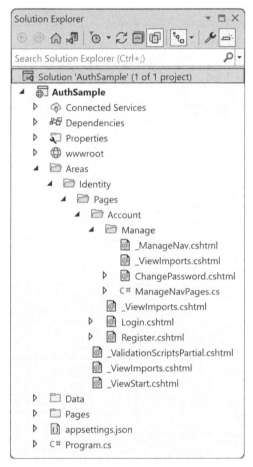

Figure 12.6 – The Solution Explorer view of the AuthSample project

For more details relating to customizations, you can refer to `https://docs. microsoft.com/en-us/aspnet/core/security/authentication/ scaffold-identity?view=aspnetcore-6.0`.

Now, let's understand how to integrate an ASP.NET Core application with external login providers.

Integration with external login providers

In this section, we will learn how to integrate an ASP.NET Core application to use external login providers, such as Microsoft Account, Google, Facebook, Twitter, and more. Additionally, we will look at how to authenticate using an OAuth 2.0 flow so that users can use their existing credentials to sign up and access our application. A common pattern to integrate an ASP.NET Core application with any external login provider is given as follows:

1. Acquire credentials (usually, the client ID and secret) to access OAuth APIs for authentication from the respective developer portal.

2. Configure the credentials in the application settings or user secrets.

3. Next, we need to add the respective NuGet package to the project at **Add Middleware Support** to use the OpenID and OAuth 2.0 flows.

4. In `Program.cs`, add the `AddAuthentication` method to register the authentication middleware.

Configuring Google

To configure Google as an external login provider, you need to perform the following steps:

1. Create OAuth credentials at `https://developers.google.com/identity/sign-in/web/sign-in`.

2. Configure the credentials in the user secrets. You can use the `dotnet` CLI to add secrets to your project, as follows:

```
dotnet user-secrets set "Authentication:Google:ClientId"
"<client-id>"
dotnet user-secrets set
"Authentication:Google:ClientSecret" "<client-secret>"
```

3. Add the `Microsoft.AspNetCore.Authentication.Google` NuGet package to your project, and add the following code to `Program.cs`:

```
services.AddAuthentication()
        .AddGoogle(options =>
        {
            IConfigurationSection googleAuthNSection =
                Configuration.GetSection
                ("Authentication:Google");
            options.ClientId =
            googleAuthNSection["ClientId"];
```

```
        options.ClientSecret =
        googleAuthNSection["ClientSecret"];
    });
```

4. Similarly, you can add multiple providers.

To learn how to integrate with other popular external authentication providers, you can refer to `https://docs.microsoft.com/en-us/aspnet/core/security/authentication/social/?view=aspnetcore-6.0`.

After you have completed the preceding steps, you should be able to use Google credentials to log in to your application. This concludes this section on using ASP.NET Core Identity with external login providers in your application for authentication. In the next section, let's see what OAuth is.

Understanding OAuth 2.0

OAuth 2.0 is a modern and industry-standard protocol for securing web APIs. It simplifies the process by providing specific authorization flows for web apps, single-page apps, mobile apps, and more to access secured APIs.

Let's consider a use case where you want to build a web portal in which users can sync and view photos/videos from their favorite applications such as Instagram, Facebook, or other third-party applications. Your application should be able to request data from third-party applications on behalf of the user. One approach involves the storing of a user's credentials in relation to each third-party application, and your application sends or requests data on behalf of the user.

This approach can lead to many problems. They are outlined as follows:

- You need to design your application to securely store user credentials.

- Users might not be comfortable with their credentials being shared and stored by third-party applications in your application.

- If a user changes their credentials, they need to be updated back in your application.

- In the case of a security breach, fraudsters can gain unrestricted access to a user's data in third-party applications. This can lead to potential revenue and reputation loss.

OAuth 2.0 can handle all of the preceding use cases by addressing all of these concerns. Let's see how it does this, as follows:

1. The user logs in to your application. To sync pictures/videos, the user will be redirected to a third-party application, and they will need to sign in with their credentials.

2. OAuth 2.0 reviews and approves the app's request to fetch resources.

3. The user is redirected back to your application with the authorization code.

4. To sync pictures/videos, your application can acquire a token by exchanging the authorization code and then making an API call to a third-party application along with the token.

5. For each request, the third-party application validates the token and responds accordingly.

In OAuth flows, there are four parties involved: **Client**, **Resource Owner**, **Authorization Server**, and **Resource Server**. Refer to the following screenshot:

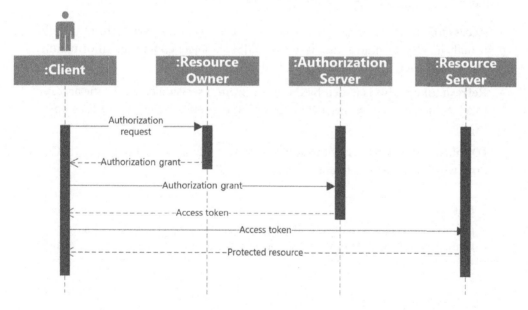

Figure 12.7 – An OAuth2 flow

From the preceding screenshot, we can see the following:

- **Client**: This refers to an application that acquires a token from the authorization server and makes requests to the resource server on behalf of the resource owner.

- **Resource Owner**: This is an entity that owns resources/data and is capable of granting access to clients.

- **Authorization Server**: This authenticates the resource owner and issues tokens to clients.

- **Resource Server**: This is the server that hosts resources or data relating to the resource owner, uses a bearer token to validate, and responds to or rejects requests coming from clients.

Tokens

The authorization server authenticates the user and provides an ID token, access token, and refresh token, which are used by native/web applications to access protected services. Let's understand each of them a bit more:

- **Access token**: This is issued by the authorization server as part of the OAuth flow, usually in JWT format; a Base64-encoded JSON object containing information about the issuer, user, scope, expiry, and more.

- **Refresh token**: This is issued by the authorization server along with the access token, which is used by the client application to request a new access token before it expires.

- **ID tokens**: This is issued by the authorization server as part of the OpenID Connect flow, which can be used to authenticate the user.

> **Note**
> OpenID Connect is an authentication protocol built on top of OAuth2. It can be used to verify the identity of a user on an authentication server.

Authorization grant types

OAuth 2.0 defines a number of ways for a client to acquire tokens to access secured resources—these are called **grants**. It defines five grant types: authorization code flow, implicit flow, on-behalf-of flow, client credentials flow, and device grant flow. They are outlined here:

- **Authorization code flow**: This flow is suitable for web, mobile, and single-page apps, where your application needs to get your data from another server. The authorization code flow begins with the client redirecting the user to authenticate at the authorization server. If successful, the user gives their consent to permissions required by the client and is redirected back to the client with the authorization code.

  Here, the client's identity is verified by the configured redirection **Uniform Resource Identifier** (**URI**) in the authorization server. Next, the client requests the access token by passing the authorization code and, in return, gets the access token, the refresh token, and the expiry date. The client can use the access token to call the web API. Since access tokens are short-lived, before they expire, the client should request a new access token by passing the access token and the refresh token.

- **Implicit flow**: This is a simplified version of code flow suitable for single-page, JavaScript-based applications. With implicit flow, instead of issuing an authorization code, the authorization server only issues an access token. Here, the client identity is not verified, as there is no need to specify a redirect URL.

- **On-behalf-of flow**: This flow is best suited to situations where a client invokes a call to a web API (say, A) that, in turn, needs to invoke another API (say, on B). The flow goes like this: the user sends a request along with a token to A; A requests a token for B from the authorization server by providing a token of A and credentials such as the client ID and client secret of A. Once it acquires the token for B, it invokes the API on B.

- **Client credentials flow**: This flow is used in cases where server-to-server interaction is needed (say, A to B, where A acquires the token to interact with B using its credentials—usually, this is the client ID and the client secret—and then invokes the API with the acquired token). This request runs under the context of A instead of the user. The required permissions should be granted to A to perform the necessary actions.

- **Device grant flow**: This flow is used in cases where users need to sign in to devices with no browsers, such as smart TVs, IoT devices, or printers. The user visits a web page on mobile or PC to authenticate and enters the code displayed on the device to acquire the token and refresh the token for the device to connect.

Now that we understand what OAuth is, in the next section, let's understand what Azure AD is, how to integrate it with our e-commerce application, and how to use it as our identity server.

Introduction to Azure AD

Azure AD is an **Identity and Access Management (IAM)** cloud service offering from Microsoft. It is a single identity store for both internal and external users so that you can configure applications to use Azure AD for authentication. You can synchronize on-premises Windows AD to Azure AD; therefore, you can enable a **single sign-on (SSO)** experience for your users.

Users can log in using their work or school credentials or personal Microsoft accounts such as Outlook.com, Xbox, and Skype. It also allows you to natively add or delete users, create groups, do a self-service password reset, enable Azure MFA, and much more.

With **Azure AD B2C**, you can customize how your users sign up, sign in, and manage their profiles. Additionally, it allows your customers to use their existing social credentials such as Facebook and Google to sign in and access your applications and APIs.

Azure AD is compliant with industry-standard protocols such as **OpenID Connect**, also known as **OIDC** and **OAuth 2.0**. OIDC is an identity layer built on top of the OAuth 2.0 protocol and is used to authenticate and retrieve a user's profile information. OAuth 2.0 is used for authorization to obtain access to an HTTP service using different flows such as implicit grant flow, on-behalf-of flow, client credentials flow, code flow and device grant flow.

A typical authentication flow in web apps goes like this:

1. The user tries to access the secure content of an application (say, **My Orders**).
2. The user is redirected to the Azure AD sign-in page if they are not authenticated.
3. Once the user has submitted their credentials, they are validated by Azure AD, which sends a token back to the web app.
4. A cookie is saved to the user's browser and displays the user-requested page.
5. On subsequent requests, a cookie is sent to the server that is used to validate the user.

Azure AD B2C enables your customer to use their preferred social, enterprise, or native identities to access your applications or APIs. It can scale to millions of users and billions of authentications per day.

Let's try to integrate our e-commerce application with Azure AD B2C. At a high level, we need to perform the following steps to integrate it:

1. Create an Azure AD B2C tenant.
2. Register an application.
3. Add identity providers.
4. Create user flows.
5. Update the app code to integrate.

> **Note**
>
> As a prerequisite, you should have an active Azure subscription with a contributor role. If you don't have one, you can sign up for a free account at `https://azure.microsoft.com/en-in/free/`.

The Azure AD B2C setup

Using Azure AD B2C as an identity service will allow our e-commerce users to sign up, create their own credentials, or use their existing social credentials such as Facebook or Google. Let's look at the steps that we need to perform to configure Azure AD B2C as an identity service for our e-commerce application, as follows:

1. Log in to the Azure portal, making sure you are in the same directory that contains your subscription.
2. On the **Home** page, click on **Create Resource** and search for **B2C**. Then, select **Azure Active Directory B2C** from the list of options.
3. Select **Create a new Azure AD B2C Tenant**, as illustrated in the following screenshot:

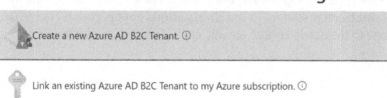

Home > New > Azure Active Directory B2C >

Create new B2C Tenant or Link to existing Tenant

Create a new Azure AD B2C Tenant. ⓘ

Link an existing Azure AD B2C Tenant to my Azure subscription. ⓘ

Figure 12.8 – Azure AD B2C

4. Provide the required details and click on **Review + create**. Then, complete the following fields:

Organization name: This is the name of your B2C tenant.

Internal domain name: This is the internal domain name of your tenant.

Country/Region: Select the country or region where your tenant should be provisioned.

Subscription and **Resource Group**: Provide subscription and resource group details.

These fields are shown in the following screenshot:

Home > New > Azure Active Directory B2C > Create new B2C Tenant or Link to existing Tenant >

Create a tenant   ✕
Azure Active Directory

* Basics   * **Configuration**   Review + create

Directory details

Configure your new directory

Organization name * ⓘ | Packt Ecommerce   ✓ |

Initial domain name * ⓘ | packtecommerce   ✓ |

                                                                                        packtecommerce.onmicrosoft.com

Country/Region ⓘ | United States   ∨ |

                                          ✅ Datacenter location - United States

                                          Datacenter location is based on the country/region selected above. Azure Active Directory B2C service is
                                          available worldwide.

| Review + create | | < Previous | | Next : Review + create > |

Figure 12.9 – The New Azure AD B2C Configuration section

5. Review your details and click on **Create**. The creation of your new tenant might take a few minutes. Once it has been created, you will see a confirmation message in the notification section. In the **Notifications** popup, click on the tenant name to navigate to the newly created tenant, as illustrated in the following screenshot:

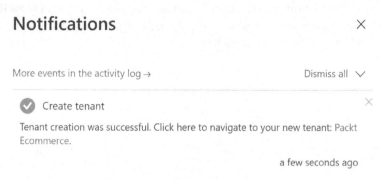

Figure 12.10 – Confirmation of the creation of the Azure AD B2C service

6. In the following screenshot, note that **Subscription status** is given as **No Subscription**. Additionally, a warning message says that you should **link a subscription to your tenant**. You can click on the link to fix it, else you can skip to *Step 9* to continue to configure Azure AD:

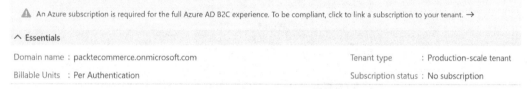

Figure 12.11 – A warning message showing no subscription has been linked

7. The link will open the same screen that you saw in *Step 3*. This time, click on **Link an existing Azure AD B2C Tenant to my Azure subscription** to continue, as illustrated in the following screenshot:

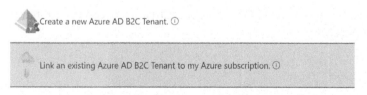

Figure 12.12 – Linking an Azure AD B2C tenant to a subscription

8. Select your B2C tenant subscription from the drop-down list, provide a **Resource group** value, and click on **Create** to link the subscription and the tenant, as illustrated in the following screenshot:

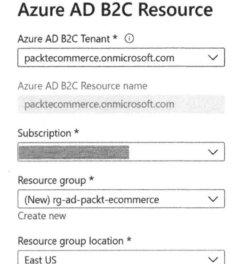

Azure AD B2C Resource

Azure AD B2C Tenant * ⓘ

packtecommerce.onmicrosoft.com   ∨

Azure AD B2C Resource name

packtecommerce.onmicrosoft.com

Subscription *

⬛⬛⬛⬛⬛⬛⬛⬛⬛   ∨

Resource group *

(New) rg-ad-packt-ecommerce   ∨
Create new

Resource group location *

East US   ∨

Create

Figure 12.13 – Subscription selection

9. You can navigate to your B2C tenant by selecting the **Open B2C Tenant** link in the overview section of the B2C tenant to continue with the next steps of the configuration, as follows:

-   You need to register your application with the Azure AD B2C tenant to use it as the identity service.

-   You need to choose the identity providers that users can use to sign in to your application.

- Choose user flows to define the experience for your users to sign up or sign in, as illustrated in the following screenshot:

Welcome to Azure Active Directory B2C

 Register an application

The application registration is used to secure your directory by allowing only your applications to make requests and to make sure your users are sent to a trusted place after signing in. Get started

 Add identity provider(s)

Identity providers are the different types of accounts your users can use to sign into your application. Get started

 Create a user flow

User flows define the experience for your users signing up and signing into your application. Get started

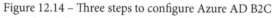

Figure 12.14 – Three steps to configure Azure AD B2C

10. Under **Manage**, click on **App Registrations** and provide the necessary details as follows. Then, click on **Register** to create the AD application:

Name: Display the name of your application.

Supported account types: Choose **Accounts in any identity provider or organizational directory** so that we can allow users to use their existing credentials to sign up or sign in.

Redirect URI: You need to provide the URL of your application to which the user will be redirected after successful authentication. For now, we can leave it blank.

Permissions: Select **Grant admin consent to openid and offline_access permissions**.

The fields are illustrated in the following screenshot:

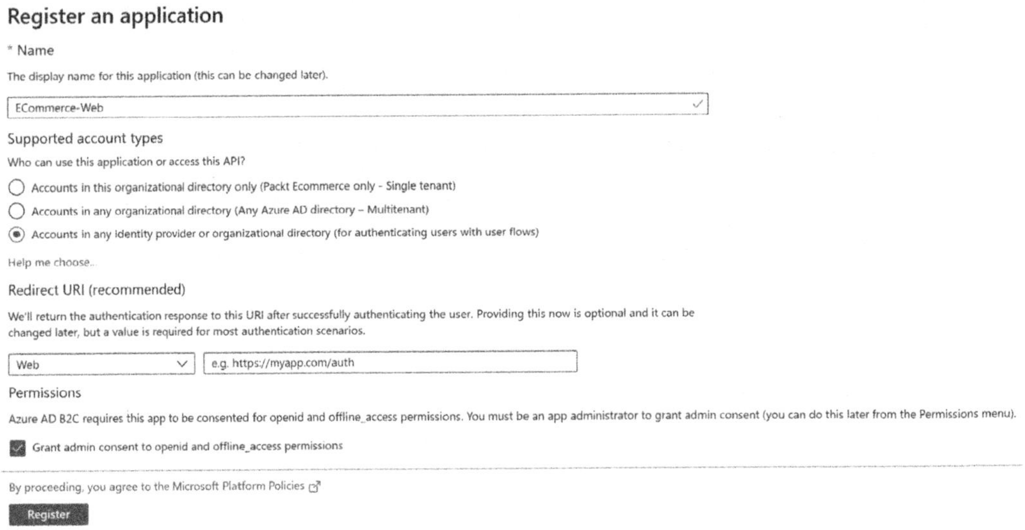

Register an application

* Name

The display name for this application (this can be changed later).

| ECommerce-Web | ✓ |

Supported account types

Who can use this application or access this API?

○ Accounts in this organizational directory only (Packt Ecommerce only - Single tenant)

○ Accounts in any organizational directory (Any Azure AD directory – Multitenant)

◉ Accounts in any Identity provider or organizational directory (for authenticating users with user flows)

Help me choose..

Redirect URI (recommended)

We'll return the authentication response to this URI after successfully authenticating the user. Providing this now is optional and it can be changed later, but a value is required for most authentication scenarios.

| Web   ∨ | e.g. https://myapp.com/auth |

Permissions

Azure AD B2C requires this app to be consented for openid and offline_access permissions. You must be an app administrator to grant admin consent (you can do this later from the Permissions menu).

☑ Grant admin consent to openid and offline_access permissions

By proceeding, you agree to the Microsoft Platform Policies ☐

Register

Figure 12.15 – Registering a new Azure AD application

> **Note**
>
> To set up and debug locally, we can configure with `localhost`. This needs to be replaced with the URL where your app is hosted.

11. Now, let's choose **Identity Providers** under **Manage** to configure, as follows:

Local accounts: This option allows users to register and sign in to our application in a traditional way—with a username and password. The following screenshot illustrates this:

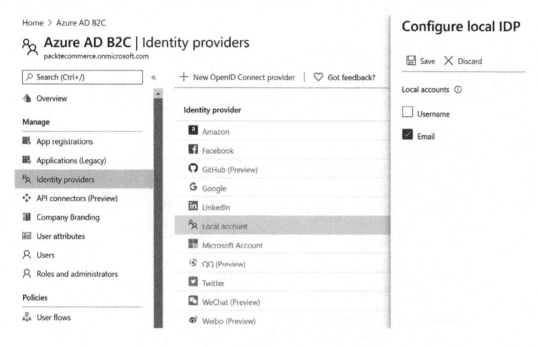

Figure 12.16 – Selecting an identity provider

12. Let's configure Google as the identity provider for our application. You can follow the steps outlined at `https://docs.microsoft.com/en-in/azure/active-directory-b2c/identity-provider-google` to acquire the client ID and secret. The details you need to provide are shown in the following screenshot:

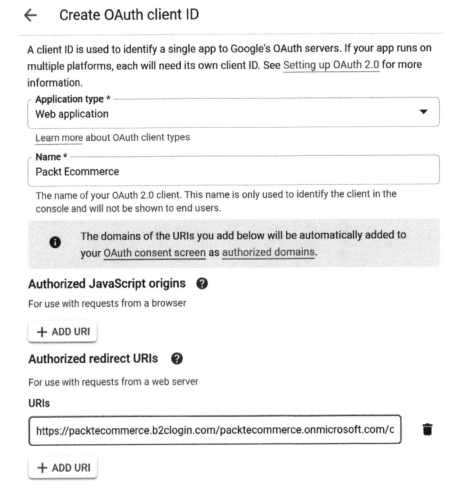

Figure 12.17 – Google: New OAuth client

After you provide the required details and select save, the client ID and secret are generated, as shown in the following screenshot:

OAuth client created

The client ID and secret can always be accessed from Credentials in APIs & Services

> ℹ OAuth is limited to 100 sensitive scope logins until the OAuth consent screen is verified. This may require a verification process that can take several days.

Your Client ID

`2q3jdh.apps.` 📋

Your Client Secret

`3j` 📋

OK

Figure 12.18 – The Google OAuth client

13. Once you have created **Auth Client,** click on **Google** from **identity providers,** and then provide the **Client ID** and **Client secret** values to complete the configuration. Refer to the following screenshot:

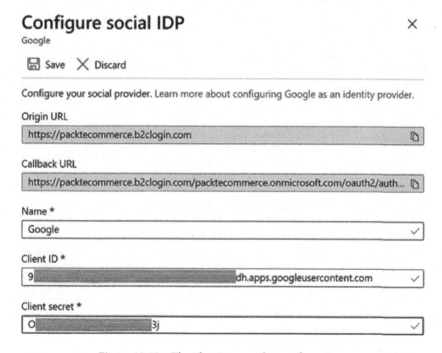

Figure 12.19 – The identity provider configuration

14. Let's configure Facebook as another identity provider for our e-commerce application. You can follow the steps outlined at `https://docs.microsoft.com/en-in/azure/active-directory-b2c/identity-provider-facebook`.

15. Once you have created the **Client Auth** settings, click on **Facebook** from **identity providers**, and then provide the **Client Id** and **Client Secret** values to complete the configuration. Refer to *Figure 12.19* for an overview of this.

16. Now, let's configure the user flow. The user flow allows you to configure and customize the authentication experience for your users. You can configure multiple flows in your tenant and use them in your application. User flows allow you to add MFA and also customize the information that you capture from a user at the time of registration—for example, their given name, country, postal code, and, optionally, whether you want to add them to claims. You can also customize the UI for a better user experience. To create a flow, click on **User Flows** under **Policies** and choose a flow type, as illustrated in the following screenshot:

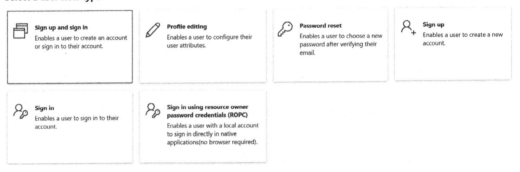

Figure 12.20 – A new user flow

17. Provide the necessary details, and click on **Create** to save:

Name: This is the name of your flow to uniquely identify.

Identity providers: Select your identity providers.

Optionally, you can choose additional user attributes such as **Name**, **Postal Code**, and more, as illustrated in the following screenshot:

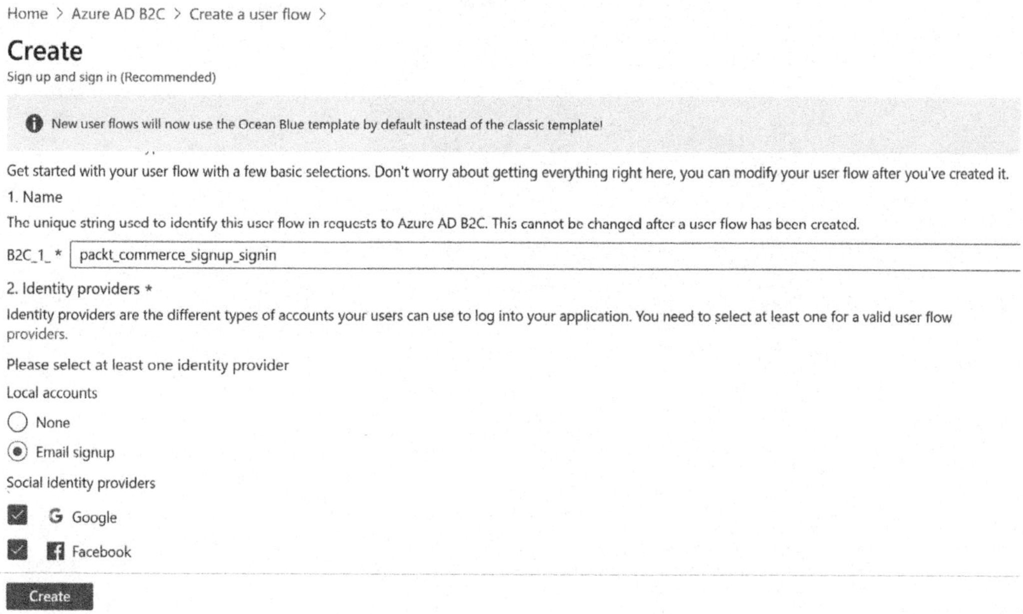

Home > Azure AD B2C > Create a user flow >

Create
Sign up and sign in (Recommended)

> ℹ New user flows will now use the Ocean Blue template by default instead of the classic template!

Get started with your user flow with a few basic selections. Don't worry about getting everything right here, you can modify your user flow after you've created it.

1. Name

The unique string used to identify this user flow in requests to Azure AD B2C. This cannot be changed after a user flow has been created.

B2C_1_ * | packt_commerce_signup_signin

2. Identity providers *

Identity providers are the different types of accounts your users can use to log into your application. You need to select at least one for a valid user flow providers.

Please select at least one identity provider

Local accounts

◯ None

◉ Email signup

Social identity providers

☑ G Google

☑ 🟦 Facebook

[Create]

Figure 12.21 – The user flow configuration

You can choose additional attributes in the **User attributes and token claims** section, as shown in the following screenshot:

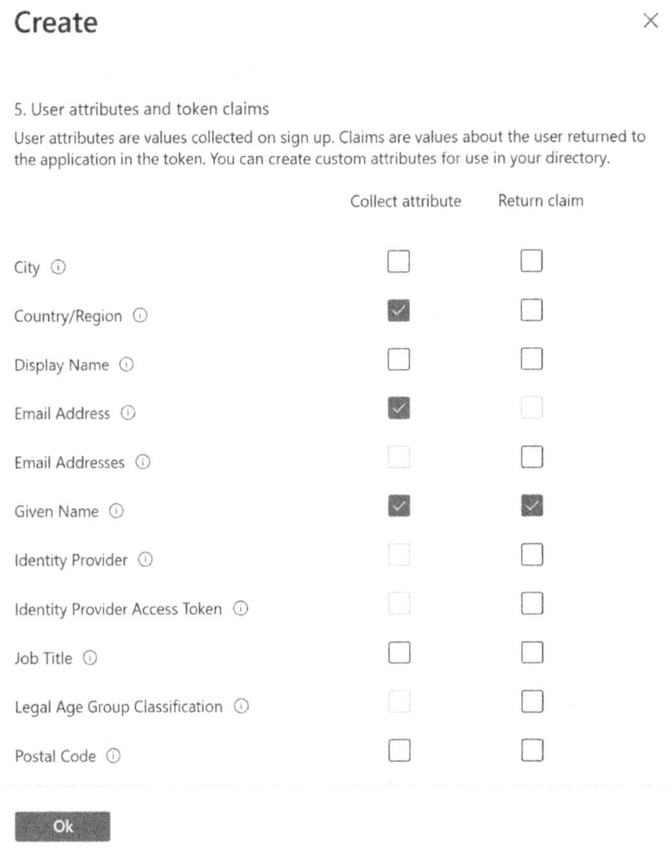

Figure 12.22 – The additional attribute and claim configuration

18. Similarly, we should also set up a password reset policy. This is required for local accounts. To create one, under **Create User Flow**, choose **Password Reset** and provide the necessary details. You can refer to *Figure 12.20*.

19. Having completed the minimum required setup of Azure AD B2C, we are ready to test the flow. Select the user flow that was created and click on **Run user flow**. You can view the sign-up and sign-in pages that were created for you, which you can find in the following screenshot:

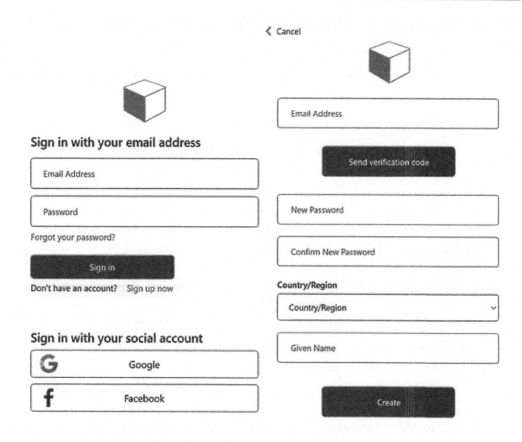

Figure 12.23 – The sign-in and sign-up screens

Let's look at the changes that we need to do in `Packt.Ecommerce.Web` to integrate with Azure AD.

Integrating our e-commerce application with Azure AD B2C

We will configure authentication on the web application to use Azure AD B2C. Let's make the necessary changes to our application to integrate with the B2C tenant, as follows:

1. Add the following two NuGet packages to our `Packt.Ecommerce.Web` project:

    `Microsoft.Identity.Web`: This is the main package required to integrate with Azure AD.

    `Microsoft.Identity.Web.UI`: This package generates the UI for signing in and signing out. In `Program.cs`, we need to add an authentication service using the `OpenIdConnect` scheme along with the `Azure AD B2C` configuration, as follows:

    ```
    services.AddAuthentication(OpenIdConnectDefaults.
    AuthenticationScheme).
    AddMicrosoftIdentityWebApp(Configuration.
    GetSection("AzureAdB2C"));
    services.AddRazorPages().AddMicrosoftIdentityUI();
    ```

2. Under the `Configure` method, add the following code before the `app.UseAuthorization()` method:

    ```
    app.UseAuthentication();
    ```

3. We need to add `AzureAdB2C` to `appsettings.json`, as follows:

    `Instance`: `https://<domain>.b2clogin.com/tfp`. Replace `<domain>` with the name you have chosen while creating the B2C tenant.

    `ClientId`: This is the AD application ID that you created while setting up Azure AD B2C.

    `Domain`: `<domain>.onmicrosoft.com`. Here, replace `<domain>` with the domain name you chose while creating the B2C tenant.

    Update `SignUpSignInPolicyId` and `ResetPasswordPolicyId`, as follows:

    ```
    "AzureAdB2C": {
        "Instance":
        "https://packtecommerce.b2clogin.com/tfp/",
        "ClientId": "1ae40a96-60d7-4641-bb81-
          bc3a47aad36d",
        "Domain": "packtecommerce.onmicrosoft.com",
        "SignedOutCallbackPath": "/signout/B2C_1_susi",
    ```

```
        "SignUpSignInPolicyId": "B2C_1_packt_commerce",
        "ResetPasswordPolicyId": "B2C_1_password_reset",
        "EditProfilePolicyId": "",
        "CallbackPath": "/signin-oidc"
    }
```

4. You can add an `[Authorize]` attribute to controllers or action methods—for instance, you can add it to `OrdersController` in `OrdersController.cs` to force users to authenticate themselves to access the `Orders` information.

5. The last step is to update the reply URI. To do so, navigate to **AD Application** in your tenant. Navigate to the **Authentication** section under **Manage**, update **Reply URI**, and set implicit grant permissions.

The reply URI is the URL of your application to which users will be redirected after successful authentication. To set up an application and debug them locally, we can configure the localhost URL, but once you deploy the application to a server, you will need to update the URL of the server.

Under **Implicit grant**, select **Access tokens** and **ID tokens**, which are required for our ASP.NET Core application, as illustrated in the following screenshot:

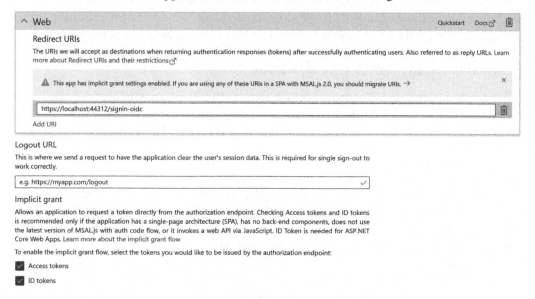

Figure 12.24 – The reply URL configuration

Now, run your application and try accessing the **Orders** page. You will be redirected to the sign-in and sign-up pages, as shown in *Figure 12.23*. This concludes the integration of our e-commerce application with Azure AD B2C.

Azure AD offers many more options and customizations to suit your needs. For more details, you can look at `https://docs.microsoft.com/en-in/azure/active-directory-b2c`.

> **Note**
>
> You can use Duende Identity Server to set up your own identity server. This uses OpenID Connect and the OAuth 2.0 framework to establish identity. It is available via NuGet and can be easily integrated with ASP.NET Core applications. For more details, you can refer to `https://docs.duendesoftware.com/identityserver/v6`.

In the next section, let's see how to use Windows Authentication.

Introduction to Windows Authentication

ASP.NET Core applications can be configured to use Windows Authentication, whereby users are authenticated against their Windows credentials. Windows Authentication is the best choice when your application is hosted on a Windows server and your application is only available on the intranet. In this section, we will learn how to use Windows Authentication in an ASP.NET Core application.

In Visual Studio, choose **Windows** in the **Change Authentication** window while creating a new ASP.NET Core project. If you choose the CLI to create the project, use the `--auth Windows` parameters to create a new web app using Windows Authentication, as follows:

```
dotnet new webapp --auth Windows -o WinAuthSample
```

If you open `launchSettings.json`, you will notice that `WindowsAuthentication` is set to `true` and `anonymousAuthentication` is set to `false`, as illustrated in the following code snippet. This setting is only applicable when running an application in **Internet Information Services Express (IIS Express)**:

```
"iisSettings": {
    "windowsAuthentication": true,
    "anonymousAuthentication": false,
```

```
"iisExpress": {
  "applicationUrl": "http://localhost:21368",
  "sslPort": 44384
}
}
```

When you host an application on IIS, you need to configure `WindowsAuthentication` to `true` in `web.config`. By default, `web.config` is not added to the .NET Core web application, so you need to add it and make the necessary changes, as depicted in the following code snippet:

```
<location path="." inheritInChildApplications="false">
    <system.webServer>
      <security>
        <authentication>
          <anonymousAuthentication enabled="false"/>
          <windowsAuthentication enabled="true"/>
        </authentication>
      </security>
    </system.webServer>
</location>
```

The preceding configuration makes every endpoint secure. There will be no impact, even if we set `AllowAnonymous` on every controller or action. If you want to make any endpoint anonymously accessible, you need to set `anonymousAuthentication` to `true` and set `Authorize` on the endpoints that you want to make secure. In addition to that, you need to register the authentication service with the scheme as `Windows`, as follows:

```
services.AddAuthentication(IISDefaults.AuthenticationScheme)
```

This is all you need to do to enable Windows Authentication in your application. For more details, you can refer to `https://docs.microsoft.com/en-us/aspnet/core/security/authentication/windowsauth?view=aspnetcore-6.0`.

In the next section, we will look at a few best practices to be followed to secure client and server applications.

Understanding best practices to secure client and server applications

There are several best practices that are recommended to secure your web application. The .NET Core and Azure services make it easy to ensure their adoption. The following are key ones you could consider:

- Enforce HTTPS for web applications. Use `UseHttpsRedirection` middleware to redirect requests from HTTP to HTTPS.

- Use modern authentication frameworks based on OAuth 2.0 and OIDC to secure your web or API app.

- If you are using the Microsoft identity platform, use open source libraries such as MSAL.js and MSAL.NET to acquire or renew tokens.

- Configure strong password requirements and lock your account in the case of continuous failed login attempts—for example, five consecutive failed attempts. This can prevent a brute-force attack.

- Enable MFA for privileged accounts such as back-office admin, back-office staff accounts, and more.

- Configure session timeouts, invalidate your session on logout, and clear cookies.

- Enforce authorization on all secured endpoints and on the client side.

- Store keys/passwords in a secured location such as key vaults.

- If you are using Azure AD, register each logical/environment-specific application separately.

- Do not store sensitive information in plain text.

- Ensure proper exception handling.

- Perform a security/malware scan on files that are uploaded.

- Prevent cross-site scripting attacks—always HTML-encode user input data.

- Prevent SQL injection attacks by parameterizing SQL queries and using stored procedures.

- Prevent cross-site request forgery attacks—use a `ValidateAntiForgeryToken` filter on an action, a controller, or globally.

- Enforce **Cross-Origin Requests (CORS)** in middleware using this policy.

While the provided best practices and guidance are good to start with, you need to always consider an application's context and continuously assess and enhance your application to address security vulnerabilities and threats.

Summary

In this chapter, we understood what authentication is and the key elements of authentication in ASP.NET Core. We explored the different options offered by the ASP.NET Core framework and learned how ASP.NET Core Identity helps to quickly add authentication to your application. We discussed OAuth 2.0 and grant flows and understood how they make things easier when you need to authenticate and connect to multiple API services.

Also, we looked at configuring Azure AD as your identity service, using external authentication providers such as Google or Facebook in your application, and using Windows Authentication in an ASP.NET Core application. We concluded this chapter by discussing a few best practices to follow while developing server-side and client-side applications.

In the next chapter, we will see what authorization is and how it helps to control access to your resources.

Questions

1. What information can be derived from a JWT?

   a. Issuer

   b. Expiry

   c. Scopes

   d. Subject

   e. All of the above

   Answer: e

2. What are the recommended OAuth grant flows for single-page apps?

    a. Client credentials flow

    b. Implicit flow

    c. Code grant flow

    d. On-behalf-of flow

    Answer: b and c

3. What are the minimum required NuGet packages to integrate with Azure AD?

    a. `Microsoft.AspNetCore.Identity`

    b. `Microsoft.Identity.Web.UI`

    c. `Microsoft.AspNetCore.Identity.UI`

    d. `Microsoft.Identity.Web`

    Answer: d

Further reading

To learn more about authentication, you can refer to the following resources:

- `https://docs.microsoft.com/en-us/aspnet/core/security/authentication/?view=aspnetcore-6.0`

- `https://docs.microsoft.com/en-in/azure/active-directory-b2c`

13

Implementing Authorization in .NET 6

One of the important aspects of building secure applications is to ensure that users have access only to the resources that they need. In the real world, when you check in to a hotel, a front-desk employee validates your ID and credit card and assigns a key card to access your room. Based on the type of room you have chosen, you may have privileges, such as access to the lounge, pool, or gym, among others. Here, the validation of your ID and credit card and assigning a key card is called **authentication**, and permitting you to access the various resources is called **authorization**. So, to explain it further, using a key card, we cannot identify who you are but can determine what you can do.

Authorization is a mechanism by which you determine what users can do and grant or deny access to a resource of your application. For instance, users of our e-commerce application should be able to browse products, add them to the cart, and check out to buy them, and only admin or back-office users should be able to add or update product information, update the price of products, and approve or reject orders.

In this chapter, we will learn what authorization is and the various ways to implement authorization using the ASP.NET Core framework. The following topics are covered in this chapter:

- Understanding authorization in .NET 6
- Simple authorization
- Role-based authorization
- Claims-based authorization
- Policy-based authorization
- Custom authorization
- Authorization in client and server applications

Technical requirements

For this chapter, you need basic knowledge of Azure, Azure AD B2C, C#, .NET Core, and Visual Studio 2022.

Back to a few basics

Before we dig into more details, let's understand the differences between authentication and authorization.

Authentication and authorization may look similar and be used interchangeably, but fundamentally they are different. The following table illustrates the differences:

Authentication	Authorization
A process with which you identify who is accessing your application	A process with which you determine what a user can access
Authentication takes place first	Occurs after establishing the identity of a user
Authenticated by verifying credentials such as username and password	Determined by claims, roles, or policies
Usually uses OpenID protocol to determine users' identity	Uses OAuth protocol to govern access

Table 13.1

> **Note**
>
> Refer to *Chapter 12, Understanding Authentication*, for more details on how authentication works in ASP.NET 6.

To summarize this, authentication and authorization go hand in hand. Authorization works only after the identity of the user has been established, and an authentication challenge is triggered by authorization when a user tries to access a secure resource. In the upcoming sections of this chapter, we will understand how to implement authorization in ASP.NET 6 applications.

Understanding authorization

Authorization in ASP.NET Core is handled by a **middleware**. When your application receives the first request from an unauthenticated user to a secured resource, an authentication challenge is invoked by the middleware, and depending on the authentication scheme, the user is either redirected to log in or access is forbidden. Once the identity of the user has been established after authentication, the authorization middleware checks whether the user can access the resource or not. In subsequent requests, the authorization middleware uses the identity of the user to determine whether access is allowed or forbidden.

To configure authorization middleware in your project, you need to invoke `UseAuthorization()` in `Program.cs`. It is mandatory to register authorization middleware only after authentication middleware, as authorization can be performed only after establishing the user's identity. Refer to the following code:

```
var builder = WebApplication.CreateBuilder(args);
..
var app = builder.Build();
app.UseAuthentication();
app.UseAuthorization();
app.UseEndpoints(endpoints =>
{
endpoints.MapControllerRoute(
    name: "default",
    pattern: "{controller=Home}/{action=Index}/{id?}");
    endpoints.MapRazorPages();
});
```

In the preceding code block, you'll notice that app.UseAuthorization() is invoked after app.UseAuthentication() and before app.UseEndpoints().

ASP.NET 6 provides simple, declarative role- and claims-based authorization models and rich policy-based models. In the following sections, we will learn more details about these.

Simple authorization

In ASP.NET Core, authorization is configured using AuthorizationAttribute. You can apply the [Authorize] attribute on a controller, action, or Razor page. When you add this attribute, access to that component is restricted only to authenticated users. Refer to the following code block:

```
public class HomeController : Controller
{
[Authorize]
public IActionResult Index()
{
    return View();
}
public IActionResult Privacy()
{
    return View();
}
}
```

In the preceding code, you'll notice that the [Authorize] attribute is added to the Index action. When a user tries to access /Home/Index from the browser, the middleware checks whether the user is authenticated or not. If not, the user is redirected to the login page.

If we add the [Authorize] attribute to a controller, access to any action under that controller is restricted only to authenticated users. In the following code, you'll notice that the [Authorize] attribute is added to HomeController, making all actions under it secure:

```
[Authorize]
public class HomeController : Controller
{
```

```
public IActionResult Index()
{
    return View();
}
[AllowAnonymous]
public IActionResult Privacy()
{
    return View();
}
}
```

At times, you may want to allow a few areas of your application to be accessible to any user; for example, the login or reset password page should be open to all, regardless of whether the user is authenticated or not. To meet such requirements, you can add the [AllowAnonymous] attribute to a controller or an action and make them available to unauthenticated users as well.

In the preceding code, you'll notice that the [AllowAnonymous] attribute is added to the Privacy action, though we have the [Authorize] attribute on the controller. That requirement is overridden by the [AllowAnonymous] attribute on the action method and so the Privacy action is accessible by all users.

> **Note**
>
> The [AllowAnonymous] attribute overrides all authorization configurations. If you set [AllowAnonymous] on a controller, setting the [Authorize] attribute on any action methods under it will have no impact. In this case, the Authorize attribute on the action methods is completely ignored.

So far, we have seen how to secure a controller or an action method. In the next section, we will see how to enable authorization globally in an ASP.NET Core application.

Enabling authorization globally

So far, we have seen how to secure a controller or an action method using the [Authorize] attribute. Setting the authorize attribute on every controller or action is not sustainable in large projects; you may miss configuring it on newly added controllers or action methods, which can lead to a security vulnerability.

ASP.NET Core allows you to enable authorization globally by adding a fallback policy in your application. You can define a fallback policy in `Program.cs`. The fallback policy will be applied to all requests where no explicit authorization requirement is defined:

```
var builder = WebApplication.CreateBuilder(args);
builder.Services.AddAuthorization(options =>
{
options.FallbackPolicy = new AuthorizationPolicyBuilder()
        .RequireAuthenticatedUser()
        .Build();
});
```

Adding a policy globally enforces users to be authenticated to access any action method in your application. This option is beneficial as you don't have to specify the `[Authorize]` attribute for every controller/action in your application.

You can still set the `[AllowAnonymous]` attribute on a controller or action method to override the fallback behavior and make it anonymously accessible.

Now that we understand how to implement simple authorization, in the next section, let's understand what role-based authorization is and how it simplifies implementation.

Role-based authorization

It is quite common for certain areas of your application to be available to only certain users. Instead of granting access at the user level, general practice is to group users into roles and grant access to roles. Let's consider a typical e-commerce application, in which *users* can place orders, *support* staff can view, update, or cancel orders and resolve user queries, and the *admin* role approves or rejects orders, manages inventory, and so on.

Role-based authorization can address such requirements. When you create a user, you may assign it to one or more roles, and when we configure the `[Authorize]` attribute, we can pass one or more role names to the `Roles` property of the `Authorize` attribute.

The following code restricts access to all action methods under the `Admin` controller to users who belong to the `Admin` role:

```
[Authorize(Roles ="Admin")]
public class AdminController : Controller
{
public IActionResult Index()
{
```

```
      return View();
   }
}
```

Similarly, you can specify comma-separated role names in the `Roles` property of the `Authorize` attribute, so that users who belong to either of the configured roles will have access to the action methods under that controller.

In the following code, you'll notice `User`, `Support` is supplied as a value of the `Roles` property of the `[Authorize]` attribute; users belonging to the `User` or `Support` roles can access the action methods of `OrdersController`:

```
[Authorize(Roles ="User,Support")]
public class OrdersController : Controller
{
public IActionResult Index()
{

   return View();
}
}
```

You can also specify multiple authorization attributes. If you do so, the user must be a member of all roles specified to access it.

In the following code, multiple `[Authorize]` attributes are configured on `InventoryController` for the `InventoryManager` and `Admin` roles. To access the `Inventory` controller, a user must have the `InventoryManager` and `Admin` roles:

```
[Authorize(Roles ="InventoryManager")]
[Authorize(Roles ="Admin")]
public class InventoryController : Controller
{
public IActionResult Index()
{

   return View();
}
[Authorize(Roles ="Admin")]
public IActionResult Approve()
{

   return View();
```

```
        }
    }
```

You can further restrict access to the action methods under the `Inventory` controller by specifying authorization attributes. In the preceding code, users must have the `InventoryManager` and `Admin` roles to access the `Approve` action.

Programmatically, if you want to check whether a user belongs to a role, you can use the `IsInRole` method of `ClaimsPrinciple`. In the following example, you'll notice that `User.IsInRole` accepts `roleName` and, based on the user's role, it returns `true` or `false`:

```
public ActionResult Index()
{
if (User.IsInRole("Admin"))
{
    // Handle your logic
}
return View();
}
```

So far, we have seen how to secure a controller or an action by specifying role names in an authorization attribute. In the next section, we will see how to centralize these configurations in one place using policy-based role authorization.

Policy-based role authorization

We can also define role requirements as policies in `Program.cs`. This approach is quite useful, as you can create and manage your role-based access requirements in one place and use policy names instead of role names to control access. To define a policy-based role authorization, we need to register an authorization policy with one or more role requirements in `Program.cs` and provide a policy name to the `Policy` property of the `Authorize` attribute.

In the following code, `AdminAccessPolicy` is created by adding a requirement with the `Admin` role:

```
var builder = WebApplication.CreateBuilder(args);
builder.Services.AddAuthorization(options =>
```

```
{
    options.AddPolicy("AdminAccessPolicy",
        policy => policy.RequireRole("Admin"));
});
```

In your controller, you can specify the policy to be applied as follows, and access to `AdminController` is restricted to users with the `Admin` role:

```
[Authorize(Policy ="AdminAccessPolicy")]
public class AdminController : Controller
{
public IActionResult Index()
{
    return View();
}
}
```

You can specify multiple roles while defining a policy. Users belonging to any one of the roles can access resources when that policy is used to authorize users. For example, the following code will allow a user with the `User` or `Support` roles to access resources:

```
options.AddPolicy("OrderAccessPolicy",
        policy => policy.RequireRole("User","Support"));
```

You can use an `OrderAccessPolicy` policy with the `Authorize` attribute either on the controller or action methods to control access.

Now that we understand how to use role-based authorization, in the next section, we will create a simple application and configure it to use role-based authorization.

Implementing role-based authorization

Let's create a sample application implementing role-based authorization using ASP.NET Core Identity:

1. Create a new ASP.NET Core project. You can use the following dotnet **command-line interface (CLI)** command to create it. This will create a new ASP.NET Core **Model-View-Controller (MVC)** application using `Individual` accounts as the `Authentication` mode and `SQLite` as the database store:

   ```
   dotnet new mvc --auth Individual -o AuthSample
   ```

2. You need to enable role services by invoking `AddRoles<IdentityRole>()` in `Program.cs`. You can refer to the following code to enable it. You'll also notice `RequireConfirmedAccount` is set to `false`. This is required for this sample as we create users programmatically:

```
{
var builder = WebApplication.CreateBuilder(args);
var connectionString = builder.Configuration.
GetConnectionString("DefaultConnection");
builder.Services.
AddDbContext<ApplicationDbContext>(options =>
    options.UseSqlite(connectionString));
builder.Services.
AddDatabaseDeveloperPageExceptionFilter();
builder.Services.AddDefaultIdentity<IdentityUser>(options
=>
    options.SignIn.RequireConfirmedAccount = false)
    .AddRoles<IdentityRole>()
    .AddEntityFrameworkStores<ApplicationDbContext>();
builder.Services.AddControllersWithViews();
}
```

3. Next, we need to create roles and users. For this, we will add two methods, `SetupRoles` and `SetupUsers`, to `Program.cs`. We can make use of the `RoleManager` and `UserManager` services to create roles and users. In the following code, we create three roles. Using `IServiceProvider`, we get an instance of the `roleManager` service and then we make use of the `RoleExisysAsync` and `CreateAsync` methods to create it:

```
//Add this method to Program.cs
async Task SetupRoles(IServiceProvider serviceProvider)
{
var rolemanager = serviceProvider
    .GetRequiredService<RoleManager<IdentityRole>>();
string[] roles = { "Admin", "Support", "User" };
foreach (var role in roles)
{
    var roleExist = await rolemanager.
RoleExistsAsync(role);
    if (!roleExist)
```

```
    {
        await rolemanager.CreateAsync(new
            IdentityRole(role));
    }
    }
}
```

4. Similarly, we create users and assign one of the roles using the `userManager` service. In the following code, we create two users – admin@abc.com, assigned the admin role, and support@abc.com, assigned the support role:

```
//Add this method to Program.cs
async Task SetupUsers(IServiceProvider serviceProvider)
{
var userManager = serviceProvider
    .GetRequiredService<UserManager<IdentityUser>>();
var adminUser = await userManager.
FindByEmailAsync("admin@abc.com");
if (adminUser == null)
{
    var newAdminUser = new IdentityUser
    {
        UserName = "admin@abc.com",
        Email = "admin@abc.com",
    };
var result = await userManager
    .CreateAsync(newAdminUser, "Password@123");
if (result.Succeeded)
    await userManager.AddToRoleAsync(newAdminUser,
      "Admin");
}
var supportUser = await userManager
    .FindByEmailAsync("support@abc.com");
if (supportUser == null)
{
    var newSupportUser = new IdentityUser
    {
        UserName = "support@abc.com",
```

```
            Email = "support@abc.com",
        };
    var result = await userManager
        .CreateAsync(newSupportUser, "Password@123");
    if (result.Succeeded)
        await userManager.AddToRoleAsync(newSupportUser,
            "Support");
    }
}
```

5. To invoke these two methods, we need an instance of IserviceProvider. The following code gets the instance to IServiceProvider to set up roles and users data:

```
//
//
var app = builder.Build();
using (var scope = app.Services.CreateScope())
{
    var services = scope.ServiceProvider;
    await SetupRoles(services);
    await SetupUsers(services);
}
```

6. Inside the Home controller, add the following code. To simplify the implementation, we are using the Index view. In a real-life scenario, you need to return the view that is created for the respective action methods:

```
[Authorize(Roles = "Admin")]
public IActionResult Admin()
{
return View("Index");
}
[Authorize(Roles = "Support")]
public IActionResult Support()
{
return View("Index");
}
```

7. Optionally, we can add logic to `Layout.cshtml` to display links to navigate based on the logged-in user's role. The following sample makes use of `IsInRole` to check the user's role and display a link:

```
<li class="nav-item">
<a class="nav-link text-dark" asp-area=""
asp-controller="Home" asp-action="Index">Home</a>
</li>
@if (User.IsInRole("Admin"))
{
<li class="nav-item">
    <a class="nav-link text-dark" asp-area=""
asp-controller="Home" asp-action="Admin">Admin</a>
</li>
}
@if (User.IsInRole("Support"))
{
<li class="nav-item">
    <a class="nav-link text-dark" asp-area=""
asp-controller="Home" asp-action="Support">Support</a>
</li>
}
```

With the preceding step, the sample implementation is complete, and you can run the application to see how it works.

Run the application, log in with admin@abc.com, and you will notice that the **Admin** menu item is visible and **Support** is hidden:

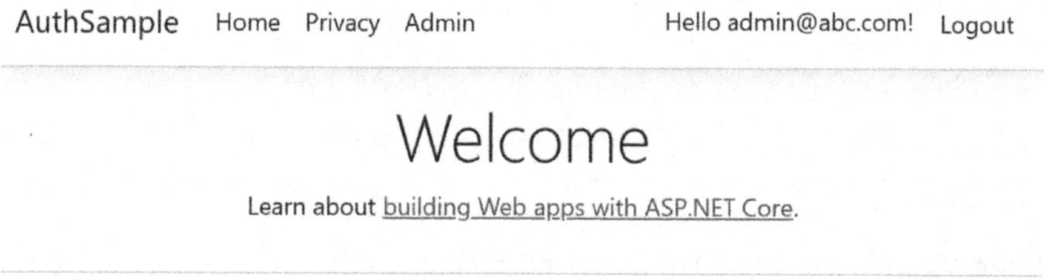

AuthSample   Home   Privacy   Admin   Hello admin@abc.com!   Logout

Welcome

Learn about building Web apps with ASP.NET Core.

Figure 13.1 – Admin user login view

When you log in with support@abc.com, you will notice the **Support** menu item is visible and the **Admin** item is hidden:

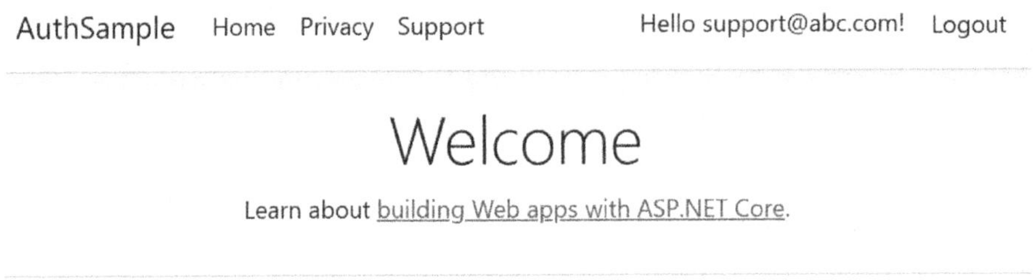

AuthSample   Home Privacy Support   Hello support@abc.com!   Logout

Welcome

Learn about building Web apps with ASP.NET Core.

Figure 13.2 – Support user login view

In the next section, we will see how to use claims for authorization.

Claims-based authorization

A **claim** is a key-value pair associated with identity after successful authentication. A claim can be a date of birth, gender, or zip code, for example. One or more claims can be assigned to a user. Claims-based authorization uses the value of a claim and determines whether access to a resource can be granted or not. You can use two approaches to validate a claim; one way is to just check whether the claim exists or not and the other approach is to check whether the claim exists with a particular value.

To use claims-based authorization, we need to register a policy in Program.cs. You need to pass a claim name and optional values to the RequireClaim method to register. For example, the following code registers PremiumContentPolicy with the requirement of the PremiumUser claim:

```
var builder = WebApplication.CreateBuilder(args);
builder.Services.AddAuthorization(options =>
{
    options.AddPolicy("PremiumContentPolicy",
        policy => policy.RequireClaim("PremiumUser"));
});
```

In the following code, the PremiumContentPolicy authorization policy is used on PremiumContentController. It checks whether the PremiumUser claim exists in the user claims to authorize the user's request; it doesn't care what value is in the claim:

```
[Authorize(Policy ="PremiumContentPolicy")]
public class PremiumContentController : Controller
```

```
{
public IActionResult Index()
{
        return View();
}
}
```

You can also specify a list of values while defining a claim. They will be validated to grant access to a resource. For example, as per the following code, the user request is authorized if the user has the Country claim with the values of US, UK, or IN:

```
var builder = WebApplication.CreateBuilder(args);
builder.Services.AddAuthorization(options =>
{
    options.AddPolicy("ExpressShippingPolicy",
        policy => policy.RequireClaim(ClaimTypes.Country,
            "US", "UK", "IN"));
});
```

Programmatically, if you want to check whether a user has a claim, you use the HasClaim method of ClaimsPrinciple by specifying a match condition.

To fetch a claim value, you can use the FindFirst method. The following code illustrates an example:

```
@if (User.HasClaim(x => x.Type == "PremiumUser"))
{
    <h1>Yay, you are Premium User!!!, @User.FindFirst(x =>
        x.Type == ClaimTypes.Country)?.Value</h1>
}
```

As seen in the *Implementing role-based authorization* section, while adding a user to an application, you can also add a claim to the user using the UserManager service. In the following code, you'll notice the AddClaimAsync method is invoked with IdentityUser and Claim:

```
var user = await userManager.FindByEmailAsync("user@abc.com");
if (user == null)
{
var newUser = new IdentityUser
```

```
{
    UserName = "user@abc.com",
    Email = "user@abc.com",
};
var result = await userManager.CreateAsync(newUser,
"Password@123");
if (result.Succeeded)
{
await userManager
    .AddToRoleAsync(newUser, "User");
await userManager
    .AddClaimAsync(newUser, new Claim("PremiumUser",
        "true"));
await userManager
    .AddClaimAsync(newUser, new Claim(ClaimTypes.Country,
        "US"));
await userManager
                .AddClaimAsync(newUser, new Claim(ClaimTypes.
DateOfBirth, "1-5-2003"));
}
}
```

In the preceding code, you will notice two claims created and associated with the user using the AddClaimAsync method. In the next section, we will see how to use policy-based authorization.

Policy-based authorization

Policy-based authorization allows you to write your own logic to handle authorization requirements that suit your needs. For example, you have a requirement to verify a user's age and authorize the placing of an order only if the user is above 14 years of age. You can use the policy-based authorization model to handle such requirements.

To configure policy-based authorization, we need to define a requirement and a handler, and then register the policy with the requirement. Let's understand these components:

- A **policy** is defined with one or more requirements.

- A **requirement** is a collection of data parameters used by the policy to evaluate the user's identity.

- A **handler** is responsible for evaluating data from the requirement against the context and determining whether access can be granted or not.

In the following section, we will see how to create a requirement and a handler, and register an authorization policy.

Requirements

To create a requirement, you need to implement the `IAuthorizationRequirement` interface. This is a marker interface, so you don't have any members to implement. For example, the following code creates `MinimumAgeRequirement`, with `MinimumAge` as a data parameter:

```
public class MinimumAgeRequirement: IAuthorizationRequirement
{
public int MinimumAge { get; set; }
public MinimumAgeRequirement(int minimumAge)
{
    this.MinimumAge = minimumAge;
}
}
```

Requirement handlers

Requirement handlers encapsulate logic to allow or deny a request. They use requirement properties against `AuthorizationHandlerContext` to determine access. A handler may inherit `Authorizationhandler<TRequirement>`, where `TRequirement` is of the `IauthorizationRequirement` type, or implement `IAuthorizationHandler`.

In the following example, `MinimumAgeAuthorizationHandler` is created by inheriting `AuthorizationHandler` with `MinimumAgeRequirement` as `TRequirement`. We need to override `HandleRequirementAsync` to write custom authorization logic where the user's age is calculated from the `DateOfBirth` claim. If the user's age is greater than or equal to `MinimumAge`, we invoke `context.Succeed` to grant access. If the claim is not present or doesn't meet the age criteria, access is forbidden:

```
public class MinimumAgeAuthorizationHandler
 : AuthorizationHandler<MinimumAgeRequirement>
{
protected override Task HandleRequirementAsync(
```

```
AuthorizationHandlerContext context,
MinimumAgeRequirement requirement)
{
    if (context.User.HasClaim(
        c => c.Type == ClaimTypes.DateOfBirth))
    {
        var dateOfBirth = Convert.ToDateTime(
            context.User.FindFirst(x =>
            x.Type == ClaimTypes.DateOfBirth).Value);

        var age = DateTime.Today.Year - dateOfBirth.Year;

        if (dateOfBirth > DateTime.Today.AddYears(-age))
          age--;

        if (age >= requirement.MinimumAge)
        {
            context.Succeed(requirement);
        }
        else
        {
            context.Fail();
        }
    }
        return Task.CompletedTask;
}
}
```

To mark a requirement as successful, you need to invoke `context.Succeed` by passing a requirement as a parameter. You don't have to handle failure, as another handler for the same requirement may succeed. If you want to forbid a request, you can invoke `context.Fail`.

> **Note**
>
> Handlers must be registered for service collection in `Program.cs`.

Registering a policy

A policy is registered with a name and a requirement in `Program.cs`. You can register one or more requirements while defining a policy.

In the following example, a policy with a requirement is created by invoking `policy.Requirements.Add()` and passing a new instance of `MinimumAgeRequirement`. You'll also notice `MinimumAgeAuthorizationHandler` is added to the service collection with a singleton scope:

```
var builder = WebApplication.CreateBuilder(args);
builder.Services.AddAuthorization(options =>
{
options.AddPolicy("Over14", policy =>
    policy.Requirements.Add(new
      MinimumAgeRequirement(14)));
});
builder.Services.AddSingleton<IAuthorizationHandler,
    MinimumAgeAuthorizationHandler>();
```

We can then configure an authorization policy on the controller or action to restrict access based on the user's age:

```
[Authorize(Policy ="Over14")]
public class OrdersController : Controller
{
public IActionResult Index()
{
        return View();
}
}
```

If we register a policy with more than one requirement, then all requirements must be satisfied for successful authorization.

In the next section, we will learn how to further customize authorization.

Custom authorization

In the previous section, we learned how to use policy-based authorization and implement custom logic to handle authorization requirements. But, it is not always possible to register authorization policies in `Program.cs` like that. In this section, we will see how to use `IAuthorizationPolicyProvider` to dynamically build policy configurations in your application.

The `IAuthorizationPolicyProvider` interface has three methods to be implemented:

- `GetDefaultPolicyAsync`: This method returns the default authorization policy to be used.

- `GetFallbackPolicyAsync`: This method returns the fallback authorization policy. It is used when no explicit authorization requirement is defined.

- `GetPolicyAsync`: This method is used to build and return an authorization policy for the provided policy name.

Let's look into an example where you want to authorize a request to several controllers/actions based on different age criteria, say `Over14`, `Over18`, `Over21`, `Over60`, and so on. One way to implement it is to register all these requirements as policies and use them on your controllers or actions. But, using this approach, the code is less maintainable and not sustainable in a large application with many policies. Let's see how we can make use of the authorization policy provider.

We need to create a class implementing `IAuthorizationPolicyProvider` and also implement `GetPolicy` and other methods.

In the following example, the `MinimumAgePolicyProvider` class implements `GetPolicyAsync`. The input for this method is the policy name. Since our policy name is something such as `Over14` or `Over18`, we can use string functions and extract the age from them, and a requirement is initialized with the required age and registered as a new policy:

```
public class MinimumAgePolicyProvider :
IAuthorizationPolicyProvider
{
        const string PREFIX = "Over";
        public Task<AuthorizationPolicy?>
          GetPolicyAsync(string policyName)
        {
            if (policyName.StartsWith(PREFIX,
```

```
          StringComparison.OrdinalIgnoreCase) &&
        int.TryParse(policyName.Substring(
          PREFIX.Length), out var age))
        {
            var policy = new
              AuthorizationPolicyBuilder();
            policy.AddRequirements(new
              MinimumAgeRequirement(age));
            return Task.FromResult
              <AuthorizationPolicy?>(policy.Build());
        }
        return
          Task.FromResult<AuthorizationPolicy?>(null);
    }
}
```

> **Note**
>
> For the implementation of `MinimumAgeRequirement`, please refer to the *Policy-based authorization* section.

ASP.NET Core uses only one instance of `IAuthorizationPolicyProvider`. So, you should either customize a `Default` and `Fallback` authorization policy or, alternatively, use a backup provider.

In the following code, you'll see a sample implementation of the `GetDefaultPolicyAsync` and `GetFallbackPolicyAsync` methods in the `MinimumAgePolicyProvider` class.

`AuthorizationOptions` is injected into the constructor, and it is used to initialize `DefaultAuthorizationPolicyProvider`. The `BackupPolicyProvider` object is used to implement the `GetDefaultPolicyAsync` and `GetFallbackPolicyAsync` methods:

```
public MinimumAgePolicyProvider(IOptions<AuthorizationOptions>
options)
{
this.BackupPolicyProvider =
    new DefaultAuthorizationPolicyProvider(options);
}
```

```
Private DefaultAuthorizationPolicyProvider BackupPolicyProvider
{ get; }
public Task<AuthorizationPolicy> GetDefaultPolicyAsync()
=> this.BackupPolicyProvider.GetDefaultPolicyAsync();
public Task<AuthorizationPolicy?> GetFallbackPolicyAsync()
=> this.BackupPolicyProvider.GetFallbackPolicyAsync();
```

This concludes the implementation of `MinimumAgePolicyProvider`. You can now use the authorization policy on your controller or action methods. In the following code, you'll notice two policies are used, one with `Over14` on top of the controller and another with `Over18`, on the `Index` action method:

```
[Authorize(Policy ="Over14")]
public class OrdersController : Controller
{
    [Authorize(Policy ="Over18")]
public IActionResult Index()
{
        return View();
}
}
}
```

Users with an age above 14 will have access to any action methods under `OrdersController`, and users older than 18 will only have access to the `Index` action.

In the next section, we will learn how to create and use a custom authorization attribute.

Custom authorization attributes

In the previous example, a policy name with an age was passed as a string, but the code is not clean that way. It would be good if you could pass `age` as a parameter to the authorization attribute. For this, you need to create a custom authorization attribute inheriting the `AuthorizeAttribute` class.

In the following sample code, the `AuthorizeAgeOverAttribute` class is inherited from the `AuthorizeAttribute` class. The constructor of this class accepts age as input. In the setter, we construct and set a policy name by concatenating `PREFIX` and `Age`:

```
public class AuthorizeAgeOverAttribute : AuthorizeAttribute
{
const string PREFIX = "Over";
public AuthorizeAgeOverAttribute(int age) => Age = age;
public int Age
{
    get
        {
            if
            (int.TryParse(Policy.Substring(PREFIX.Length),
            out var age))
                {
                    return age;
                }
            return default(int);
        }
        set
        {
            Policy = $"{PREFIX}{value.ToString()}";
        }
    }
}
```

To use the `AuthorizeAgeOver` attribute, we must register the `AuthorizationHandler` and `AuthorizationPolicyProvider` services in `Program.cs`. In the following code, the `MinimumAgeAuthorizationHandler` and `MinimumAgePolicyProvider` types are registered as `Singleton` for `IAuthorizationHandler` and `IauthorizationPolicyProvider`, respectively:

```
builder.Services.AddSingleton<IAuthorizationHandler,
        MinimumAgeAuthorizationHandler>();
builder.Services.AddSingleton<IAuthorizationPolicyProvider,
        MinimumAgePolicyProvider>();
```

Now that the custom attribute implementation is complete, we can use it on controller or action methods. In the following example, you can see a sample implementation, where age is passed as a parameter to our custom authorization attribute, `AuthorizeAgeOver`:

```
[AuthorizeAgeOver(14)]
public class OrdersController : Controller
{
[AuthorizeAgeOver(18)]
public IActionResult Index()
{
        return View();
}
}
```

In the next section, we will learn how to configure roles in an Azure AD application and use role-based authentication.

Authorization in client and server applications

In previous chapters, we learned how to use **Azure Active Directory** (**AAD**) as an identity service to authenticate users, but to use role-based authorization, we need to make a few configuration changes in Azure AD. In this section, we will see how to enable and create custom roles in an Azure AD application and do so in our e-commerce application to authorize users.

When a user logs in to an application, Azure AD adds assigned roles and claims to the user's identity.

> **Prerequisites**
>
> You should already have Azure AD and an AD app set up. If you don't, you can refer to the *Introduction to Azure Active Directory* section of *Chapter 12, Understanding Authentication*, to get set up.

Let's look into the steps that need to be performed on an Azure AD application to enable roles:

1. In the Azure portal, navigate to your **Active Directory** tenant.

2. In the left menu, under **Manage**, select **App registrations**:

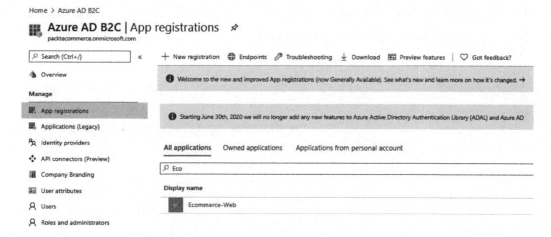

Figure 13.3 – Azure AD application

3. Search and select your AD application from the **App registrations** page. Refer to the following screenshot:

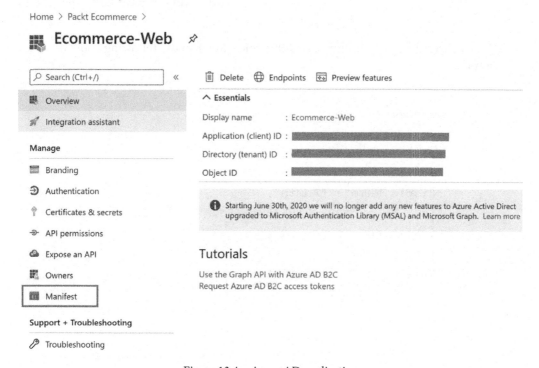

Figure 13.4 – Azure AD application

4. Click on **Manifest** from the left menu to edit it, as shown in the previous screenshot.

Figure 13.5 – Editing the manifest

5. Locate `appRoles` to configure multiple roles. Refer to the following code to add a role:

```
{
"allowedMemberTypes": [
      "User"
    ],
    "description": "Admin Users",
    "displayName": "Admin",
    "id": "6ef9b400-0219-463c-a542-5f4693c4e286",
    "isEnabled": true,
    "lang": null,
    "origin": "Application",
    "value": "Admin"
}
```

You need to provide values for `displayName`, `value`, `description`, and `id`. The value for `id` is `Guid`, and it must be unique for each role you add. Similarly, for `value`, you need to provide the role name that you refer to in your code, and it should be unique.

6. Save the manifest to complete it.

Saving a manifest with the required details will enable custom roles in an Azure AD application. In the next section, we will learn how to assign users to these custom roles.

Assigning roles to users

The next step is to assign roles to users. The assignment of roles to users can be done using the Azure portal or programmatically using the Graph API. In this section, we'll use the Azure portal to assign roles, and the same can also be achieved using theGraph API. For more information, you can refer to `https://docs.microsoft.com/en-us/graph/azuread-identity-access-management-concept-overview`:

1. In the Azure portal, navigate to the **Azure Active Directory** tenant.
2. Click on **Enterprise applications** from the left menu and search for and select your AD application.
3. Go to **Manage | Users and Groups | Add User**.
4. Search for and select the user, and click on **Ok**.
5. Click on **Select Role** to choose the role you want to assign.
6. Click **Assign** to save the selection.

You can continue these steps to assign roles to multiple users.

To secure controllers or actions, you can add an `Authorize` attribute along with the roles. In the following code, the `Admin` controller is accessible only to users with the `Admin` role:

```
[Authorize(Roles ="Admin")]
public class AdminController : Controller
{
public IActionResult Index()
{
    return View();
}
}
```

So far, we have learned how to enable roles in Azure AD and use the role-based model for authorization. In the next section, we will see how to access roles and claims using the user's identity in views.

User identity in views

A user claim principle can be used in views to conditionally show or hide data as required. For example, the following code checks the `IsAuthenticated` property of the user identity to determine whether the user is authenticated or not. If the user is not authenticated, a link to `Sign in` is displayed; otherwise, the username with a `Sign out` link is displayed:

```
<ul class="navbar-nav">
    @if (User.Identity.IsAuthenticated)
    {
        //// HTML code goes here
    }
    else
    {
        ////
    }
</ul>
```

Similarly, we can use `IsInRole` or `HasClaim` and write our logic to show content to or hide content from the user:

```
@if (User.HasClaim(x => x.Type == "PremiumUser"))
{
    <h1>Yay, you are Premium User!!!, @User.FindFirst(x =>
x.Type == ClaimTypes.Country)?.Value</h1>
}
```

For more details, you can refer to `https://docs.microsoft.com/en-us/azure/active-directory/develop/howto-add-app-roles-in-azure-ad-apps`.

Summary

In this chapter, we learned what authorization is and the different ways to implement it using the ASP.NET Core framework. We learned how to restrict or anonymously allow users to access resources using simple, declarative role- and claims-based models, and we learned how to implement custom logic to authorize user requests using a rich policy-based authorization model.

We learned how to dynamically add authorization policies using authorization policy providers and build custom authorized attributes. We also learned how to configure custom roles in Azure AD and use them in an ASP.NET Core application. Depending on your authorization requirements, you can use one or more authorization models to secure your applications.

In the next chapter, we will learn how to monitor the health and performance of an ASP.NET Core application.

Questions

After reading the chapter, you should be able to answer the following questions:

1. Which of the following is the primary service that determines whether authorization is successful or not?

   a. IAuthorizationHandler

   b. IAuthorizationRequirement

   c. IAuthorizationService

   d. IAuthorizationPolicyProvider

   Answer: c

2. In the following code, access to the Support action is restricted to only the Support role:

   ```
   [AllowAnonymous]
   public class HomeController : Controller
   {
        public IactionResult Index()
   {
       return View();
   }
   [Authorize(Roles ="Support")]
   ```

```
public IactionResult Support()
{
        return View();
}
}
```

a. True

b. False

Answer: b

Further reading

To learn more about authorization, you can refer to `https://docs.microsoft.com/en-us/aspnet/core/security/authorization/introduction?view=aspnetcore-6.0`.

Part 5: Health Checks, Unit Testing, Deployment, and Diagnostics

Just like for us, the health of any enterprise application should be easily checkable and, in the case of any anomalies, we should be informed upfront so that we can take corrective action without this resulting in downtime. In this part, we will integrate the new .NET 6 health and performance check APIs with our application and also unit-test our application. We will then learn how to deploy our application in the modern DevOps way and also see how to monitor, diagnose, and troubleshoot an application in production.

This part comprises the following chapters:

14
Health and Diagnostics

Modern software applications have evolved to be complex and dynamic and are distributed in nature. There is a high demand for these applications to be able to work round the clock, anywhere, on any device. To achieve this, it is important to know that our application is available and responds to requests at all times. Customer experiences will play a big role in the future of service and the revenue of an organization.

Once the application is live, it is critical to monitor the application's health. Regular application health monitoring will help us to proactively detect any failures and address them before they cause more damage. Application monitoring has now become a part of day-to-day operations. To diagnose any failure on a live application, we need to have the right telemetry and diagnostic tools. The telemetry that we capture will also help us identify those problems not directly seen or reported by users.

Let's learn about application health monitoring and what is on offer in .NET 6.

In this chapter, we will learn about the following topics:

- Introducing health checks
- The health check API in ASP.NET Core 6
- Monitoring the application with Application Insights
- Performing remote debugging

By the end of this chapter, you'll have a good grasp of building the health check API for .NET 6 apps and Azure Application Insights for capturing telemetry and diagnosing problems.

Technical requirements

You will need the following software to work through the tasks in this chapter:

- Visual Studio 2022 Community Edition with the Azure development workload installed (certain sections require Enterprise Edition)
- An Azure subscription

A basic understanding of Microsoft .NET and how to create resources in Azure is expected.

The code used in this chapter can be found at `https://github.com/ PacktPublishing/Enterprise-Application-Development-with-C-10- and-.NET-6-Second-Edition/tree/main/Enterprise%20Application`.

Introducing health checks

A health check is a comprehensive review of an application that helps us to understand the current state of the application and use visible indicators to take corrective measures. Health checks are exposed as HTTP endpoints by applications. The health check endpoints are used as health probes for certain orchestrators and load balancers to route traffic away from a failing node. Health checks are used to monitor application dependencies, such as databases, external services, and cache services.

In the next section, we will learn about the support for building the health check API in ASP.NET Core 6.

The health check API in ASP.NET Core 6

ASP.NET Core 6 has a built-in middleware (available via the `Microsoft.Extensions.Diagnostics.HealthChecks` NuGet package) to report the health status of the application components exposed as an HTTP endpoint. This middleware makes it so easy to integrate health checks for databases, external systems, and other dependencies. It is also extensible, so we can create our own custom health checks.

In the next section, we will add a health check endpoint to our `Ecommerce` portal.

Adding a health check endpoint

In this section, we will add a health check endpoint to our `Packt.Ecommerce.Web` application:

1. In order to add a health check endpoint, we need to first add the `Microsoft.Extensions.Diagnostics.HealthChecks` NuGet package reference to the `Packt.Ecommerce.Web` project, as shown in the following screenshot:

Figure 14.1 – NuGet reference, Microsoft.Extensions.Diagnostics.HealthChecks

Now, we need to register `HealthCheckService` with the dependency container. The `Microsoft.Extensions.Diagnostics.HealthChecks` package has the `AddHealthChecks` extension method defined to add `HealthCheckService` to the container. We can call the `AddHealthChecks` method from the `Program.cs` file to add the `DefaultHealthCheckService` module:

```
// Removed code for brevity.
// Add health check services to the container.
builder.Services.AddHealthChecks();
```

2. Let's go ahead and configure the health check endpoint to our web application. Map the health endpoint using the `MapHealthChecks` method, as shown in the following code, in the `Program.cs` file. This will add the health check endpoint route to the application. This will internally configure the `HealthCheckResponseWriters.WriteMinimalPlainText` framework method to emit the response. `WriteMinimalPlainText` will just emit the overall status of the health check services:

```
// Removed code for brevity.
app.UseEndpoints(endpoints =>
{
    endpoints.MapControllerRoute(
        name: "default",
        pattern:
        "{controller=Products}/{action=Index}/{id?}");
    endpoints.MapHealthChecks("/health");
});
```

3. Run the application and browse to the `<<Application URL>>/health` URL. You will see following the output:

```
Healthy
```

Figure 14.2 – Health check endpoint response

The health endpoint we added provides basic information on service availability. In the next section, we will see how we can monitor the status of dependent services.

Monitoring dependent URIs

An enterprise application depends on multiple other components, such as databases and Azure components including `KeyVault`, and other microservices (such as our `Ecommerce` website) depend on the Order service, Product service, and so on. These services can be owned by other teams within the same organization or, in some cases, they might be external services. It is often a good idea to monitor dependent services. We can leverage the `AspNetCore.HealthChecks.Uris` NuGet package to monitor the availability of dependent services.

Let's go ahead and enhance our health endpoint to monitor the Product and Order services:

1. Add the NuGet package reference to `AspNetCore.HealthChecks.Uris`. Now, modify the health check registration to register the Product and Order services, as shown in the following code snippet:

    ```
    // Add health check services to the container.
    services.AddHealthChecks()

    .AddUrlGroup(new Uri(this.Configuration.
    GetValue<string>("ApplicationSettings:ProductsApiEndpoint
    ")), name: "Product Service")

    .AddUrlGroup(new Uri(this.Configuration.
    GetValue<string>("ApplicationSettings:OrdersApiEndpoint
    ")), name: "Order Service");
    ```

    The health check middleware also provides details about the status of individual health checks.

2. Let's now modify our health check middleware to emit the details as shown in the following code:

    ```
    // Removed code for brevity.
    app.UseEndpoints(endpoints =>
    {
        endpoints.MapControllerRoute(
            name: "default",
            pattern: "{controller=Products}/{action=Index}/
    {id?}");
    ```

```
            endpoints.MapHealthChecks("/health", new
            HealthCheckOptions
        {
            ResponseWriter = async (context, report) =>
            {
                context.Response.ContentType =
                    "application/json";
                var response = new
        {
            Status = report.Status.ToString(),
            HealthChecks = report.Entries.Select(x => new
            {
                Component = x.Key,
                Status = x.Value.Status.ToString(),
                Description = x.Value.Description,
            }),
            HealthCheckDuration = report.TotalDuration,
        };
            await context.Response.WriteAsync(
                JsonConvert.SerializeObject(response))
                .ConfigureAwait(false);
            },
        });
    });
```

In this code, the health check middleware is overwritten to write the details of the status, health check duration, component name, and a description as its response by providing `HealthCheckOptions` with `ResponseWriter`.

3. Now, if we run the project and navigate to the health check API, we should see the following output:

```
←    →    ↻       🔒   https://localhost:44365/health
```

```
▼ {
      "Status": "Healthy",
   ▼ "HealthChecks": [
      ▼ {
            "Component": "Product Service",
            "Status": "Healthy",
            "Description": null
        },
      ▼ {

            "Component": "Order Service",
            "Status": "Healthy",
            "Description": null
        }
      ],
      "HealthCheckDuration": "00:00:00.7641736"
  }
```

Figure 14.3 – Health check endpoint response with status

We have learned how to customize the response of the health check endpoint and how to leverage a third-party library to monitor the status of dependent URIs. If you wish to integrate the check for a database used via Entity Framework Core, you can leverage the `Microsoft.Extensions.Diagnostics.HealthChecks. EntityFrameworkCore` library. More information about using this library can be found at `https://docs.microsoft.com/en-us/aspnet/core/host-and-deploy/health-checks?view=aspnetcore-6.0#entity-framework-core-dbcontext-probe`.

A wider collection of health check packages for different services can be found at `https://github.com/Xabaril/AspNetCore.Diagnostics.HealthChecks`. In the next section, we will learn how to build a custom health check.

Building a custom health check

The health check middleware in ASP.NET Core 6 is extensible, meaning that it allows us to extend and create a custom health check. We will learn how to build and use custom health checks by building a process monitor. In some scenarios, there might be a need to monitor a specific process running on the machine. If the process (for example, an anti-malware service) is not running, or if the license of a third-party SaaS offering is expiring/expired, we might flag them as health issues.

Let's start creating the `ProcessMonitor` health check in the `Packt.Ecommerce.Common` project:

1. Add a project folder named `HealthCheck` to `Packt.Ecommerce.Common` and add two classes, `ProcessMonitor` and `ProcessMonitorHealthCheckBuilderExtensions`, as shown in the following screenshot:

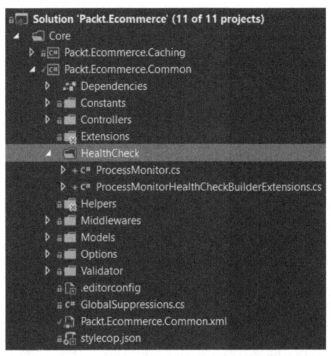

Figure 14.4 – Project structure after adding a custom health check

The custom `HealthCheck` middleware requires the NuGet reference to be `Microsoft.Extensions.Diagnostics.HealthChecks`.

2. The custom health check in ASP.NET Core 6 should implement the `IHealthCheck` interface. This interface defines the `CheckHealthAsync` method that will get called when the request comes to the health endpoint API.

3. Implement the `ProcessMonitorHealthCheck` class as shown in the following code:

```
public class ProcessMonitorHealthCheck : IHealthCheck
{
    private readonly string processName;
    public ProcessMonitorHealthCheck(string
```

```
    processName) => this.processName = processName;
   public Task<HealthCheckResult>
     CheckHealthAsync(HealthCheckContext context,
     CancellationToken cancellationToken = default)
     {
         Process[] pname =
          Process.GetProcessesByName(this.processName);
         if (pname.Length == 0)
         {
             return Task.FromResult(new
                 HealthCheckResult(context.Registration
                 .FailureStatus, description: $"Process
                 with the name {this.processName} is not
                 running."));
         }
         else
         {
             return Task.FromResult(
                 HealthCheckResult.Healthy());
         }
     }
 }
```

In the CheckHealthAsync method, fetch the list of processes with the name specified in processName. If there is no such process, then return as health check failed, otherwise, return the state as failed.

4. Now that we have the custom health check middleware, let's add an extension method to register. Modify the ProcessMonitorHealthCheckBuilderExtensions class as shown in the following code snippet:

```
public static class
ProcessMonitorHealthCheckBuilderExtensions
    {
        public static IHealthChecksBuilder
          AddProcessMonitorHealthCheck(
            this IHealthChecksBuilder builder,
            string processName = default,
            string name = default,
```

```
        HealthStatus? failureStatus = default,
        IEnumerable<string> tags = default)
    {
        return builder.Add(new
          HealthCheckRegistration(
          name ?? "ProcessMonitor",
          sp => new
          ProcessMonitorHealthCheck(processName),
          failureStatus,
          tags));
    }
}
```

This is an extension method to `IHealthCheckBuilder`. We can see that adding `ProcessMonitorHealthCheck` in the code snippet registers it with the container.

5. Let's now make use of the custom health check that we have built. In the following code, we registered the `ProcessMonitorHealthCheck` health check for `notepad`:

```
// Add health check services to the container.
Builder.Services.AddHealthChecks()
.AddUrlGroup(new Uri(this.Configuration.
GetValue<string>("ApplicationSettings
:ProductsApiEndpoint")), name: "Product Service")
.AddUrlGroup(new Uri(this.Configuration.
GetValue<string>("ApplicationSettings
:OrdersApiEndpoint")), name: "Order Service")
.AddProcessMonitorHealthCheck("notepad", name: "Notepad
monitor");
```

6. Now, when you run the application and navigate to the health check API, you will see the output shown in *Figure 14.5* if `notepad.exe` is running on your machine:

```
                      https://localhost:44365/health
{
    "Status": "Healthy",
    "HealthChecks": [
        {
            "Component": "Product Service",
            "Status": "Healthy",
            "Description": null
        },
        {
            "Component": "Order Service",
            "Status": "Healthy",
            "Description": null
        },
        {
            "Component": "Notepad monitor",
            "Status": "Healthy",
            "Description": null
        }
    ],
    "HealthCheckDuration": "00:00:03.9274025"
}
```

Figure 14.5 – Response from the health check endpoint

We can enable **cross-origin resource sharing (CORS)**, authorization, and host restriction on our health check endpoints. For details, please refer to `https://docs.microsoft.com/en-us/aspnet/core/host-and-deploy/health-checks?view=aspnetcore-6.0`.

In some scenarios, the health check APIs are split into two types based on the state of the application that they probe. They are the following:

- **Readiness probes**: These indicate that the application is running normally but is not ready to take requests.

- **Liveliness probes**: These indicate whether the application has crashed and must be restarted.

Both readiness and liveliness probes are used to control the health of the application. A failing readiness probe will stop the application from serving traffic, whereas a failing liveliness probe will restart the node. We use readiness and liveliness probes in hosting environments, such as Kubernetes.

We have learned about how to add the health check API to an ASP.NET Core 6 application. In the next section, we will learn about Azure Application Insights and how it helps to monitor an application.

Monitoring the application with Application Insights

Monitoring the application is key to providing end users with a top-class experience. Application monitoring is needed to drive business return on investment and retain a competitive advantage in the current era of super-fast digital markets. The parameters we should be focusing on are page/API performance, most-used pages/APIs, application errors, and system health, among others. There should be alerts set up for when there is an anomaly in the system so that we can correct it and minimize the impact on our users.

You were already introduced to integrating Application Insights into an application and its key features in *Chapter 7, Logging in .NET 6*. Let's open Application Insights in the Azure portal and understand its different offerings. On the overview dashboard, along with the Azure subscription, location, and instrumentation key, we see key metrics as follows:

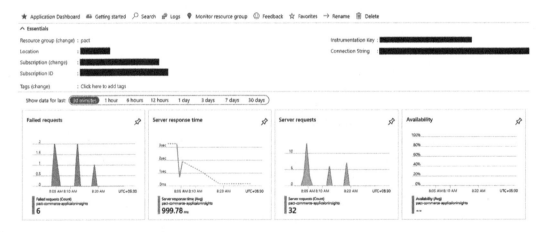

Figure 14.6 – Application Insights dashboard

The **Failed requests** graph shows the number of requests that failed in the selected duration. This is the key metric we should pay attention to; many failures represent instability in the system. **Server response time** represents the average response time of the server for the calls. If the response time is too high, more users will see a lag in the application responsiveness, which might lead to frustration and we could lose our users as a result.

The **Server requests** graph represents the total number of calls to the application; this will give us the patterns of the usage in the system. The **Availability** graph represents the uptime of the application. The availability tests that we will configure later in this chapter will show the **Availability** graph. By clicking on each graph, we can get more details pertaining to the respective metric, including requests and exception details. We can change the duration to view the graphs for the chosen interval.

The graphs on the overview dashboard show recent metrics. This can be useful in a situation where we wish to know the working of the system for a particular time in the past.

In the next section, we will learn about some of the most important offerings from Application Insights, looking at Live Metrics, telemetry events, and remote debugging features.

Live Metrics

Live Metrics is enabled by default. Live metrics are captured with a latency of 1 second, unlike the analytics metrics, which are aggregated over time. The data for Live Metrics is streamed only when the Live Metrics pane is open. The collected data only persists while it is on the chart. During Live Metrics monitoring, all the events are transmitted from the server and they won't be sampled. We can also filter the events by the server if the application is deployed in a web farm.

Live Metrics shows various charts, such as the incoming and outgoing requests, along with the overall health of the memory and CPU utilization. On the right-hand pane, we can see the captured telemetry, which will list the requests, dependency calls, and exceptions. Live Metrics is leveraged where we want to evaluate a fix that is released to production by watching the failure rates and performance. We will also monitor these while running a load test to see the effects of the load on the system.

For applications such as our `Ecommerce` app, it is important to know how users are using the application, the most-used features, and how users are traversing through the application. In the next section, we will learn about usage analysis in Application Insights.

Usage analysis with Application Insights

In *Chapter 11, Creating an ASP.NET Core 6 Web Application,* you learned how to integrate Application Insights with views. When Application Insights is integrated with views, Application Insights helps us with powerful insights into how people are using an application. The **Users** blade under the **Usage** section of Application Insights provides details about the number of users using the application. The user is identified by using anonymous IDs stored in browser cookies. Please note that a single person using different browsers and machines is counted as more than one user. The **Sessions** and **Events** blades represent the sessions of user activity and how often certain pages or features are used respectively. You can also generate reports on users, sessions, and events based on custom events, which you learned about in *Chapter 7, Logging in .NET 6.*

Another interesting tool available under usage analysis is **User Flows**. The **User Flows** tool visualizes how users navigate through different pages and features of an application. User flows provide the events that happened before and after the given event during the user session. *Figure 14.7* shows the user flows at a given time. This tells us that from the home page, users are mainly navigating to the **Product Details** page or the **Account Sign In** page:

Figure 14.7 – User flow in our Ecommerce application

Let's add a couple of custom events and see what the user flow is like against those custom events. Add one custom event, as shown in the following code snippet, in the `Create` action method of `OrderController` in the `Packt.Ecommerce.Web` application. This will track a custom event when the user clicks on the **Place Order** button on the **Cart** page:

```
this.telemetry.TrackEvent("Create Order");
```

Similarly, let's add a custom event tracking when the user clicks on the **Add to Cart** button on the **Product Details** page. To do this, add the following code snippet:

```
this.telemetry.TrackEvent("Add Item To Cart");
```

After adding the custom events, the user flow will show the different activities of the application with respect to these events. User Flows is a handy tool to know how many users are navigating away from a page and what they click on a page. Please refer to the Azure Application Insights documentation provided in the *Further reading* section at the end of the chapter to learn more about the other interesting offerings for usage analysis, including cohorts, funnels, and retention.

When there are enough telemetry events, you can use an Application Insights feature called **Smart Detection**, which automatically detects anomalies in the system and alerts us to them. In the next section, we will learn about Smart Detection.

Smart Detection

Smart Detection does not need any configuration or code changes. It works on the telemetry data captured from the system. Alerts will be displayed under the **Smart Detection** blade in the system and these alerts will go to users with the **Monitoring Reader** and **Monitoring Contributor** roles. We can configure additional recipients for these alerts under the **Settings** option. Some of the Smart Detection rules include **Slow page load time**, **Slow server response time**, **Abnormal raise in daily data volume**, and **Degradation in dependency volume**.

One of the important aspects we need to monitor for an application is availability. In the next section, we will learn how to leverage Application Insights to monitor application availability.

Application availability

In Application Insights, we can set up availability tests for any `http` or `https` endpoints accessible from the internet. This does not require any changes to our application code. We can configure the health check endpoint at (`<App Root URL>/health`) for an availability test.

To configure an availability test, go to the Application Insights resource in the Azure portal and perform the following steps:

1. Select **Availability** under the **Investigate** menu, as shown here:

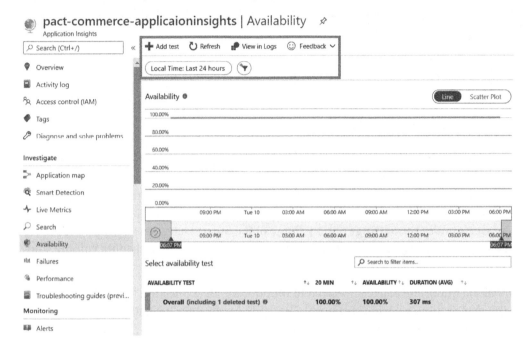

Figure 14.8 – Application Insights' Availability section

2. Click on **Add test** to add an availability test, as highlighted in the preceding screenshot.

3. In the **Create Test** dialog, specify the name for the test (say, `Commerce availability test`), select **URL Ping Test** for **Test Type**, and in the **URL** field, enter the health check URL as `<<App root url>>/health`. Leave the other options at their default values and click on **Create**.

4. Once the test is configured, Application Insights will call the configured URL every 5 minutes from all the configured regions. We can see the availability test results as follows:

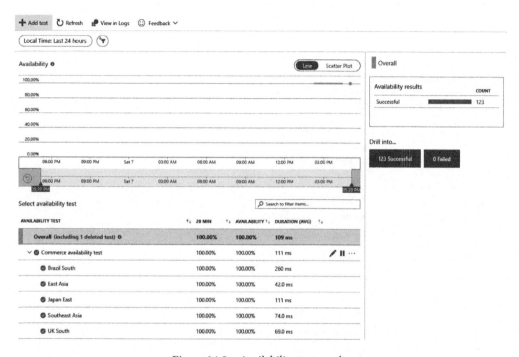

Figure 14.9 – Availability test results

5. The default regions selected while creating the tests were **Brazil South**, **East Asia**, **Japan East**, **Southeast Asia**, and **UK South**. We can add or remove any of the regions on which the availability test will be run. It is recommended to configure at least five regions.

6. If we want to add a new region at a later point in time, we can edit the availability test and select the new region (for example, **West Europe**) as shown in the following screenshot and then click on **Save**:

Figure 14.10 – Editing availability test regions

We can also configure a multi-step web test as an availability test in Application Insights.

> **Note**
>
> You can use the following documentation to help you configure a multi-step web test: `https://docs.microsoft.com/en-us/azure/azure-monitor/app/availability-multistep`.

Application Insights provides a very good tool to query the telemetry events captured. In the next section, we will learn about the **Search** feature in Application Insights.

Search

The **Search** feature in Application Insights helps to explore telemetry events such as requests, page views, and exceptions. We can also query the traces that we have coded in the application. **Search** can be opened from the **Overview** tab or from the **Search** option of the **Investigate** tab:

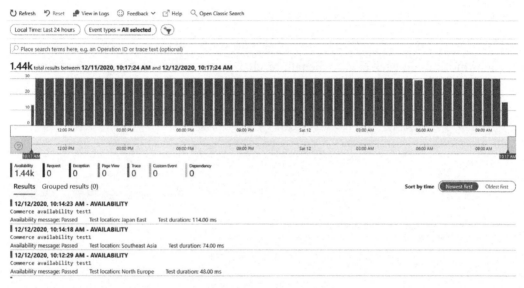

Figure 14.11 – Search results

With the **Transaction Search** feature, we can filter the telemetry events displayed based on time and **Event Type**.

We can also filter on their properties. By clicking on a specific event, we can view all the properties of the event along with the telemetry of the event. To view the requests with status code **500**, filter the events based on the response code as follows:

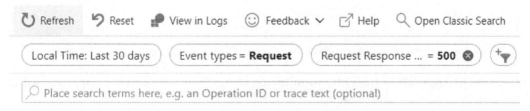

Figure 14.12 – Filtering search results

Once we apply the filter, in the search results, we will only see requests with the response code 500, as shown in the following screenshot:

Figure 14.13 – Filtered search results

To know more about what caused the failure, click on the event. Clicking on the event will show the details of the related telemetry, as shown in the following screenshot:

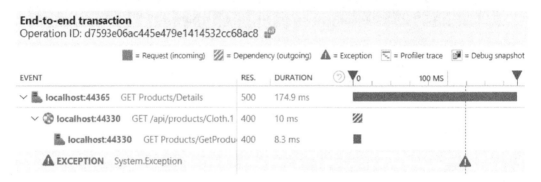

Figure 14.14 – End-to-end transaction details

We can even drill down more by clicking on the exception. This will show details such as the method name and the stack trace, which will help us identify the cause of the failure.

With Application Insights, we can write custom queries on the telemetry data that was captured to get more meaningful insights. In the next section, we will learn about writing queries.

Logs

To write queries on the telemetry data that is captured, let's navigate to it as follows:

1.   Go to **Application Insights | Monitoring | Logs**. This will show the **Logs** page with sample queries that we can run:

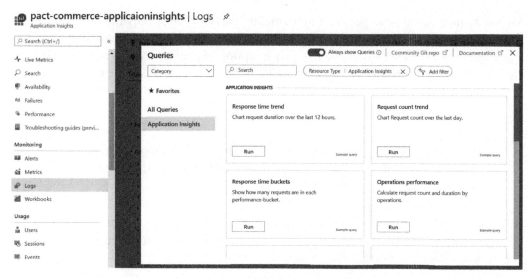

Figure 14.15 – Application Insights logs

2. Select **Request count trend** in the suggested sample queries. This will generate a query for us and run it. Once the run is complete, we will see the results and the chart populated, as shown in the following screenshot:

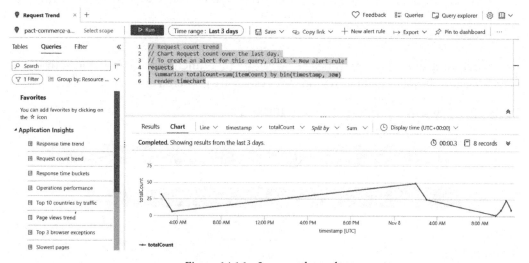

Figure 14.16 – Log search results

The telemetry that is captured in Application Insights goes into different tables covering requests, exceptions, dependencies, traces, and page views. The query generated here summarizes the telemetry data from the request table and renders a time chart where the time axis is split by 30 minutes.

We select the time range as per our requirements. We can even specify the time range in the query rather than selecting from the menu options. These queries created here can be saved and rerun at a later time. There is also an option to configure alerts here, which we learned about in *Chapter 7, Logging in .NET 6*. The language used here to write the queries is Kusto.

> **Note**
>
> Refer to the following documentation to learn about Kusto Query Language:
> `https://docs.microsoft.com/en-us/azure/data-explorer/kusto/concepts/`.

Kusto is based on relational database constructs. With Kusto Query Language, we can write complex analytical queries. Kusto supports group-by aggregation, computed columns, and join functions.

Let's take another example, where we want to identify the 95th percentile service response time for each client city. The query for this will be written as follows:

```
requests
| summarize 95percentile=percentile(duration, 0.95) by client_
City
| render barchart
```

In the preceding query, we are using the `percentile` function to identify the 95th percentile and summarize it per region. The results are rendered as a bar chart.

For the preceding query, we see the following graph:

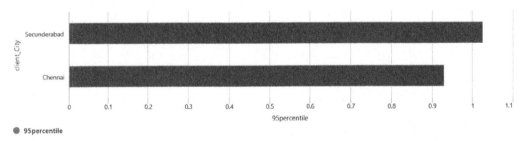

Figure 14.17 – Kusto percentile summary results

From the rendered graph, we can infer that the response time for a request coming from **Chennai** is faster than for requests from **Secunderabad**.

Now, let's find any exceptions that caused a request failure and summarize them by request and exception type. To get the result for this, we will join the `requests` table with `exceptions` and summarize them based on request name and exception type, as shown in the following query:

```
requests
| join kind= inner (
exceptions
) on operation_Id
| project requestName = name, exceptionType = type
| summarize count=sum(1)  by requestName, exceptionType
```

If we run the query, we get the results summarized by the name of the request and the type of the exception, as shown in the following screenshot:

requestName ▽	exceptionType ▽	count
> GET Products/Index	System.Net.Sockets.SocketException	18
> POST Cart/Index	System.Net.Sockets.SocketException	16
> GET Products/Details	System.Exception	20
> GET Products/Index	System.InvalidOperationException	15

Figure 14.18 – Kusto failing request exception

Search is a powerful feature of Application Insights to diagnose and fix failures in a production site. It is recommended to click through the different features of Application Insights and explore them.

When you create an Application Insights resource, a **Log Analytics workspace** will be created that persists the telemetry captured through Application Insights. Using **Log Analytics** workspaces along with application metrics, we can also query and monitor the key metrics related to Azure resources such as RU/s consumed in Cosmos DB. All the queries we ran in this section were executed on the **Log Analytics** workspace. We can create a dashboard in the Azure portal and pin all the charts related to the key metrics we wanted to track for the application.

> **Note**
>
> Refer to the Azure documentation to learn more about Log Analytics:
> `https://docs.microsoft.com/en-us/azure/azure-monitor/logs/log-analytics-overview`.

In this section, we learned how to monitor the application deployed in Azure using Azure Monitor. To analyze and troubleshoot any production failures better, we might want to know the state of an application when a specific error occurred. In the next section, we will learn how the **Snapshot Debugger** feature of Application Insights enables us to achieve this.

Configuring the Snapshot Debugger

The Snapshot Debugger monitors the exception telemetry of our application. It automatically collects snapshots of the top exceptions that occurred in the application with the current state of the source code and variables.

> **Note**
>
> The Snapshot Debugger feature is only available in the Enterprise version of Visual Studio.

Let's now go ahead and configure the Snapshot Debugger for our Ecommerce application:

1. Add the Microsoft.ApplicationInsights.SnapshotCollector NuGet package to the Packt.Ecommerce.Web project.

2. Add the following using statement to Startup.cs:

    ```
    using Microsoft.ApplicationInsights.SnapshotCollector;
    ```

3. Add a Snapshot Collector to your services by adding the following line to the ConfigureServices method:

    ```
    services.AddApplicationInsightsTelemetry(this.
    Configuration["ApplicationInsights:InstrumentationKey"]);
    builder.Services.AddSnapshotCollector((configuration)
    => this.Configuration.
    Bind(nameof(SnapshotCollectorConfiguration),
    configuration));
    ```

4. To simulate a failure, add the following code to the GetProductsAsync method of the EcommerceService class. This code will throw an error if there are any products available:

    ```
    public async Task<IEnumerable<ProductListViewModel>>
    GetProductsAsync(string filterCriteria = null)
    ```

```
{
        // Code removed for brevity
        if (products.Any())
        {
                throw new InvalidOperationException();
        }
        return products;
}
```

5. Now, let's go ahead and run the application. We see an error on the home page. Refresh the page again, as the debugging snapshot is for errors that occur at least twice.

6. Now, open the **Search** tab in Application Insights. Filter by the **Exception** event types:

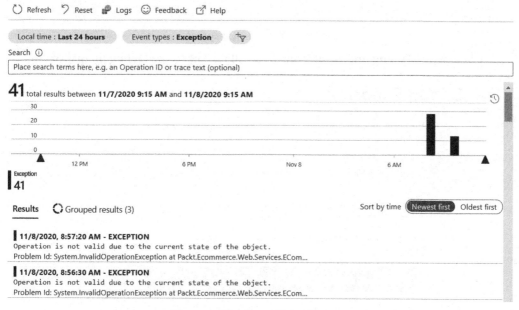

Figure 14.19 – Exceptions telemetry

7. Click on the exception to go to the details page. On the details page, we see that the debug snapshot has been created for the exception, as highlighted in the following screenshot:

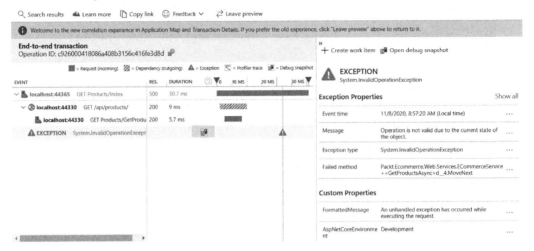

Figure 14.20 – Debug snapshot

8. Click on the **Debug Snapshot** icon. This will take us to the **Debug Snapshot** page:

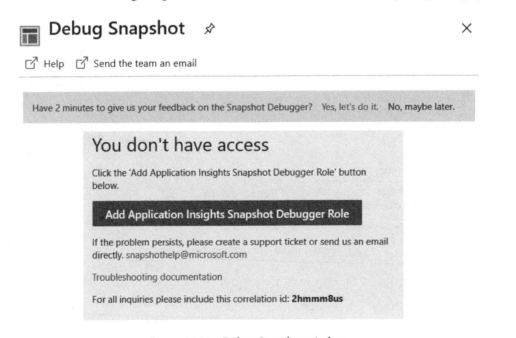

Figure 14.21 – Debug Snapshot window

9. To view the debug snapshots, the **Application Insights Snapshot Debugger Role** is required. As the debug state might have sensitive information, this role is not added by default. Click on the **Add Application Insights Snapshot Debugger Role** button. This will add the role to the currently logged-in user.

10. Once the role addition is complete, we can then see the debug snapshot details populated on the page, along with a button to download the snapshot:

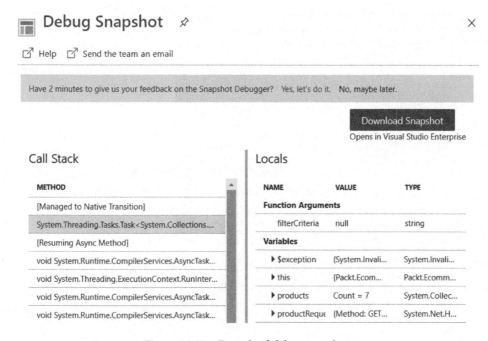

Figure 14.22 – Download debug snapshot

11. Click on the **Download Snapshot** button. The extension of the downloaded debug snapshot file is `diagsession`. Open the downloaded `diagsession` file in Visual Studio:

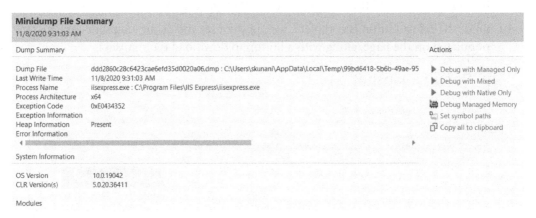

Figure 14.23 – Debug snapshot view in Visual Studio

12. Now, click on **Debug with Managed Only** to start the debug session. Once the debug session is open, we see the exception is broken at the line where we throw `InvalidOperationException`:

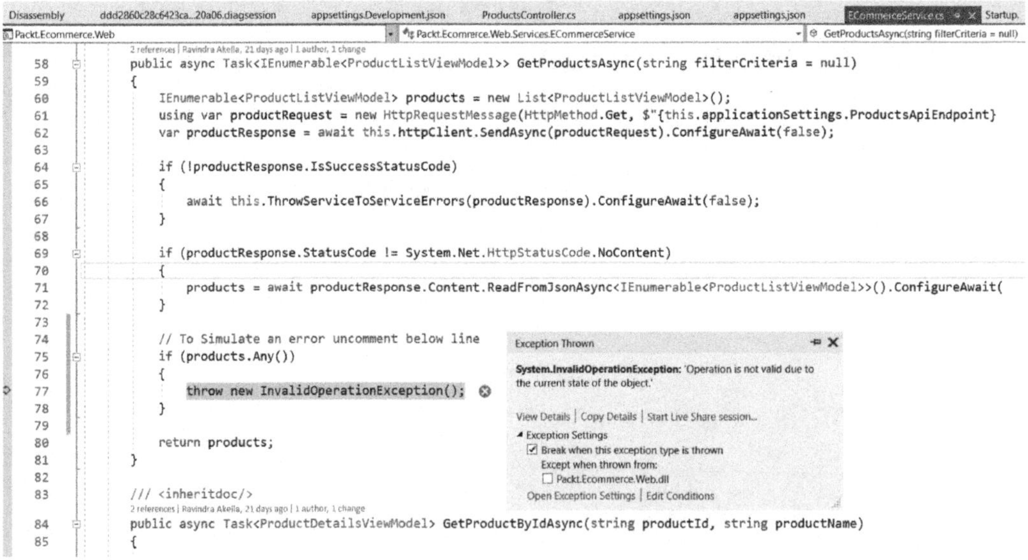

Figure 14.24 – Debugging snapshot in Visual Studio

In this debug session, we may add a watch to the local variables and class variables to understand the state they are in, which will aid in debugging.

> **Note**
>
> Refer to the following documentation to understand more about the Snapshot Debugger configurations: `https://docs.microsoft.com/en-us/azure/azure-monitor/app/snapshot-debugger-vm`.

As the application grows and is integrated with multiple other services, it will be challenging to troubleshoot and debug those issues that occur in production environments. In some cases, it is not possible to reproduce them in the pre-production environment. With the telemetry that we capture and the tools available with Application Insights, we will be able to analyze the problem and address the issue. The Snapshot Debugger is a powerful tool to troubleshoot critical issues. Application Insights collects telemetry data and sends it in batches via a background process. The impact of using Application Insights on our application is small.

There might be instances where we want to debug a live application. With Visual Studio, we are able to attach a debugger to a remotely running application to debug it. In the next section, we will learn how to achieve this.

Performing remote debugging

In this section, we will learn how to attach a debugger to our deployed application in Azure App Service. Debugging a remote application is easy with the tooling provided by Visual Studio. Deploying an application in Azure App Service is covered in *Chapter 16, Deploying the Application in Azure*. We can attach a debugger to an already-deployed service by performing the following:

1. Launch the **Publish** window by right-clicking on the **Packt.Ecommerce.Web** project and select **Publish** from the context menu. You can also launch the **Publish** window by setting the **Build** | Publish **Packt.Ecommerce.Web** menu item.

2. Create a **Publish** profile to **Packt.Ecommerce.Web** by selecting the Azure App Service resource in the Publish Wizard.

3. Once the **Publish** profile is created, you can attach the debugger to the application instance running in Azure App Service by selecting **Attach Debugger** from the **Hosting** options, as shown in the following screenshot:

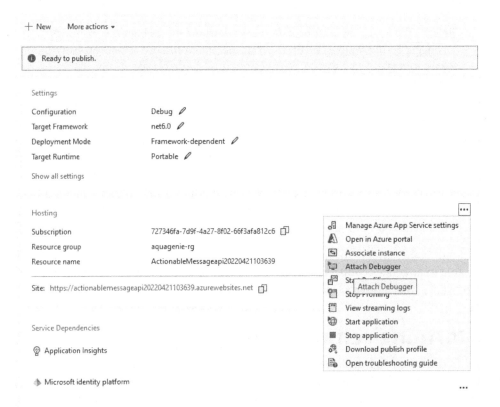

Figure 14.25 – Visual Studio's Publish window

4. Once the debugger is attached, the application will be opened in the browser from Azure App Service. We can add breakpoints in Visual Studio and debug the application as we would in a local development environment. To debug effectively, we need the debug version of the application deployed to Azure App Service.

Though this is a powerful feature for debugging remotely deployed applications, we should be extra cautious when attaching the debugger to the production instance, as we will be seeing live customer data. We can attach the debugger to the staging slot of Azure App Service to debug and fix the issue, and from there, swap the staging slot to promote the fix to production. There are many more important features in Application Insights and Azure Monitor that are not covered in this chapter. It is strongly recommended to explore them further in the Azure documentation.

Summary

This chapter introduced you to the concepts of health checks and diagnosing problems with applications using Application Insights. We have learned how to build a health check API and add a health check module to our `Ecommerce` application, which will help us monitor the health of an application. This chapter also covered some of the key features of Azure Application Insights, which is a powerful tool to capture telemetry and diagnose problems.

We have learned how Application Insights detects anomalies and alerts with the Smart Detection feature. We have also learned about snapshots and remote debugging, which help to troubleshoot problems in live applications running in production environments.

In the next chapter, we are going to learn about different testing methodologies to ensure the quality of an application before deploying it to production.

Questions

After reading this chapter, we should be able to answer the following questions:

1. Periodic monitoring of the application is not that important for an application once it is deployed to production. True or false?

   a. True

   b. False

   Answer: b

2. What is the interface that a custom health check module should implement?

   a. `IHealth`

   b. `IApplicationBuilder`

   c. `IHealthCheck`

   d. `IWebHostEnvironment`

   Answer: c

3. What is the latency in displaying Live Metrics data in Application Insights?

   a. 1 minute

   b. 1 second

   c. 10 seconds

   d. 5 seconds

   Answer: b

4. What is the query language used to write queries in Application Insights logs?

    a. SQL

    b. C#

    c. JavaScript

    d. Kusto

    Answer: d

Further reading

- Azure Application Insights documentation: `https://docs.microsoft.com/en-us/azure/azure-monitor/app/app-insights-overview`

15
Testing

The success of any application depends on how easy it is for users to use it. The longevity of any software product depends directly on the quality of the product.

Testing is an important aspect of the **Software Development Life Cycle (SDLC)** and ensures that a product meets the customer's requirements and the quality requirements. Testing is also important, as the cost of fixing bugs increases as we move toward the later stages of the SDLC.

In this chapter, we will learn about the different types of testing and the tools that Visual Studio provides for testing, as well as looking at third-party tools that we can use to ensure the quality of the products we build in .NET 6.

In this chapter, we will learn about the following:

- Types of testing
- Unit testing
- Functional testing
- Understanding the importance of load testing

By the end of this chapter, you will know everything you need to know about ensuring the quality of a product.

Technical requirements

You will need Visual Studio 2022 Community Edition. (Certain sections require Enterprise Edition.)

Along with Visual Studio, you will need JMeter, which can be downloaded from here: `https://jmeter.apache.org/download_jmeter.cgi`. You will also need a basic understanding of Microsoft .NET.

Introducing testing

Software testing is a way to check whether an application is performing according to expectations. These expectations could be to do with functionality, responsiveness, or the resources that the software consumes while running.

Software testing can be broadly categorized into the following two categories based on the way it is performed:

- **Manual testing**: In manual testing, testers execute test cases manually by using the application under test and validating the expected outcome. Manual testing requires more effort than the alternative.

- **Automated testing**: Automated testing is performed by special automated testing software. This automated software runs on the application under test in a specialized environment and validates the expected output. Automated testing saves a lot of time and manpower. In some cases, it might take a lot of effort to have 100% automation and maintain the automation with considerably less **Return on Investment (ROI)**.

In terms of the information known about the internals of the application under test (such as the code flow and dependent modules integration), software testing can also be broadly categorized in the following ways:

- **Black-box testing**: In black-box testing, the individual responsible for testing does not have information about the internals of the system. The focus here is on the behavior of the system.

- **White-box testing**: In white-box testing, the tester has information about the internal structure, design, and implementation of the system. The focus of white-box testing is testing the alternate paths that exist in the implementation.

In software testing, we validate different aspects of an application. Software testing also has the following variants, based on the aspect of an application that it validates and the tools or frameworks it uses:

- **Unit testing**: Unit testing focuses on the smallest unit of an application. Here, we validate individual classes or functions. This is mostly done during the development phase.

- **Functional testing**: This is often termed **integration testing**. The main objective of this is to ensure that an application is performing as per the requirements.

- **Regression testing**: A regression test ensures that any recent changes have not adversely affected application performance and that the existing functionality is not affected by any changes. In regression testing, all or some of the functional test cases are executed, depending upon the change introduced in the application.

- **Smoke test**: A smoke test is done after every deployment to ensure that the application is stable and ready for rollout. This is also known as a **Build Verification Test (BVT)**.

- **Load test**: A load test is used to determine the overall effectiveness of the system. During a load test, we simulate the projected load on an integrated system.

- **Stress testing**: In stress tests, we push the system beyond the intended capacity or load. This helps us identify the bottlenecks in the system and identify the points of failure. Performance testing is the umbrella term used for both stress and load testing.

- **Security testing**: Security testing is performed to ensure the flawless execution of the application. In security testing, we focus on evaluating various elements of security aspects such as integrity, confidentiality, and authenticity, among others.

- **Accessibility testing**: Accessibility testing is designed to determine whether differently-abled individuals will be able to use an application.

Now that we have seen the different types of testing, in the sections ahead, we will be covering unit testing, functional testing, and load testing in detail, as they are critical to ensuring the stability of an application.

> **Note**
>
> To explore more on security, try security testing with static code analysis tools: `https://docs.microsoft.com/en-us/azure/security/develop/security-code-analysis-overview`. More on accessibility can be found here: `https://accessibilityinsights.io/`.

Performance tests, accessibility tests, and security tests are the tests that we perform to assess the non-functional aspects of the application, such as performance, usability, reliability, security, and accessibility.

Now, let's see how to perform unit testing for our e-commerce application.

Unit testing

Unit testing is a way to test the smallest isolated unit of an application. It is an important step in software development that helps isolate a problem early.

Unit testing has a direct impact on the quality of the software we build. It is always recommended to write a unit test as soon as you write any method. If we follow the methodology of **test-driven development** (**TDD**), we write the test case first and then proceed to implement the functionality.

In the next section, we will learn about creating unit tests and running them from Visual Studio.

Unit testing in Visual Studio

We chose to use Visual Studio as it has powerful tooling to create and manage test cases.

With Visual Studio, we can create, debug, and run unit test cases. We can also check the code coverage of the tests that are executed. Additionally, it has a **Live Unit** test feature, which runs unit test cases while we modify the code and shows the results in real time.

We will explore all these features in the subsequent sections.

Creating and running unit tests

Let's go ahead and create a unit test project to perform unit testing on the `Packt.ECommerce.Order` project.

Perform the following steps to create unit test cases:

1. Add a new project of the **xUnit Test Project** type to the solution in the `Tests` folder, and name the project `Packt.ECommerce.Order.UnitTest`:

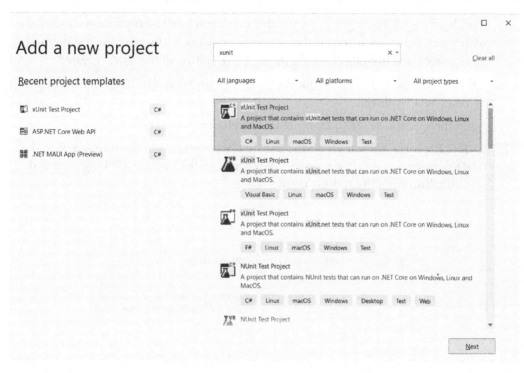

Figure 15.1 – Visual Studio xUnit test project

2.   Add a project reference of `Packt.ECommerce.Order` to the newly created test project.

3.   Add a new class to the test project and name it `OrdersControllerTest`. We are going to add all the test cases related to `OrdersController` in this class.

4.   Now, let's add a simple test to test the constructor of the `OrdersController` controller. The test we will be performing is to assert the successful creation of the `OrderController` controller. Let's now add the test, as shown in the following code:

```
[Fact]
public async Task Create_Object_OfType_OrderController ()
{
        OrdersController testObject = new
            OrdersController(null);
        Assert.NotNull(testObject);
}
```

The `Create_Object_OfType_OrderController` test method is attributed with `Fact`; this is required for the `xUnit` framework to discover the test method. Here, we are asserting by checking the `null` condition of the object created.

5. Visual Studio provides **Test Explorer** to manage and run tests. Let's open it by going to **Test | Test Explorer**.

6. Build the solution to see the tests in **Test Explorer**.

7. In **Test Explorer**, we can see all the tests that were present in the solution. Run the `OrderController_Constructor` test we created by right-clicking on it and selecting **Run** from the context menu:

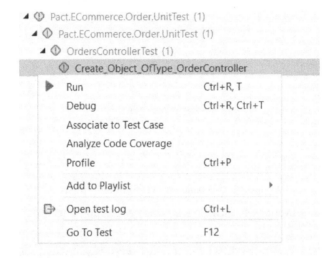

Figure 15.2 – Test Run context menu from the Test Explorer window

8. Once the test is executed, we can see the test result in the right pane. From the result, we can see that the test was executed and run successfully, as follows:

Figure 15.3 – Test results from Test Explorer

We have created and executed a simple test in Visual Studio. In the next section, we will learn how to mock the dependencies of `OrdersController` to validate the functionality.

Mocking dependencies with Moq

Often, a method under test calls other external methods or services, which we call dependencies. To ensure the functionality of the method under test, we isolate the behavior of dependencies by creating mock objects for the dependencies.

In an application, classes may be dependent on other classes; for instance, our OrdersController class is dependent on OrderService. While testing OrdersController, we should be isolating the behavior of OrderService.

To understand mocking, let's create the unit test for the GetOrdersAsync action method of OrdersController.

Let's have a look at the GetOrderById method for which we are writing the unit test case:

```
//This is the GetOrderById action method in OrdersController.cs
[HttpGet]
[Route("{id}")]
public async Task<IActionResult> GetOrderById(string id)
{
    var order = await
      this.orderService.GetOrderByIdAsync(id)
      .ConfigureAwait(false);
    if (order != null)
    {
        return this.Ok(order);
    }
    else
    {
        return this.NotFound();
    }
}
```

In this method, the call is made to GetOrderByIdAsync of orderService in order to fetch the orders based on the id instance passed in. The controller action will return the order id retrieved from OrderService; otherwise, the NotFound action is returned.

As we have seen, there are two paths for the code flow:

- One path is for when the order is present.
- The other is for when the order is not present.

With a unit test, we should be able to cover both paths. So, now, the question that arises is, how do we simulate these two cases?

What we want here is to mock the response of OrderService. To mock the response of OrderService, we can leverage the Moq library. To leverage Moq, we need to add a NuGet reference to the Moq package to the Packt.ECommerce.Order.UnitTest test project.

Let's add the test method in the OrdersControllerTest class, as shown in the following code, to test GetOrderById of OrdersController to validate the case where the order object is returned by OrderService:

```
[TestMethod]
public async Task When_GetOrdersAsync_with_ExistingOrder_
receive_OkObjectResult()
{
    var stub = new Mock<IOrderService>();
    stub.Setup(x => x.GetOrderByIdAsync(
      It.IsAny<string>())).Returns(Task.FromResult(new
      OrderDetailsViewModel { Id = "1" }));
    OrdersController testObject = new
      OrdersController(stub.Object);
    var order = await
      testObject.GetOrderById("1").ConfigureAwait(false);
    Assert.IsType<OkObjectResult>(order,
      typeof(OkObjectResult));
}
```

From the code, we can observe the following:

- Since IOrderService is injected to OrderController via controller injection, we can inject a mocked OrderService to OrderController, which will help us to test all the code paths of OrderController by altering the mock object behavior.

- We leverage the `Mock` class to create a stub (also known as a mock) for `IOrderService` and overwrite the `GetOrderByIdAsync` behavior, as shown in the preceding code.

- We create an instance of the `Mock` object for the `IOrderService` interface and set up the behavior for `GetOrderByIdAsync` by calling the `Setup` method on the `Mock` object.

- The `GetOrderByIdAsync` method is mocked such that for any parameter value that it receives, the `mock` object will return the object of `OrderDetailsViewModel` with `Id` as 1.

- Since we injected the mocked object into `OrderService` via constructor injection, whenever there is a call to any method in `IOrderService`, the call will go to the mocked implementation of `IOrderService`.

- Finally, we assert the test result by validating the type of result that is returned from `OrderController` to `OkObjectResult`.

Now, let's add a test case to validate the behavior, where we receive the `NotFound` result if the order is not present, as shown in the following code:

```
[TestMethod]
public async Task When_GetOrdersAsync_with_No_ExistingOrder_
receive_NotFoundResult()
{
    var stub = new Mock<IOrderService>();
    stub.Setup(x =>
    x.GetOrderByIdAsync(It.IsAny<string>()))
    .Returns(Task.FromResult<OrderDetailsViewModel>(null));
    OrdersController testObject = new
        OrdersController(stub.Object);
    var order = await testObject
        .GetOrderById("1").ConfigureAwait(false);
    Assert.IsType<NotFoundResult>(order,
        typeof(NotFoundResult));
}
```

In this test case, we simulated the behavior of the order not being present by returning a `null` value from the `OrderService` stub. This will make the `GetOrderById` action method of `OrdersController` return `NotFoundResult`, and this is validated in the test case.

> **Note**
>
> The `OrderService` class depends on `IHttpClientFactory`,
> `IOptions`, `Mapper`, and `DistributedCacheService`. So, to add
> a unit test for this, we should be mocking them all. You can take a look at the
> `When_GetOrderByIdAsync_with_ExistingOrder_receive_`
> `Order` test method in the `OrderServiceTest` test class of the GitHub
> code samples for more details.

In this section, we have seen how to leverage the `xUnit` framework to create unit
tests. There are several other test frameworks available to create unit tests in .NET. Two
such frameworks worth mentioning here are MSTest and NUnit. Though there are a
few differences in the way the tests are executed between these frameworks, all these
frameworks are brilliant and provide features such as mocking and parallel execution.
Because of its simplicity and extensibility, xUnit has a little advantage over competing
frameworks. We can also write data-driven tests using `Theory` in xUnit, as shown in the
following code snippet:

```
[Theory]
[InlineData(999, 19.98)]
[InlineData(2000, 100)]
public void When_ComputeTotalDiscount_with_
OrderTotalAmount(double number, double expectedResult)
{
<<Code removed for brevity>>
    OrdersService testObject = new
        OrdersService(httpClientFactory, mockOptions, mapper,
        mockCacheService.Object);
    var result = testObject.ComputeTotalDiscount(number);
    Assert.Equal(result, expectedResult);
}
```

In the preceding code snippet, the test method is executed with the test data passed
through the `InlineData` attribute.

In unit testing, our aim is to test a specific class by mocking the behavior of dependent classes. If we test these classes along with other dependent classes, we call that **integration testing**. We write integration tests at various levels: at the level of a specific module or assembly, at the microservice level, or the entire application level.

Now that we have added unit test cases to our e-commerce solution, in the next section, we will check the code coverage for these tests.

Code coverage

Code coverage is a measure to describe how much of the code is covered by our test cases. Visual Studio provides a tool to find the code coverage of unit tests. We can run **Test | Analyze Code Coverage** for all tests, as shown here:

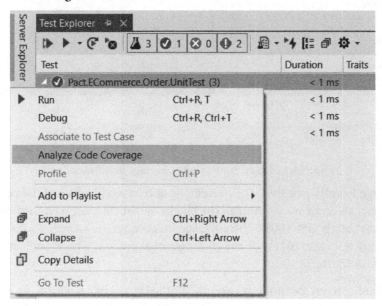

Figure 15.4 – The Analyze Code Coverage context option in Text Explorer

This can also be done from the **Context** menu in **Test Explorer**.

> **Note**
>
> The **Analyze Code Coverage** feature is only available in the Enterprise Edition of Visual Studio. If you are using the Community Edition, you can use the Visual Studio free extension, `https://marketplace.visualstudio.com/items?itemName=FortuneNgwenya.FineCodeCoverage`, to view the code coverage results.

This will run all the test cases and identify any code blocks that are not tested. We can see the code coverage results in the following **Code Coverage Results** window:

Hierarchy	Not Covered (Blocks)	Not Covered (% Blocks)	Covered (Blocks)	Covered (% Blocks)
▲ 📊 2020-11-28 14_09_49.coverage	408	86.62%	63	13.38%
▷ 🔲 packt.ecommerce.dto.models.dll	89	98.89%	1	1.11%
▲ 🔲 packt.ecommerce.order.dll	319	96.37%	12	3.63%
▷ {} Packt.Ecommerce.Order	100	100.00%	0	0.00%
▲ {} Packt.Ecommerce.Order.Controllers	40	76.92%	12	23.08%
▷ 🔧 OrdersController	0	0.00%	2	100.00%
▷ 🔧 OrdersController.<AddOrderAsync>d__4	9	100.00%	0	0.00%
▷ 🔧 OrdersController.<GetOrderById>d__3	0	0.00%	10	100.00%
▷ 🔧 OrdersController.<GetOrdersAsync>d__2	11	100.00%	0	0.00%
▷ 🔧 OrdersController.<UpdateOrderAsync>d__5	20	100.00%	0	0.00%
▷ {} Packt.Ecommerce.Order.Services	179	100.00%	0	0.00%
▷ 🔲 pact.ecommerce.order.unittest.dll	0	0.00%	50	100.00%

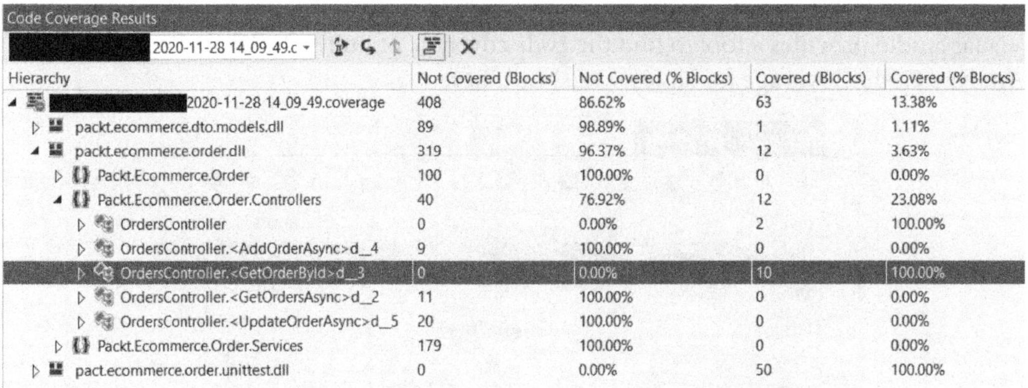

Figure 15.5 – Visual Studio Code Coverage Results window

Code Coverage Results will show the percentage of covered blocks and the percentage of not-covered blocks. Since we covered all the blocks of `GetOrderByIdAsync`, the code coverage for that method is **100%**. The coverage for `GetOrdersAsync` is **0.00%**, as we did not have any test cases to test it. The code coverage gives us a good indication of how effective our unit testing is.

It is recommended to create unit test cases for all the classes in a solution. By adding unit tests to validate all the classes and functionality, a higher percentage of code will be covered by unit test cases. With higher code coverage, we will be able to catch more errors early in the development while making changes to a solution. We should ensure that all the test cases pass before we commit changes. In the next chapter, *Chapter 16, Deploying the Application in Azure*, we will learn how to integrate running test cases with Azure DevOps pipelines.

So far, we have tested individual modules or classes by mocking dependencies and writing unit test cases. It is also important to test functionality after integrating and deploying an entire solution. In the next section, we will learn about how to perform functional testing for our e-commerce application.

> **Tip**
>
> Visual Studio's code metrics and code analysis tools are useful to ensure
> the maintainability and readability of the code that we write. You can find
> details on code metrics here: `https://docs.microsoft.com/`
> `en-us/visualstudio/code-quality/code-metrics-`
> `values?view=vs-2022.`
>
> For code analysis, go here: `https://docs.microsoft.com/en-us/`
> `dotnet/fundamentals/code-analysis/overview.`

Functional testing

In functional testing, we validate the application we have built against the functional
requirements. Functional testing is performed by providing some input and asserting the
response or output of the application. While performing functional testing, we consider
the application as a whole; we are not validating individual internal components.

Functional testing can be split into three tasks:

1. Identifying the functionalities of the system to be tested

2. Determining the input with the expected output

3. Executing these tests to assess whether the system is responding according to
   expectations

The execution of functional tests can be done manually by performing the test steps on the
application, or we can automate them using tools. The time to market for an application
can be drastically reduced by automating functional tests.

In the next section, we will learn about automating functional test cases.

Automating functional test cases

Executing functional test cases manually is still relevant in application testing. However,
given the fact of shorter deployment cycles and customers expecting new features quickly,
manual testing can be prohibitively time-consuming and inefficient in terms of identifying
bugs early. Using automation, we can gain new efficiencies, accelerate the testing process,
and improve software quality. There are multiple tools and frameworks available to
automate functional test cases.

In this section, we will learn about the most popular automation framework, **Selenium**. Let's begin:

1. To start with, let's create an `MSTest` project and name it `Packt.ECommerce.FunctionalTest`.

2. To this project, add the `Selenium.WebDriver`, `Selenium.WebDriver.ChromeDriver`, and `WebDriverManager` NuGet packages. These packages are required for us to run Selenium tests.

3. Let's start with a simple test that validates the title of our e-commerce application. To do this, create a `HomePageTest` test class and a `When_Application_Launched_Title_Should_be_ECommerce_Packt` test method, as we did in the *Unit testing* section, as shown in the following code:

    ```
    [TestClass]
    public class HomePageTest
    {
        [TestMethod]
        public void When_Application_Launched_Title
          _Should_be_ECommerce_Packt()
    {
    }
    }
    ```

4. To execute our functional tests, we should launch a browser and use that browser to navigate to the e-commerce application. The `MSTest` framework provides a special function to perform the initialization and cleanup operations required for our tests. We will be creating a Chrome web driver to perform a functional test.

    Let's go ahead and add the initialize and cleanup methods, as shown in the following code:

    ```
    [TestClass]
    public class HomePageTest
    {
        ChromeDriver _webDriver = null;
        [TestInitialize]
    public void InitializeWebDriver()
    ```

```
    {
            var d = new DriverManager();
            d.SetUpDriver(new ChromeConfig());
            _webDriver = new ChromeDriver();
    }
    [TestMethod]
    public void When_Application_Launched_Title
      _Should_be_ECommerce_Packt()
    {
    }
    [TestCleanup]
    public void WebDriverCleanup()
    {
            _webDriver.Quit();
    }
}
```

In the preceding code, the InitializeDriver method is attributed with TestInitialize to notify the framework that this is the test initialization method. In test initialization, we are creating ChromeDriver and initializing the class variable. After the completion of the test case, we should close the browser instance; we do this in the WebDriverCleanup method by calling the Quit method. To notify the test framework that it is the cleanup method, it should be attributed as TestCleanup.

5.   Now, let's go and add the test case to navigate to the e-commerce application and validate the title, as shown in the following code:

```
[TestMethod]
public void When_Application_Launched_Title_Should_be_
ECommerce_Packt()
{
    _webDriver.Navigate().GoToUrl("https://localhost:
      44365/");
    Assert.AreEqual("Ecommerce Packt",
      _webDriver.Title);
}
```

Call `GoToUrl` on our Chrome web driver to navigate to the e-commerce application. Once navigated, we can validate the title of the page by asserting the `Title` property of the web driver.

6. Go ahead and run the test case from **Test Explorer** by right-clicking on the `When_Application_Launched_Title_Should_be_ECommerce_Pact` test case and selecting **Run**. This will open the Chrome browser and navigate to the specified e-commerce URL, and then it will assert the title of the page. After the execution of the test case, the browser will be closed. We see the results in **Test Explorer**, as shown in the following screenshot:

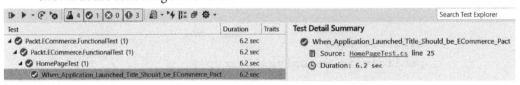

Figure 15.6 – Solution structure after the creation of the test project

7. Now, we will extend the functional test to validate the search functionality. To test this functionality, we should enter text in the search box and click on the **Search** button. Then, check the results to see whether the returned test results are only for the searched product.

8. Let's automate the test case by adding the `When_Searched_For_Item` test method, as shown in the following code:

```
[TestMethod]
public void When_Searched_For_Item()
{
    _webDriver.Navigate().GoToUrl("https://localhost
        :44365/");
    var searchTextBox =
    _webDriver.FindElement(By.Name("SearchString"));
    searchTextBox.SendKeys("Orange Shirt");
    _webDriver.FindElement(By.Name("searchButton"))
        .Click();
    var items =
    _webDriver.FindElements(By.ClassName("product-
    description"));
```

```
        var invaidProductCout = items.Where(e => e.Text
        != "Orange Shirt").Count();
        Assert.AreEqual(0, invaidProductCout);
    }
```

In this test case, after navigating to the home page, enter the search text in the **SearchString** field and click on the **Search** button. Assert by validating the search results to see whether any product is not returned as the `search` string.

Selenium makes it so easy to write functional tests. We should try to automate all functional test cases, such as user management, adding products to the cart, and placing an order. With all the functional test cases automated, we will be in a better position to test and validate the functionality of new releases and maintain the quality of our application. There are other functional testing tools available, such as QTP and Visual Studio Coded UI tests.

We have looked at functional testing, which validates the functionality of an application. It is equally important to assess the responsiveness of an application to see how it responds to a particular load. In the next section, we will learn how we can perform performance testing on our e-commerce application. We can leverage automated functional test cases to perform BVT or regression testing.

> **Note**
>
> Refer to the documentation to explore more about Selenium testing:
> `https://www.selenium.dev/documentation/en/`.

Load testing

Users expect an application to respond quickly to their actions. Any sluggishness in response will lead to user frustration, and ultimately, we will lose them. Even if an application works fine under a normal load, we should know how our application behaves when there is a sudden peak in demand and be prepared for it.

The main goal of load testing is not to find bugs but to eradicate the performance bottlenecks of the application. A load test is done to provide stakeholders with information about the speed, scalability, and stability of their application. In the next section, we will learn how to perform a load test using JMeter.

Load testing with JMeter

JMeter is an open source testing tool built by the Apache Software Foundation. It is one of the most popular tools available to perform load testing. JMeter can simulate a heavy load on an application by creating virtual concurrent users of a web server.

Let's go ahead and create a JMeter load test for our e-commerce application.

To learn how to use JMeter to do a load test, we will be creating a test with two home pages and product search pages. Try the following steps to create the load test:

1. Launch Apache JMeter from the download location. We will see the window as follows:

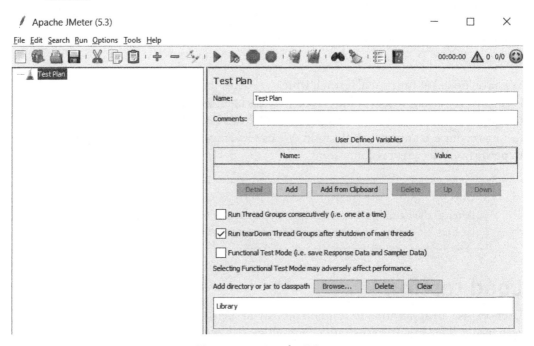

Figure 15.7 – Apache JMeter

2. Add a thread group by right-clicking on **Test Plan** in the left pane and selecting **Add | Threads (Users) | Thread Group**. The thread group defines the pool of users that will execute the test case against our application. With it, we can configure the number of users simulated, the time to start all the users, and the number of times to perform the test.

3. Let's name the thread group Load and Query Products and set the number of users to 30. Set **Ramp-up period (seconds)** to 5 seconds, as shown in the following screenshot:

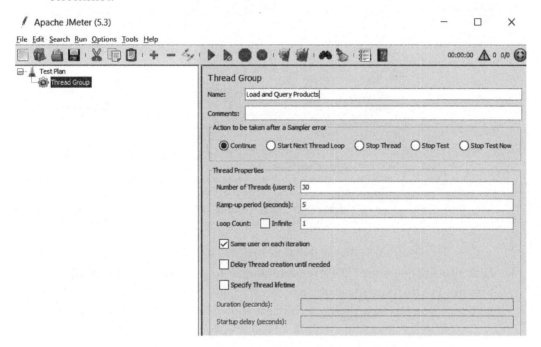

Figure 15.8 – Adding a thread group in Apache JMeter

This will simulate a user load of 30 within 5 seconds. Using **Thread Group**, we can also control the number of times the test should run.

4. To add the test request, right-click on **Thread Group** and select **Add | Sampler | HTTP Request**.

    Let's set **Protocol** as `https`, **Server Name or IP** as `localhost`, and **Port Number** as `44365` (the port number of the locally running e-commerce portal). Name this test `Home Page`, as shown in the following screenshot:

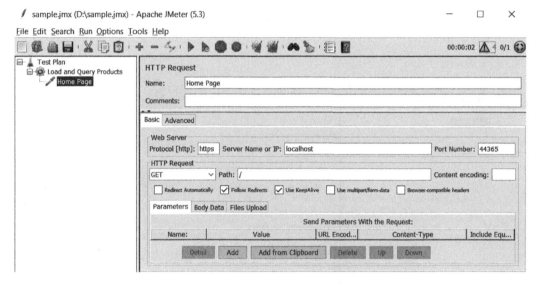

Figure 15.9 – Adding the Home Page HTTP request in JMeter

Let's also add one more HTTP request sampler to get the details of a specific product. For this request, set the `productId` query parameter as `Cloth.3` and `productName` as `Orange%20Shirt`, as shown in the following screenshot:

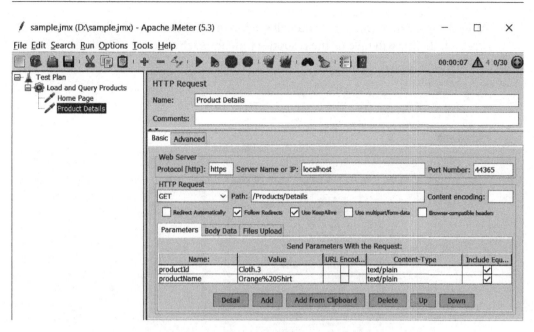

Figure 15.10 – Adding the Product Details page HTTP request in JMeter

5. Save this test plan by clicking on the **Save** button and naming it `ECommerce`.

6. To view the results, we should add a listener to this test. Right-click on the test group and select **Add | Listener | View Results in Table**.

7. Once the listener is added, go ahead and run the test by selecting **Run | Start**.

8. After the test run is complete, you will see the results as shown in the following screenshot. This will give us the response time for each request:

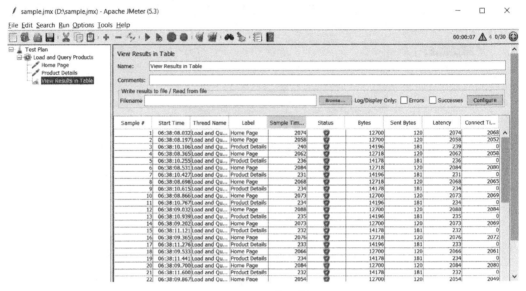

Figure 15.11 – Test results table in JMeter

There are multiple listeners available in JMeter to view the results, such as **Summary report** and **Graph results**, which will give another representation of the test results. We can configure different kinds of samplers easily with JMeter, as well as configuring requests with different HTTP methods and dynamic tests, where requests are dependent on another API's response. Once a test plan is in JMeter, we can leverage the JMeter command-line utility to run it from multiple data centers to simulate a load across geographies and collate the results.

The flexibility that JMeter provides, along with its extensive documentation, makes it the most-used performance testing tool. JMeter can also be leveraged to perform functional testing.

We can use the Azure Load Testing service to generate high-scale load using the JMeter test that we created in this section. The infrastructure required to execute your JMeter script and load test your application is abstracted by Azure Load Testing. Azure Load Testing gathers precise resource data for Azure-based applications to assist you in identifying performance bottlenecks across your Azure application components.

> **Note**
>
> At the time of writing this book, Azure Load Testing is in preview. More details about load testing can be found in the Azure documentation at `https://docs.microsoft.com/en-us/azure/load-testing/overview-what-is-azure-load-testing`. It is recommended to run a load test with one and a half to two times the anticipated load. After running the performance test, it is recommended to use **Application Insights** to analyze the server response time of requests, how dependent APIs are responding during the load conditions, and more importantly, any failures that occur while the test is in progress.

> **Tip**
>
> It is recommended to run automated tests using Azure DevOps pipelines. Use the documentation to see how to integrate tests with an Azure DevOps pipeline:
>
> Selenium: `https://docs.microsoft.com/en-us/azure/devops/pipelines/test/continuous-test-selenium?view=azure-devops`
>
> JMeter tests: `https://github.com/Azure-Samples/jmeter-aci-terraform`

Summary

In this chapter, we explored a very important aspect of software development: testing. We have learned about the different kinds of testing and the stages at which we should be using them in the SDLC.

We learned about the concepts of unit testing and how to focus our testing on specific calls by mocking dependencies using the Moq framework. We were also introduced to the creation of automated functional tests using Selenium to test the functionality of our e-commerce application before releasing it to production.

Toward the end, we learned about JMeter, which is the most-used tool for performing load testing. The next chapter will focus on deploying applications in Azure.

Questions

1. True or false? We should only start to think about testing an application after the completion of its development.

    a. True

    b. False

    Answer: b

2. Which of the following is a kind of software testing?

    a. Security testing

    b. Functional testing

    c. Accessibility testing

    d. All of the above

    Answer: d

3. True or false? A higher code coverage percentage for unit tests is desirable to achieve a shorter time to market.

    a. True

    b. False

    Answer: a

16
Deploying the Application in Azure

Deployment is a set of activities we perform to make software applications available for use. The general approach is to take the code, and then build, test, and deploy it to the target systems. Depending on the type of application and the business requirements, the approach that you take to deploy your code might vary. It could be as simple as taking the target system down, replacing existing code with a new version, and then bringing the system up; or, it may involve other sophisticated approaches such as blue-green deployment, where you deploy code to a staging environment that is identical to production, run your tests, and then redirect the traffic to staging to make it to production.

Modern software development adopts Agile and DevOps to shorten the development cycle and deliver new features, updates, and bugs frequently and reliably to provide more value to customers. To enable this, you will need a set of tools to plan, collaborate, develop, test, deploy, and monitor.

In this chapter, we will learn what Azure DevOps is and the tools it offers for rapid and reliable delivery.

The following topics are covered in this chapter:

- Introducing Azure DevOps
- Understanding the CI pipeline
- Understanding the CD pipeline
- Deploying an ASP.NET 6 application

Technical requirements

For this chapter, you need basic knowledge of Azure, Visual Studio 2022, Git, and an active Azure subscription with a contributor role. If you don't have one, you can sign up for a free account at `https://azure.microsoft.com/en-in/free`.

The code for the chapter can be found here: `https://github.com/PacktPublishing/Enterprise-Application-Development-with-C-10-and-.NET-6-Second-Edition/tree/main/Chapter16`.

Introducing Azure DevOps

To bring a product idea to life, irrespective of your team size, you will need an efficient way to plan your work, collaborate within your team, and build, test, and deploy. Azure DevOps helps you to address these challenges and offers various services and tools for your success. Azure DevOps services can be accessed via the web or from popular development IDEs such as Visual Studio, Visual Studio Code, and Eclipse. Azure DevOps services are available in the cloud as well as on-premises using Azure DevOps Server.

Azure DevOps offers the following services:

- **Boards**: Offers a set of tools to plan and track your work, defects, and issues using Scrum and Kanban methodologies
- **Repos**: Offers source control to manage your code using Git or **Team Foundation Version Control (TFVC)**
- **Pipelines**: Offers a set of services to support **continuous integration (CI)** and **continuous delivery (CD)**
- **Test Plans**: Offers a set of test management tools to drive the quality of your application with end-to-end traceability
- **Artifacts**: Allows you to share packages from public and private sources, as well as integrating with CI and CD pipelines

In addition to these services, Azure DevOps also helps you to manage wikis for your team, manage dashboards, use widgets to share progress and trends, and configure notifications. It also allows you to add or develop custom extensions and integrate with popular third-party services such as Campfire, Slack, and Trello.

Azure DevOps services offer free and paid subscriptions. To sign up for a free account, follow the steps outlined at `https://docs.microsoft.com/en-us/azure/devops/user-guide/sign-up-invite-teammates?view=azure-devops`.

The following is a screenshot of the home screen from a sample project:

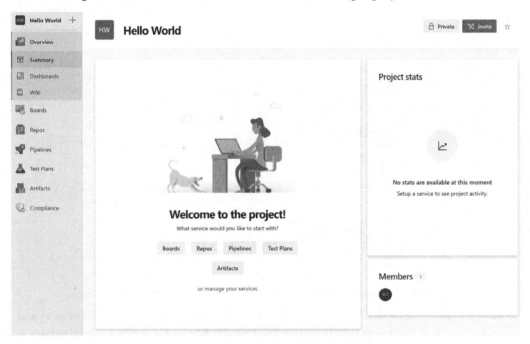

Figure 16.1 – Azure DevOps home page

Let's understand Azure DevOps and each of these services in detail.

Boards

Boards helps you to define a process for your project and track your work. When you create a new project in Azure DevOps, you have the option to choose a process template as Agile, Basic, Scrum, or a **Capability Maturity Model Integration (CMMI)** process. The process template determines the work item types and workflows that you can use in your project. Work items help you to track your work, and workflows help you track the progress of your work items. The following figure shows the hierarchy of work items and the workflow of the Scrum process template:

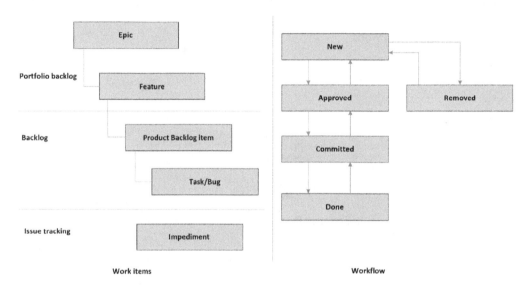

Figure 16.2 – Hierarchy of work items and the workflow in a Scrum process

To further customize or define your workflows and work item types, you can choose to create your own process template based on the previously mentioned process templates.

Let's understand more about work items and workflows.

Work items

Work items help you to track features, requirements, and bugs in your project. You can group requirements in a hierarchy. Usually, we start with a high-level requirement called an **epic**, which can be further broken down into **features** and **product backlog items**. Product backlog items are deliverables that are prioritized, assigned to a team member, and delivered in a sprint. **Tasks** are created for backlog items and bugs to track defects against product backlog items.

The collaboration feature enables communication within your team through discussion or questions on a work item. You can mention a team member or link another work item and view the history of all actions or discussions at any time. You can also choose to follow a work item to get alerts when it is updated.

Workflows

Workflows help you to review the progress and health of your project. For instance, a product backlog item is created with the **New** state. Once it is reviewed and approved by a product owner, it is moved to **Approved**, then it is prioritized and assigned to a team member in a sprint and moved to **Committed**, and when it is complete, it is moved to **Done**. Workflows help you to track the health of your project.

You can use a Kanban board to view the state of all work items and easily move work items to different states using the drag-and-drop feature. The following screenshot illustrates a Kanban board consisting of work items in different states:

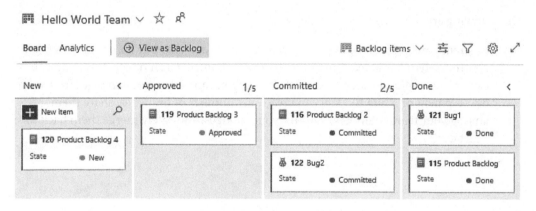

Figure 16.3 – Kanban dashboard

> **Note**
> If you create your own process template, you can customize work items or create new work items and customize or define your workflows to suit your business needs.

To learn more about process templates and how they differ, you can refer to https://docs.microsoft.com/en-us/azure/devops/boards/get-started/what-is-azure-boards?view=azure-devops&tabs=scrum-process#work-item-types.

Next, let's understand more about Repos.

Repos

Repos offers version control tools with which you can manage your code. A version control system allows you to track the changes made by your team to code. It creates a snapshot of each change, which you can review at any time and revert to it if required. Azure DevOps offers **Git** and **TFVC** as your version control systems.

Git is currently the most widely used version control system and is increasingly becoming the standard for version control systems. Git is a distributed version control system with a local copy of the version control system in which you can view the history or commit changes locally, even if you are offline, and it will sync to the server once connected to a network. TFVC, however, is a centralized version control system with only one version of each file on the dev machine, and the history is maintained on the server. For more information on Git, you can refer to `https://docs.microsoft.com/en-in/azure/devops/repos/git/?view=azure-devops`, and for TFVC, you can refer to `https://docs.microsoft.com/en-in/azure/devops/repos/tfvc/?view=azure-devops`.

The following are the key services of **Repos**:

- **Branches** are a reference of your code with the history of your commits. A version control system has at least one branch, usually named `main` or `master`, and you can create another branch from it. This way, you can isolate your changes for feature development or a bug fix. You can create any number of branches, share them among your team members, commit your changes, and safely merge them back to `master`.

- **Branch policies** help you to protect your branches during development. When you enable a branch policy on a branch, any change must be made via pull requests only, so that you can review, give feedback, and approve changes. As a branch policy, you can configure a minimum number of required approvers, check for linked work items and comment resolution, and enforce the build to be successful to complete pull requests.

The following screenshot illustrates policies defined on a branch:

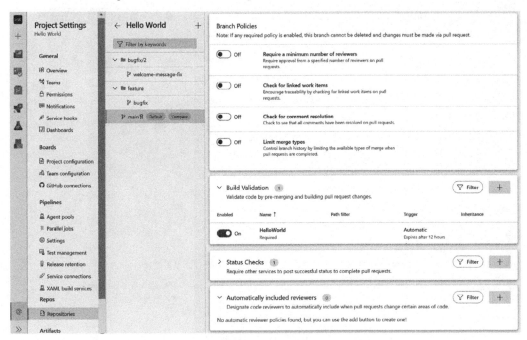

Figure 16.4 – Branch policies

Here, a policy is created to validate the build before the code is merged to the branch.

- **Pull requests** allow you to review code, add comments, and ensure they are resolved before the code is merged to your branch. Based on the configured branch policy, you can add mandatory reviewers to review and approve changes. You can associate work items to pull requests to enable traceability of changes. The following screenshot illustrates a sample pull request:

Figure 16.5 – Pull request

The pull request has a title and description, and users can review files and compare them with the previous versions, check the status of builds and linked work items, and approve.

Next, let's understand Pipelines.

Pipelines

Pipelines allows you to configure, build, test, and deploy your code to any target system. Using Pipelines, you can enable CI and CD for consistent and quality delivery of your code. You can use pipelines targeting many application types built using popular languages such as .NET, Java, JavaScript, Node.js, PHP, and C++, and target them to deploy to either cloud or on-premises servers. You can define pipelines using YAML files or a UI-based classic editor.

CI automates builds and tests for your project to ensure quality and consistency. CI can be configured to run on schedule or when new code is merged into your branch or both. CI generates artifacts that are used by CD pipelines to deploy to target systems.

CD enables you to automatically deploy code to the target system and run tests. CD can be configured to run on a schedule.

Next, let's understand more about Test Plans.

Test Plans

Azure DevOps provides a set of tools to drive quality in your projects. It provides browser-based test management solutions with all the capabilities required for manual and exploratory testing. It provides the capability to organize **test cases** under **test suites** or **test plans** with which you can track the quality of a feature or a release. These are explained as follows:

- **Test cases** are used to validate individual parts of your application. They contain test steps, which you can use to assert a requirement. You can reuse a test case by importing it into test suites or test plans.
- **Test suites** are a group of test cases executed to validate a feature or a component. You can create static test suites, requirement-based suites, and query-based suites.
- **Test plans** are a group of test suites or test cases used to track the quality of each iteration of a release.

Next, let's understand more about Artifacts.

Artifacts

Artifacts makes it easy to share code among teams. You can easily create and share Maven, npm, or NuGet package feeds from public and private sources, and they are easy to use in CI and CD pipelines. Artifacts are based on standard packaging formats and can be easily integrated with development IDEs, such as Visual Studio, as a package source.

Azure DevOps enables coordination and collaboration within teams and helps you to deliver projects consistently with high quality. With CI and CD, you can automate the build and deployment of your code.

In the next section, let's understand the CI pipeline.

Understanding the CI pipeline

CI is a practice in which you automate the building and testing of your code. In Azure DevOps, you can create pipelines and configure them to trigger automatically when code is merged to your target (master/main) branch, run on a schedule, or both. You may choose to create a pipeline using YAML files or a UI-based classic editor.

The following figure illustrates the typical flow of code from a developer's machine to the cloud:

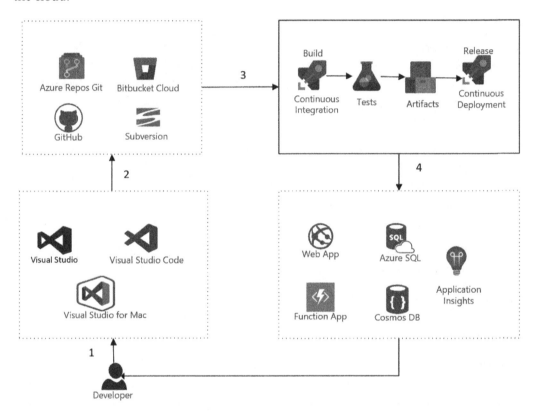

Figure 16.6 – Typical flow of code

From the preceding screenshot, we see the following:

1. The developer uses development tools such as Visual Studio, Visual Studio Code, or Visual Studio for Mac to develop code.

2. Code changes are moved to the repository.

3. The CI pipeline is triggered, validates the build, runs tests, and publishes artifacts. The CD pipeline is triggered, and it deploys code to target systems.

4. The developer uses Application Insights to continuously monitor and improve the application.

> **Note**
>
> **YAML** (short for **YAML Ain't Markup Language**) is the preferred way to define your pipelines. It offers the same capabilities as a classic editor. You can check these files to repositories and manage them like any other source file. For more details, you can refer to `https://docs.microsoft.com/en-us/azure/devops/pipelines/yaml-schema?view=azure-devops&tabs=schema%2Cparameter-schema`.

Let's understand the core components and flow of a pipeline.

Understanding the flow and components of a pipeline

A **pipeline** is a definition of a set of actions to be performed to build and test your code. A pipeline definition contains a **trigger**, **variables**, **stages**, **jobs**, **steps**, and **tasks**. When we run a pipeline, it executes **tasks** defined in the pipeline definition. Let's understand each of these components in the following sections.

Trigger

A **trigger** is a configuration that defines when a pipeline should run. You can configure a pipeline to run automatically when new code is merged to your repository, at a scheduled interval, or after the completion of another build. All these configurations are defined in the `trigger` section of a pipeline.

In the following code snippet, the pipeline is configured to trigger when code is pushed to the `master` branch or any branch under the `releases` folder. Optionally, we can also specify path filters in the pipeline so that it is triggered only when code is changed that satisfies path conditions:

```
trigger:
  branches:
    include:
    - master
    - releases/*
  paths:
```

```
    include:
    - web
    exclude:
    - docs/README.md
```

You can also configure a pipeline to run automatically based on a schedule. In the following code snippet, a pipeline is configured to run every day at 9:30 A.M. Schedules are specified using a cron expression and you can specify multiple schedules. If you set always to true, the build is triggered even if there is no change in the code:

```
schedules:
- cron: "30 9 * * *"
    displayName: Daily build
    branches:
        include:
        - master
    always: false
```

Variables

Variables can be defined with a value and reused at multiple places in your pipeline. You can define variables at root, a stage, or in a job. There are three different types of variables that can be used in pipelines – user-defined, system variables, and environmental variables:

```
variables:
  buildConfiguration: 'Release'

. . . .

. . . .
- task: DotNetCoreCLI@2
    displayName: Publish
    inputs:
    command: 'publish'
    publishWebProjects: false
    projects: '**/*HelloWorld.csproj'
    arguments: '--configuration $(BuildConfiguration) --output
$(build.artifactstagingdirectory)/web'
```

In the preceding code snippet, the `buildConfiguration` variable is defined with the `Release` value and is used in the `arguments` section of the task. The `build.artifactstagingdirectory` system variable contains the location of the artifacts directory.

Stages

Stages are a collection of jobs run sequentially by default. You can also specify conditions on the preceding stage execution state or add approval checks to control when a stage should run.

The following is a sample pipeline definition with multiple stages:

```
stages:
- stage: Build
  jobs:
  - job: build
    steps:
    - script: echo building code
- stage: Test
  jobs:
  - job: windows
    steps:
    - script: echo running tests on windows
  - job: linux
    steps:
    - script: echo running tests on Linux
- stage: Deploy
  dependsOn: Test
  jobs:
  - job: deploy
    steps:
    - script: echo deploying code
```

In the preceding sample, three stages are configured, each running sequentially. The `Test` stage contains two jobs that can run in parallel, and the `Deploy` stage has a dependency on the `Test` stage.

The following is a screenshot of the pipeline execution summary of the preceding sample, and you can click on each stage to view the logs:

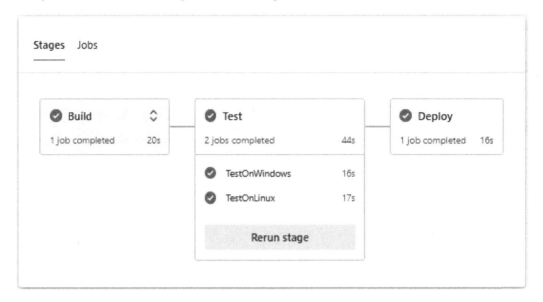

Figure 16.7 – Summary of a pipeline run

Jobs

Jobs are a collection of steps run on an agent pool. In addition, you can configure to run jobs conditionally or add dependencies on preceding jobs. In the following code snippet, a job is defined with a step and a condition on the testNull variable:

```
variables:
- name: testNull
  value: ''
jobs:
  - job: BuildJob
    steps:
    - script: echo Building!
    condition: eq('${{ variables.testNull }}', '')
```

In the preceding code, the job is configured with a condition to run only when testNull is empty.

Steps and tasks

Steps are groups of tasks in your pipeline. These could be to build your code, run tests, or publish artifacts. Each step is executed on the agent and has access to the pipeline workspace.

Tasks are the building blocks for the automation of your pipeline. There are many built-in tasks that you can use, or you can create your own custom task and use it in pipelines. For instance, the following code snippet uses the `DotNetCoreCLI@2` task to build `csproj`:

```
- task: DotNetCoreCLI@2
  displayName: build
  inputs:
   command: 'build'
   projects: '**/*.csproj'
   arguments: '--configuration $(BuildConfiguration)'
```

To learn more about pipelines, you can refer to `https://docs.microsoft.com/en-in/azure/devops/pipelines/create-first-pipeline?view=azure-devops&tabs=java%2Ctfs-2018-2%2Cbrowser`.

In the next section, let's learn more about the CD pipeline.

Understanding the CD pipeline

CD is a process by which you automate the deployment of code to target environments. CD pipelines use artifacts produced by CI pipelines and deploy to one or more environments. Like the CI pipeline, we can use YAML files or a classic editor to define a CD pipeline. You can specify conditions on the preceding stage execution state or add approval checks to deploy, which is a very common scenario for production deployments.

You can also configure to run automated UI tests to perform a sanity check post-deployment. Based on the sanity check results, you can configure it to automatically promote code to a higher environment.

At any point in time, if the deployment to a stage fails, we can re-deploy code from previous releases. Depending on the configured retention policy under the project settings, Azure DevOps retains build artifacts so that it is easy to deploy code of any version at any time. If you find any issues with the application post-deployment, you can easily find the last known good release and deploy code to minimize the business impact.

Let's understand more about this in the following section.

Continuous deployment versus CD

Continuous deployment is automated deployment to the target system whenever new code is merged to your repository, whereas CD makes the application available to deploy at any time to the target system. Azure DevOps offers multi-staged pipelines; you can configure pipelines with stages to achieve this.

Continuous deployment is usually configured on lower environments, such as dev or test, whereas for higher environments such as staging or production, you should consider CD so that you can validate changes on lower environments and approve to deploy code to higher environments.

The following screenshot illustrates a multi-stage pipeline, with automated build and release to dev, and waiting for approval in the test stage. In this case, releasing code to testing requires approval:

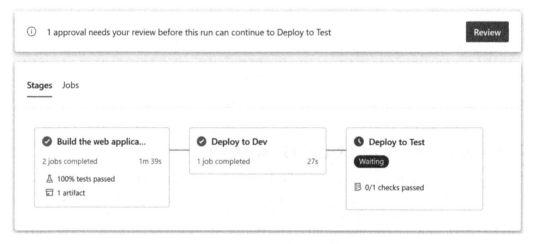

Figure 16.8 – Multi-stage pipeline pending approval

To learn more about how to configure approvals and check on Azure pipelines, you can refer to https://docs.microsoft.com/en-in/azure/devops/pipelines/process/approvals?view=azure-devops&tabs=check-pass.

To view the details of a pipeline run, you can click on any stage to view the logs of that run. Logs help us to troubleshoot deployment failures. The following screenshot illustrates the logs of a pipeline run:

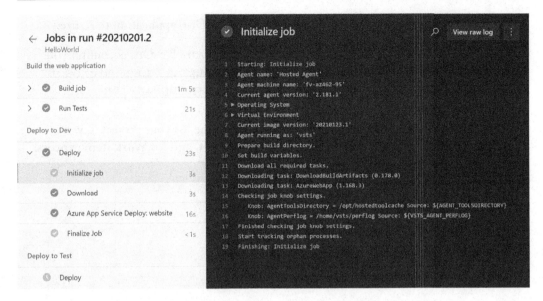

Figure 16.9 – Pipeline execution details

In the preceding screenshot, you will notice that you can view stages, jobs, and tasks configured in the pipeline, and you can click on tasks to view logs.

In the next section, we will learn how to create a pipeline to build and deploy an application.

Deploying an ASP.NET 6 application

So far in this chapter, we have explored Azure DevOps, understood the tools and services it offers, and then learned about CI and CD pipelines. In this section, we shall learn how to create an Azure DevOps project, clone the repository, push code to the repository, and create a CI and CD pipeline to deploy code to Azure App Service.

> **Note**
> Do check the *Technical requirements* section to ensure you have everything set up before you deploy the sample application.

You can follow along with these steps to deploy an ASP.NET 6 application to Azure:

1. Log in to your Azure DevOps account. Create an Azure DevOps account if you don't have one; you can follow the steps given at `https://docs.microsoft.com/en-us/azure/devops/user-guide/sign-up-invite-teammates?view=azure-devops`.

2. On the home page of Azure DevOps, provide a name for your project, say, `HelloWorld`, then for **Version control**, choose **Git**, and for **Work item process**, you can choose **Agile**:

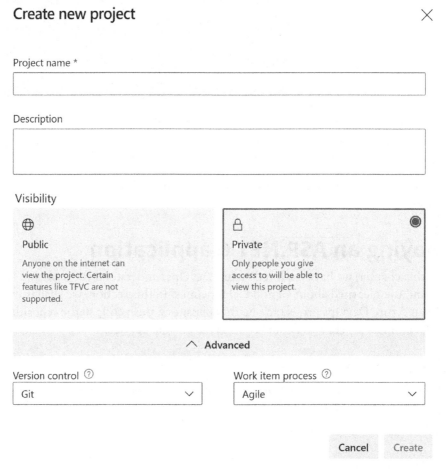

Figure 16.10 – New Azure DevOps project

3. Now, let's create a service connection, which we will use in the pipeline to connect and deploy code to Azure App Service.

    From the left menu, navigate to **Project settings | Service connections | Create service connection | Azure Resource Manager | Service Principal (automatic):**

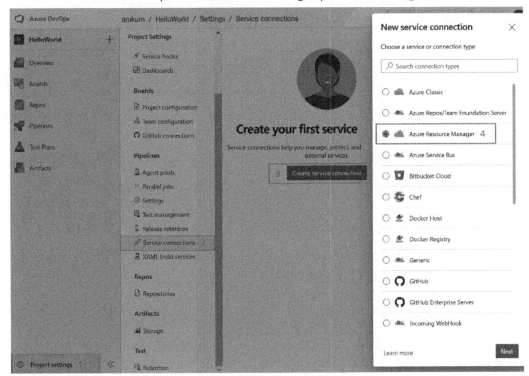

Figure 16.11 – New service principal

The service principal enables pipelines to connect to your Azure subscription to manage resources or deploy your code to Azure services.

4. Select a subscription and provide a name for the connection to create a service connection. Azure DevOps uses this service connection to connect Azure resources and deploy code:

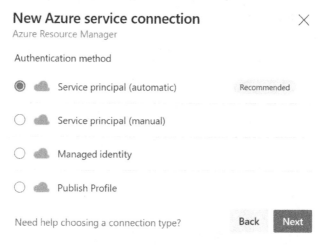

Figure 16.12 – New service principal

5. Once the project is created, you should see a page similar to the following. From the left menu, under **Repos**, select **Branches**:

Figure 16.13 – Azure DevOps Home | Repos screen

6. Copy the link, which we will use to clone the repository to our local machine:

Figure 16.14 – Clone repository

7. To clone the repository to your system, open Command Prompt and navigate to a folder to which you want to clone the code, then run the following command.

   Replace <organization> with your Azure DevOps organization:

   ```
   git clone https://<organization>@dev.azure.
   com/<organization>/HelloWorld/_git/HelloWorld
   ```

8. Since our repository is new and empty, we need to add code to it. The following dotnet CLI commands would help us to create an ASP.NET 6 application and an xUnit project, create a solution file, and add a web and tests project to it. Run each command in sequence to continue:

   ```
   dotnet new mvc --auth Individual -o HelloWorld
   dotnet new xunit -o HelloWorld.Tests
   dotnet new sln
   dotnet sln add HelloWorld/HelloWorld.csproj
   dotnet sln add HelloWorld.Tests/HelloWorld.Tests.csproj
   ```

9. Run the following commands to build code and run tests to verify whether it is all good:

   ```
   dotnet build
   dotnet test
   ```

Now that we have tested the code, next let's see how the pipeline is created for CI and CD for using the code.

Creating a pipeline for CI and CD

After running the tests, we need to see how the CI and CD pipeline is created. Perform the following steps:

1. Next, we need to create a pipeline for CI and CD. You can use the code available at `https://github.com/PacktPublishing/Enterprise-Application-Development-with-C-10-and-.NET-6-Second-Edition/blob/master/Chapter16/Pipelines/HelloWorld/azure-ci-pipeline.yml` and save it in the root directory of the repository. Let's name it `azure-ci-pipeline.yml`.

   This pipeline is configured to trigger when new code is merged to the `main` branch.

2. It is configured to have three stages – build, dev, and test – where the build stage is configured to build code, run unit tests, and publish artifacts. The dev and test stages are configured to deploy code to Azure App Service.

3. Dependencies are configured at the dev and test stages, where the dev stage depends on build, and the test depends on the dev stage.

   Let's examine a few important sections of this YAML file.

   The following snippet contains a section to define variables:

   ```yaml
   trigger:
   - main
   variables:
     BuildConfiguration: 'Release'
     buildPlatform: 'Any CPU'
     solution: '**/*.sln'
     azureSubscription: 'HelloWorld-Con' # replace this
     # with your service connection name to connect Azure
     #subscription
     devAppServiceName: 'webSitejtrb7psidvozs' # replace
     #this with your app service name
     testAppServiceName: 'webSitejtrb8psidvozs' # replace
     #this with your app service name
   ```

You will notice three variables are declared in the YAML file. Provide the appropriate values before you save the file:

- `azureSubscription`: Provide the name of your service connection.
- `devAppServiceName`: Provide the name of the app service for dev deployment.
- `testAppServiceName`: Provide the name of the app service for test deployment.

To build code, we use the `DotNetCoreCLI@2` task and configure `command`, `projects`, and, optionally, `arguments`:

```
- task: DotNetCoreCLI@2
  displayName: Build
  inputs:
    command: 'build'
    projects: '**/*.csproj'
```

`command` is configured as `build` and the path is set to `csproj` for `projects` to build the code. This task runs .NET CLI commands, so we can also configure this task with other .NET CLI commands, such as `run`, `test`, `publish`, `restore`, and so on.

4. To publish the code, the `PublishBuildArtifacts@1` task is used. It is configured with `PathtoPublish`, `ArtifactName`, and `publishLocation`:

```
- task: PublishBuildArtifacts@1
  inputs:
    PathtoPublish:
      '$(Build.ArtifactStagingDirectory)/web'
    ArtifactName: 'drop'
    publishLocation: 'Container'
```

`PathtoPublish` is configured with the location of the artifact directory where build artifacts are available, `ArtifactName` as `drop`, and `publishLocation` as `Container` to publish artifacts to Azure Pipelines. Alternatively, we can also configure `publishLocation` as `FileShare`.

The following code snippet does the required actions to deploy code:

```
- download: current
  artifact: drop
- task: AzureWebApp@1
  displayName: 'Azure App Service Deploy: website'
  inputs:
    azureSubscription: '$(azureSubscription)'
    appType: 'webApp'
    appName: '$(devAppServiceName)'
    package: '$(Pipeline.Workspace)/drop/*.zip'
    deploymentMethod: 'auto'
```

In the deployment job, the first step is to download the artifact, and the artifact's name should be the same as the one that is configured in the `PublishBuildArtifacts@1` task, in this case, `drop`.

The `AzureWebApp@1` task is used to deploy artifacts to Azure App Service. The required parameters are `azureSubscription`, `appType`, `appName`, `package`, and `deploymentMethod` (as `auto`).

Now that the artifact is ready, we see how the code is committed and code changes are pushed.

Pushing the code

Now that the code and pipeline are ready, the next step is to commit and push these changes to the Azure DevOps repository:

1. In Command Prompt, run the following commands to commit changes locally and push them to Azure DevOps:

    ```
    git add .
    git commit -m "Initial Commit"
    git push
    ```

2. In Azure DevOps, navigate to **Pipelines** and click **Create Pipeline** to create a new pipeline:

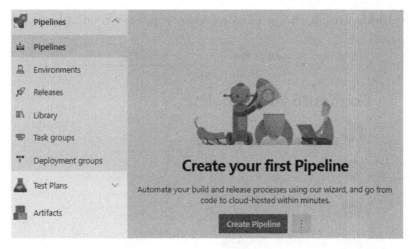

Figure 16.15 – New pipeline

3. To configure the pipeline, we need to perform four steps. Select the service in which your repository resides, select the repository, configure the pipeline, and save. For this implementation, select **Azure Repos Git** to continue, and then select your repository:

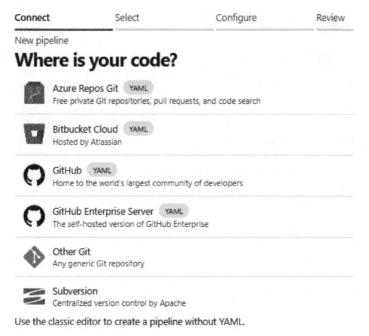

Figure 16.16 – Source control selection

4. In the **Configure** tab, choose **Existing Azure Pipelines YAML file** to continue:

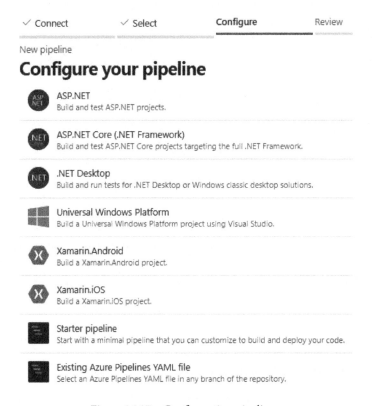

Figure 16.17 – Configuration pipeline

5. Select the pipeline file we saved earlier in the repository and click **Continue**, and then click **Run** to trigger the pipeline:

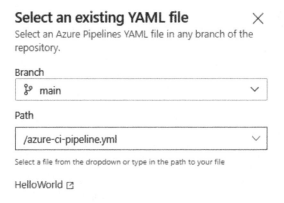

Figure 16.18 – YAML file selection

6. This will open a page in which we can see the state of the pipeline. The following screenshot is taken from the pipeline run. You will notice three stages have been created:

Figure 16.19 – Summary of the pipeline run

In the build stage, you will notice two jobs in progress.

The dev stage and test stage are waiting for the build to complete.

Optionally, you can enable deployment slots on Azure App Service and configure the pipeline to deploy code to a non-production deployment slot, say, *pre-prod*. Once you check the sanity of the deployed code, you can swap the *production* slot with *pre-prod*. The swap is instantaneous and, without any downtime, you can make the latest changes available to users. If you notice any issues, you can swap back to the previous slot to go back to the last known good version. For more information, you can refer to `https://docs.microsoft.com/en-us/azure/app-service/deploy-staging-slots`.

7. After the pipeline execution is complete, navigate to **Environments** under **Pipelines** from the left menu. You will notice the dev and test environments are created:

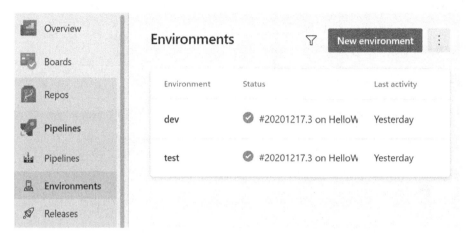

Figure 16.20 – Environments

8. Click on the **test** stage and in the more actions selection, select **Approvals and checks** to continue:

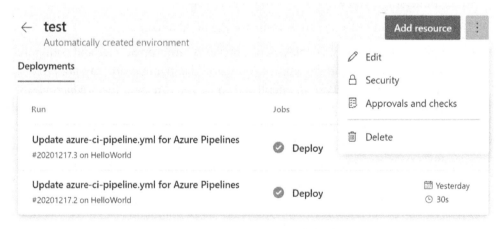

Figure 16.21 – Approvals and checks

9. You will find many options to choose from, such as **Approvals, Branch control, Business Hours,** and so on:

Figure 16.22 – Add checks

10. Select **Approvals** to continue and it will open a dialog where we can select users/ groups as approvers. Provide the necessary details and click **Create**:

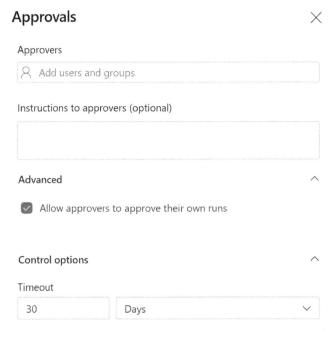

Figure 16.23 – Add approvals

11. Re-run the pipeline to test the changes. You will notice the pipeline is waiting to execute at the test stage:

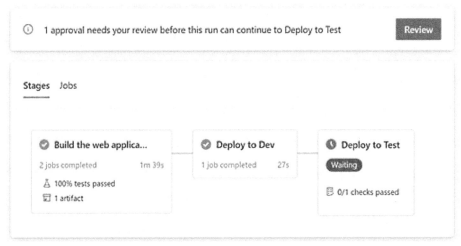

Figure 16.24 – Multi-stage pipeline with pending approvals

12. Click on **Review**, which will open a dialog to approve or reject. Click **Approve** to finish the deployment:

Figure 16.25 – Approve or reject

To summarize, in this section, we started with the creation of a new project in Azure DevOps, then cloned the repository to a local system, created a simple ASP.NET Core application using the .NET CLI, created a pipeline in YAML to build, test, and publish artifacts and deploy them to Azure App Service, and committed and pushed code back to the repository. Next, we created a new CI/CD pipeline by selecting a YAML file in our repository and triggered the pipeline. In **Environments**, we configured approval checks and triggered the pipeline to see how it works.

Summary

In this chapter, we understood what Azure DevOps is, as well as the tools and services it offers. We understood how services such as Boards, Repos, Pipelines, Test Plans, and Artifacts help us to efficiently execute a project.

Next, we looked at CI and CD pipelines and their core components. We also learned how they help us to automate the building and deployment of code. We concluded this chapter by learning how to create an ASP.NET 6 application, and a pipeline to build and deploy to Azure App Service using CI and CD pipelines.

I hope this book has helped you to enhance your .NET skills and motivated you to try out and build more of its applications. There are further topics that you can explore by referring to the notes and the *Further reading* sections of the chapters.

For enterprise applications, we have also covered the happy path scenarios for a typical e-commerce application, and it can be further extended based on the requirements defined in *Chapter 1, Designing and Architecting the Enterprise Application*. There are examples to extend the authentication/authorization for an end-to-end flow, using an API gateway for service-to-service communication and authentication, and implementing the notification service, for you to learn more.

We wish you the best in your C# and .NET projects. Happy learning!

Questions

1. How does continuous deployment differ from CD?

    a. CD works with databases and continuous deployment supports web applications.

    b. Continuous deployment is released to an environment *every* time, whereas CD is released to an environment at *any* one time.

    c. Continuous deployment requires the cloud, while CD works with on-premises servers.

    d. Continuous deployment is released to an environment at *any* one time, whereas CD is released to an environment *every* time.

    Answer: b

2. What are the characteristics of the CD approach? (Choose two)

    a. A focus on cycle time reduction

    b. A small amount of complex releases

    c. Resource-based management of the process

    d. Self-managed and responsive teams

    Answers : a and d

3. Which component provides the first feedback on the quality of committed application code changes?

    a. Automated deployment

    b. Automated provisioning

    c. Automated build

    d. Automated test

    Answer: c

Further reading

To learn more about Azure DevOps, you can refer to `https://docs.microsoft.com/en-in/azure/devops/user-guide/services?view=azure-devops`, and for pipelines, you can refer to `https://docs.microsoft.com/en-in/azure/devops/pipelines/get-started/pipelines-get-started?view=azure-devops`.

Index

B

Packt.com

Subscribe to our online digital library for full access to over 7,000 books and videos, as well as industry leading tools to help you plan your personal development and advance your career. For more information, please visit our website.

Why subscribe?

- Spend less time learning and more time coding with practical eBooks and Videos from over 4,000 industry professionals

- Improve your learning with Skill Plans built especially for you

- Get a free eBook or video every month

- Fully searchable for easy access to vital information

- Copy and paste, print, and bookmark content

Did you know that Packt offers eBook versions of every book published, with PDF and ePub files available? You can upgrade to the eBook version at packt.com and as a print book customer, you are entitled to a discount on the eBook copy. Get in touch with us at customercare@packtpub.com for more details.

At www.packt.com, you can also read a collection of free technical articles, sign up for a range of free newsletters, and receive exclusive discounts and offers on Packt books and eBooks.

Other Books You May Enjoy

If you enjoyed this book, you may be interested in these other books by Packt:

Modernizing Your Windows Applications with the Windows App SDK and WinUI

Matteo Pagani, Marc Plogas

ISBN: 9781803235660

- Understand the key concepts of the Windows App SDK and WinUI
- Integrate new features by creating new applications or by enhancing your existing ones
- Revamp your app's UI by adopting Fluent Design and new interaction paradigms such as touch and inking
- Use notifications to engage with your users more effectively
- Integrate your app with the Windows ecosystem using the Windows App SDK
- Use WinML to boost your tasks using artificial intelligence
- Deploy your application in LOB and customer-facing scenarios with MSIX

Software Architecture with C# 10 and .NET 6 - Third Edition

Gabriel Baptista, Francesco Abbruzzese

ISBN: 9781803235257

- Use proven techniques to overcome real-world architectural challenges
- Apply architectural approaches such as layered architecture
- Leverage tools such as containers to manage microservices effectively
- Get up to speed with Azure features for delivering global solutions
- Program and maintain Azure Functions using C# 10
- Understand when it is best to use test-driven development (TDD)
- Implement microservices with ASP.NET Core in modern architectures
- Enrich your application with Artificial Intelligence
- Get the best of DevOps principles to enable CI/CD environments

Packt is searching for authors like you

If you're interested in becoming an author for Packt, please visit authors.
packtpub.com and apply today. We have worked with thousands of developers and
tech professionals, just like you, to help them share their insight with the global tech
community. You can make a general application, apply for a specific hot topic that we are
recruiting an author for, or submit your own idea.

Share Your Thoughts

Now you've finished *Enterprise Application Development with C# 10 and .NET 6*, we'd love
to hear your thoughts! Scan the QR code below to go straight to the Amazon review page
for this book and share your feedback or leave a review on the site that you purchased it
from.

https://packt.link/r/1-803-23297-8

Your review is important to us and the tech community and will help us make sure we're
delivering excellent quality content.

Made in the USA
Las Vegas, NV
11 February 2023

67323609R00321